The Ecology of British and American Empire Writing, 1704–1894

Edinburgh Critical Studies in Atlantic Literatures and Cultures
Series Editors: Laura Doyle, Colleen Glenney Boggs and Maria Cristina Fumagalli

Available titles
Sensational Internationalism: The Paris Commune and the Remapping of American Memory in the Long Nineteenth Century
J. Michelle Coghlan

American Travel Literature, Gendered Aesthetics, and the Italian Tour, 1824–1862
Brigitte Bailey

American Snobs: Transatlantic Novelists, Liberal Culture and the Genteel Tradition
Emily Coit

Scottish Colonial Literature: Writing the Atlantic, 1603–1707
Kirsten Sandrock

Yankee Yarns: Storytelling and the Invention of the National Body in Nineteenth-Century American Culture
Stefanie Schäfer

Reverberations of Revolution: Transnational Perspectives, 1770–1850
Edited by Elizabeth Amann and Michael Boyden

Consuming Empire in U.S. Fiction, 1865–1930
Heather Wayne

Derek Walcott's Painters: A Life with Pictures
Maria Cristina Fumagalli

Literature, Art and Slavery: Ekphrastic Visions
Carl Plasa

The Ecology of British and American Empire Writing, 1704–1894
Louis Kirk McAuley

Forthcoming titles
Emily Dickinson and Her British Contemporaries: Victorian Poetry in Nineteenth-Century America
Páraic Finnerty

The Atlantic Dilemma: Reform or Revolution Across the Long Nineteenth Century
Kelvin Black

Visit the series website at: www.edinburghuniversitypress.com/series/ECSALC

The Ecology of British and American Empire Writing, 1704–1894

Louis Kirk McAuley

EDINBURGH
University Press

Edinburgh University Press is one of the leading university presses in the UK. We publish academic books and journals in our selected subject areas across the humanities and social sciences, combining cutting-edge scholarship with high editorial and production values to produce academic works of lasting importance. For more information visit our website: edinburghuniversitypress.com

© Louis Kirk McAuley 2024, 2025

Edinburgh University Press Ltd
13 Infirmary Street
Edinburgh EH1 1LT

First published in hardback by Edinburgh University Press 2024

Typeset in 11/13pt Adobe Sabon
by Cheshire Typesetting Ltd, Cuddington, Cheshire

A CIP record for this book is available from the British Library

ISBN 978 1 3995 2714 9 (hardback)
ISBN 978 1 3995 2715 6 (paperback)
ISBN 978 1 3995 2716 3 (webready PDF)
ISBN 978 1 3995 2717 0 (epub)

The right of Louis Kirk McAuley to be identified as the author of this work has been asserted in accordance with the Copyright, Designs and Patents Act 1988, and the Copyright and Related Rights Regulations 2003 (SI No. 2498).

Contents

List of Figures	vi
Series Editors' Preface	viii
Acknowledgments	ix
Introduction: Unruly Natures	1
1. The Evolution of Robinson Crusoe's World-Ecological Consciousness	60
2. The Poetics of Biological Invasion and Crop Monoculture in Early Caribbean Literature	110
3. Capitalism, Domestic Violence, and the "Botany of Desire" in Leonora Sansay's *Secret History; Or, the Horrors of St. Domingo*	158
4. Robert Louis Stevenson and the "Horror of Creeping Things"	212
Afterword	279
Bibliography	284
Index	299

Figures

0.1 "Hawaiian House, Hilo" from the photo albums of Sir Graham Balfour. Courtesy of the Special Collections, National Library of Scotland, Edinburgh. 35
0.2 "Hawaiian House, Hilo" (detail showing what appears to be a black and white cat), from the photo albums of Sir Graham Balfour. Courtesy of the Special Collections, National Library of Scotland, Edinburgh. 35
0.3 Thomas Sutherland (1785–1838) after James Hakewill (1778–1843), "Golden Vale, Portland" from *A Picturesque Tour of the Island of Jamaica from Drawings Made in the Years 1820 and 1821,* London: Hurst and Robinson and E. Lloyd, 1825, hand-coloured aquatint. Courtesy of the Yale Center for British Art, Paul Mellon Collection. 37
1.1 "Selkirk amusing himself with his Cats." Illustration from John Howell's children's book devoted to the *Life and Adventures of Alexander Selkirk, the real Robinson Crusoe* (New York: M. Day & Co., 1841). Courtesy of the Boston Public Library. 69
1.2 "Selkirk catching a Goat." Illustration from John Howell's children's book devoted to the *Life and Adventures of Alexander Selkirk, the real Robinson Crusoe* (New York: M. Day & Co., 1841). Courtesy of the Boston Public Library. 72
2.1 "St Christophers 1779," from *The Journal of John Ker, Surgeon's Mate in the Royal Navy – a manuscript account describing his service in the West Indies, 1778–1782.* Courtesy of the Special Collections, National Library of Scotland, Edinburgh. 119
3.1 Giovanni Tiepolo, "The Triumph of Flora" (c. 1743). Available in the public domain via Wikimedia Commons. 192
4.1 Thomas Moran, "The Wilds of Lake Superior" (1864). Available in the public domain via Wikimedia Commons. 219

4.2 "Hawaiians peeling Taro," from the photo albums of
    Sir Graham Balfour. Courtesy of the Special Collections,
    National Library of Scotland, Edinburgh. 227
4.3 Vailima (Stevenson's home in Samoa), with Mt. Vaea
    in the background. Courtesy of the Special Collections,
    National Library of Scotland, Edinburgh. 230
4.4 *Mimosa pudica*, from Henry Charles Andrews, *The
    Botanist's Repository* (1807–8). Courtesy of the Beinecke
    Rare Book and Manuscript Library, Yale University. 244
4.5 Clearing ground (wrestling with vegetable life) at Vailima
    (Stevenson's home in Samoa). Courtesy of the National
    Library of Scotland, Edinburgh. 247
4.6 "The Sensitive Plant," from P. W. Latham's "The
    Floral Festival" in *The Family Circle* periodical (New
    York, 1856). Courtesy of the American Antiquarian
    Society, Worcester, MA. 260

Series Editors' Preface

Modern global culture makes it clear that literary study can no longer operate on nation-based or exceptionalist models. In practice, American literatures have always been understood and defined in relation to the literatures of Europe and Asia. The books in this series work within a broad comparative framework to question place-based identities and monocular visions, in historical contexts from the earliest European settlements to contemporary affairs, and across all literary genres. They explore the multiple ways in which ideas, texts, objects and bodies travel across spatial and temporal borders, generating powerful forms of contrast and affinity. The Edinburgh Critical Studies in Atlantic Literatures and Cultures series fosters new paradigms of exchange, circulation and transformation for Atlantic literary studies, expanding the critical and theoretical work of this rapidly developing field.

Laura Doyle, Colleen Glenney Boggs, and
Maria Cristina Fumagalli

Acknowledgments

Working on a project of this scale invariably results in the accrual of significant debts of gratitude. And given the limitations of space, it would be impossible to acknowledge everyone who has contributed in some way to the composition of this book. However, it gives me pleasure to mention some of the people (and institutions) without whose assistance this project would not have been possible. First and foremost, I wish to thank the US-UK Fulbright Commission and the National Library of Scotland, Edinburgh, for generously providing me with a Fulbright Scholarship to carefully engage in the archival research that makes working on a project like this such an enlightening (and altogether enjoyable) experience. Not only was I enabled to closely examine the Scottish materials that I've incorporated into this book, greatly contributing to my new-found critical appreciation of the work of Robert Louis Stevenson, but it also gave me a chance to walk across great portions of the highlands and islands of Scotland, and thereby develop the sort of eco-poetic appreciation of place that both Stevenson and Saint Lucian poet, Derek Walcott, recommend. I especially wish to thank Chris Taylor, Dora Petherbridge, and the librarians overseeing the Archives and Manuscript Collections for making me feel at home in the library and whose invaluable knowledge of Scottish literature and culture helped guide my research throughout. I cherish the time I spent there. Other libraries and archives that played a role in my research include the National Library of Jamaica, American Antiquarian Society, New York Public Library, Library Company of Philadelphia, and British Library. The Royal Botanic Garden in Edinburgh enabled me to examine a first edition copy of James Grainger's *The Sugar-Cane*, inside of which I discovered an unpublished, elegiac poem by Dr. Tailour, titled "On the Death of Dr. Grainger" (see Chapter 2).

I wish to thank my colleagues (faculty, graduate students, and staff) in the Department of English at Washington State University for their overall collegiality and support throughout this process, especially our current Chair, Donna Potts, for understanding when I needed to set aside my Associate Chair duties to focus on this book instead. However, I owe a special debt of gratitude to my former Chair and faculty mentor, and present Dean of the College of Arts and Sciences, Todd Butler, for his unwavering support of my research and writing. Although I don't see him nearly as often as when we both had offices in Avery Hall, Todd continues to offer invaluable advice and support whenever our paths cross in Pullman. Alongside Todd, I owe colleagues outside WSU similarly special thanks, Miriam Wallace and Evan Gottlieb, whose commitment to Eighteenth-Century Studies remains an inspiration, and whose ongoing support helped make it possible for me to buy the time (through grants and fellowships) I needed to complete this project. I offer warm thanks to the Department of English at the University of Dayton, for appointing me the Lawrence Ruff Visiting Chair in Eighteenth-Century Studies (Fall 2019), a position which allowed me to concentrate on Leonora Sansay's novel, *Secret History*, and during which time I enjoyed working with three bright undergraduates in my seminar on "*Contra*-diction." I thank the English faculty and staff at Dayton, especially Andy Slade (Chair), Tom Morgan, Teresa Saxton, and Laura Vorachek, for their warm welcome and insightful feedback offered during my Ruff Lecture. My former advisors at SUNY Buffalo, Deidre Lynch and James Bunn, also merit special consideration – Deidre, for introducing me to the wonders of Eighteenth-Century Studies, and Jim, for the initial inspiration to develop connections between literature and ecology. Jim's sage advice – remember to think strangely – continues to inform my work.

At Edinburgh University Press, I wish to thank Emily Sharp and Elizabeth Fraser for seeing this project through to publication. Although I owe many thanks to former EUP Commissioning Editor, Michelle Houston, for the initial faith she put in me (and this project), I am grateful for the way in which Emily ensured a smooth transition after Michelle's departure, and for her careful stewardship of the final product. The blind peer-review process at EUP was a most rewarding experience, offering invaluable feedback that significantly transformed and improved the book's overall critical framework. And I am deeply indebted to the editors of the Edinburgh Critical Studies in Atlantic Literatures and Cultures series, Laura Doyle, Colleen Glenney Boggs, and Maria Cristina Fumagalli, for their steady support throughout this long process. I consider it a great honor to be included in this important series.

Finally, I wish to thank my family and friends for their kind support and comforting cheer. This project was completed during a global pandemic, over which time I lost my father, a dear friend, and father-in-law. That the project was not derailed by this upheaval, but completed, speaks to the role that family and friends play in uplifting us through difficult times, including the ongoing climate crisis, the most direct experience of which for those of us living in Pullman, Washington (and neighboring Moscow, Idaho), would be the few weeks, if not months that we now spend every year coping with smoke-filled air from wildfires raging across the inland Northwest. Linda Russo has been a constant source of support, and whose love, understanding, and fellow recognition of connections across species continues to inspire me. Furthermore, that she lets me be my goofy self at home without question (or much complaint) makes everything possible. And, considering the attention I give to Alexander Selkirk's cats in Chapter 1, I must acknowledge the two most adorable indoor cats I know, Ishi and Elsie, whose affection for Linda and me (and sisterly love for one another) never fails to elicit laughter and smiles. Sharing our home and sympathies with these feline companions has certainly enriched our everyday lives.

Significantly abbreviated early versions of Chapters 2 and 4 have appeared in *The Edinburgh Companion to Atlantic Literary Studies*, edited by Leslie Eckel and Clare Elliot (Edinburgh University Press, 2016), and *ISLE: Interdisciplinary Studies in Literature and Environment* (Oxford University Press), Volume 26, no. 3 (Summer 2019), 570–93.

For Linda

Introduction: Unruly Natures

Several months following the shipwrecked Robinson Crusoe's washing ashore a so-called remote island in the Atlantic Ocean some uncertain distance from South America, an event which is supposed to have occurred on or around 30 September 1659, Daniel Defoe's iconographic castaway notices something uncanny . . . the appearance of some deeply familiar green sprouts emerging from the island's fertile soil. Always a careful observer of his material surroundings, Crusoe notes in his Journal that it was about a month after the "great rains" that

> I saw some few stalks of something green, shooting out of the ground, which I fancy'd might be some plant I had not seen, but I was surprised and perfectly astonish'd, when, after a little longer time, I saw about ten or twelve ears come out, which were perfect green barley of the same kind as our *European*, nay, as our *English* barley.[1]

Although the real historical figure who inspired Defoe's immensely popular tale, Alexander Selkirk, a Scotsman, was stranded on the Juan Fernández archipelago in the Pacific Ocean for over four years (and upon an island that is now commonly referred to as Isla Robinson Crusoe), the author's decision to situate his narrative in the Atlantic Ocean has multiple implications, not least of which is the narrative's resonance with what Alfred W. Crosby dubbed the Columbian Exchange – i.e. the purposeful and accidental ebb and flow of Old and New World species across the Atlantic.[2] In *Colonial Botany*, for example, Londa Schiebinger and Claudia Swan note that, "on his second voyage, in 1494, Columbus brought to the West Indies sugar-cane cuttings, eventually one of the world's most lucrative cash crops."[3] To be sure, in the Early Modern period, botany was big business, as "European colonial expansion touched off an unprecedented widespread movement of flora globally that ... deeply restructured the world agricultural map."[4] Defoe's choice of setting, therefore, invites us to read *Robinson Crusoe* in light of this emerging global economy, including, specifically, the British Empire's transplantation of both human and extra-human natures overseas. And, in this regard, whether in terms of Defoe's conflation of the Pacific and Atlantic Oceans[5] or his treatment of Crusoe's nascent capitalism as a totalizing force, initiating an "epochal reorganization of global natures,"[6] *Robinson Crusoe* merits consideration as a sort of world-literature – that is, if we treat world-literature, as Michael Niblett does in his compelling recent study of the aesthetics of commodity frontiers, *World Literature and Ecology* (2020), as the "literature of the capitalist world-system."[7] The novel is not merely about Crusoe's remodeling this island in the Atlantic into a familiar Old World landscape – a circumstance that makes the novel relevant to a number of important ecocritical studies, including Jill Casid's *Sowing Empire* (2005), in which Crusoe's island garden figures as one of the "most influential imperial relandscapings of the eighteenth century,"[8] or, say, Rebecca Woods's study of the roles played by British breeds in the "economics and ecologies of empire in the nineteenth century," *The Herds Shot Round the World* (2017).[9] Nor is this, as I see it, a novel primarily concerned with Crusoe's Englishness (or identity politics, per se). The very notion of individuality upon which traditional, ego- or anthropocentric readings of the novel depend – and here I'm thinking primarily of Ian Watt's influential formulation in *The Rise of the Novel* – gets upended by the attention that Defoe gives *not* to insects, parasites, or pathogens (i.e. to the various less visible and microscopic ways in which the human body figures as host, though that would obviously be a useful approach). Rather, it's the development of Crusoe's especially keen understanding of the cooperation of human and extra-human natures in this not merely transatlantic, but *transoceanic* (Atlantic-Pacific), global economy that, I argue, highlights the novel's truly world-ecological significance. That is, *Crusoe* is certainly a tale of fences, as Casid suggests, and these fences seem (at times) peculiarly designed not merely to protect either his livestock (goats) or his environment from their overgrazing, but also to preserve his Englishness.[10] However, by drawing attention to Crusoe's sharing the island with various plant and animal species, including the imperfect creatures (rats) whose vanishing act forms the basis of Lucinda Cole's important analysis of the novel, I aim to offer a rather more *heterarchical* reading of the novel in which the remoteness of Crusoe's island is called into question, and the human is decentered / re-positioned alongside other equally restless environmental engineers, or, rather, *unruly natures* (according to Cole, the agricultural economy of Crusoe's island – his survival or food security – depends upon the rats' mysterious disappearance, which, as she cleverly demonstrates, makes no practical sense: the numbers of cats versus rats simply don't add up).[11] Resembling the non-human actors that figure in Bruno Latour's discussion of Robert Boyle's work on the physical nature of air, unruly natures proliferate in Defoe's novel, as it were, jeopardizing the very nature-culture dichotomy (and anthropocentrism) upon which our so-called modern constitution depends. In this regard, I offer what might be described as a "non-modern," posthumanist reading of the novel in which the human coalesces with the animal, plant, and mineral, or in which, as Latour suggests, "nature and society are not two distinct poles, but one and the same production of successive states of societies-natures, of collectives."[12]

As I see it, the significance of this particular barley scene lies in its providing us with a glimpse of Crusoe's world-ecological awakening. For example, Crusoe's first impulse is to link the barley's appearance upon the island to God's Providence; that is, he is apt to invest religious significance in the barley's so-called miraculous growth:

> I had hitherto acted upon no religious foundation at all, indeed I had very few notions of religion in my head ... But after I saw barley grow there, in a climate which I know was not proper for corn, and especially that I knew not how it came there, it startled me strangely, and I began to suggest, that God had miraculously caus'd this grain to grow without any help of seed sown, and that it was so directed purely for my sustenance on that wild miserable place.
>
> This touch'd my heart a little, and brought tears out of my eyes, and I began to bless my self, that such a prodigy of Nature should happen upon my account; and this was the more strange to me, because I saw near it still all along by the side of the rock, some other straggling stalks, which prov'd to be stalks of rice, and which I knew, because I had seen it grow in *Africa* when I was ashore there. (63)

Upon discovering these green stalks of English barley, Crusoe's thoughts immediately turn to God's providence. Or, as Cole puts it, "the providential preservation of grain against the threat of hungry rats leads to a meditation on the nature of this agricultural miracle."[13] At this juncture, Crusoe's thinking reflects the primacy of biblical narratives in determining Europeans' relationship to the

New World. However, while this seemingly providential preservation of the English barley plays a central role in Cole's very compelling analysis of the significance of Crusoe's disappearing rats, anyone as familiar with the novel as Cole knows that Crusoe's first impulses and impressions are often incorrect, and that such first thoughts are almost always succeeded by second guesses, and possibly third and fourth thoughts and impressions.[13] In this case, as Crusoe weighs the matter further still, he soon realizes that he is responsible for the grain's accidental introduction to the island:

> at last it occur'd to my thoughts, that I had shook a bag of chickens meat out in that place, and then the wonder began to cease; and I must confess, my religious thankfulness to God's Providence began to abate too upon the discovering that all this was nothing but what was common, tho' I ought to have been as thankful for so strange and unforeseen Providence, as if it had been miraculous for it was really the work of Providence as to me, that should order or appoint, that 10 or 12 grains of corn should remain unspoil'd, (when the rats had destroy'd all the rest,) as if it had been dropt from Heaven; as also, that I should throw it out in that particular place, where it being in the shade of a high rock, it sprang up immediately; whereas, if I had thrown it any where else, at that time, it had been burnt up and destroy'd. (64)

Although Crusoe claims that he "ought to have been as thankful for so strange and unforeseen Providence," the important thing is that he no longer regards God as responsible for the barley's (and the corn and rice's) taking root, but instead remembers his part in this transfer of English barley (L. *Hordeum vulgare*) to a remote oceanic island. This transition from a Providential to mere accidental, or co-produced explanation of the origins of the sprouted barley alerts us to the possibility of Crusoe's developing an ecological consciousness. And, in this regard, Defoe's novel draws a parallel between Crusoe's ecological awakening and what María M. Portuondo describes as Early Modern efforts to "create a new framework to explain the reality of the New World."[14] Portuondo's focus on Spanish cosmography and the New World, including those cosmographers who were employed by the Council of the Indies, one of two institutions established by the royal court of Spain to "coordinate the colonization and exploitation of the New World," corresponds with the Spanish presence in *Robinson Crusoe*.[15] Much as Crusoe's survival depends on his developing new and distinct ways of producing knowledge, so too did the members of Spain's Council of the Indies require accurate information to help them "govern the empire effectively." "Philosophical speculation had no place in this program," observes Portuondo, "not because of fear of deviating from orthodoxy ... but because such musings rarely yielded tangible results that could be applied to the pressing problems of the expanding empire."[16] Similarly, the expansion and governance of Crusoe's island empire rests upon close, empirical investigation of his surroundings, as it were, leading to a peculiarly ecological understanding of how everything, including the barley, ties together.

That is, while one expects to see Crusoe transition from a hypothetical state of nature to civilization over the course of the novel, as it were, in keeping with contemporary political philosophy such as John Locke's *Second Treatise of Government*, this is only partly true. Changes in Crusoe's sleep habits demarcate such a transition. At first, owing to his lack of candlelight, Crusoe insists, that, "as soon as ever it was dark, which was generally by seven-a-clock, I was oblig'd to go to bed" (62). But, as soon as he figures out how to render goat fat to produce a lamp made from tallow, a clay dish, and "wick of some oakum," Crusoe's old sleep habits are restored, and the imaginative transition back to civilization is at least partially complete. Similarly, Cole regards Crusoe's perfection of food accumulation and storage as integral to the "reassertion of an European, civilized identity on Crusoe's island" – i.e. circumstances she links to the mysterious absence of such imperfect creatures as the rats which were accidentally introduced to the island alongside Crusoe's English barley.[17] Indeed, that Crusoe's sleep is not disturbed by rats gnawing on his feet, as was the case with the real historical castaway, Alexander Selkirk, suggests the potential limitations of Defoe's island ecology. Cole correctly notes, for example, that, "the agricultural economy of Crusoe's island depends ... on the absence of the [imported, or invasive] rats that plagued Selkirk and the millions of others across the modern world, all struggling to protect their grain supplies against rodent infestation,"[18] but this leads her to make, I think, a less convincing claim (vis-à-vis John Bender) about the apparitional nature of Defoe's novel: "the island's imagined environment is not an open, dynamic ecosystem but a closed, zoomorphic world in which Crusoe hunts, gathers, farms, and stores under metaphysically secured conditions."[19]

This claim about the metaphysical security of Crusoe's island is not nearly as convincing because it is also the case, I argue, that Crusoe becomes increasingly ecologically conscious as he continues to make a home for himself (and his capitalist ideals) *in* nature. Although he first links the barley's growth to God's providence, he soon develops an appreciation for the specific natures of barley, corn, and rice.[20] And so, in keeping with Latour's non-anthropocentric (or heterarchical) theory of actants, in which humans, animals, and plants all act upon one another in dynamic and interlocking systems,[21] Crusoe becomes increasingly less preoccupied with questions of identity, and more concerned about his place in not merely the island's ecosystem, as it were – but in the broader transatlantic, if not transoceanic, global ecology and economy, a notion that Defoe explores further in his sequel, *The Farther Adventures of Robinson Crusoe* (1719). Whether in terms of the barley's so-called miraculous growth or the most famous scene in which a mysterious footprint appears in the sand, Crusoe develops an understanding of the world that greatly exceeds the boundaries of his imperial imagination. My reading of Crusoe's evolving, notably heterarchical view of the world, thus, corresponds with Ayesha Ramachandran's efforts to disentangle these key terms – empire and world – that often get confused in postcolonial critiques of empire and Enlightenment. Initially, readers may be encouraged to view Crusoe's island as part of a world that signifies "all the territory available for conquest," but the footprint scene clearly points to the "territories and peoples *not* part of a state's [i.e. Crusoe's] control."[22] The novel presents a concept of the world as comprised of various unruly natures – a concept of the world that, as Ramachandran puts it, "offers an alternative order and an alternate means of identification that both resists and transcends the hegemonic energies of empire – even though it threatens to be co-opted into displays of imperial ambition."[23] As a quintessential piece of empire writing, I argue, Defoe's novel builds on this tense opposition of world views, as it were, inviting readers to imagine a world that simultaneously lends itself to (cooperates or corresponds with) and exceeds / resists / opposes Crusoe's imperial ambition. In this regard, does not *Crusoe* fulfill Latour's goal of relocating the human in the "continuous exchange of forms"?[24]

More importantly, as recent work in invasion biology suggests, perhaps the best explanation for the barley's so-called miraculous establishment upon Crusoe's island lies in the fact that he's actually not the first human to have intervened in the island's natural history – i.e. that, as Daniel Simberloff explains, "disturbed habitats are particularly susceptible to invasion."[25] In fact, it is the peculiar nature of barley to grow in disturbed habitats, including along roadsides. And it is precisely the disturbed nature of Crusoe's island, and its vulnerability to biological invasion that undercuts any notion of its so-called metaphysical security.

Of course, the other thing that we might notice about this important barley scene is that Crusoe accidentally introduces not just one, but two species here. Crusoe fails to mention whatever happens to the European rats: a species that, along with the Javan mongoose, has "played a major role in the decline of ground-nesting birds in the Caribbean."[26] Cole (as noted earlier) offers a compelling analysis of the rats' disappearance, linking it to issues of food security. She insists that the "economy Crusoe constructs depends not simply on the *presence* of European corn, but the *absence* of the rats that plagued Selkirk and the millions in Europe who tried desperately to protect grain supplies from vermin,"[27] and she neatly links this issue of food accumulation and storage to the development of particular social virtues: compassion and benevolence, such as that which Crusoe extends to Friday and others. However, it's worth noting here too that such neglect neatly parallels the furtive economy of some of the most infamous biological invasions. It may be years or decades before the ecological damage caused by these rats catches Crusoe's eye. And exactly how quick may depend, of course, upon whether or not the rats' work jeopardizes Crusoe's livelihood (capitalism) (see, for example, Chapter 2, in which I discuss the attention paid to rats by James Grainger in his West Indian georgic, *The Sugar-Cane*). It would have been practically impossible for Crusoe to remain unaware of the rats' population growth for very long because rats reproduce at an alarming rate by comparison to cats. "At the end of six months," Cole explains, "two shipboard rats and their offspring could have produced 77,960 rodents, overrunning the island and wreaking ecological havoc," as compared to "fifty or one hundred cats."[28] And so, the disappearance of Crusoe's rats would appear to be ideologically linked to Defoe's efforts to promote overseas trade.[29]

****

In 1857, a French-born astronomer and lithographer named Etienne Leopold Trouvelot moved to Medford, Massachusetts, a town composed of former farmland roughly seven miles northwest of Boston (Medford would become a center of industry by the end of the nineteenth century). Remembered by astronomers for his beautiful, lithographic representations of planetary objects, Trouvelot's greatest claim to fame or, rather, infamy, stems from his tangential interest in zoology. Trouvelot collected animal species, which he occasionally donated to Harvard University's Museum of Comparative Zoology, and, with the eruption of the American Civil War in the 1860s and New England's mills cut off from their regular supply of southern cotton (L. *Gossypium*), he began experimenting with North American moths to see if they could be used to produce silk to replace cotton. A homespun commercial silk industry would certainly have helped to bolster the Union's economy, but Trouvelot had no such luck with any of the local moths / indigenous species. And so, he set his sights further afield. After traveling to Europe in search of such a useful moth species, Trouvelot settled on the gypsy moth (*Lymantria dispar*), the eggs of which he received in Medford in 1868. Unfortunately, Trouvelot's winged companions (his fluttering unpaid laborers) did not produce the valuable silk he had hoped for, and, to make matters worse, these little creatures with an insatiable appetite for the leaves of hardwood trees escaped from their poorly constructed cage in his backyard, thereby setting in motion one of the greatest environmental catastrophes related to invasive species in U.S. history. As Daniel Simberloff writes:

> The gypsy moth spread rapidly (partly by the movement of egg masses on vehicles and infested timber), easily escaping from an expensive eradication campaign launched by the state of Massachusetts. By 1934 it was established throughout New England, by 1994 it had spread through the mid-Atlantic states and into parts of the South and Midwest, and it is now established as far south as Tennessee and as far west as Wisconsin as it inexorably expands its range. The caterpillars feed on over 300 tree species, but especially on oak, aspen, willow, larch, and birch, causing massive defoliation, which affects birds, insects, and other forest-dwelling animals. Continued defoliation often causes tree death, and 25 – 30% of trees typically die in an outbreak region. Particularly susceptible tree species decline in frequency as they are replaced by species less affected by the gypsy moth, again with follow-on effects on animal species that used the declining tree species as food or nesting habitat.[30]

In fact, the environmental consequences of Trouvelot's introduction of the gypsy moth to North America are difficult to fathom because the campaign to eradicate this invader involved a widespread aerial assault with DDT (dichloro-diphenyl-tricholoro-ethane), a manmade pesticide that, oddly enough, was first "synthesized by a German chemist in 1874," as it were, just roughly six short years following the gypsy moth's arrival in Medford.[31] DDT, of course, and the U.S. Department of Agriculture's Plant Pest Control Division's indiscriminate chemical warfare against the moth figure prominently in Rachel Carson's hugely influential environmentalist text, *Silent Spring*, which appeared in 1962. Carson details the moth's spread to the nearby states of New York and Pennsylvania via the New England hurricane of 1938, and, of course, she notes the pervasive environmental impacts of the Department's 1957 DDT spraying program, which not only did not achieve its objective – the moth's eradication – but, instead, killed a variety of other animal species (birds, bees, crabs, fish, etc.). Indeed, I say the environmental havoc wrought by Trouvelot's experiment is difficult to fathom because such pesticides are so very insidious. Contaminating soil, water, and food, "they have the power," notes Carson, "to make our streams fishless and our gardens and woodlands silent and birdless."[32]

Of course, the gypsy moth is not entirely to blame here, as Carson links the "sudden rise and prodigious growth of an industry for the production of man-made or synthetic chemicals with insecticidal properties" to the science of the Second World War – specifically, the development of agents of chemical warfare. And she carefully highlights the growth of this industry, which, in the United States, increased from 124,259,000 pounds in 1947 to over 600,000,000 in 1960: "the wholesale value of these products was well over a quarter of a billion dollars."[33] However, I mention the economic value of this industry because it calls into focus yet another unintended consequence of Trouvelot's misguided appropriation of the otherwise innocent gypsy moth – i.e. his efforts to "identify, secure, and channel unpaid work [including the work of extra-human natures] outside the commodity system into the circuit of capitalism."[34] Trouvelot's failure to jump-start a silk industry in New England during the Civil War helped fuel an enormously lucrative biochemical industry devoted to the indiscriminate eradication of plant pests / invasive species not unlike the gypsy moth. I offer these historical leaps from 1704 and 1719 to 1857 and 1957 as an example of the ways in which the animal, plant, and mineral interventions that form the subject of this book encourage a sort of detachment from the boundaries of time (literary periodization) and space (national, economic, and geographical limitations). Such *unruly natures* invite us to play a game of historical (or, rather, world-ecological) leap-frog. Like Vandana Shiva whose work in biopiracy insightfully links the Columbus charter and 1493 Papal "Bull of Donation" to the 1947 General Agreement on Tariffs and Trade (GATT) treaty as part of same project of colonization,[35] I regard Defoe's novel and

Trouvelot's experiment with gypsy moths as variations upon an ongoing theme of capitalist appropriation, and, more importantly, both scenarios encourage reflection upon what Latour calls the testimony of non-humans.[36]

That is, I begin with these two examples of European men either accidentally or decisively introducing animal and plant species to the Americas because they both conveniently illustrate several key concerns of this book – not merely the inviolable union of economy and ecology, but the heterarchical nature of empire building, and, as far as *Robinson Crusoe* is concerned, the *registration* of these interventions in works of British and American literature that do not merely reflect, but inform and resist this historical unfolding. Indeed, this is first and foremost a literary study.

I use the term heterarchical to stress the agency of extra-human natures in the imperial expansion of Great Britain and America. As Cole suggests, citing the work of Michel Serres and Bruno Latour, "within this context, nonhumans are more than Cartesisan objects or mere vehicles of our thoughts and intention; instead, they *do* things in specific sociohistorical, ecological, institutional, and psychological environments."[37] Borrowing Latour's term, *actants*, she explains: "they are, like humans, *actants* in the world ... [they] 'modify other actors'; they are not subjects, but 'interveners.'"[38] This recognition of the ways in which animals and plants compel changes in those around them is repeatedly featured in the literature of empire, as British settlers-colonists-planters (i.e. empire builders), from Selkirk to Grainger, were not only apt to pay close attention to those species that either supported or threatened colonial efforts, but were themselves effectively transformed in various ways (whether physiologically or psychologically) as a result. Similarly, as a number of scholars have observed, Europeans were apt to capitalize upon indigenous knowledge to support their establishment of plantations in the Americas, or, more generally, to facilitate the spread of their imperial ambitions across the globe. Shiva focuses mainly upon intellectual property rights (IPRs) and the more recent, post-GATT treaty patenting of indigenous knowledge,[39] whereas, in the *Alchemy of Empire* (2016), Rajani Sudan explores how the British co-opted Indian techne – specifically, the practices and processes surrounding the production of mud, mortar, ice, smallpox matter, cloth, and paper – for the sake of colonialism and empire. For example, "ice making," writes Sudan, "becomes part of the technology of transforming an alien climate into one more recognizably English."[40] Judith Carney similarly investigates the importation of West African rice culture to the Americas. She insightfully observes, that, "the African diaspora was one of plants as well as people." "Enslaved West Africans," says Carney, "brought an indigenous knowledge system that would establish rice as a subsistence and plantation crop over a broad region from South Carolina to tropical South America."[41] This may seem ironic, of course, as we imagine such fictions of empire as Defoe's *Robinson Crusoe* to be largely about Crusoe's (i.e. capitalism's) capacity to effectively transform (i.e. impose European norms upon) a world that lies out there, as if it were separated from humanity. But repeatedly these texts break down this Cartesian notion of separation, highlighting (often in strange and surprising ways) the actions of animals, plants, and minerals.

Perhaps the most obvious example of such an intervention / transformation would be the superhuman agility that Selkirk claims to have developed in order to keep pace with the goats with which he shared the island of Juan Fernández, whereas Grainger offers some idea of how the accidental importation of rats to the West Indies forced planters to adopt new more or less devastating, from an ecological perspective, strategies to protect their lucrative cane fields, as well as precious food supplies. Other examples that I consider here include the migrating female land crab's inspiration for a feminist uprising in Leonora Sansay's Gothic novel, *Secret History*, and the way in which the presence of an invasive plant species in Samoa – namely, *Mimosa pudica* (or sensitive plant) – obliges Robert Louis Stevenson to rethink his / the human place in nature, thereby filling him with an utterly unsettling, or destabilizing / decentering horror – the "horror of creeping things."[42]

And so, in keeping with Cole and other similarly focused scholarship in the field of animal studies, such as Virginia Anderson's *Creatures of Empire* (2006), Tobias Menely's *The Animal Claim* (2015), and Rebecca Woods's *The Herds Shot Round the World* (2017), my work is concerned with how these sorts of human-extra-human collaborations shift, as Cole puts it, "fundamental questions from the identity of actors to their functions; the 'who am I?' of western philosophy is superseded by another question: 'what is my place in the system?'"[43] Other valuable contributions to the field of animal studies, such as John Miller's *Empire and the Animal Body* (2012), have helped refocus attention on the non-human, offering, as it were, a distinctly postcolonial edge to reading "resistance to the catastrophic environmental abuse perpetrated by the industrial west."[44] However, because I think it worth exploring the conspiracy of particular extra-human natures in this world historical process (a capitalist complex of notably uneven developments, given that some species in certain contexts benefitted from transoceanic commerce, whereas others clearly did, or do not), the texts that I've chosen are not (as I see it) primarily ego- or anthropocentric, but effectively decenter the human, in as much as they encourage us to consider human-animal-plant-mineral relations within not merely a transatlantic, but transoceanic, global context.

That I am chiefly concerned with the registration of such interventions in empire writing suggests this project's close relationship to Michael Niblett's recent book, *World Literature and Ecology* (2020). As a literary study, I would say this book commences with a similarly great appreciation for literature's capacity to produce or engineer historical realities and environments. Indeed, I too am concerned with the registration of specific "environment-making processes" in fiction and poetry, and, as Niblett suggests, "to speak of 'registration' is not to suggest that literary texts merely reflect or passively record the dynamics of commodity frontiers":

> Cultural practice is itself an ecological force, an integral pivot in humanity's capacity to rework life, land, and the body.[45]

I completely agree with Niblett's notion here about literature as an ecological force. As a sort of how-to manual, a West Indian georgic like James Grainger's *The Sugar-Cane* (1764), for example, clearly engages in environmental engineering, as Tobias Menely's book, *Climate and the Making of Worlds* (2021), suggests too. (Indeed, Menely goes so far as to claim that "poetry offers an archive of geohistory because poems formalize the activity of making as a transformative redirection of planetary energy.")[46] Registration as such corresponds with Early Modern concepts of the art of worldmaking. "Worldmaking has a complex ideological history that derives from physico-theology and was only later exported into modern philosophical discourse," explains Ramachandran: "at its core is the idea of creation – the belief that a world can be made and transformed, rather than being a preestablished entity awaiting discovery."[47] However, I also think it worth noting here (as does Niblett to a considerable extent) the sometimes furtive, or not so obvious ways in which various natures (animals, plants, and minerals), in fact (or as *actants*) inform the production of literature. That is, while my work focuses on a similar set of commodity frontiers (mostly sugar and copra) in a transoceanic (Atlantic-Pacific) context, the timing of this study is obviously distinct from Niblett's, taking into account a wholly different set of pivotal stages in the development of a truly world-historical-ecological matrix, in which, as Niblett suggests (vis-à-vis Jason Moore) humans are knit together with the rest of nature "within a gravitational field of endless accumulation."[48]

The earlier focus serves to undermine the pre-eminence of the nature-culture divide, much as Ramachandran's work invites us to reconsider Descartes's metaphysics through close critical examination of Descartes the natural philosopher "who seeks a convincing and wider-ranging explanation of the natural world."[49] And it also provides us with a glimpse of how the processes of empire building, such as the transportation of goats to the Juan Fernández archipelago, taught Enlightenment-era authors, not unlike Daniel Defoe, James Grainger, and John Singleton, to see themselves as part of a transoceanic, global economy, as well as inextricably linked to (not separated from) a variety of extra-human natures. Botanists at this point in time clearly imagined themselves as "gardeners of the earth," suggests Marie-Noëlle Bourguet, effectively reshaping "nature's distribution of floras by moving seeds and plants across the seas."[50] And, importantly, with certain exceptions (Crusoe's barley), the transoceanic mobilization of plants was not an easy task, but one that required a keen understanding of not merely the "relation between plants and climate," as Bourguet's work suggests, but a broad network of plant-animal-mineral relations unfolding in a global context.

Future developments clearly add to this transoceanic view of things. Grainger's attentiveness to various imperfections in West Indian sugar production, for example, including Book IV which happens to be riddled with anxiety over the likelihood of a slave uprising (and the inevitable emergence of independent nations throughout the Americas), may be linked to the Haitian Revolution, on the one hand – a revolution that, in keeping with Michelle Burnham's illuminating suggestion regarding how transoceanic narrative structures "return revolution to its older, astronomical definition of rotation rather than its more familiar association with a dramatic linear break and change,"[51] would both reorient the United States westward towards California and the Pacific Ocean,[52] and make Cuba the epicenter of a sugar boom in the nineteenth century. (Noting that "there were periods in which the annual increase in sugar production was 25 percent," Antonio Benítez-Rojo refers to this phase in Cuban history as the Creole, or plantation machine).[53] Accordingly, Leonora Sansay's Gothic novel, *Secret History*, invites us to think about the cyclical nature of capitalist exploitation, in so far as she traces this boom and bust pattern in sugar production from Haiti to Cuba (Chapter 3). On the other hand, it's possible to connect the dots between Grainger's various ideas about pest control and the futile struggles to contain the damage caused by invasive species in late nineteenth-century Hawaii and Samoa. And such connections (which form the arc of this book, from Selkirk to Stevenson) do more than just detach us from troubling geopolitical and economic boundaries of nation (and continent), as it were, in keeping with Burnham's efforts to read American literature in a "maritime global context."[54] Such connections in effect decenter the human, despite the ostensible anthropocentrism of all this empire building. In other words, Niblett's excellent point about how "variations in the geopolitical location of commodity frontiers might differently inflect literary production"[55] speaks to the necessity of this and further place-based studies that consider how specific natures in particular locations impact literary production (and vice versa).

However, while this book certainly draws upon the aforementioned animal studies, it is as much concerned with the work of animals, as it is with other forms of so-called cheap nature – namely, the actions of plants and minerals within literature / upon literary production. Or, rather, this book highlights the transformative human-animal-plant-mineral connections foregrounded in British and American empire writing, a diverse assortment of texts that beg to be read transoceanically.

Moreover, whether Trouvelot was motivated primarily by avarice (or maybe political allegiance) to import the European gypsy moth to New England, he clearly imagined himself filling a gap in the U.S. economy created by the Civil War. And, while the outcome, or slowly unfolding environmental catastrophe, would appear to reinforce what environmental historian Jason Moore describes as Green thought's standard arithmetic – namely, that economy (capitalism) + nature = crisis, I would argue that there is little difference between Trouvelot's grave (and very real) misfortune and Crusoe's contrasting good fortune, however fictional. That is, both scenarios reflect Moore's point, that, despite the scientific revolution's prioritization of purposive control over nature, capitalism may *not* do with Nature as it pleases. The historical process, explains Moore, "is radically different":

> While the manifold projects of capital, empire, and science are busy making Nature with a capital "N" – external, controllable, reducible – the web of life is busy shuffling about the biological and geological conditions of capitalism's process.[56]

The reality is a bit more like what happens to Trouvelot (and Crusoe), in which a particular unruly nature (an extra-human actant) does what it will despite, but not exactly regardless of Trouvelot's capitalist ambition. The histories of invasive species like the gypsy moth not only delineate the limits of human control, but also give wing to emergent alternative views, including a non-anthropocentric view of the world as this interlocking system within which humans, animals, plants, and minerals co-operate.

Here too I am reminded of Macarena Gómez-Barris's valuable point, that, "extractive zones contain within them the submerged perspectives that challenge obliteration."[57] Is not Trouvelot's backyard in Medford, like Crusoe's island, an extractive zone, as it were, geared towards the conversion of plant and animal life into "extractible data and natural resources for material and immaterial accumulation" (to support the Union)? And does not the gypsy moth belong to a sort of hidden world that forms the "nexus of human and nonhuman multiplicity"?[58] Is the gypsy moth not of a piece with the "transitional and intangible spaces" that figure in Gómez-Barris's work as geographies that "cannot be fully contained by the ethnocentrism of speciesism, scientific objectification, or by the extractive technocracies that advance oil fields, construct pipelines, divert and diminish rivers, or cave-in mountains through mining."[59]

Perhaps in much simpler terms, the narrative that I wish to tell about Trouvelot and, more importantly, Crusoe, is *not* a cautionary tale, per se – *not* a story about the aspiring capitalist's alienation from or deadly manipulation of their surroundings (an externalized Nature), but one that reinforces Graham Huggan and Helen Tiffin's point, in *Postcolonial Ecocriticism: Literature, Animals, Environment* (2010), that "such invasions by animals and plants were by no means systematic; nor did the animals and plants themselves (or, for that matter, practices of animal husbandry and cultivation) in the new environments . . . remain unchanged."[60] That is, Trouvelot's experience provides us with a glaring example of human history as co-produced by manifold species, much as the barley's so-called miraculous, or providential taking root supports Crusoe's overarching capitalist enterprise. The trouble is simply that the gypsy moth's specific nature was not suited to the grand task Trouvelot had designed for it – i.e. the establishment of a lucrative silk industry in the north-eastern United States. Trouvelot's failure is partly a failure to recognize the specific nature and agency of the European gypsy moth (L. *Lymantria dispar*), much as Crusoe initially misinterprets the barley's (*Hordeum vulgare*) miraculous growth as having religious, not ecological significance: it is supposed to reflect God's providence, and not the cooperation of specific natures. Or, rather, to build upon the title of Daniel Defoe's exceedingly popular novel, each of these scenarios constitutes a strange surprising adventure.

Defoe occasionally uses the term "adventure" in an economic sense, as is the case when Crusoe gives an account of one of his early (and only successful) voyages to the west coast of Africa:

> I embrac'd the offer, and entering into a strict friendship with this Captain ... I went the voyage with him, and carried a small <u>adventure</u> with me, which by the disinterested honesty of my friend the Captain, I encreased very considerably; for I carried about 40*l*. in such toys and trifles as the Captain directed me to buy ... This was the only voyage which I may say was successful in all my <u>adventures</u> ... For I brought home *L. 5.9 ounces* of gold dust for my <u>adventure</u>, which yielded me in *London* at my return, almost 300*l*. and this fill'd me with those aspiring thoughts which have since so compleated my ruin. (16) (Underscoring mine.)

Notable here is the significant difference between "adventure," which denotes an investment fund, so to speak, and the plural form, "adventures," which Defoe employs in a more familiar sense to indicate Crusoe's partaking in a hazardous or exciting activity. But what makes each of his adventures so very strange and surprising is that, despite Crusoe's relentless rationalization of experience, or, say, life on earth, things don't always go as planned. There is an element of providence, which I interpret *not* as God's providence – but the influence of specific natures, in this case barley's adaptability to this disturbed tropical habitat / climate and the gypsy moth's voracious appetite (and taste) for over 300 different species of hardwood trees. Or, rather, I highlight these two similar, yet drastically different scenarios because this book partly aims to complicate the overriding narrative of colonialist exploitation, in which the "genuinely natural ways of indigenous ecosystems were irretrievably undone as 'wild' lands were cleared for farming or opened up to pastoralism."[61] For, as Huggan and Tiffin suggest, "skewed as they were in favour of the colonizing culture, such exchanges were nevertheless often more complex in practice than the apparently simple pattern of invasion, land-clearing and destruction might lead us to suppose."[62] In other words, one of the objectives here is to explore how the texts included in this study complicate this basic pattern of invasion, land-clearing and destruction, as well as to consider how (in certain cases) the authors themselves may have been transformed through their interactions with specific natures (or non-human *actants*). And, in this respect at least, my approach has some connection to recent work in postcolonial ecocriticism, including Huggan and Tiffin's aptly titled, *Postcolonial Ecocriticism,* and Laura Wright's *"Wilderness into Civilized Shapes,"* which explores "the ambiguous and fraught nature" of that relationship between "colonization and environmental degradation" as both historically and geographically determined.[63] Like Wright, in particular, the texts that I've chosen for inclusion in this study do not merely talk back to each other, thereby complicating any preconceived notions about an overriding settler-colonialist narrative that may be evenly applied to different geopolitical locations. Here again I am reminded of Niblett's point about how the experience of "capitalist modernization" is "lived differently in different locations."[64] This multiplicity would no doubt have presented itself as a challenge to colonists / empire builders, as Ramachandran notes, that, for Early Modern world-makers, "to comprehend the world ... required deft oscillation between local details [not unlike those contained in Grainger's *Sugar-Cane*] and global frameworks and a reconfiguration of the particular against the universal."[65] But, more importantly, the texts that I focus upon here are also often riddled with contradiction, implying, of course, that interpretation remains an enterprise fraught with various ambiguities, as the authors themselves appear quite conflicted. For the Scottish authors included here these internal conflicts may be reminiscent of the duality that often characterizes the Scottish literary imagination, as Susan Manning has so convincingly demonstrated in *Fragments of Union* (2002).[66]

Furthermore, I think both scenarios provide us with a notion of capitalism as "already co-produced by manifold species."[67] After all, what was Trouvelot looking for in Europe but cheap nature – that is, a way to make nature work for him at little cost. And that he settled upon a cunning, unruly little creature whose appetite bears a strong family or, indeed, *uncanny* resemblance to either the capitalist's insatiable hunger for fossil fuels or Crusoe's restless acquisition of material goods brings us to the final question of strangeness. (It may be worth noting here that, for Sigmund Freud, the uncanny "proceeds from something familiar that has been repressed," which, in this case, I interpret as the forgotten or repressed knowledge of the intimacy between humans and non-humans, or the nature-in-humanity / humanity-in-nature.)[68] These scenarios are strange precisely because the manifold species involved either seriously test the limits or, more likely, showcase the remarkable scope and/or capaciousness of human sympathy (eighteenth-century parlance for empathy), which David Hume treats as the faculty of mind that enables one to "receive by communication [another's] inclinations and sentiments, however different from, or even contrary to our own."[69]

Whether in terms of recent psychological work detailing literature's capacity to teach empathy or, say, Evan Gottlieb's compelling literary study of the unification of England and Scotland, *Feeling British* (2007), philosophies of sympathy (especially Enlightenment theories of this faculty of mind) have enjoyed a sort of renaissance within the humanities over the past decade or so.[70] But Tobias Menely's important book, *The Animal Claim* (2015), deserves special mention here, for having pushed these debates about Enlightenment ideas of sympathy, including Hume's theory of it, squarely into the center of Animal Studies. Enlightenment-era thinkers like Hume and Rousseau were keen to stress either sympathy or compassion's role in enabling cross-species communication, providing a pathway between animals and humans, nature and culture. As Menely carefully points out, "Hume sees us as most resolutely human, in our capacity to convey passions and join interests, where we are most akin to our fellows creatures, for '*sympathy*, or the communication of passions, takes place among animals, no less than among men'."[71] Or, rather, "sympathy not only bridges the species divide, joining creatures in common felicity, but in an even more forceful overcoming of identity's hold, draws us from our contentment into a recognition of another's suffering."[72] Opponents of vivisection in the nineteenth century, of course, rely upon this human capacity to identify with, or imagine the feelings of other animals – a scenario writ large in works like H. G. Wells's *The Island of Doctor Moreau* (1896). But, as Menely suggests, the most radical thing that Hume does in his *Treatise of Human Nature* is develop a theory of communicative feeling that takes into account the significance of creaturely voices to the very formation of human conceptions of self and community. Our notions of self and community are not merely born out of communication with other humans, as it were, always already derived from the affective signs of another's feelings – the impressionable force fields of human faces, etc.[73] But, in rooting his theory of sympathy within an overarching belief in the universality of such communication across animal species, Hume alerts us to the possibility – nay, the very unavoidability – of our ideas of self and community developing in affective communication with other non-human creatures.

It is not simply that this faculty of mind – sympathy – forms the basis of human feelings for animals, but, rather, that animal feelings inform human conceptions of self and community. And so, I use this key term throughout as a convenient articulation for how humans are bound together with the rest of nature in the web of life, as it were, though I explore Hume's (and Menely's) treatment of this "fundamental 'correspondence of *passions* in men and animals,'"[74] especially as it relates to Stevenson's ecological imagination / intimacy with various extra-human natures, in greater detail in Chapter 4. And I add that it's *not merely* the voices and physical expressions of animals that count here. Drawing upon eighteenth-century botanist, William Bartram's radical conception of the likenesses between plants and animals, I am just as apt to highlight how the actions of plants inform these processes of human identification too. That is, in addition to Hume's theory of sympathy, Bartram's claim, in his *Travels through North and South Carolina, Georgia, and East and West Florida, the Cherokee Country, The Extensive Territories of the Muscogulges, or Creek Confederacy, and the Country of the Chactaws* (1791), "that vegetable beings are endued with some sensible faculties or attributes, familiar to those that dignify animal nature,"[75] begs us to stand up and take notice of the profound relevance of eighteenth-century literature and culture to present-day ecological thinking about sentient plants (see, for example, Susan Simard's groundbreaking work in forest ecology, *Finding the Mother Tree: Discovering the Wisdom of the Forest* (2021).[76] If Hume deserves our attention for his linking humans and other animals in this great chain of communicative feeling – so too does Bartram for his reminding us that plants are much more like animals than we have hitherto imagined. That is, while some non-students of British literature may find fault with Bartram's overly poetic (i.e. non-scientific) approach, including the curious formal comparisons of animals and plants that occur in his beautiful illustrations, on a very basic level he neatly anticipates present-day scientific revelations about the animal-like actions of plants. For as Paul Simons observes, "the 'vegetable' world is alive with sensitivity and movement." In fact, plants are endowed with a number of "senses not normally considered plant-like,"[77] which is a topic that gets explored further in Chapter 4.

And so, in as much as reading literature improves empathy (or theory of mind),[78] so too does empire writing draw us (as readers) into a matrix of human-animal-plant-mineral relations. Animals do not merely make claims (ethical and otherwise) on our attention, as Menely points out, but so do plants merit consideration as similarly sympathetic creatures. In Chapter 4, for example, I explore how plant sensitivity alters Robert Louis Stevenson's conception of his (or the human) place in nature.

Furthermore, the link between sympathy and economics is an interesting one because, as T. M. Devine notes, prominent Scottish Enlightenment thinkers and theorists of sympathy like Adam Smith were apt to dismiss the economic advantages of slavery in favor of wage labor. Francis Hutcheson, for example, "emphasized sympathy and fellow-feeling between individuals as the foundation of ethical behavior" – a "thesis of intrinsic 'benevolence' that, as Devine notes, was practically impossible to reconcile with "the oppression of slavery."[79] Albeit, Hume's factoring of resemblance and contiguity into his analysis of the power of sympathy may have been used to help explain why so many Britons were apt to ignore the racist and inhuman treatment of Africans upon the Caribbean sugar plantations; Hume argues that the degree to which one feels sympathy for another depends on their close resemblance (or likeness) and proximity (the great distance between the British isles and, say, Jamaica would, according to Hume's theory, be apt to downplay, if not discourage any sympathetic feelings for the enslaved Africans brutalized by the plantation economy over there / overseas). However, his insistence that benevolence is incapable of counteracting the most powerful of human passions – i.e. greed – nevertheless plays a significant role in the global spread of capitalism, in so far as Olaudah Equiano's (and others') most basic argument for the abolition of the transatlantic slave trade draws upon Hume's idea, that, "there is no passion ... capable of controlling the interested affection [greed], but the very affection itself, by an alteration of its direction."[80] In his autobiography, *The Interesting Narrative of the Life of Olaudah Equiano, or Gustavus Vassa, The African* (1789), for example, Equiano carefully designed his ultimate argument for abolition to appeal to the interested affections of British Members of Parliament. It is on the basis of profitability that Equiano argues for the abolishment of the slave trade and corresponding establishment of a commercial intercourse with Africa: "I doubt not, if a system of commerce was established in Africa, the demand for manufactures would most rapidly augment, as the native inhabitants would insensibly adopt the British fashions, manners, customs, &c. In proportion to the civilization, so will be the consumption of British manufactures."[81] The insensibility with which Africans will become, according to Equiano, *like* their British trading partners in fashion, manners, and customs neatly resonates with Hume's salient point about sympathy – that "a good-natur'd man finds himself in an instant of the same humour with his company."[82] Whereas for Hume, writing in the aftermath of the Act of Union, sympathy may be the glue that binds a nation like Britain together, as Gottlieb suggests in *Feeling British*,[83] for Equiano, sympathy *and* greed both are fundamental to the global economy.

And so, the two scenarios that I have cited here – the first which might be described as Defoe's allegorical treatment of the transplantation of Old World cereal grasses (barley and rice) to the Americas, and Trouvelot's disastrous introduction of the gypsy moth to North America – both figure as convenient examples of what I call unruly natures. Crusoe and Trouvelot provide us with an idea of how particular animals and plants intervene in this historical unfolding of a transoceanic, global economy, and how – like invasive species – they insinuate themselves and transform (and are themselves transformed by) the literature of empire. Accordingly, they both seriously complicate Cartesian notions of humankind's separation from nature, and they test (if not expand) the limits of human sympathy. Is the facilitation of various sympathetic interspecies connections not one of the consequences of Defoe's novel, for example? Can we sympathize with Trouvelot's insatiable gypsy moth? But, more importantly, both of these scenarios showcase the ways in which capitalism bundles specific cooperative (as well as uncooperative) natures together in the web of life. In keeping with Moore's suggestion, that, "the history of capitalism is one of successive historical natures,"[84] the agrochemical industry's lucrative battle to contain so-called pests not unlike Trouvelot's gypsy moth rages on, while Crusoe's appropriated grasses – including barley, corn, and rice – continue to serve as a low-cost food in support of the accumulation of capital.

Although one might be more apt to compare the gypsy moth's feasting upon the hardwood forests in North America to the U.S. economy's insatiable consumption of fossil fuels, Crusoe's reliance upon cereal grasses, I argue, similarly aptly conveys the *nature* of his capitalism. That the former leads to an obvious environmental crisis of epic proportions, whereas the latter evidently contributes to Crusoe's survival is perhaps merely a matter of perception. Never mind how easy it is for us to forget about Crusoe's rats, the accumulation of capital depends upon fossil fuels to support production, much as it does the work/energy of cereal grasses. Indeed, both Trouvelot's ill-fated experimentation with gypsy moths and Crusoe's cultivation of English barley, however accidental, are useful illustrations of Moore's overarching claim that capitalism works through nature, and nature works through capitalism. Even though one might argue that because Crusoe is a fictional character in a novel written by Defoe, a "dogged promoter of overseas trade,"[85] there is nothing at all surprising about the novel's contrasting fortunate outcome – that is, the ending was obviously carefully designed to endorse a particular political agenda. Such a reading does not alter the union of economy and ecology that lies at the center of Defoe's remarkably prescient novel. That Crusoe's survival depends upon cereal grasses (and goats, cats, and the disappearance of rats too) directly reflects the co-production of capitalism by manifold species.

Empire / Nature Writing

In his groundbreaking 2015 study, *Capitalism in the Web of Life: Ecology and the Accumulation of Capital,* Jason Moore premises his exploration of capitalism as world-ecology – not the ecology of the world, per se, but a "patterned history of power, capital, and nature, dialectically joined"[86] – upon two critical inversions of so-called Green Thought's most fundamental questions. First, for Moore, it is not a matter of how (or when) humanity became separated (or possibly alienated) from nature, but, rather, humanity's ongoing unification with the rest of nature *in* the web of life. Environmental thinkers, as Moore explains, may be keen to embrace the concept of the human-in-nature. William Cronon, for example, in his seminal essay, "The Trouble with Wilderness," challenges the notion of wilderness as wild nature separated from humanity.[87] However, the idea that human organization, including capitalism, may be similarly unified with nature tends to be a much less palatable notion, and, of course, for all the obvious reasons. Moore's contribution to Green Thought lies in his encouraging us to completely (not partially) reject the old Cartesian binary of Society/Nature – i.e. the question of separation (how and when) – which invariably resurfaces in any effort to explain capitalism as an economic force (and social relation) that does something to an otherwise externalized Nature out there.

And this leads us to the second inversion. For Moore, it is not a matter of how humans defile, degrade, or decimate nature, so much as the following question: "how is human history a *co-produced* history, through which humans have put nature to work – including other humans – in accumulating wealth and power?"[88] This is the central thrust of Moore's insightful contribution to the study of world-ecology – namely, that capitalism is not only historically coherent as far back as the sixteenth century, but "co-produced by human and *extra-human natures* in the web of life" (italics mine), and that its coherence rests upon a law of value that is a law of cheap nature – i.e. a steady supply of low-cost food, labor, energy, and raw materials.[89] This latter element takes into account capitalism's appropriation of the unpaid work/energy of both human and extra-human natures, including women. And I think it worth noting here too, that, Moore prefers the term work/energy because it "helps us to rethink capitalism as a set of relations through which the 'capacity to do work' – by human and extra-human natures – is transformed into value."[90] Indeed, for Moore, work/energy includes not merely commodifiable labor power and/or geophysical energy – say, for example, the hydro-electrical power of the Columbia River – but organic life: "from photosynthesis to hunting prey to bearing children."[91] To this list I would add various other metabolic processes, including digestion, which partly explains capitalism's profound reliance upon grazers, including Crusoe's goats.

Drawing inspiration from Moore's work, the story that I wish to tell in this book is *not* a cautionary tale about humanity's impact upon / defilement of an otherwise innocent, external Nature. Nor is it simply a tale about how particular works of literature, such as James Fennimore Cooper's *The Pioneers, or the Sources of the Susquehanna* (1823) or Dorothy Wordsworth's *Grasmere Journals* (1800–3), may help us to develop a greater respect and appreciation for Nature out there. Rather, it is a story about the *"relations* that co-produce manifold configurations of humanity-in-nature, organisms and environments, life and land, water and air."[92] As "the stories of human organization," including capitalism, are "co-produced by *bundles* of human and extra-human nature,"[93] suggests Moore, this book is at least partially concerned with the rooting of our present-day environmental crisis within a particular literary legacy – i.e. British and American empire writing. But, mostly, it is about the interactions of nature and culture within a literature squarely situated at the heart of the *Capitalocene*, a globally fueled phenomenon *not* contingent upon the advent of any singular piece of technology, such as the steam engine, but, as Moore suggests, the "relations of power, capital, and nature that rendered fossil capitalism so deadly in the first place."[94] I prefer not to employ the commonplace umbrella term Anthropocene in this study because I think it mistakenly returns the human to the center of things, reinforces a dualist (Human versus Nature) framework, and/or neglects to account for the conspiracy of particular extra-human natures, as it were, which is one of the central concerns of this book. I also agree with Moore and other scholars who insist that the Anthropocene makes for much too easy a story – an oversimplified narrative that treats "humanity as an undifferentiated whole," that does not "challenge the naturalized inequalities, alienation, and violence inscribed in modernity's strategic relations of power and production."[95] Similarly, Macarena Gómez-Barris insists, that, "we use the term too generally, addressing 'humanity' as a whole without understanding histories of racial thought and settler colonialism that are imposed upon categorizations of biodiversity spaces where the biotechnologies of capitalism accelerate."[96] The Anthropocene, writes Gómez-Barris, "like the militarized production of the extractive zone, demarcates the temporalities and spatial catastrophe of the planetary through a universalizing idiom and viewpoint that hides the political geographies embedded within the conversion of complex life."[97] Instead, I prefer the term Capitalocene to stress the role of co-production (the various interventions of extra-human actors / natures), and to hopefully avoid presenting an overly simplistic, monolithic / monocultural view of humanity as a unified geological force, one that obscures key differences and diversity.

That is, this is a book about empire writing's role in the formation of human-extra-human relationships, though (again) I use an instrumental eighteenth-century philosophical term – namely, *sympathy* (as defined by two principal members of the Scottish Enlightenment, David Hume and Adam Smith) – to indicate such partnerships. Perhaps most importantly, I define empire writing as a body of literature that not only reflects the expansion and consolidation of European interests across the globe, and, in particular, the meteoric rise of the British and American Empires – but a remarkably wide range of texts that also effectively make that history possible, in as much as capital produces space.[98] Like Michelle Burnham, I bring together what to some may appear to be a relatively strange assortment of texts, in large part to emphasize my archival, materialist focus on the transportation of various organisms overseas, but also to showcase literature's capacity to transform both the reading public's world view *and* the world itself. And, of course, this strange mixture of materials reflects the assorted ways in which Early Modern scientists struggled to make sense of (if not control) an otherwise uncertain world. As Portuondo points out, "when early modern historians refer to *science*, we are using the word anachronistically but also as an expedient way of referring to a group of quite distinct ways of producing knowledge about the natural world," including "natural philosophy, experimentalism, natural history, natural magic, and mixed mathematics."[99]

Again, I share Niblett's conception of literature as "ecological force"[100] – a form of ecological engineering, as it were – and I am chiefly concerned with the registration of particular animal, plant, and mineral interventions within these texts. In fact, I wish to propose that empire writing *is* always already nature writing because humans do not build empires on their own, or without – i.e. separated from – nature, but, rather, as a number of valuable critical studies, including Alfred W. Crosby's *Ecological Imperialism*, Virginia DeJohn Anderson's *Creatures of Empire*, and Rebecca Woods's *The Herds Shot Round the World*, suggest, through the establishment of various important biotic alliances or, as I see it, interventions.[101] Some of these relationships are purposeful, such as humankind's ongoing reliance upon livestock to convert otherwise so-called useless grasses into valuable protein, whereas others are accidental and pose as some form of ecological interference, so to speak: the introduction of Crusoe's rats, for example. In either case, these particular natures invariably actively participate in the production of empire writing.

Accordingly, I begin with the marooning of a Scottish sailor, Alexander Selkirk, upon the Juan Fernández archipelago in the Pacific Ocean in 1704 because, on the one hand, my primary concern is with how these human-extra-human relationships (pathways between nature and culture, ecology and economy) figure or form in particular eighteenth- and nineteenth-century British and American literatures – that is, over a nearly 200-year period of incredible significance for the development of the British Empire and the United States. And, of course, Selkirk is frequently cited as the inspiration for Daniel Defoe's ever-popular novel about adventure capitalism in the Atlantic World, *The Life and Strange Surprizing Adventures of Robinson Crusoe* (1719), though this tendency to emphasize Defoe's situation of Crusoe's fictional island within the Atlantic Ocean obscures, I argue, the novel's transoceanic (Atlantic-Pacific), real world historical and ecological significance.

That is, I begin with Selkirk not merely because the accounts that circulated of his survival upon the island "four Years and four Months" helped create a market for voyages (seafaring literatures) among British merchants with money to invest in far-flung commercial ventures across the globe, as Andrew Lambert points out, but also because of the island's strategic location in the Pacific Ocean, roughly 415 miles off the west coast of Chile.[102] The archipelago figures as an important link between the Pacific and Atlantic, thereby emphasizing not merely the transatlantic, but transoceanic nature of empire building even at this early stage. Indeed, Woodes Rogers summarized the island's considerable geopolitical significance in his *A Cruising Voyage Round the World* (1712): "I have insisted the longer upon this island, because it might be at first of great use to those who would carry on any Trade to the *South-Sea*."[103] In this instance I would say Rogers's work practices what Burnham describes as a narrative dynamics of expectation, in which the "expectation of future profits" buries or downgrades "the pain of present losses."[104] The considerable attention that Rogers gives to the island, and not merely Selkirk's experience upon it, serves as a testament to its significance to the global economy. Or, indeed, as Lambert puts it, "Juan Fernández was the key to an entire ocean."[105] My concern here is with both the island's contribution to the British imagination (to building readers' expectations of future profit), *and*, more importantly, its very real function as a convenient rest stop for scorbutic sailors aboard European ships engaged in global commerce. To employ one of Burnham's key terms, the island factors into Rogers's calculus of risk. Its presence offers a possible solution to the problem of scurvy plaguing long-distance voyages,[106] but also (as a point of refreshment and resupply) raises readers' expectations of increased profit margins owing to this potential reduction of overhead costs and losses.

On the other hand, I take Selkirk, *Robinson Crusoe*, and, in Chapters 2 and 3, the sugar revolution that informs the so-called manifest destiny of the British Empire and the United States both into account for the same reason that Charles S. Elton, one of the founders of the field of animal ecology, focuses so much of his attention upon the fate of remote islands in his influential book, *The Ecology of Invasions by Animals and Plants* (1958): islands are infamously susceptible to invasion by both human *and* extra-human natures.[107] Thus, I focus upon Selkirk to not only push back against the false image of a remote and pristine tropical island Eden that weighs heavily into the early propaganda of American settlement,[108] but also to showcase the very *work* of particular natures in this historical development, which, I might add, merits consideration as one of repetition *and* multiplication.[109] Indeed, a transoceanic view of history "offering" what Geraldine Heng describes as "repetitions with change"[110] ties in nicely with the problem of such unruly natures as invasive species.

First, as far as the myth of island remoteness is concerned, my work builds upon Elizabeth DeLoughrey's treatment of the "dynamic and shifting relationship between land and sea" in her compelling study of Caribbean and Pacific island literatures, *Routes and Roots*.[111] In particular, DeLoughrey's engagement with Barbadian poet Kamau Brathwaite's theory of the tidal dialectic – that is, a methodological tool used to foreground "how a dynamic model of geography can elucidate island history and cultural production"[112] – in part helps her to "position island cultures in the world historical process," as well as to explain her overarching focus upon "shared histories, particularly as they are shaped by geography" – i.e. histories which exceed or transcend "national, colonial, and regional frameworks."[113] For Brathwaite, the term refers to the dynamics of Caribbean-ness: "it takes me back & drags me tidalectic into this tangled urgent meaning to & fro . . ."[114] That is, the cyclical rhythms of the ocean figure in Brathwaite's notion of Caribbeanness, which he marshals in opposition to the "conquering technological thrust" of Eurocentric "straight-line thinking and rigidity," as it were. Similarly, in *The Repeating Island* (1996), Cuban novelist and essayist Antonio Benítez-Rojo insists that "Caribbeanness is a system full of noise and opacity, a nonlinear system, an unpredictable system, in short a chaotic system beyond the total reach of any specific kind of knowledge or interpretation of the world."[115]

Of course, one may be inclined to treat a novel like *Robinson Crusoe* as a colonialist cover-up – as precisely the sort of "conquering technological thrust" that Brathwaite opposes with his capsule paradigm, or dynamic model of Caribbeanness. Or, rather, one might be tempted to read the novel in light of imperialist propaganda, if not in keeping with DeLoughrey's point about how "western models of passive and empty [island] space such as *terra* and *aqua nullius* . . . were used to justify territorial expansion."[116] Novels certainly merit consideration as both epistemological and ecological forces, capable of reshaping the world historical process. And were we to limit our analysis to the cultural landscapes of *Robinson Crusoe*, the obvious overtones of racism and patriarchal homosociality certainly appear to reinforce the sort of Eurocentric biases that Brathwaite's dynamic concept of Caribbeanness opposes. Sexism and misogyny also factor into Defoe's remarks upon the dual occupation / treatment of indigenous women as both wives *and* servants in his sequel, *The Farther Adventures of Robinson Crusoe* (1719), a circumstance that reinforces Burnham's observation that indigenous women were "enmeshed everywhere in episodes of material exchange for goods and for sex."[117] It's worth noting too that the anthropomorphic confusion of particular social groups with animals, including the implicit allusion to Highland Scots embedded in James Grainger's infamously ridiculous description of rats as a "whisker'd vermine-race" (see *The Sugar-Cane*, Book II)[118] certainly dovetails with prevalent nineteenth-century racist tendencies, such as the "black-animal subtext," which is, as Bénédict Boisseron observes, "deeply ingrained in the cultural genetics of the global north, an inherited condition informed by a shared history of slavery and colonization."[119]

However, this is not the sort of confusion that I have in mind when I refer to human-extra-human sympathies. And, more importantly, Defoe makes a point of emphasizing repeatedly that Crusoe's island is neither passive nor empty, but frequented by both Europeans and indigenous Americans, as well as various extra-human natures who all leave behind considerable footprints, ecological and otherwise. The infamous footprint scene, in which Crusoe's mind is blown away by the appearance of a mysterious footprint in the sand, for example, is such a pivotal moment in the novel because it is here we see Defoe poignantly challenge the myth of wilderness that Wright regards as integral to Western colonialist misrepresentations of the Americas.[120] Moreover, the key terms in the novel's title – *strange*, *surprising* (terms that figure in Crusoe's startling recognition of the nature of barley) – suggest an alternative approach, one that is attentive to the manifold natures involved in the composition of Crusoe's history, as it were.

That is, if we follow Crusoe's lead here, and give careful consideration to the nature of barley – to its wonderfully fibrous root system, its tendency to grow in disturbed habitats, along roadsides, etc. – then the novel effectively invites us to develop a similarly strange and surprising (if not uncanny) understanding of human intimacy (or sympathy) with animals, plants, and minerals. Accordingly, the texts that I've chosen here are riddled with similar such animal, plant, and mineral interventions – whether Grainger's attention to non-native species, Singleton's preoccupation with the formation of gullies, and the ecofeminist inspiration that Sansay derives from the female land crabs' spectacular migration to the sea – so that each text bears out, however surprisingly, some version of either Brathwaite or Benítez-Rojo's tidal dialectical model of Caribbeanness, which, as Edward Baugh notes, "shuns linearity, consolidation, and stasis ... It is a movement of fluidity and flux and tides, of waves endlessly repeating themselves outward and returning."[121] The cyclical nature of Leonora Sansay's *Secret History*, for example, ties in nicely with this transoceanic view, as she invites readers to reflect upon repeated instances of violence attending women's entanglement in the global economy – the confused circuitry of economic and sexual desire.

Vandana Shiva's critical work in biopiracy similarly calls our attention to the exploitation of women's bodies / appropriation of their labor. Shiva insightfully links the bioengineering of seeds (hybrid varieties that are non-regenerative, or do not produce true-to-type seed) by multinational chemical corporations like Monsanto to the mechanization of the female body, "in which a set of fragmented, fetishized, and replaceable parts are managed by professional medical experts."[122] Most provocatively, she insists that the "source of patriarchal power over women and nature lies in separation and fragmentation":

> Nature is separated and subjugated to culture; mind is separated from and elevated above matter; female is separated from male, and identified with nature and matter. The domination over women and nature is one outcome; the disruption of cycles of regeneration is another. Disease and ecological destruction arise from this interruption of the cycles of renewal of life and health.[123]

The solution to these conjoined crises of health and ecology, suggests Shiva, lies in the rebuilding of connections, in a politics of partnership with nature, "as it is being shaped in the everyday lives of women and communities."[124] The communal component here calls to mind Gómez-Barris's study of anarcho-feminist indigenous critique in Potosí, Bolivia, a city built around the extraction of silver from nearby Cerro Ricco (Rich Mountain), a site that is sacred to the Aymara Indigenous people. Not only does Gómez-Barris call into focus the critical dependency of the silver mining industry upon the labor of women and children, but she also details the incredible efforts undertaken by women to resist "extreme exploitation within the mining industry" – anarcho-feminist efforts that would open "the hemisphere's horizon of radical politics beyond that of a heteronormative and masculinist vision."[125] Gómez-Barris notes how "women and children provide labor to the extractive zone by supporting the heterosexual 'mining family' at home, while also working within the slag waste piles that lie just south of Cerro Ricco, the million-ton heap of the mining sector's wasted materials":

> Over the course of five centuries, hundreds of thousands of women and children have labored as porters, recycling mining extraction's toxic materials.[126]

She then proceeds to closely examine various forms of anarcho-feminist Indigenous resistance to the silver mining industry, including the Chola market woman, whose active presence in the public sphere has helped to create new social systems and extend kinship networks, "thereby growing the spaces of influence for Andean cultural forms,"[127] and Mujeres Creando Communidad, an organization which, according to one of its founders, Julieta Paredes, embraces "exchange with the other's life history as a source of political insight."[128] As Gómez-Barris explains, the work of Mujeres Creando relies on communal feminisms to develop new sources of relationality, as well as to invoke anti-capitalist ideas.[129]

Again, I think it worth noting the communal element of resistance here, as I read Sansay's novel, *Secret History*, as similarly geared towards the formation of a radical ecofeminist community. My reading acknowledges the ongoing subjection of women to one of the most traumatic forms of capitalist appropriation: sexual violence. Although, as Shiva observes, patents and genetic engineering have made it possible for Capital to carve out additional colonies in the "interior spaces of the bodies of women, plants, and animals,"[130] this process began long before the publication of Sansay's novel in 1808. Has the enslaved African woman as rape victim tasked with bearing her master's illegitimate child not had the interior space of her body colonized by Capital? Gómez-Barris's remarks about Cholas – namely, that they "challenged middle-class and upper-class feminists by raising such issues as 'couple violence,' and the need for a new morality"[131] – corresponds directly with one of Sansay's main concerns: the commonplace subjection of women to domestic and sexual violence. Similarly, the shifting of control over pregnant women's bodies to medical specialists – a scenario that Shiva aptly describes in terms of "patriarchal science and law [working] hand in hand to establish the control by professional men over women's lives"[132] – dates to the long eighteenth century. As Lisa Forman Cody observes, in *Birthing the Nation*:

> by the turn of the nineteenth century, men-midwives and other men of science had established a cultural authority over sex and birth. Their apparent accomplishments and the ramifications of their knowledge deeply impressed the public, including Members of Parliament, who began to pass legislation on reproductive matters. As this occurred, many long-held assumptions about the sanctity of maternal life, the inherent authority of women over their own bodies, and the positive value of population growth were overturned.[133]

Burnham's critical analysis of Sansay's *Secret History* picks up on various related issues. She offers a compelling reading of the novel in which the "bodies of women expose the implication of short-term desires within a long-term system of global capitalist drive whose relentless circuits generate violence and inequality."[134] I too explore Sansay's confusion of economic and sexual desire. But I add to this mixture various sexual-scientific elements, including the biology of land crabs. And then I take the "botany of desire"[135] – in particular, Sansay's reliance upon both tropical flora and the discourse of sugar to convey the desirability of women in this context – a step further, arguing that the novel presents misogyny (cyclical violence against women), and *not* greed as the driving force or mechanism behind capitalism (indeed, I cite the millions of women who continue to be subject to some form of modern slavery in our present-day global economy as reinforcement of my reading).[136] The ending of the novel, for example, cycles backward from the revolutionary bust of sugar production in late eighteenth-century Haiti to what would soon become a boom period for planters of sugar cane in nineteenth-century Cuba, thereby offering a view of history that is non-linear, "repetition with change" (Heng).[137]

This book is most certainly concerned with similar questions of fluidity and flux, and with the shared histories that develop in connection with, say, the "voyaging subject who is not physically or culturally circumscribed by the terrestrial boundaries of island space," as DeLougrey puts it.[138] However, I cite Hume's theory of sympathy here precisely to foreground the agency of animals, plants, and minerals in such world historical processes. The tidal dialectic, as I see it, includes other extra-human organisms that similarly refuse to be circumscribed by the terrestrial boundaries of island or, for that matter, continental space. Numerous animals and plants have been discovered traveling on lush rafts of flotsam far out at sea, including, as Alan Burdick notes, "thirty-foot palm trees."[139] Or, for example, consider the following rather more well-known account of insect migration, which appeared in Charles Darwin's chronicle of his five-year journey aboard the HMS *Beagle*:

> Several times when the ship has been some miles off the mouth of the Plata, and at other times when off the shores of Northern Patagonia, we have been surrounded by insects. One evening, when we were about ten miles from the Bay of San Blas, vast numbers of butterflies, in bands or flocks of countless myriads, extended as far as the eye could range ... Some moths and hymenoptera accompanied the butterflies, and a fine beetle (Calosoma) flew on board. Other instances are known of this beetle having been caught far out at sea; and this is the more remarkable, as the greater number of the Carbide seldom

or never take wing. The day had been fine and calm, and the one previous to it equally so, with light and variable airs. Hence we cannot suppose that the insects were blown off the land, but we must conclude that they <u>voluntarily</u> took flight . . .

On another occasion, when seventeen miles off Cape Corrientes, I had a net overboard to catch pelagic animals. Upon drawing it up, to my surprise, I found a considerable number of beetles in it, and although in the open sea, they did not appear much injured by the salt water . . . At first I thought that these insects had been blown from the shore, but upon reflecting that out of the eight species four were aquatic, and two other partly so in their habits, it appeared to me most probable that they were floated into the sea by a small stream which drains a lake near Cape Corrientes. On any supposition it is an interesting circumstance to find live insects swimming in the open ocean seventeen miles from the nearest point of land . . . The most remarkable instance I have known of an insect being caught far from the land, was that of a large grasshopper (Acrydium), which flew on board, when the Beagle was to windward of the Cape de Verd Islands, and when the nearest point of land, not directly opposed to the trade-wind, was Cape Blanco on the coast of Africa, 370 miles distant.[140] (Underscoring mine.)

Humans like Crusoe are not the only subjects to be infected with a sort of wanderlust, and, curiously enough, that Darwin makes a point of emphasizing the voluntary nature of, say, the Calosoma beetle's waywardness reinforces this point. Thus, the shared histories that figure in this book represent a fluid confusion of human and extra-human natures. As Burnham rightly emphasizes over again in her work, a transoceanic view necessarily invites us to break away from both traditional, linear-progressive concepts of history and the ideological boundaries of nation and continent. Citing Epeli Hau'ofa's observation, that, "Pacific island peoples have long engaged in a kind of 'world enlargement' that makes 'nonsense of all national and economic boundaries, borders that have been defined only recently, crisscrossing an ocean that had been boundless for ages before Captain Cook's apotheosis,'"[141] Burnham invites us to remember the fluid, connective nature of water, and to "reimagine global relations in more oceanic terms."[142] My point here is to consider the various ways in which extra-human natures in effect act as reminders of these truths too. Ignorant of such arbitrary boundaries, animals and plants are apt to travel (and thrive) wherever it suits them. That is, animals and plants continue to make nonsense of "all national and economic boundaries." And were it not for the ecology of invasions by animals and plants, Robert Louis Stevenson's *vegetating* – his sympathetic adoption of a plant's-eye view of things in Samoa (Chapter 4) – might well be construed as a variation of what Hau'ofa describes as the Pacific Islanders' world enlargement. Here again I am reminded of Gómez-Barris's efforts to "decolonize the Anthropocene by cataloguing life otherwise," as it were, through careful attention paid to what she calls *submerged perspectives*.[143] "To name the visible and invisible forces between the human and nonhuman, between animate and inanimate life, is to perceive a too-often-ignored network of relationality," writes Gómez-Barris.[144] Such a realization is an effect of Stevenson's adoption of a plant's-eye view of things. The trouble lies in that sometimes these boundless / transoceanic human-extra-human collaborations produce scenarios in which there is an overwhelming loss in either regional or global biodiversity – a circumstance that makes me think that *world shrinkage* would be the more apt terminology to describe the outcome of all this confusing wanderlust, including the infamous work of such unruly natures as, say, Australia's brown tree snake.

Introduced (whether purposefully or accidentally) by seafaring humans to islands throughout the world, Crusoe's goats, rats, and cats stand out as species that have had huge ecological impacts.[145] Grazing mammals like goats are good at deforesting islands, a devastating circumstance that affects all other species there, whether directly or indirectly (via climate change), whereas rats have been linked to the extinction of birds and bats: skillful climbers, "ship rats extinguished the populations of all three endemic New Zealand bats in just one year on Big South Cape Island (2,300 acres) off Stewart Island, at the same time eliminating five bird species there. One of the three bats is probably now globally extinct, and another is endangered."[146] Much has been reported recently about the average U.S. domesticated cat's voluminous appetite for birds and other prey. Loss, Will, and Marra estimate, for example, that, in the United States alone, free-ranging domesticated cats "kill 1.3 – 4.0 billion birds and 6.3 – 22.3 billion mammals annually ... and are likely the single greatest source of anthropogenic mortality for US birds and mammals."[147] Noting that cats are "among the 100 worst non-native invasive species in the world," they point out that "free-ranging cats on islands have caused or contributed to 33 (14%) of the modern bird, mammal, and reptile extinctions recorded by the International Union for Conservation of Nature (IUCN) Red List."[148] Simberloff notes too, for example, that "on subantarctic Marion Island in the southern Indian Ocean, cats were introduced in 1949 and are now estimated to kill over 400,000 birds per year, mostly ground-nesting petrels."[149] It's worth noting here too, that, in the late nineteenth century (or roughly the same time that Robert Louis Stevenson published *Island Nights' Entertainments* in 1893), the Hawaii-based British entomologist, ornithologist, and naturalist, Robert Cyril Lawton Perkins documented in his field journals the considerable ecological havoc wrought by the cooperation of several particular natures, including the introduction of cats, and the clearing of forests for coffee plantations. "The four first birds of Oahu (got 40 years ago)," observes Perkins, "are now utterly extinct & between the mongoose (which swarms there), cats and mynah birds, not to mention the wholesale clearing, which is taking place for coffee planting, those on Hawaii must follow before many years."[150] The following photo taken by Stevenson's cousin, Graham Balfour (see Figure 0.1 and detail), provides us with a glimpse of the incorporation of cats into Hawaiian culture (please note: the Balfour photo included in Chapter 4 more clearly depicts a cat).

Numerous other examples abound, including the harmless-sounding rosy wolf snail and the Indian mongoose, which seems to be nearly as omnipresent on the Big Island of Hawaii as the gray squirrel is in North America. Or, in other words, as one of the leading invasion biologists, Daniel Simberloff explains, "introduced species on islands have often had staggering impacts":

> On the Hawaiian Islands, Society Islands, and other small islands in the Pacific, the rosy wolf snail, introduced from Florida and Central America in a futile attempt to lower populations of the introduced giant African snail, has caused the extinction of at least 50 species of terrestrial snails. The small Indian mongoose, introduced in attempts to control rats in agricultural fields [including sugar cane in Jamaica in 1872 – see Chapter 2] and occasionally to control venomous snakes, has caused extinction and endangerment of mammals, birds, reptiles, and amphibians in the West Indies, Hawaiian Islands, Fiji, Okinawa, Amami, Mauritius, and several Adriatic Islands.[151]

The list could go on, and, of course, continental ecosystems are susceptible to the ecological effects of invasive species too. Remember Trouvelot's European gypsy moth. Not only does the gypsy moth (a voracious consumer of oak and aspen leaves) presently occupy at least "200,000 square miles of the northeastern United States and eastern Canada," but its defoliation also increases a tree's overall vulnerability to other damaging insects and disease, so that, as Simberloff points out, "in some areas, repeated defoliation has

Introduction 35

Figure 0.1 "Hawaiian House, Hilo" from the photo albums of Sir Graham Balfour. Courtesy of the Special Collections, National Library of Scotland, Edinburgh.

Figure 0.2 "Hawaiian House, Hilo" (detail showing what appears to be a black and white cat), from the photo albums of Sir Graham Balfour. Courtesy of the Special Collections, National Library of Scotland, Edinburgh.

caused up to 90% mortality of preferred host trees, thus greatly changing forest composition."[152]

Other infamous examples of invasive species include the brown tree snake (see Chapter 4), which "has eliminated 15 native forest bird species on Guam, leaving but one species in forests that are now eerily silent" (as eerily silent as the tropical rainforest that figures in Stevenson's fiction of empire, *The Beach of Falesá* (1893)), or the Burmese python, which is supposed to be responsible for drastic reductions in mammal populations inside Everglades National Park, Florida: "observations of raccoons declined by 99.3%, opossums by 98.9%, and bobcats by 87.5%. Rabbits, red foxes, and gray foxes ceased to be recorded entirely."[153] In other words, as I argue in Chapter 4, if we follow Stevenson's lead and sympathetically adopt a plant's (or animal's) view of the world, then are we not necessarily encouraged to acknowledge the nonsense of national and economic boundaries, as well as to think in transoceanic terms about history? Does the Australian brown tree snake's transformation in / transformation of Guam's tropical forests not encourage us to view history as non-linear, as cyclical in nature or (again), as Heng suggests, "repetitions with change"?[154] The texts that I focus on here are riddled with such animal, plant, and mineral interventions that invite us to think in similarly transoceanic terms about time and place.

I also think it worth noting that while certain texts featured here may read (at times) like the sort of paradise discourse that, according to Sharae Deckard, haunts the Enlightenment vis-à-vis consumer demand for the "addictive stimulations of tea, coffee, tobacco, and sugar,"[155] others adopt more of what might be described as a postlapsarian approach. Over the course of the eighteenth century, observes Deckard, paradise was not only transformed "from a *place* to a *state* of consumption" – as the "myth of paradise as endless supply and plenty propelled further exploitation and spending, devouring the earth's resources at an ever-accelerating rate."[156] A poem like *The Sugar-Cane*, for example, in so far as it operates on the nitty-gritty level of production, as it were, helping to perfect (in considerable detail) the cultivation and processing of sugar cane to satisfy this growing consumer demand, resonates with Deckard's analysis of paradise transformed. However, as I noted earlier, Grainger frequently takes into account various imperfections in sugar production too, from persistent pests (invasive species) to the inevitability of revolution, and, in a contrasting, big-picture poem like John Singleton's *General Description of the West Indian Islands* (1767),[157] the attention given to the formation of gullies (see Chapter 2), not unlike the one depicted in the following image from James Hakewill's *Picturesque Tour of the Island of Jamaica* (1824), shatters any sort of paradisiacal associations with Caribbean life.

Introduction 37

Figure 0.3 Thomas Sutherland (1785–1838) after James Hakewill (1778–1843), "Golden Vale, Portland" from *A Picturesque Tour of the Island of Jamaica from Drawings Made in the Years 1820 and 1821,* London: Hurst and Robinson and E. Lloyd, 1825, hand-coloured aquatint. Courtesy of the Yale Center for British Art, Paul Mellon Collection.

Note the tree that is uprooted at the edge of what appears to be a gully in the bottom center of this image, not to mention the goats grazing away on the boughs of this particular victim of soil erosion resulting from the conversion of so many acres into a vast monoculture of sugar cane. The "deep gullies" that repeatedly appear in Charlotte Smith's Gothic work, *The Story of Henrietta*, and which figure as the "peculiar lurking place of fugitive negroes [runaway slaves]," similarly present us with an idea of so-called paradise transformed, or devastated to satisfy the interests of European men (planters-capitalists).[158] Originally published as the second volume in the five-volume series *The Letters of a Solitary Wanderer* (1800), Smith's novel links this geographical feature of the islands (a by-product of soil erosion owing to intensive crop monoculture) to the awful brutality of slavery and other horrors of the plantation economy, whereas Singleton's work, in particular, raises important questions about the alarming rate at which Caribbean resources were being exploited to satisfy Europeans' growing demand for stimulants (forests were decimated to make room for and literally fuel the fires required for the processing (refinement) of sugar cane, anxiously triggering a newly devised set of forest conservation laws, including the King's Hill Forest Act of 1791).[159] Accordingly, in Chapter 2 I closely analyze Singleton's *A General Description*. In this poem, Singleton offers no generic descriptions of an island Eden, but something more along the lines of the ironic paradises that, according to Deckard, crop up in postcolonial literatures such as Hervé Guibert's *Paradise*, which utilizes an "aesthetic of degradation."[160] Building on Sudan's valuable point (vis-à-vis Latour), in *The Alchemy of Empire*, that substances have histories,[161] I read the monoculture of sugar cane in not merely biological, but geological terms, as clearly linked to soil erosion. Both Singleton's *General Description* and Leonora Sansay's Gothic novel, *Secret History* reflect upon the nature-culture of the sugar boom and bust in terms of degradation, dissolution, and depravity, and, in so doing, obliterate any lingering West Indian paradise myths. Sansay's reliance upon Gothic horror is especially affective in this regard. Her novel pierces the veil of what Burnham might call a spectacle of excess.[162] Dispensing with any preconceived paradise-like notions of the plantation economy, Sansay reveals how violence towards women lies at the heart of an "early nineteenth-century imperial culture of pleasurable consumption."[163]

Furthermore, I think one should add that even pro-empire writings like *Robinson Crusoe* and *The Sugar-Cane* are riddled with complications that in effect undermine the discourse of paradise. Indeed, if empire is, as Neel Ahuja suggests, a "project in the *government* of species" (italics mine), then it stands to reason that empire writing must either implicitly or explicitly acknowledge the potential *unruliness* of particular natures, as well as the labor (or work) required to contain such unruliness.[164] And both *Crusoe* and *The Sugar-Cane* do just this.

In *Colonizing Nature*, Beth Tobin aims to "reconstruct the conditions under which tropical plants, flowers, and fruit as well as landscapes were produced and consumed" by Europeans.[165] I similarly intend to demystify the "real relations of production," as it were, in keeping with Tobin's valuable efforts. However, instead of Edenic representations of tropical nature that were carefully constructed to encourage British imperialism – i.e. the "discursive processes by which labor and history were elided from the representation of tropical nature"[166] – this book focuses upon particular authors' engagements with specific natures, in order to recollect the "biological and geological conditions of capitalism's process."[167] British attempts to colonize Nature were no doubt informed by the tropical island Eden's appearance in travel literature, botanical treatises, poetry, etc., as Tobin and others like Deckard, in *Paradise Discourse*, have suggested, but, as Grainger's *The Sugar-Cane* very clearly points out too (Chapter 2), this process occurs as part of a flow of flows, in which specific *unruly* natures play an integral role.

Accordingly, I concentrate much of my attention upon invasive (as well as other *unruly* introduced and non-native) species to showcase this element of co-production, and to remember the ways in which oceans function *not* as barriers, as it were, conveniently dividing the earth into separate landmasses, but information networks constantly carrying news (zoological, botanical, meteorological, etc.) from one part of the globe to another. The infamous Captain William Bligh's successful transplantation of breadfruit to the Caribbean would be one such example of this sort of transoceanic communication that was clearly motivated by a capitalistic agenda (not unlike Trouvelot's) – namely, the appropriation of cheap natures. (Interestingly, the Saint Vincent Botanic Garden, which was under the general management of a Scotsman and University of Edinburgh graduate, Dr. Alexander Anderson, served as the primary site for the cultivation of the breadfruit seeds that were introduced to the Caribbean by Captain Bligh in 1793; evidently, "all of the breadfruit trees in Saint Vincent are derived from suckers of these original introductions.")[168] Of course, it's worth noting that the transplantation of breadfruit to the Saint Vincent Botanic Garden represents just one example of widespread efforts by European botanists to reconfigure the world's floras. Thanks to Bourguet's considerable work on botany and climate in eighteenth-century France, we know that "in the late 1770s thermometers were present throughout the island" of Saint-Domingue, along with barometers and a few hygrometers.[169] This suggests the considerable extent to which Europeans broadly understood the mobilization of plants as a technical challenge, the success of which was linked to their close attention to climate – i.e. fluctuations in humidity and temperature. The value of Grainger's *Sugar-Cane*, thus, partly lies in publicizing meteorological data about the island of St. Christopher in poetic form. Furthermore, such transplantations, and related efforts to establish a "direct correspondence between the colonies of the eastern and western parts of the Torrid Zone"[170] reflect, in my view, a world that has already shrunk considerably by the end of the eighteenth century – a world in which biodiversity is sacrificed for the sake of the approximation of one place to another.

Bearing all of this transportation of information, goods, and bodies (humans, animals, and plants) overseas in mind, one of the goals of this book is to suggest ways in which we might rethink our geocentrism to consider the truth behind Rachel Carson's insistence, "the sea lies all about us."[171] The very name of our planet – Earth – elides the overwhelming presence and significance of the "enveloping seas,"[172] some vast percentage of which remains a mystery. And so, for scholars engaging in literary studies, perhaps a first step would be to acknowledge that every novel is a sort of seafaring novel because the capitalist society responsible for the novel's development into a highly valued literary genre rises with wave upon wave of not merely transatlantic, but transoceanic commerce, just as the British and American Empires were built upon the trans-shipment of goods and bodies – i.e. human and extra-human natures – overseas. Even today, as Margaret Cohen notes, "ships continue to convey over ninety percent of the world's freight."[173]

Of course, I am not alone in proposing that we read novels oceanically. Margaret Cohen suggests as much, linking the novel's rise to the adventure capitalism of overseas exploration and seafaring. There is (as noted earlier) DeLoughrey's careful engagement of tidal dialectics in her compelling study of Caribbean and Pacific Island literatures, *Routes and Roots*, and, of course, there's Michelle Burnham's tremendous reading of American literature in a "maritime global context." However, I am (not unlike Burnham) most keen to point out that novels / texts may merit consideration as seafaring literature regardless of whether they offer any sort of direct engagement with / representation of the sea. Burnham, for example, makes a great point about how on a formal level – in terms of their "explicit engagement with non-linear cyclical plots and narrative structures" – novels may be soaked through with saltwater, "whether or not the ocean and sea travel are part of their content."[174] Indeed, such profound recognition of the scope and significance of oceanic commerce informs not only Cohen's *The Novel and the Sea* (2010), but also Burnham's *Transoceanic America* (2019). In particular, Burnham's efforts to read the American novel transoceanically – that is, in light of the "explosion of transoceanic commerce in the age of revolutions," and with particular attention paid to connections between the Pacific and Atlantic – deserves special mention here for several reasons.

First, building upon Burnham's work, I make a point of trying to read and think about British and American literature transoceanically, though I focus primarily upon the ecology (and not merely the economy) of Europeans (from Selkirk to Stevenson) criss-crossing the Atlantic and Pacific oceans. At the outset of *Transoceanic America*, Burnham raises the following important question: "What network of connections – between Salem and Calcutta, St. Helena and New York, Canton and Philadelphia, Hawai'i and Boston – do we begin to see when we read American literature in a maritime global context?" Although my work is similarly concerned with the connections that form between distant places when literature is read transoceanically, I tend to focus not on cross-cultural reverberations, so to speak, as does Burnham, who, for example, interprets *The Travels of Hildebrand Bowman* (1778) as an allegorical pairing of the American Revolution with "indigenous anti-colonial uprisings" in the South Pacific.[175] Instead, my attention is drawn first and foremost to the often strange and surprising (*Crusoe*) pathways between cultures *and* natures that open up as a result. In *A Footnote to History*, for example, Robert Louis Stevenson's imaginative yoking together of Scotland and Samoa clearly invites us to think about shared histories of cultural imperialism (between Pacific Islanders and Highland Scots), though his conflation of these two distant places also begs to be read (on an ecological level) in light of world shrinkage – that is, in terms of the biological approximation of one place to another. The latter view, I argue, ties in nicely with Stevenson's curious preoccupation with a particular invasive plant species, *Mimosa pudica* (the sensitive plant), which (as I explain in Chapter 4), he says, was brought to Samoa by a "fool" who "used to lecture and sentimentalize over the tender thing."[176]

Second, Burnham's materialist focus on goods and bodies clearly resonates with my emphasis on the transportation of animals and plants overseas, and that she situates her analysis of American novels such as Charles Brockden Brown's *Ormond; Or, the Secret Witness* (1799) within a broad field of non-fiction works, especially numerical genres – "mathematical textbooks, accounting manuals, and insurance handbooks – that place both male and female readers in a global, transoceanic world of goods and exchanges"[177] corresponds with the strange assortment of texts that I count as empire writing here, as though the vastness of the Pacific and Atlantic oceans demands as much – a comparably wide range of texts. Whereas any transoceanic study of literature must take into account a variety of non-fiction travel narratives, Burnham pays especially close attention to "numerical record-keeping in the annals of maritime travel," in keeping with her proposition, that, the "calculative residue" of all this numerical record-keeping "differentiates novelistic from other kinds of narratives."[178] The "coiled tension" that characterizes a novel like Brown's *Ormond* not only reflects (on a formal level) a transoceanic (or non-linear) view of history, suggests Burnham. [Other novels by Brown, such as *Edgar Huntly; Or, Memoirs of a Sleepwalker* (1799) and *Arthur Mervyn; Or, Memoirs of the Year 1793* (1799), are similarly built upon cyclical narrative structures.] Such a suspenseful novel as *Ormond* also invites readers to employ a strategy of calculation that is resonant with Pacific travel writing. "Because novel plots and novel reading shared with mathematical genres strategies for determining promise and risk," suggests Burnham, "they provided an affective training ground for managing prediction and disappointment as well as for calculating probability and danger."[179] In place of Burnham's emphasis on numerical genres, I draw upon a similarly rich archive of both published and unpublished non-fiction works, from Caribbean newspapers, periodicals, and natural histories to journals, diaries, and letters composed by various relevant individuals, including, for example, John Ker, a surgeon's mate in the Royal Navy, and Lady Mary Nugent, the wife of Jamaica's Lieutenant Governor (1801–05).

Taken together, all of these texts regardless of genre highlight the considerable extent to which men and women variously located throughout the British (and American) Empire(s) were encouraged to see themselves as situated within not merely a "global, transoceanic world of goods and exchanges," but (again) a world-historical-ecological matrix, in which, as Niblett suggests (vis-à-vis Jason Moore) humans are knit together with the rest of nature "within a gravitational field of endless accumulation."[180] In her posthumously published journal, *The Narrative of a Journey from Scotland to the West Indies, North Carolina, and Portugal; in the years 1774 to 1776* (1921), for example, Janet Schaw's remarks upon the Dutch-controlled, free port island of St. Eustatius – a "place of vast traffic from every part of the globe"[181] – makes it perfectly clear how Caribbean-based planters imagined themselves as central to the formation of a truly transoceanic, global economy: "it were endless to enumerate the variety of merchandize in such a place, for in every store you find every thing ..."[182] "In every store you find every thing." Schaw's claim succinctly provides us with an idea of how sugar production transformed the West Indies into a bustling center of transoceanic commerce. In fact, according to Schaw, St. Eustatius was so thoroughly devoted to the sale of manufactured goods – "the whole riches of the Island consist in its merchandize" – that "they are obliged to the neighbouring Islands for subsistence; which they in return furnish them with contraband commodities of all kinds."[183] Schaw's celebration of St. Eustatius's commercial boom inadvertently alerts us to the island's ecological bust, or inability to sustain life.

And, finally, I must acknowledge how greatly I appreciate the careful attention that Burnham pays to the exploitation of women in this transoceanic economy. Indeed, Burnham's important recognition of the impossibility of separating the commercial from the scientific and the sexual is especially noteworthy, and has direct bearing upon my reading of Leonora Sansay's Gothic novel, *Secret History*. Like Burnham, who highlights the novel's articulation of the ways in which "circuits of desire are caught up in circuits of commerce that, by 1808, are inescapably transoceanic and tragically destructive,"[184] I too am concerned with how the exploitation of women's bodies (as well as Creole women's familiarity with the violence underscoring capitalism's appropriation of so-called cheap natures, including women's unpaid labor) factors into this world-historical-ecological process. The main difference lies in the attention I give to evolutionary biology and the botany of desire – or, rather, to Sansay's clever floral arrangement of what Burnham describes as an "obscene world of capitalist appetite."[185] I read Sansay's novel as prefiguring the provocative, ecofeminist connections that Vandana Shiva establishes between the bioengineering of seeds and the mechanization of human reproduction – i.e. Capital's invasion and exploitation of the interior spaces of the bodies of women, plants, and animals.[186]

Furthermore, because, as a number of scholars, including Burnham, have carefully noted, that our present-day global economy is very much rooted in the plantation system that was fine-tuned to support lucrative sugar production in the West Indies beginning in the seventeenth century,[187] the bulk of my attention here (Chapters 2 and 3) focuses upon literature relevant to this sugar revolution. Indeed, as Sidney W. Mintz points out in his remarkable study, *Sweetness and Power: The Place of Sugar in Modern History*, the Caribbean sugar plantations played a vital role in the rise of capitalism, which involved not merely the destruction of European feudalism, but the

> creation of a system of world trade ... the creation of colonies, the establishment of experimental economic enterprises in various world areas [agribusinesses], and the development of new forms of slave-based production in the New World, using imported slaves – perhaps Europe's biggest single external contribution to its own economic growth.[188]

Of course, one must acknowledge not merely the centrality of violence here (and especially, I argue in Chapter 3, violence against women), as Sven Beckert and others like Burnham have noted, that, "violence made the expansion of global capitalism possible at the hands of European empires that navigated oceans in pursuit of commodities, markets, and labor."[189]

One must also take into account the element of speed, which was a factor in both the clearing of forests to make room for agricultural production, and the production of sugar for European consumers (a remarkably time-sensitive process that I detail in Chapter 3). That one may establish connections between climate change (the overarching twenty-first-century threat of world-ecological collapse) and the wholesale transformation of Caribbean islands to support this time-sensitive, farm-factory model of sugar production in the eighteenth century (a model designed to avoid spoilage, as well as keep pace with Europeans' growing demand for stimulants: sugar, coffee, chocolate, and tea) would certainly appear to lend credence to Paul Virilio's conception of speed as the engine of destruction.[190] And Moore notes, for instance, that

> the rise of capitalism after 1450 was made possible by an epochal shift in the scale, speed, and scope of landscape transformation in the Atlantic world and beyond. The long seventeenth century's forest clearances of the Vistula Basin and Brazil's Atlantic Rainforest [notably, not too far from where Defoe chooses to set Crusoe's island] occurred on a scale, and at a speed between five and ten times greater than anything seen in medieval Europe.[191]

Last but not least, we must also take into account the scientific revolution's role in the appropriation of new forms of unpaid labor. Indeed, the transatlantic slave trade was significant enough for James Grainger to devote the entire fourth book of *The Sugar-Cane* to the topic of slave maintenance. While this fourth book has (not surprisingly) received the most critical attention (it is the most frequently anthologized example of Grainger's work), the preceding three books, I argue, are equally important because they serve as a testament to Grainger's Trouvelot-like efforts to "identify, secure, and channel unpaid work outside the commodity system into the circuit of capitalism,"[192] including the work of the Indian mongoose, which he recommends as a potential solution to the invasive rat problem (the so-called imperfect creatures that similarly plagued Selkirk) upon the sugar plantations of St. Christopher (St. Kitts). Indeed, "the history of capitalism is one of successive historical natures."[193]

And so, I begin with Selkirk (and especially Selkirk's goats) (Chapter 1), and then I continue to closely analyze texts composed by or about persons residing upon Caribbean (Chapters 2 and 3) and Pacific (Chapter 4) islands because these islands not only continue to bear the greatest environmental burden of all this imperial business / transoceanic traffic, but they also reflect this element of co-production precisely in terms of their susceptibility to biological invasion, which by definition represents a sort of collaboration between human and non-human animals and plants. Indeed, human participation is built into the very definition of invasive species – i.e. "species that arrive with *human assistance*, establish populations, and spread" (italics mine)[194] – and, as Simberloff observes, "islands are famous for having many introduced species and suffering huge transformations at the hands of these species."[195] Of course, I am not going to rehearse the history of the British Empire here, an unfolding that has been thoroughly documented elsewhere (see, for example, *The Oxford History of the British Empire* and *The Oxford History of the British Empire Companion Series*, especially William Beinart and Lotte Hughes's *Environment and Empire*),[196] except to note that a critical link exists between biodiversity loss, including species extinction, and the transportation of animals and plants upon which this massive new, and increasingly mobile empire was built over the course of the long eighteenth and nineteenth centuries. That is, I acknowledge the British Empire to be, as Ahuja suggests, in *Bioinsecurities*, a "project in the government of species."[197] Defoe's *Robinson Crusoe*, which details the step-by-step remodeling of a so-called remote desert island in the Atlantic Ocean, prefaces this historical, or, rather, world-ecological unfolding, in as much as Crusoe's survival depends upon not merely his careful appropriation of cheap natures, especially cereal grasses, cats, and goats, but the development of particular interspecies relations. The story of Robinson Crusoe, not unlike the history of the British Empire itself, dovetails with the ecology of invasions by animals and plants.

****

In short, *The Ecology of British and American Empire Writing, 1704–1894*, explores the literary legacy of world-ecology through close analysis of the interactions that take place between human and extra-human natures at the heart of the Capitalocene. It brings environmental studies (and especially invasion biology) to bear upon texts composed by (or about) persons residing at the so-called outer limits of the British (and American) Empire(s), including the story of Alexander Selkirk, Daniel Defoe's *Robinson Crusoe*, James Grainger's West Indian georgic, *The Sugar-Cane*, John Singleton's poem, *A General Description of the West-Indian Islands*, Leonora Sansay's Gothic novel set during the Haitian Revolution, *Secret History*, and Robert Louis Stevenson's Pacific poetry and fiction, among others. Because these empires were built around the transoceanic, global transfer of animals and plants, I offer biotic readings of this literature, in order to highlight various formations of humanity-in-nature / nature-in-humanity, as well as to provide practical literary examples of the ways in which oceans confuse both geographical spaces and timelines. Indeed, this book is concerned not merely with the inviolable union of economy and ecology, but the heterarchical nature of empire building, and, of course, the *registration* of particular animal, plant, and mineral interventions in works of British and American literature that do not merely reflect, but also inform and resist this world-historical-ecological process. *Robinson Crusoe*, I argue, urges us to consider the co-productive role that extra-human natures play in the accumulation of capital (Chapter 1), while *The Sugar-Cane* not only invites us to reflect upon poetry's capacity to produce environmental realities, but also focuses our attention upon the vulnerability of island ecosystems to invasive species (Chapter 2). John Singleton's *General Description* of the West Indies treats the environmental degradation caused by intensive crop monoculture in the Caribbean (Chapter 2), whereas Sansay's novel establishes a troubling connection between the brutality of capitalism and evolutionary biology vis-à-vis women's struggle for survival in a plantation economy designed to satisfy particular masculine, patriarchal desires (Chapter 3). And, finally, Stevenson's work begs to be read in light of the brown tree snake's recent horrifying invasion (and devastating domination) of Guam's ecosystem (Chapter 4), as well as studies detailing the uncanny animal-like actions of plants. From *Robinson Crusoe* to *The Beach of Falesá*, the natures of empire writing present an increasingly robust challenge to the integrity of the human, such that the fundamental question of Western philosophy – Who am I? – gets, as Cole puts it, "superseded by another question: 'What is my place in the system?'."[198]

In Chapter 1, I read *Robinson Crusoe* as a novel that complicates the so-called borderline between nature and culture. Focusing upon the all-important footprint scene, as well as the natural-historical-geopolitical significance of the Juan Fernández archipelago (including the island upon which the so-called real Robinson Crusoe, Scottish naval officer Alexander Selkirk, lived as a castaway from 1704 to 1709), I argue that Defoe's novel presents us with a unique opportunity to both debunk the myth of isolated island space and explore human history's implication in natural history.[199] A close ecocritical examination of the passages leading up to and surrounding Crusoe's discovery of the footprint, including those highlighting the peculiar natures of barley, goats, rats, and cats, suggests ways in which Defoe's immensely popular novel invites us to think about various formations of humanity-in-nature / nature-in-humanity, as well as the heterarchical nature of empire building. Crusoe's ecological awakening, as it were, precipitated by the barley's so-called miraculous growth, not to mention the mysterious appearance of a footprint in the sand, reflects what María M. Portuondo describes as Early Modern efforts to develop a new framework, including "new ways of collecting knowledge about nature," through which to explain the reality of the New World.[200]

Chapter 2 takes the world-ecological significance of the sugar revolution into account, in part through close analysis of both the real and imaginative confusion of Old and New World species in various forms of West Indian empire writing. Essays that appeared in *The Jamaica Magazine*, such as "An Account of Some Trees of Prodigious Dimensions in Scotland," for example, beg to be read in light of widespread deforestation in *both* Scotland and the Caribbean. Accordingly, this chapter considers the ways in which early Caribbean authors broadly conceive of the sugar revolution and, by extension, human history, as co-produced by manifold species. That is, I seize this opportunity to examine the world-ecological orientation of Caribbean-based authors, including James Grainger, whose efforts to perfect the cultivation and processing of sugar cane led him to make some very bold suggestions concerning the vulnerability of island ecosystems to invasive species, and John Singleton, whose poem, *A General Description of the West-Indian Islands* (1767), portrays (in sublime detail) Caribbean nature as exhausted by intensive crop monoculture. Furthermore, by taking into account the future environmental impacts of, say, Grainger's proposal to not only introduce the mongoose to St. Christopher in 1764, but also (more radically) to eat the invaders (to incorporate rats into human diets), I draw attention to the resonances between past and present environmental practices, and, in doing so, I emphasize the remarkable relevance of these early texts to present-day environmental crises. On one hand, Grainger's work reads (at times) as a product of the scientific revolution, in so far as he capitalizes upon local knowledge to exert purposive control over Nature, or govern particular *unruly* species (so-called pests of various sorts). And, in this regard, *The Sugar-Cane* merits consideration as a form of biopiracy, in keeping with Vandana Shiva's work tracing the effects of the Papal "Bull of Donation," John Locke's labor theory of property, and, most recently, the GATT treaty upon Europeans' transoceanic plunder of nature and knowledge.[201] On the other hand, Singleton's poem contains contrasting passages of considerable alarm, an "aesthetic of degradation,"[202] as it were, linking the plantation economy to ecological collapse.

In Chapter 3, I adopt an ecofeminist approach to the sugar revolution vis-à-vis Leonora Sansay's Gothic novel, *Secret History; Or, the Horrors of St. Domingo* (1808). That Sansay chooses to *not* make Haitian independence her primary object of study, but, instead, focuses upon the horrifyingly misogynistic, amorous intrigues of Europeans, I argue, invites readers to reconsider the brutal nature of capitalism in the Caribbean. Instead of *avarice*, the passion whose rehabilitation by Enlightenment philosophers neatly coincides with capitalism's rise, Sansay relies upon a series of non-human metaphors (plant and animal interventions) to link European agribusiness to gender injustices: systemic violence towards women that – not unlike the history of sugar cane (L. *Saccharum officinarum*) itself – knows no geopolitical, racial, ethnic and/or religious boundaries. It is a distinctly gendered botany of desire (Pollan) that Sansay posits as the secret history of capitalist exploitation in the Caribbean. Not only does Sansay's narrator, Mary, compare her sister's sexual appeal to the sweetness of flora, anticipating Sidney W. Mintz's efforts to showcase the "special significance ... of sugar in the growth of world capitalism."[203] She also claims that "St. Domingo was formerly a garden," which is important because the garden referred to here is emphatically *not* one of the Edenic, island paradises featured in the propaganda of American settlement, but, rather, a garden distinguished by its gross immorality – an immorality characterized by Europeans' libidinous excesses and horrifying violence. Anticipating Macarena Gómez-Barris's study of anarcho-feminist-Indigenous critique in Potosí, Bolivia, Sansay's novel treats communal feminism as the antidote to extractive capitalism. In other words, Sansay's novel links the routine victimization of women to the accumulation of capital, which, as Moore suggests, similarly depends upon the "fruits of appropriation derived from Cheap Natures, understood primarily as ... labor-power, food, energy, and raw materials."[204] Like Michelle Burnham, I read Sansay's novel as a horrifying treatment of the tragically confused circuitry of sexual desire and commerce.[205] However, I also take into account evolutionary biology, and the botany and zoology of this desire, as it were – the various ways in which particular animals and plants intervene in Sansay's Gothic narrative to situate cycles of capitalist exploitation (boom and bust) in the web of life (birth and death). Drawing upon Vandana Shiva's work in biopiracy, I read Sansay's novel as foregrounding connections between bioengineering and misogyny in the agribusiness of sugar cane.

And, finally, Chapter 4 explores how both walking and weeding contributed to Robert Louis Stevenson's writing (especially his Pacific poetry and prose) and to his increasing awareness of what contemporary economists and ecologists routinely call our shrinking world. Whereas Ann C. Colley draws our attention to the nature of Stevenson's memory in her compelling 2004 study, *Robert Louis Stevenson and the Colonial Imagination*,[206] this chapter takes into account Stevenson's memory of particular natures, or the various ways in which his writing encourages us to not only remember the "world of things" (Serres),[207] but also to sympathetically recognize the animal-like actions of plants. Like Colley, I am concerned with particulars here, but instead of the particularities of cultural exchange, I focus upon Stevenson's inter-subjective relationship to non-human (or environmental) particularities, especially as they relate to larger, global questions and concerns about biological invasion. Not only does Stevenson's frequent nostalgic and psychogeographic conflation of Scotland and Samoa reflect a keen transoceanic attentiveness to the shrinking of his world – i.e. to the various purposeful and accidental threats that global commerce poses to biodiversity. (Here, again, I am reminded of Marie-Noëlle Bourguet's work on the mobilization of plants, and, in particular, European efforts to establish a "direct correspondence between the colonies of the eastern and western parts of the Torrid Zone.")[208] Stevenson also implicitly establishes a troubling parallel between capitalism's acceleration of turnover time and a particular invasive plant species' takeover of Samoa's forests, a natural-historical unfolding that he aptly refers to in his letters as the "horror of creeping things."[209] Weeding in Samoa, I argue, enables Stevenson to sympathetically adopt a plant's-eye and, thus, world-ecological view of Pacific islands – a strange new perspective that, in turn, prompts him to rethink his (the human) place in nature. Like Macarena Gómez-Barris, whose valuable work engages the "possibility of renewed perception,"[210] this chapter explores how the sensitive plant affectively transformed Stevenson's view of the human and, more broadly, world-ecology.

In short, at this critical juncture in which the biodiversity of planet Earth appears to be shrinking fast and furiously, this book invites us to take a close, biotic look at British and American empire writing to consider the various ways in which particular animals, plants, and minerals actively intervene in this literature to decenter the human, thereby highlighting the heterarchical nature of empire building. From Selkirk's so-called imperfect creatures (rats), Crusoe's English barley, and Singleton's deep gullies to Sansay's female land crabs and Stevenson's sensitive plant, the fate of such unruly natures remains inextricably linked to our own. As noted earlier, if Empire is, as Neel Ahuja suggests, a "project in the *Government* of species" (italics mine), then it stands to reason that empire writing must either implicitly or explicitly acknowledge the potential *unruliness* of particular natures.[211] And it is through close attention to such unruliness that, I argue, these texts acknowledge the co-productive agency of animals and plants, offering a transoceanic view of time and place: one that both troubles the geopolitical (and geographical) boundaries of nation (and of island and continent), and presents world literature / history as non-anthropocentric, linear and progressive, but integral to world-ecology and, thus, cyclical *in* nature.

Notes

1. Daniel Defoe, *The Life and Strange Surprizing Adventures of Robinson Crusoe of York, Mariner*, etc. (London: W. Taylor, 1719), edited by John Richetti (New York: Penguin Books, 2001), 63. Further citations will be parenthetical.
2. See, for example, Alfred W. Crosby, *Ecological Imperialism: The Biological Expansion of Europe, 900–1900* (Cambridge: Cambridge University Press, 2004).
3. Londa Schiebinger and Claudia Swan, eds, "Introduction," *Colonial Botany: Science, Commerce, and Politics in the Early Modern World* (Philadelphia: University of Pennsylvania Press, 2005), 2.
4. Schiebinger and Swan, *Colonial Botany*, 9.
5. Aside from Woodes Rogers's account of Alexander Selkirk's nearly 4.5-year sojourn on Juan Fernández in *A Cruising Voyage Round the World* (1712) and Richard Steele's treatment of the same in *The Englishman* (1713), scholars have identified a number of other source texts for *Crusoe* that speak to the transoceanic nature of Defoe's work, including, for example, Robert Knox's *An Historical Relation of the Island of Ceylon* (1681), and John Poyntz's *The Present Prospect of the Famous and Fertile Island of Tobago* (1683). See Richard H. Grove, *Green Imperialism: Colonial expansion, tropical island Edens and the origins of environmentalism, 1600–1860* (Cambridge: Cambridge University Press, 1995), 228.

6. Michael Niblett, *World Literature and Ecology: The Aesthetics of Commodity Frontiers, 1890–1950* (Cham: Palgrave Macmillan, 2020), 7.
7. Niblett, *World Literature and Ecology*, 6.
8. Jill Casid, *Sowing Empire: Landscape and Colonization* (Minneapolis: University of Minnesota Press, 2005), 95.
9. Rebecca J. H. Woods, *The Herds Shot Round the World: Native Breeds and the British Empire, 1800–1900* (Chapel Hill: University of North Carolina Press, 2017), 3.
10. Casid, *Sowing Empire*, 97.
11. Lucinda Cole, *Imperfect Creatures: Vermin, Literature, and the Sciences of Life, 1600–1740* (Ann Arbor: University of Michigan Press, 2016), 146–7.
12. Bruno Latour, *We Have Never Been Modern* (1991), translated by Catherine Porter (Cambridge, MA: Harvard University Press, 1993), 139.
13. Cole, *Imperfect Creatures*, 145.
14. María M. Portuondo, *Secret Science: Spanish Cosmography and the New World* (Chicago: University of Chicago Press, 2009), 1.
15. Portuondo, *Secret Science*, 4.
16. Portuondo, *Secret Science*, 4–5.
17. Cole, *Imperfect Creatures*, 22.
18. Cole, *Imperfect Creatures*, 145–6.
19. Cole, *Imperfect Creatures*, 147. See also John Bender, *Ends of Enlightenment* (Palo Alto, CA: Stanford University Press, 2012).
20. Strangely, Defoe appears (at times) to mix up the terms corn and barley. See, for example, p. 64, in which case Crusoe speaks of "10 or 12 grains of corn," as he endeavors to explain the sprouting of what he previously described as *English* barley.
21. Cole, *Imperfect Creatures*, 9.
22. Ayesha Ramachandran, *The Worldmakers: Global Imagining in Early Modern Europe* (Chicago: University Press of Chicago, 2015), 17.
23. Ramachandran, *Worldmakers*, 17.
24. Latour, *We Have Never Been Modern*, 138.
25. Daniel Simberloff, *Invasive Species: What Everyone Needs to Know* (Oxford: Oxford University Press, 2013), 48–9.
26. Herbert A. Raffaele and James W. Wiley, *Wildlife of the Caribbean* (Princeton: Princeton University Press, 2014), 92.
27. Cole, *Imperfect Creatures*, 22.
28. Cole, *Imperfect Creatures*, 146.
29. Jason H. Pearl, "Desert Islands and Urban Solitudes in the *Crusoe* Trilogy," *Studies in the Novel* 44, no. 2 (Summer 2012), 125. See also Bruce McLeod, *The Geography of Empire in English Literature, 1580–1745* (New York: Cambridge University Press, 1992).
30. Simberloff, *Invasive Species*, 10.

31. Rachel Carson, *Silent Spring* (1962), 50th Anniversary Edition (Boston: Mariner Books, 2002), 20.
32. Carson, *Silent Spring*, 188.
33. Carson, *Silent Spring*, 17.
34. Jason W. Moore, *Capitalism in the Web of Life: Ecology and the Accumulation of Capital* (London: Verso, 2015), 17.
35. Vandana Shiva, *Biopiracy: The Plunder of Nature and Knowledge* (Boston: South End Press, 1997), 1–2.
36. Latour, *We Have Never Been Modern*, 22–4.
37. Cole, *Imperfect Creatures*, 8–9. See also Michel Serres, *The Parasite* (Minneapolis: University of Minnesota Press, 2007), and Latour, *We Have Never Been Modern*.
38. Cole, *Imperfect Creatures*, 9. See also Bruno Latour, *Politics of Nature: How to Bring the Sciences into Democracy*, translated by Catherine Porter (Cambridge, MA: Harvard University Press, 2004), 75.
39. See, for example, Shiva's discussion of the neem tree in *Biopiracy*, 69–72.
40. Rajani Sudan, *The Alchemy of Empire: Abject Materials and the Technologies of Colonialism* (New York: Fordham University Press, 2016), 7.
41. Judith Carney, "Out of Africa: Colonial Rice History in the Black Atlantic," *Colonial Botany: Science, Commerce, and Politics in the Early Modern World*, edited by Londa Schiebinger and Claudia Swan (Philadelphia: University of Pennsylvania Press, 2005). 204.
42. Robert Louis Stevenson, *The Letters of Robert Louis Stevenson*, Vol. 7 (New Haven: Yale University Press, 1995), 93.
43. Cole, *Imperfect Creatures*, 9.
44. John Miller, *Empire and the Animal Body: Violence, Identity, and Ecology in Victorian Adventure Fiction* (London: Anthem Press, 2012), 4.
45. Niblett, *World Literature and Ecology*, 3.
46. Tobias Menely, *Climate and the Making of Worlds: Toward a Geohistorical Poetics* (Chicago: University of Chicago Press, 2021), 15.
47. Ramachandran, *Worldmakers*, 8.
48. Quoted in Niblett, *World Literature and Ecology*, 7.
49. Ramachandran, *Worldmakers*, 150.
50. Marie-Noëlle Bourguet, "Measurable Difference: Botany, Climate, and the Gardener's Thermometer in Eighteenth-Century France," *Colonial Botany: Science, Commerce, and Politics in the Early Modern World*, edited by Londa Schiebinger and Claudia Swan (Philadelphia: University of Pennsylvania Press, 2005), 270.
51. Michelle Burnham, *Transoceanic America: Risk, Writing, and Revolution in the Global Pacific* (Oxford: Oxford University Press, 2019), 18.

52. Elizabeth Maddox Dillon and Michael Drexler, eds, *The Haitian Revolution and the Early United States: Histories, Textualities, Geographies* (Philadelphia: University of Pennsylvania Press, 2016), 10.
53. See Antonio Benítez-Rojo, "Sugar and the Environment in Cuba," translated by James Maraniss, *Caribbean Literature and the Environment: Between Nature and Culture*, edited by Elizabeth DeLoughrey, Renée K. Gosson, and George B. Handley (Charlottesville: University of Virginia Press, 2005), 40–1.
54. Burnham, *Transoceanic*, 4.
55. Niblett, *World Literature and Ecology*, 12.
56. Moore, *Capitalism*, 2–3.
57. Macarena Gómez-Barris, *The Extractive Zone: Social Ecologies and Decolonial Perspectives* (Durham, NC: Duke University Press, 2017), 12.
58. Gómez-Barris, *Extractive Zone*, 5.
59. Gómez-Barris, *Extractive Zone*, 12.
60. Graham Huggan and Helen Tiffin, *Postcolonial Ecocriticism: Literature, Animals, Environment* (Abingdon: Routledge, 2010), 8.
61. Huggan and Tiffin, *Postcolonial Ecocriticism*, 8.
62. Huggan and Tiffin, *Postcolonial Ecocriticism*, 8.
63. Laura Wright, *"Wilderness into Civilized Shapes": Reading the Postcolonial Environment* (Athens: University of Georgia Press, 2010), 14.
64. Niblett, *World Literature and Ecology*, 6.
65. Ramachandran, *Worldmakers*, 7.
66. Susan Manning, *Fragments of Union: Making Connections in Scottish and American Writing* (Houndmills and New York: Palgrave, 2002).
67. Moore, *Capitalism*, 4.
68. Sigmund Freud, "The Uncanny," first published in *Imago*, translated by Alix Strachey (1919).
69. David Hume, *A Treatise of Human Nature* (1739–40) (Oxford: Clarendon Press, 1978), 316.
70. Evan Gottlieb, *Feeling British: Sympathy and National Identity in Scottish and English Writing, 1707–1832* (Lewisburg, PA: Bucknell University Press, 2007). See also, for example, *Subversion and Sympathy: Gender, Law, and the British Novel*, edited by Martha Nussbaum and Alison LaCroix (Oxford: Oxford University Press, 2013); and Seth Lobis, *The Virtue of Sympathy: Magic, Philosophy and Literature in Seventeenth-Century England* (New Haven, CT: Yale University Press, 2015).
71. Tobias Menely, *The Animal Claim: Sensibility and the Creaturely Voice* (Chicago: University of Chicago Press, 2015), 3.
72. Menely, *Animal Claim*, 2.

73. For a neurological discussion of facial expression and body feedback, see Jonathan Turner, *On the Origins of Human Emotions: A Sociological Inquiry into the Evolution of Human Affect* (Palo Alto, CA: Stanford University Press, 2000). See also Alphonso Lingis, *Dangerous Emotions* (Berkeley: University of California Press, 2000).
74. Menely, *Animal Claim*, 61.
75. William Bartram, *Travels through North and South Carolina, Georgia, and East and West Florida, the Cherokee Country, The Extensive Territories of the Muscogulges, or Creek Confederacy, and the Country of the Chactaws. Containing An Account of the Soil and Natural Productions of Those Regions; Together with Observations on the Manners of the Indians*, Second Edition (London: J. Johnson, 1794), xiii.
76. Suzanne Simard, *Finding the Mother Tree: Discovering the Wisdom of the Forest* (New York: Knopf, 2021). See also Peter Wohlleben, *The Hidden Life of Trees: What They Feel, How They Communicate – Discoveries from a Secret World* (Vancouver, BC: Greystone Books, 2016).
77. Paul Simons, *The Action Plant: Movement and nervous behavior in plants* (Oxford, and Cambridge, MA: Blackwell, 1992), 1–2.
78. See Maja Djikic, Keith Oatley, and Mihnea C. Moldoveanu, "Reading other minds: Effects of literature on empathy," *Scientific Study of Literature* 3, no. 1 (2013), 28–47.
79. T. M. Devine, *Scotland's Empire: The Origins of the Global Diaspora* (London: Penguin, 2003), 246.
80. Hume, *Treatise*, 492.
81. Olaudah Equiano, *The Interesting Narrative and Other Writings*, edited by Vincent Carretta (New York: Penguin, 1995), 233.
82. Hume, *Treatise*, 317.
83. See, for example, Gottlieb, *Feeling British*.
84. Moore, *Capitalism*, 19.
85. Pearl, "Desert Islands," 125. See also McLeod, *Geography of Empire*.
86. Moore, *Capitalism*, 8.
87. William Cronon, "The Trouble with Wilderness; or, Getting Back to the Wrong Nature," *Uncommon Ground: Rethinking the Human Place in Nature*, edited by William Cronon (New York: W. W. Norton, 1995), 69–90.
88. Moore, *Capitalism*, 9.
89. Moore, *Capitalism*, 14–15.
90. Moore, *Capitalism*, 14.
91. Moore, *Capitalism*, 15.
92. Moore, *Capitalism*, 5.
93. Moore, *Capitalism*, 7.
94. Moore, *Capitalism*, 172. I share Moore's insistence, that, if we are to effectively combat climate change, then it is better not to link the

so-called Anthropocene to the advent of any particular technology, thereby ignoring the basic conditions of capitalism's rise – but steam and coal have had significant environmental impacts. Simberloff aptly points out, for example, that as travel by steamship greatly sped up the Atlantic Ocean crossing, "nursery stock imported into the United States ... drastically increased the number of introduced insect species." See Simberloff, *Invasive Species*, 39.

95. Moore, *Capitalism*, 170. See also Vandana Shiva, *Monocultures of the Mind: Perspectives on Biodiversity and Biotechnology* (London: Zed Books, 1993); and Frank Biermann, et al., "Down to Earth: Contextualizing the Anthropocene," *Global Environmental Change*, no. 39 (2016), 341–50.
96. Gómez-Barris, *Extractive Zone*, 4.
97. Gómez-Barris, *Extractive Zone*, 4.
98. See Henri Lefebvre, *The Production of Space*, translated by Donald Nicholson-Smith (Malden, MA: Wiley-Blackwell, 1992).
99. Portuondo, *Secret Science*, 2.
100. Niblett, *World Literature and Ecology*, 3.
101. See Crosby, *Ecological Imperialism* and Virginia DeJohn Anderson, *Creatures of Empire: How Domestic Animals Transformed Early America* (Oxford: Oxford University Press, 2006).
102. Andrew Lambert, *Crusoe's Island: A Rich and Curious History of Pirates, Castaways and Madness* (London: Faber & Faber, 2016), 49.
103. Woodes Rogers, *A Cruising Voyage Round the World: First to the South-Seas, thence to the East-Indies, and homewards by the Cape of Good Hope . . .* (1712) (Amsterdam: N. Israel, 1969), 137.
104. Burnham, *Transoceanic*, 14.
105. Lambert, *Crusoe's Island*, 29.
106. For more on scorbutic sailors, see Jonathan Lamb, *Scurvy: The Disease of Discovery* (Princeton: Princeton University Press, 2016).
107. See esp. Chapter 4, "The Fate of Remote Islands," in Charles S. Elton's foundational study, *The Ecology of Invasions by Animals and Plants* (1958), with a new forward by Daniel Simberloff (Chicago: University of Chicago Press, 2000), 77–93. See also Simberloff, *Invasive Species*, 41–8.
108. See, for example, Sharae Deckard, "Early Modern Paradise and the Age of Imperialism," in *Paradise Discourse, Imperialism, and Globalization: Exploiting Eden* (New York and London: Routledge, 2010), 7–11.
109. For a discussion of the tropical island Eden's significance in the British imperial imagination, see Grove, *Green Imperialism*; and Beth Tobin, *Colonizing Nature: The Tropics in British Arts and Letters, 1760–1820* (Philadelphia: University of Pennsylvania Press, 2005).
110. Geraldine Heng, "Reinventing Race, Colonization, and Globalisms across Deep Time: Lessons for the Longer *Durée*," *PMLA* 130, no.2 (March 2015), 360.

111. Elizabeth M. DeLoughrey, *Routes and Roots: Navigating Caribbean and Pacific Island Literatures* (Honolulu: University of Hawaii Press, 2007), 3.
112. DeLoughrey, *Routes and Roots*, 2.
113. DeLoughrey, *Routes and Roots*, 3.
114. Kamau Brathwaite, *Barabajan Poems, 1492–1992* (Kingston, Jamaica and New York: Savacou North, 1994), 182.
115. Quoted in Edward Baugh, "Literary Theory and the Caribbean: Theory, Belief, and Desire, or Designing Theory," *Journal of West Indian Literature* 15, no. 1/2 (November 2006), 5.
116. DeLoughrey, *Routes and Roots*, 3.
117. Burnham, *Transoceanic*, 12.
118. James Grainger, *The Sugar-Cane: A Poem in Four Books. With Notes* (1764), *Caribbeana: An Anthology of English Literature of the West Indies, 1657–1777*, edited by Thomas W. Krise (Chicago and London: University of Chicago Press, 1999), 200.
119. Bénédict Boisseron, *Afro-Dog: Blackness and the Animal Question* (New York: Columbia University Press, 2018), ix. Grainger would no doubt have been familiar with how the term "vermin" was used to disparage and dehumanize Highland Scots, especially those involved in the 1745 Jacobite uprising. See W. A. Speck, *The Butcher: The Duke of Cumberland and the Suppression of the '45* (Caernarfon Gwynedd, Cymru: Welsh Academic Press, 1995), 147.
120. Wright, *"Wilderness,"* 11.
121. Baugh, "Literary Theory and the Caribbean," 7.
122. Shiva, *Biopiracy*, 57.
123. Shiva, *Biopiracy*, 63.
124. Shiva, *Biopiracy*, 64.
125. Gómez-Barris, *Extractive Zone*, 114–15.
126. Gómez-Barris, *Extractive Zone*, 114.
127. Gómez-Barris, *Extractive Zone*, 118.
128. Gómez-Barris, *Extractive Zone*, 124.
129. Gómez-Barris, *Extractive Zone*, 124.
130. Shiva, *Biopiracy*, 5.
131. Gómez-Barris, *Extractive Zone*, 118.
132. Shiva, *Biopiracy*, 59.
133. Lisa Forman Cody, *Birthing the Nation: Sex, Science, and the Conception of Eighteenth-Century Britons* (Oxford: Oxford University Press, 2005), 269.
134. Burnham, *Transoceanic*, 19.
135. This is a key term for Michael Pollan. See Pollan, *The Botany of Desire: A Plant's-Eye View of the World* (New York: Random House, 2001).
136. According to the Global Slavery Index, of the roughly 40 million people enslaved in 2016, 71 percent were women. See the Global

Slavery Index. Available at <https://www.globalslaveryindex.org/2018/findings/highlights>. Accessed 14 August 2020.
137. Heng, "Reinventing Race," 360.
138. DeLoughrey, *Routes and Roots*, 3.
139. Alan Burdick, *Out of Eden: An Odyssey of Ecological Invasion* (New York: Farrar, Straus, and Giraux, 2005), 49.
140. Charles Darwin, *Journal of Researches into the Geology and Natural History of Various Countries Visited by the H.M.S. Beagle, 1832–1836* (1839) (New York: Modern Library, 2001), 142.
141. Quoted in Burnham, *Transoceanic*, 9.
142. Burnham, *Transoceanic*, 9.
143. Gómez-Barris, *Extractive Zone*, 4.
144. Gómez-Barris, *Extractive Zone*, 2.
145. It's worth noting here that invasive species are, by definition, those which "arrive with human assistance, establish populations, and spread." See Simberloff, *Invasive Species*, 3.
146. Simberloff, *Invasive Species*, 66.
147. Scott R. Loss, Tom Will, and Peter P. Marra, "The impact of free-ranging domestic cats on wildlife in the United States," *Nature Communications* 4, no. 1396 (29 January 2013), 1.
148. Loss, et al., "The Impact," 2.
149. Simberloff, *Invasive Species*, 43.
150. Robert Cyril Lawton Perkins, *Barefoot on Lava: The Journals and Correspondence of Naturalist R. C. L. Perkins in Hawai'i, 1892–1901*, edited by Neal L. Evenhuis (Honolulu: Bishop Museum Press, 2007), 306.
151. Simberloff, *Invasive Species*, 43.
152. Simberloff, *Invasive Species*, 69.
153. Simberloff, *Invasive Species*, 66.
154. Heng, "Reinventing Race," 360.
155. Deckard, *Paradise Discouse*, 12.
156. Deckard, *Paradise Discourse*, 12.
157. See John Singleton, *A General Description of the West-Indian Islands, As far as relates to the British, Dutch, and Danish Governments, from Barbados to Saint Croix* (1767), in *Caribbeana: An Anthology of English Literature of the West Indies, 1657–1777*, edited by Thomas W. Krise (Chicago: University of Chicago Press, 1999), 292. It's worth noting here too that this edition of Singleton's poem is the one that was published in Barbados in 1767. Krise observes, that, "a much abridged version was published in London in 1776 under the title *A Description of the West-Indies: A Poem in Four Books.* See Krise, *Caribbeana*, 261.
158. Charlotte Smith, *The Story of Henrietta* (1800), edited by Janina Nordius (Kansas City: Valancourt Books, 2012), 45, 61.
159. For more on the King's Hill Forest Act, see Grove, *Green Imperialism*, 266.

160. Deckard, *Paradise Discourse*, 17.
161. Sudan, *Alchemy of Empire*, 7.
162. Burnham, *Transoceanic*, 17.
163. Burnham, *Transoceanic*, 17.
164. Neel Ahuja, *Bioinsecurities: Disease Interventions, Empire, and the Government of Species* (Durham, NC and London: Duke University Press, 2016), x.
165. Tobin, *Colonizing Nature*, 11.
166. Tobin, *Colonizing Nature*, 11.
167. Moore, *Capitalism*, 3.
168. See <http://www.bgci.org/garden.php?id=314>. Accessed 22 May 2023. See also D. J. Mabberley, "Anderson, Alexander (1748?–1811)," *Oxford Dictionary of National Biography* (Oxford University Press, 2004). Available at <http://www.oxforddnb.com/view/article/465>. Accessed 24 November 2015.
169. Bourguet, "Measurable Difference," 277.
170. Bourguet, "Measurable Difference," 280.
171. Rachel Carson, *The Sea Around Us* (1951), Special Edition (Oxford: Oxford University Press, 1991), 212.
172. Carson, *Sea Around Us*, 39.
173. Margaret Cohen, "Literary Studies on the Terraqueous Globe," *PMLA* 125, no.3 (2010), 658.
174. Burnham, *Transoceanic*, 17–18.
175. Burntham, *Transoceanic*, 18.
176. Stevenson, *Letters*, Vol. 7, 26.
177. Burnham, *Transoceanic*, 16.
178. Burnham, *Transoceanic*, 11.
179. Burnham, *Transoceanic*, 16.
180. Quoted in Niblett, *World Literature and Ecology*, 7.
181. Schaw, *Journal of a Lady of Quality; Being a Narrative of a Journey from Scotland to the West Indies, North Carolina, and Portugal, in the years 1774 to 1776*, edited by Evangeline Walker Andrews, in collaboration with Charles McLean Andrews (New Haven: Yale University Press, 1923), 35.
182. Schaw, *Journal*, 137.
183. Schaw, *Journal*, 136.
184. Burnham, *Transoceanic*, 19.
185. Burnham, *Transoceanic*, 19.
186. Shiva, *Biopiracy*, 5, 43–64.
187. See, for example, Michelle Burnham, "Female Bodies and Capitalist Drive: Leonora Sansay's *Secret History* in Transoceanic Context," *Legacy* 28, no. 2 (2011), 177–204.
188. Sidney W. Mintz, *Sweetness and Power: The Place of Sugar in Modern History* (New York: Penguin, 1986), 55.

189. Burnham, *Transoceanic*, 11. See also Sven Beckert, *Empire of Cotton: A Global History* (New York: Knopf, 2015).
190. See Paul Virilio, *Speed and Politics* (1977), translated by Mark Polizzotti (Cambridge, MA: MIT Press, 2006).
191. Moore, *Capitalism*, 182. See also Michael Williams, *Deforesting the Earth: From Prehistory to Global Crisis* (Chicago: University of Chicago Press, 2003).
192. Moore, *Capitalism*, 17.
193. Moore, *Capitalism*, 19.
194. Simberloff, *Invasive Species*, 3.
195. Simberloff, *Invasive Species*, 41.
196. See, for example, *The Oxford History of the British Empire*, Volumes I–V, especially Volumes I–III (The Origins of Empire, the Eighteenth and Nineteenth Centuries), edited by Nicholas Canny, P. J. Marshall, and Andrew Porter, respectively (Oxford: Oxford University Press, 2001). See also *The Oxford History of the British Empire Companion Series*, especially *Environment and Empire*, edited by William Beinart and Lotte Hughes (Oxford: Oxford University Press, 2009).
197. Ahuja, *Bioinsecurities*, x.
198. Cole, *Imperfect Creatures*, 9.
199. Lawrence Buell, *The Environmental Imagination: Thoreau, Nature Writing, and the Formation of American Culture* (Cambridge, MA: Belknap Press, 1996), 7.
200. Portuondo, *Secret Science*, 11.
201. See Shiva, *Biopiracy*, 1–5.
202. Deckard, *Paradise Discourse*, 17.
203. Mintz, *Sweetness and Power*, xxvii.
204. Moore, *Capitalism*, 17.
205. Burnham, *Transoceanic*, 19.
206. Ann C. Colley, *Robert Louis Stevenson and the Colonial Imagination* (Aldershot: Ashgate, 2004).
207. Michel Serres, *The Natural Contract*, translated by Elizabeth MacArthur and William Paulson (Ann Arbor: University of Michigan Press, 1995), 2.
208. Bourguet, "Measurable Difference," 280.
209. Stevenson, *Letters of Robert Louis Stevenson*, Vol. 7, 93.
210. Gómez-Barris, *Extractive Zone*, 1.
211. Ahuja, *Bioinsecurities*, x.

Chapter 1

The Evolution of Robinson Crusoe's World-Ecological Consciousness

Goats, Cats, and Rats

On 31 January 1709, two English ships commissioned to undertake a South Seas voyage, the *Duke* and the *Duchess*, arrived within observation of the remote oceanic Juan Fernández archipelago, located some 120 leagues (or roughly 415 miles) from the west coast of Chile. The next day the commander of this expedition, Bristol-based merchant ship captain Woodes Rogers, arranged for a small crew to attempt going ashore in a pinnace, but the boat swiftly turned back after a light was spotted on the island – a light that was mistakenly assumed to have originated from French ships at anchor. On 2 February, or once the coast was clear, Rogers dispatched a yall with a crew of six armed men plus Captain Dover, and, when this boat did not return from the island in a timely fashion, he "sent our Pinnace [again] with the Men arm'd, to see what was the occasion of the Yall's stay; for we were afraid that the *Spaniards* had a Garrison there, and might have seiz'd them."[1] In his account of this expedition, *A Cruising Voyage round the World* (1712), Rogers details the outcome of their first landing upon the strategically located Juan Fernández archipelago: "our Pinnace return'd from the shore, and brought abundance of Craw-fish, with a Man cloth'd in Goat-Skins, who look'd wilder than the first Owners of them."[2]

The wild man in question here, Alexander Selkirk, was a former Master aboard the *Cinque Ports*, and he was marooned on the island in 1704 after quarreling with the ship's Captain Stradling, who took command after an outbreak of scurvy led to the death of former Captain Charles Pickering (notably, the problem of scurvy is a major factor in Europeans' introduction of goats to oceanic islands not unlike Juan Fernández). Selkirk had been living on the island "four Years and four Months" before the arrival of the *Duke* and *Duchess*, though he was *not* entirely alone, nor was he the first individual to make Juan Fernández his home. Rogers's account of Selkirk's so-called desert island life, however heavily edited by Richard Steele to make a point about "natural manner[s],"[3] made the Scotsman famous, providing (as is often suggested) Daniel Defoe with the basis for British literature's most influential *adventure capitalist*, Robinson Crusoe. But some twenty-three years prior, an indigenous American, or "Moskito" Indian named Will was accidentally left behind on the island: "he [Will] was in the Woods, hunting for Goats, when Captain *Watlin* drew off his Men, and the Ship was under sail before he came back to shore"[4] – and, thus, he had to fend for himself for roughly three years, or until John Cook's *Batchelor's Delight*, and a second vessel under the guidance of Captain John Eaton arrived there in 1684. William Dampier documents this episode in the published version of his travel journal, *A New Voyage Round the World* (1697), a copy of which Defoe evidently had on hand.[5]

Will's role here recalls Rajani Sudan's point, that, "British epistemology clearly was informed and constituted by the exchange of techne that accompanied its trade interests,"[6] as well as Judith Carney's work on the role that indigenous knowledge systems – specifically, West African rice culture – played in the plantation economy of the Americas.[7] Yet aside from detailing Will's resourcefulness, including the fishing skills that explain why Buccaneers routinely enlisted indigenous men from the Mosquito Coast of Central America, Dampier pays especially close attention to Will's heartfelt reunion with a "Brother *Moskito* Man"[8] – a scenario which parallels Friday's reunion with his father in Defoe's sequel, *The Farther Adventures of Robinson Crusoe* (1719), implying that Defoe likely modeled Friday upon this marooned Miskito.[9]

Whether or not Defoe modeled Crusoe upon the similarly resourceful Selkirk, works like Dampier's *A New Voyage* and Rogers's *A Cruising Voyage*, the latter of which includes *An Introduction relating to the South-Sea Trade*, helped to not only create a market for seafaring literatures, but also to shape the newly formed Great Britain's role in the historic development of a transoceanic, global economy. Selkirk's experience, in particular, and the Juan Fernández archipelago too, played a hugely significant role in helping British readers to imagine themselves *at home in nature upon a* so-called *remote island* in such a distant part of the world.

This partly explains the moralizing twist to Rogers's account – i.e. his seizing this opportunity to wax philosophical upon the virtues of a "plain and temperate way of living"[10] – a component which he himself acknowledges as unbefitting the work of a "Mariner" / Buccaneer.[11] Of course, one would be wise to suspect Steele's editorial hand in this digression, as *The Englishman*, no. 26 (1713), which is devoted to the story of Alexander Selkirk, similarly concludes with a message against excess:

> This plain man's story is a memorable example, that he is happiest who confines his wants to natural necessities; and he that goes further in his desires, increases his wants in proportion to his acquisitions; or to use his own expression "I am now worth £800, but shall never be so happy, as when I was not worth a farthing."[12]

Although Robinson Crusoe's restless (and, arguably, reckless) accumulation of material wealth clearly contradicts this principle that Steele evidently had hoped his readers would glean from the story of Selkirk (notably, the wander-lustful Crusoe ignores his father's similar, Steele-like extolment of middle-class values), Defoe clearly recognized the importance of Selkirk's narrative in terms of promoting overseas trade through its bringing into British consciousness the natural manners (or ecological realities) of life on this particular oceanic island. And, indeed, a second point that Rogers drives home with his story of Selkirk – namely, that "Necessity is the Mother of Invention"[13] – corresponds with his overarching push to involve Britain in the South-Sea trade. The publication of Rogers's account, thus, needs to considered in light of prior efforts by European powers to preserve the secrecy of such information about the Americas. As María M. Portuondo observes in her study of Spanish cosmography and the New World, *Secret Science*, "this type of knowledge was considered to have strategic, defensive, and monetary value and needed to be safeguarded from foreign and internal enemies alike."[14]

Accordingly, in his "Introduction Concerning the South-Sea Trade," Rogers offers inspiration in the successful earlier French incursions into the Pacific:

> I was inform'd by several Merchants whom we took in those Seas, that by a modest Computation the *French* in the first Years of that Trade carry'd home above 100 Millions of Dollars, which is near 25 Millions Sterling; besides the Advantages they make by trading to the *North-Sea*, when they convoy the *Spanish* Galleons and Flota to and from the *West-Indies*.[15]

And, building on this question of international affairs, he proceeds to argue on the basis of necessity, that, Britain must "make an extraordinary Effort for settling a Trade there":

> That we are concern'd to do it for the Preservation of our Liberty and Religion, is evident enough from what has been said already; that we are likewise oblig'd to do it for the Recovery of our sinking Trade, will be evident from what follows. Our *Spanish* Commerce, which formerly supply'd us with Bullion, yields us so little now, that our Mony must insensibly ebb out of the Nation, whilst it flows into the Enemies Country thro a new Channel, of which he alone is Master; for the *French* not only supply the *South-Seas*, but carry all sorts of Goods, with Negroes, to *Portobello, La Vera Cruz, Carthagena*, and *Buenos-Ayres*: so that they have outed us both of the publick and private Trade that we formerly had with the *Spanish West-Indies*, which must necessarily stop the Fountain of our Bullion, and affect all the other Branches of our Trade thro the World. Therefore I hope every true *Briton* will approve my Zeal in proposing a way how those threatening and imminent Dangers may be prevented, and cordially join in supporting a Trade to the *South-Sea*, and other parts of the *Spanish-West Indies* . . .[16]

The significance of Selkirk's story, then, at least partly lies in answering any potential objections about the costly impracticability of supplying a ship with "Provisions and Stores to carry us thither and back again," a problem which Rogers devotes considerable space to in his *Introduction*.[17] As I've suggested already, the true value of this narrative lies in showcasing the natural manners of life on this remote island. The story of Alexander Selkirk (despite Steele's best efforts) is a tale about the co-production of human history in a distinctly transoceanic – i.e. Pacific-Atlantic – context. And it is a narrative about capitalism, in particular, focusing primarily upon the appropriation of the so-called "cheap natures" (Moore) – i.e. food, energy, and raw materials – that are available upon Juan Fernández, and which would not only be "at first of great use to those who would carry on any Trade to the *South-Sea*,"[18] as Rogers suggests, but without which such transoceanic trade would be either too costly or practically impossible.

On the one hand, the story of Selkirk affectively draws the Pacific into the foreground of British readers' imaginations, and, in this respect at least, predates, if not predicts what Michelle Burnham has described as the

> intertwined commercial, political, and literary developments that accompanied the [age of revolution's] explosion in global maritime

travel and exploration as a host of scientific and commercial voyages mutually dedicated to discovery and profit [such as the voyages of Captain James Cook] forever connected the Pacific to the rest of the world's oceans, including the Atlantic.[19]

On the other hand, much as "early capitalism mobilized technical innovation, systemic violence, and symbolic innovation to lengthen the working day *as well as* to produce and appropriate Cheap Nature so as to reduce *de facto* unit labor costs," as Moore puts it – I argue we are encouraged to remember that Selkirk was *not* alone, but marooned on an island carefully equipped with a variety of particular natures.[20]

Indeed, that both Dampier and Rogers take pains to establish the island's capacity to support human life highlights the geopolitical significance of Juan Fernández as the "key to an entire ocean."[21] The island is not only neatly situated at the European ships' entrance into the Pacific Ocean, but, as Dampier carefully observes, it has also already been carefully engineered to provide necessary refreshment for scorbutic sailors.[22] The distinction that Vandana Shiva draws between engineering and growing seems applicable here, for "when an organism or a system is mechanically manipulated to improve a one-dimensional function" – in this case, provisioning European sailors – "either the organism's immunity decreases, or it becomes vulnerable to disease and attack by other organisms, or the organism becomes dominant in an ecosystem and displaces other species, pushing them to extinction."[23] That is, aside from the island's apparent indigenous qualifications – the savannahs composed of "kindly Grass, thick and flourishing the biggest part of the Year," the "divers sorts of Trees; some large and good Timber for Building," and, last but not least, the "Cabbage Trees," which "afford a good Head, and the Cabbage very sweet" – Dampier notes, "The Savannahs are stocked with Goats in great Herds."[24] The presence of these goats Dampier links to the island's Spanish namesake:

> Goats were first put on the Island by *Juan Fernández*, who first discovered it on his Voyage from *Lima* to *Baldivia* . . . From those Goats these were propagated, and the Island hath taken its Name from this its first Discoverer, who when he returned to *Lima*, desired a Patent for it, designing to settle here; and it was in his second Voyage hither that he set ashore three or four Goats, which have since by their increase, so well stock'd the whole Island. But he could never get a Patent for it, therefore it lies still destitute of Inhabitants, tho' doubtless capable of maintaining 4 or 500 Families, by what

may be produced off the Land only. I speak much within compass; for the Savannahs would at present feed 1000 Head of Cattle, besides Goats, and the Land being cultivated would probably bear Corn, or Wheat, and good Pease, Yams, or Potatoes; for the Land in their alleys and sides of the Mountains, is of a good black mould. The Sea about it is likewise very productive of its Inhabitants. *Seals* swarm as thick about this Island, as if they had no other place in the World to live in; for there is not a Bay nor Rock that one can get ashore on, but is full of them. *Sea-Lions* are here in great Companies, and Fish, particularly Snappers and Rock-fish, are so plentiful, that two Men in an Hour's Time will take with Hook and Line as many as will serve 100 Men.[25]

His occasional psycho-geographic conflation of Juan Fernández with the highly lucrative so-called sugar islands of the West Indies notwithstanding, Dampier's estimation of the island's capacity to support 500 families is not merely political propaganda – that is, akin to the promising poetical visions of imperial wealth that one encounters in, say, Walter Raleigh's *Discovery of Guiana* – but akin to what Ayesha Ramachandran describes as a "collusion of empiricism and the poetic imagination."[26] Distinguished by his knack for various sorts of data collection, including animal, vegetable, and mineral, what Dampier also provides here is a clue to the very real, however unsuccessful, efforts by the Spanish to colonize the island. Whether or not Juan Fernández failed to receive a patent in Lima, as Dampier suggests above, the Spanish attempted twice to settle the island between 1591 and 1599,[27] which is significant because it calls to our attention the fact that the island that Selkirk inhabits in 1704 is *not* simply a breeding ground for aquatic mammals (seals and sea lions) and seabirds, but one already greatly modified, or co-produced by human-non-human activity. The savannahs, for example, the "clear pieces of [fertile] Land without Woods" that Dampier compares (in March 1684) favorably with "those only which are found so in the uninhabited parts of *America*"[28] perhaps owe their existence to an invasive species – the Pyrenean goats that the Spanish had introduced to Chile in the mid-sixteenth century[29] – as these same grazers (notorious deforesters) played an instrumental role in the aforementioned attempts to settle the Juan Fernández islands. Indeed, to use John Locke's terminology, the island that appears before Selkirk is one that had already been removed from "out of the state that nature hath provided."[30] Or, as Andrew Lambert explains, in *Crusoe's Island*, "abandoned Spanish settlements left the islands packed with goats, turnips, cress, and other European crops to supplement the astonishing richness of marine life, and the iconic cabbage trees."[31] The archipelago, thus, merits consideration as a seriously disturbed habitat, and, as biologists like Daniel Simberloff note, disturbed habitats are all the more vulnerable to invasion by non-native species.

Consider, for example, the various animal and plant species highlighted in Rogers's account of Alexander Selkirk. Aside from the 500-plus goats that Selkirk claims to have killed and/or caught over the course of his four-plus years of inhabitancy on the island's more mountainous parts, Rogers claims that his men "saw above a thousand" goats upon the South End of the island alone, which is a number that certainly helps to explain why Selkirk insists "that part of the Island was plainer" – i.e. deforested.[32] Food-wise, in addition to goat's meat, Selkirk "had plenty of Turnips, which," according to Rogers, "had been sow'd there by Capt. *Dampier*'s Men, and have now overspread some acres of Ground." There is "good Cabbage from the Cabbage-Trees," "Fruit of the Piemento Trees, which is the same as the *Jamaica* Pepper," "a black Pepper call'd Malagita, which was very good to expel Wind, and against Griping of the Guts," and "small black Plums, which are very good."[33] Perhaps the island's vegetable production is not so great as would satisfy a finicky gourmand, but, with "Fish of several sorts ... and Craw-fish in such abundance, that in a few hours we could take as many as would serve some hundreds of Men,"[34] and, of course, the aforementioned savannahs composed of a "loose black Earth"[35] capable of supporting additional agriculture (as Dampier had previously suggested), I think we can safely say that the story of Selkirk depicts Juan Fernández as not merely of geopolitical significance, but splendidly furnished with a variety of cheap natures, including wood (raw building materials),[36] sea-lions oil for lamps (energy),[37] fertile soil, and, of course, a ready-made supply of low-cost refreshment (water and food), all of which may be usefully channeled into the circuit of capital. And, in this respect at least – as an island carefully engineered (or, rather, co-produced) by the Spanish and their goats to support human life / the accumulation of capital – Juan Fernández very closely resembles the island in Defoe's *Robinson Crusoe*, which is (as noted earlier) a similarly disturbed habitat primed to welcome the accidental introduction of Crusoe's English barley. Furthermore, Rogers notes: "there's abundance of good Herbs," including a medicinal one "not much unlike Feverfew ... which tended much to the speedy Recovery of our sick Men."[38] And, last but not least, Rogers claims, that, "the Men who work'd ashore on our Rigging eat young Seals, which they prefer'd to our Ships Victuals, and said was as good as *English* lamb" – a most useful observation, given there was an almost sublime surplus of breeding seals lying about the island.[39] That Selkirk thrived upon the island for nearly four and a half years offers itself as a testament to the island's capacity – as "appropriated Cheap Nature" – to support trade to the Pacific Ocean.

Of course, not all of the species identified in Rogers's account cooperated in the formation of this transoceanic, global economy. One must also take into account various *unruly natures* too – i.e. the innumerable rats (the imperfect creatures that figure in Lucinda Cole's important analysis of *Robinson Crusoe*)[40] and cats that appear here, and that frequently reoccur in similar sorts of empire writing, including James Grainger's *The Sugar-Cane* (Ch. 2) and Graham Balfour's Hawaiian photo albums (Ch. 4). Rogers writes:

> He was at first much pester'd with Cats and Rats, that had bred in great numbers from some of each Species which had got ashore from Ships that put in there to wood and water. The Rats gnaw'd his Feet and Clothes while asleep, which oblig'd him to cherish the Cats with his Goats-flesh; by which may of them became so tame, that they would lie about him in hundreds, and soon deliver'd him from the Rats. He likewise tam'd some Kids, and to divert himself would now and then sing and dance with them and his Cats: so that ... he came at last to conquer all the Inconveniences of his Solitude ... When his Clothes wore out, he made himself a Coat and Cap of Goat-skins ...[41]

This passage contains some of the most compelling and curious images of Selkirk, a man who may have wished at times – especially when the rats were gnawing on his feet in the darkness of night – that he was either truly alone on the island or that the Cartesian binary, in which humanity remains separated from an externalized Nature out there, held true. On the one hand, it must have astonished Rogers's readers to imagine Selkirk surrounded by hundreds of formerly feral cats – cats tamed by the power of goat's flesh to serve as pest control (perhaps *The Englishman*'s readers too, though Steele downplays the quantity of cats: he says merely that "he tamed a number" of cats, "who lay about his bed, and preserved him from the enemy").[42] However, perhaps readers would have been far more astonished, if not utterly horrified by an estimate of the number of rats. That is, assuming that these cats were introduced to Juan Fernández at roughly the same time as those imperfect creatures (rats) that "gnaw'd his Feet and Clothes while asleep," and, if (as Rogers claims) Selkirk's cats truly numbered in the hundreds, then he would likely have been pestered by not hundreds, but thousands of rats (a truly horrifying situation), since, according to Cole, rats reproduce at a rate far greater than cats. Indeed, as Cole observes:

> cats produce two litters per year, with three to five surviving kittens per litter ... Rats, in contrast, are incestuous and interbreed; they produce litters of between ten and twelve offspring; the gestation period lasts only twenty-two days; females can come back into heat an hour after birth; and (unlike cats) they stay in heat all year round. At the end of six months, then, two shipboard rats and their offspring could have produced 77,960 rodents, overrunning the island and wreaking ecological havoc ... This difference in these reproductive rates is why Alexander Selkirk – while "preserved from the Enemy," Steele writes, by half-feral cats – was miserable and why, unlike Crusoe, he was starving and impoverished when rescued.[43]

Although Cole neglects to account for the number of rats that a single domesticated cat may kill over the period of one year (an astonishing figure, no doubt, given what Loss, Will, and Marra have to say about the impact of free-ranging domestic cats on wildlife in the United States, let alone vulnerable island ecosystems),[44] Cole takes good advantage of this biological fact of how quickly rats reproduce to point out the fuzzy math that figures in Defoe's repackaging of Selkirk's experience à la *Robinson Crusoe*. She insists, "the agricultural economy of Crusoe's island depends ... not simply on the providential *presence* of European corn but on the *absence* of the rats that plagued Selkirk and the millions of others across the early modern world, all struggling to protect their grain supplies against rodent infestation."[45] Rightly so, the mysterious disappearance of Crusoe's rats lies at the center of Cole's valuable critical analysis of the novel.

On the other hand, it requires an especially strange stretch of the imagination to picture this hardened Scottish sailor singing and dancing with these domesticated creatures (Figure 1.1) in order to tame his own loneliness – a circumstance that Steele neglects to mention in *The Englishman*, no. 26.[46]

First, the extraordinary number of cats mentioned here begs us to consider the fate of seemingly isolated oceanic islands like Juan Fernández, which, owing to a combination of factors – their small size, exposure to damaging meteorological events (cyclones and hurricanes), and a limited number of native species – have become "famous for both having many introduced species and

Figure 1.1 "Selkirk amusing himself with his Cats." Illustration from John Howell's children's book devoted to the *Life and Adventures of Alexander Selkirk, the real Robinson Crusoe* (New York: M. Day & Co., 1841). Courtesy of the Boston Public Library.

suffering huge transformations at the hands of these species."[47] Indeed, judging from the awesome surplus of goats, cats, and rats mentioned in Rogers's account, I think we can safely assume that the Juan Fernández islands were lacking in certain sorts of species, and therefore especially vulnerable to invasion.[48] We can be assured that "he saw no venomous or savage Creature on the Island, nor any other sort of Beast but Goats, &c. as above-mention'd [i.e. cats and rats]"[49] because that would explain precisely the otherwise incredible proliferation of goats, cats, and rats. Remote oceanic islands typically do not have any indigenous predatory mammals or, say, venomous snakes to check the population growth of such species – and so they tend to suffer greatly as a result of their introduction. Furthermore, it is perhaps not as strange as it may seem that Rogers "found no Land-Bird on the Island, but a sort of Black-Bird with a red Breast, not unlike our *English* Black-Birds; and the Humming Bird of various Colours, and no bigger than a Humble Bee"[50] – as one can certainly imagine the ecological impacts that, based on Charles Elton's biotic resistance theory, so many cats (and rats) would likely have had upon the already limited (and defenseless) indigenous bird population.[51] As Daniel Simberloff succinctly observes: "Introduced cats, rats, and the small Indian mongoose [a species that was imported to the Caribbean to serve the same purpose as Selkirk's cats – See Ch. 2] ... have eliminated many island birds as well as some mammals and amphibians."[52] Simberloff cites at least one very compelling example: the sub-Antarctic Marion Island in the Southern Indian Ocean, where feral "cats were introduced in 1949 and are now estimated to kill over 400,000 birds per year, mostly ground-nesting petrels."[53] Providing us with an idea of the damage likely caused by Selkirk's deforesting goats, on the other hand, Charles Elton observes, in his groundbreaking *The Ecology of Invasions by Animals and Plants*:

> Red deer, *Cervus elaphus*, were liberated between 1851 and 1910, and quickly multiplied in both islands of New Zealand ... The red deer have already made a profound impact upon native forests, especially in the drier types of woodland; but it is in the wetter regions that forest damage leads to most serious soil erosion. It is likely that on many watersheds the deer, helped by domestic stock, have tipped the scale towards a cycle of catastrophic soil erosion, which is felt not only in the mountains but also in those parts of the lowland valleys that receive the extra load of silt washed from above.[54]

Published in 1958, some one hundred years following the liberation of red deer in New Zealand, Elton's book provides us with some basic idea of how long it may take for a free-roaming population of grazers to effect catastrophic environmental change. Given that Selkirk's goats (1704) had been liberated on the island since at least 1591, it's easy to imagine, then, why the Swedish botanist, Carl Skottsberg, in his plan for the preservation of Juan Fernández's "original nature," calls for the "indefatigable" goats' extermination: "the stock of goats should be cut down and not allowed to increase again, or destroyed altogether (in order to supply fresh meat in case of emergency, some other less harmful animal might be introduced)."[55] Such examples remind us that oceanic islands like Juan Fernández tend to bear the greatest environmental costs of global capitalism, including the United States' so-called manifest destiny and the British Empire's exponential growth over the period covered by this book, 1704–1894.

However, it is the second, potentially more strange, or *uncanny* image that we receive of Selkirk dancing with his goats and cats that I think deserves the most ecocritical attention here, for it is precisely this sort of gesture that speaks to the inviolable union between human and extra-human natures. The great significance of this story of Alexander Selkirk lies not merely in showcasing the geopolitical value of the Juan Fernández islands, nor in serving as an important reminder of how a transoceanic, global economy continues to alter the fate (and face) of such islands. (Margaret Cohen, notes, for example, that, "ships continue to convey over ninety percent of the world's freight.")[56] Rather, the most significant thing that readers may be encouraged to take away from Rogers's account is this notion of the "double internality" that informs Moore's analysis of capitalism in the web of life. Despite what Moore describes as capitalism's governing conceit – that Nature is some external *thing* that "may be coded, quantified, and rationalized to serve economic growth, or some other higher good"[57] – Selkirk's survival upon the island depends instead upon his relating to / working through (not upon) nature. Or, rather, his experience reminds us that, as Moore insists: "capitalism is a co-produced history of human-initiated projects and processes bundled with (and within) specific natures."[58] So much depends upon the nature of goats and the fate of oceanic islands. The gloriously fertile savannahs, for example, that inform Dampier's (and Rogers's) celebration of the island's capacity to support agriculture necessary to feed some 500 families are not the indigenous features of a so-called island Eden, though obviously this sort of imperial translation reappears over again in what Sharae Deckard describes as the paradise discourse of American settlement.[59] Rather, these savannahs represent the unintended consequence of particular human-initiated projects (failed Spanish attempts to settle the island between 1591 and 1599) bundled together with the goats' insatiable hunger and freedom to proliferate upon an remote island lacking certain "venomous or savage Creature[s]."[60] And, of course, were it not for the power of goat's flesh, the similarly invasive cats might never have been tamed to deliver Selkirk from such uncooperative, unruly, or, as Cole suggests, imperfect creatures, as the rats. Are we not encouraged to read Selkirk's dancing with his goats and cats as an apt reflection of this bundling together of human and extra-human natures? As I see it, yes – in keeping with the epigraph to this chapter, the story of Alexander Selkirk invites us to adopt a world-ecological view of the Juan Fernández archipelago.

Furthermore, although Rogers seems apt to link Selkirk's physical transformation, including the extra-human agility required to catch these goats by "speed of foot" (Figure 1.2), to the plain and temperate lifestyle he was forced to adopt on the island, I am

Figure 1.2 "Selkirk catching a Goat." Illustration from John Howell's children's book devoted to the *Life and Adventures of Alexander Selkirk, the real Robinson Crusoe* (New York: M. Day & Co., 1841). Courtesy of the Boston Public Library.

encouraged to read this feature of the story as an instance of what might be called the *ecological uncanny*. Rogers writes:

> When his Powder fail'd, he took them by speed of foot; for his way of living and continual Exercise of walking and running, clear'd him of all gross Humours, so that he ran with wonderful Swiftness thro the Woods and up the Rocks and hills, as we perceiv'd when we employ'd him to catch Goats for us. We had a Bulldog, which we sent with several of our nimblest Runners, to help him in catching Goats; but he distanc'd and tir'd both the Dog and the Men, catch'd the Goats, and brought 'em to us on his back.[61]

It may be owing to simple exercise and temperance that the Scotsman has become so very swift and agile, as Rogers suggests. But if one reads this passage in light of what happens with the goats, cats, and rats as a whole, I argue this passage simultaneously begs us to consider Selkirk's physical transformation as the remembrance of some otherwise thoroughly repressed ecological reality – namely, that humanity is not separate from, but bundled together with other natures in the web of life. (It may be worth noting here that Selkirk's extra-human agility mirrors David Balfour and Alan Breck's flight through Rannoch Moor in Robert Louis Stevenson's *Kidnapped*, a scenario in which they "play at being hares" to cross the moor safely. See Chapter 4.)[62] Selkirk's nature is *not* some *thing* outside, and upon which he alone acts – but historical and internal, an integral part of humanity. Nature works through the fleet-footed Selkirk – i.e. he *is* the "savage Creature" that is required upon this remote island to check the proliferation of the "indefatigable goats," and thereby avoid a potential future catastrophe in keeping with Elton's analysis of the red deer in New Zealand. And, simultaneously, Selkirk's survival depends upon his working through nature. Selkirk told Rogers that he left a mark on the ear of the hundreds of goats that he caught, but the goats have also left an indelible mark upon Selkirk here too. Indeed, as Cole suggests, citing the work of Michel Serres and Bruno Latour, non-humans are, like humans, "*actants* in the world . . . [they] 'modify other actors'; they are not subjects, but 'interveners.'"[63] And, in what follows I argue that it is precisely this sort of new-found ecological consciousness that informs Daniel Defoe's translation of Selkirk's ecologically uncanny Pacific island experience into Crusoe's Caribbean-based adventure capitalism.

Crusoe's "Dreadful Deliverance"

Almost immediately after Robinson Crusoe washes ashore the tiny Caribbean island that serves as the primary setting for Daniel Defoe's immensely popular novel, he begins to reflect upon his so-called "dreadful deliverance" from *den wild zee* (the wild sea):

> I was wet, had not clothes to shift me, nor anything either to eat or drink to comfort me, neither did I see any prospect before me, but that of perishing with hunger, or being devoured by wild beasts; and that which was particularly afflicting to me, was, that I had no weapon either to hunt and kill any creature for my sustenance, or to defend myself against any other creature that might desire to kill me for theirs. In a word, I had nothing about me but a knife, a tobacco pipe, and a little tobacco in a box, this was all my provision, and this threw me into terrible agonies of mind, that for a while I ran about like a madman; night coming upon me, I began with a heavy heart to consider what would be my lot if there were any ravenous beasts in that country, seeing at night they always come abroad for their prey.[64]

At first glance, this seems to be a fairly straightforward passage, implying that Crusoe must have *things* about him to settle his mind. Indeed, literary scholars drawing upon economic theory frequently characterize Crusoe as someone whose life depends upon the restless acquisition of surplus material wealth. And given the circumstances, there is nothing extraordinary in Crusoe's wanting more than just "a knife, a tobacco pipe, and a little tobacco in a box" to rest comfortably after his so-called "dreadful deliverance."

However, this is nonetheless a curious passage because the natural history of the West Indies simply does not support Crusoe's assumption that there may be "ravenous beasts" on the island eager (and large enough) to devour young Englishmen. Aside from the story of Alexander Selkirk, scholars have identified a handful of potential source texts, including Robert Knox's *An Historical Relation of the Island of Ceylon* (1681). The geo- and biological dissimilarities between Southeast Asia and the West Indies, however, beg the question of Defoe's familiarity with more relevant texts, such as Richard Ligon's *A True and Exact History of the Island of Barbados* (1657) – texts that reveal the ignorance behind Crusoe's initial assumption here. Simberloff, for example, observes that "many islands, especially small ones in the oceans isolated far from major landmasses, lack certain sorts of species," including predatory mammals.[65] Either Crusoe's island is not nearly as remotely located as we have been led to believe or Crusoe's fears in this passage are entirely unwarranted. Consider, for example, Christopher Columbus's assessment of wildlife on the island of Fernandina in the Bahamas: "I saw no animals on land of any sort, save parrots and lizards. A boy told me that he saw a large snake. I saw no sheep or goats or any other animals ... if there had been any I could not have failed to see some" (*Diario*, 16 October 1492).[66] Reptiles (and, notably, no poisonous snakes) and birds account for the extent of Columbus's biological assessment of the island. Such an assessment highlights for us the limitations and relative fragility of most island ecosystems, which typically lack the sort of biodiversity that figures in their mainland counterparts. That is, while I think we should pause before labeling Crusoe's island as remote (the mere fact of his shipwreck there, and the arrival of Spaniards et al. later on suggests that the island is situated within or at least not too far outside the well-traveled triangular network of transatlantic commerce), other remote islands across the globe lack any species of large mammals, except for those introduced by humans. As Elton observed, there is an inviolable link between biological diversity and ecological health – i.e. ecosystems with less diversity are much less stable because they lack the biotic resistance that figures in larger, more "complex assemblages of species."[67] He notes: "the balance of relatively simple communities of plants and animals is more easily upset than that of richer ones . . . and more vulnerable to invasions."[68] Or, as Josef Greimler et al., observe in "The Vegetation of Robinson Crusoe Island (Isla Masatierra), Juan Fernández Archipeligo, Chile" (*Pacific Science* 2002), "oceanic islands are fragile ecosystems that are easily modified through natural and human disturbance."[69]

And so, despite Crusoe's overwhelming sense of his own vulnerability in the above passage, recent studies in biological invasion suggest that Crusoe actually poses a far greater threat to the island's natural economy than does the island's wildlife pose a threat to his self-preservation. Interestingly, Defoe draws our attention to the island's susceptibility to Crusoe's influence (or ecological footprint) vis-à-vis the English barley that "God miraculously caus'd . . . to grow without any help of seed sown" (63). Indeed, that Crusoe accidentally introduces this *foreign*, or non-native grain to the island reinforces my reading of the novel as perhaps the first to consciously (or unconsciously) challenge the myth of isolated island space that figures in much early American literature.[70] Were Crusoe a bit more ecologically aware at this juncture, he might also have interpreted the barley's miraculous growth as an early indicator of some foregoing human intervention, as Simberloff explains, "disturbed habitats are particularly susceptible to [bio-invasion]":

> Consider roadsides, railroad rights-of-way, abandoned fields, and similar places: such habitats are far more dominated by introduced plants than pristine habitats . . . perturbations of various sorts liberate resources, such as soil nutrients and light, and thereby allow introduced species to gain a foothold.[71]

Elton similarly asserts that, "invasions and outbreaks most often happen on cultivated or planted land – that is, in habitats and communities very much simplified by man":

> They have been simplified in three ways chiefly: by encouraging crops usually of foreign plants that have not a full fauna attached to them, by growing these in partial or complete monoculture, and by trying to kill all other species thought to be harmful, as well as incidentally killing or suppressing a great many more whose fate is not attended to.[72]

And worth noting here too is that barley is especially apt to grow in such disturbed habitats. In other words, the ease with which the barley takes root may not be owing to the island's Eden-like hospitality (as the imperial propaganda suggests), but, rather, some form of ecological disturbance (or liberation of resources) caused by previous human activities. And I say unconsciously because Crusoe's confusion here – that he assumes the island to be "uninhabited, except by wild beasts" (43) – begs the question: to what extent was Defoe familiar with the West Indies' natural history? That is, despite Defoe's distinctive "sharp focus on things and on phenomena" and despite Pat Rogers's suggestion, that "one of the best-attested facts concerning Defoe is his absorption in travel," Crusoe's initial fears are not grounded in the natural history of this particular bioregion. Instead, they appear to be based on his recent misadventures in Africa, which itself is rather interesting because it implicitly speaks to the confusion of Old and New World ecologies.[73] Such confusion, because it poses a threat to the biodiversity of the island's fragile ecosystem, provides us with a measure of the environmental impacts of the transoceanic trade and commerce that Defoe championed throughout his career, especially in his *Weekly Review of the Affairs of France*. Jason H. Pearl notes, for instance, that, "Defoe was a dogged promoter of overseas trade ... at one point envisioning a globalized world balanced perfectly by commercial interdependence."[74]

But perhaps it is not any potential ravenous beasts, however imaginary, that frighten Crusoe, so much as the mere unenclosed status of the island. Robert Marzec insists, for example, that what encourages Crusoe to spend his first night on the island up in a "thick bushy tree like a firr [sic]" (82) is an underlying, and peculiarly Anglo-American fear of unenclosed spaces.[75] And, given Crusoe's frenzied preoccupation with fencing himself in, one is certainly encouraged to read the novel in light of the Enclosure Movement, John Locke's labor theory of property, and even Patricia Seed's historical recounting of the English colonists' ceremonious reliance upon the construction of enclosures, including fences (a culturally determined sign of private ownership), to take possession of the New World.[76] Crusoe's cultural identity, then, is bound up with his fencing, in as much as the English landscape has been subdivided into a jigsaw-puzzle-like network of carefully demarcated private properties.

Jill Casid makes a similar point about how these fences implicate the reader in Crusoe's colonizing vision. She claims, "*Robinson Crusoe* ... is a tale of fences," but points out that "these fences, which are both marks of possession and native woodland, work to produce and reproduce the illustrated novel's reader/viewers as at once imperial subjects of colonizing vision and anticolonial protectors of island environments."[77] This latter view – the said employment of fences to protect the environment against grazing mammals – represents a form of green imperialism, in keeping with the forest conservation legislation enacted in the British sugar colonies in the late eighteenth century.[78] Accordingly, through the passages that detail Crusoe's painstaking construction of his island home, Defoe clearly demarcates his English-ness: "I was completely fenced in" (49).

However, I fear the problem with such a reading is that it perhaps inadvertently encourages us to not only focus primarily upon questions of identity (i.e. anthropocentric concerns about the preservation of Crusoe's Englishness), but also to consider Crusoe's so-called desert island as pristine *wilderness* – a term that in the eighteenth century had obvious biblical overtones signifying desolation, barrenness, savagery, waste, and moral confusion.[79] John Locke, for example, in his *Second Treatise of Government*, refers to America as an "uncultivated waste." That is, if we read Crusoe's landing as the end of nature, to use the title of Bill McKibben's provocative book on the human role in global climate change, are we not buying into a myth of Nature (upper-case N) (or, in this case, the West Indies) as remote from humanity?[80] Or, rather, does such a reading not distract us from the valuable work that Defoe's novel does in terms of highlighting Crusoe's ecological intimacy / close relationship to particular nature*s* (animals and plants)? Crusoe's insistence – "I was completely fenced in" – naively adheres to this myth of separation that, as Moore explains, haunts much environmental criticism, or green thought. But, as Defoe cleverly demonstrates by novel's end, this statement reveals Crusoe's early ignorance of how ocean currents and trade winds serve to link such so-called remote islands to the rest of the world. Crusoe will eventually discover that there is no escape from *den wild zee* (the wild sea), much as Moore insists, "humanity has always been unified with the rest of nature in a flow of flows."[81] Such a realization – that there is no escape from the sea – informs Crusoe's ongoing wanderlust, or the "Propensity to rambling" that he likens to a "chronical Distemper," in Defoe's sequel, *The Farther Adventures of Robinson Crusoe*.[82]

Indeed, for Crusoe, whose wanderlust continues unabated despite the fullness of his life at home in England at age 61, there is no escape from the wild (or encircling) sea (Carson, *The Sea Around Us*). And, accordingly, in what follows I read *Robinson Crusoe* as a novel that usefully complicates the borderline between nature and culture – i.e. the Cartesian binary between Society / Nature that Moore's work emphatically rejects. Taking into account the all-important footprint scene, I argue that *Robinson Crusoe* presents us with a unique opportunity to both debunk the myth of isolated island space, as well explore human history's implication in natural history. That is, a close ecocritical examination of the passages both leading up to and following Crusoe's discovery of this mysterious footprint in the sand suggests that Defoe's popular novel might actually be one of the earliest works to begin to grapple with a post-Cartesian notion of the humanity-, or, in this case, capitalism-in-nature / nature-in-capitalism, or simply what environmental historian William Cronon refers to as the "human place *in* nature" (italics mine).[83] The novel is commonly read as a depiction of the prototypical British imperialists' gradual conversion of a wilderness into "domesticated space rather like England" (Richetti)[84] – which is to say, most readings subscribe to a particular notion of Crusoe / Humanity / Imperialism / Capitalism as separated from and acting upon an otherwise externalized Nature. And, of course, there are certainly most compelling reasons for doing so, not least of which is Crusoe's obsession with both physical and ideological enclosures.[85] However, despite the standard presuppositions of geographical isolation that inform most readings of the novel, Crusoe's island is not a "utopia defined primarily by its boundaries."[86] Nor is it, as Cole suggests (vis-à-vis John Bender), a "closed, zoomorphic world in which Crusoe hunts, gathers, farms, and stores under metaphysically secured conditions."[87] Rather, it is like most every other island in the world, *not* entirely separated from, but linked to other geographical spaces through ocean currents and trade winds.

In *The Sea Around Us*, for example, Rachel Carson explains that a single ocean wave may travel as far as 6,000 miles, and in doing so carry information from one geographically remote region to another (I dive a bit more deeply into this subject area in Chapter 4).[88] Similarly, *Robinson Crusoe* reminds us that the ocean is not a boundary, but a channel of communication / a thoroughfare of transplantations and migrations. Indeed, the island that figures prominently in Crusoe's economic and spiritual rebirth cannot accurately be termed a wilderness in the biblical sense. Nor is it fair to describe Crusoe's island as entirely metaphysically secure, despite the fact that its agricultural economy depends very much upon the mysterious, if not practically impossible disappearance of so many rats, as Cole rightly observes. For Crusoe's initial assessment of the island's remoteness – "I had a dismal prospect of my condition, for as I was not cast away upon that island without being driven, as is said, by a violent storm quite out of the course of our intended voyage, and a great way, *viz.* some hundreds of leagues out of the ordinary course of the trade of mankind" (51) – gradually gives way to a more enlightened understanding of the island's vulnerability to ecological invasions by animals and plants. And the novel as a whole encourages us to adopt quite a different perspective on Crusoe's humanity / capitalism. Through Crusoe's initial unfamiliarity with the island, including his ignorance of any previous efforts to colonize the island, Defoe may be reflecting upon the impracticability of a Spanish policy of safeguarding information about the New World, bearing in mind, of course, that, as Portuondo puts it, "it may seem naïve to think that by keeping geographical information secret one nation could effectively hide the New World from eager interlopers."[89] But, as Crusoe becomes increasingly aware of the island's particular nature, and its relationship to the rest of the world, so too are readers encouraged to admit that capitalism is not without nature, but, rather, "co-produced by human and extra-human natures in the web of life."[90]

Oranges, Lemons, and Limes

Consider, for example, the description that Defoe provides of Crusoe's first exploration of the other side of the island. Crusoe's assessment of this space suggests *not* a barren, uncultivated waste (to use Locke's terminology) remote from humanity.[91] Instead, we receive clues of some prior biological intervention:

> At the end of this march I came to an opening ... and the country appear'd so fresh, so green, so flourishing, every thing being in a constant verdure, or flourish of *Spring*, that it look'd like a planted garden.
> I descended a little on the side of that delicious vale, surveying it with a secret kind of pleasure ... to think that this was all my own, that I was king and lord of all this country indefeasibly ... I saw here abundance of cocoa trees, orange, and lemon, and citron trees; but all wild, and very few bearing any fruit, at least not then: However, the green limes that I gathered, were not only pleasant to eat, but very wholesome ... (80)

Crusoe clearly surveys this eastern side of the island with the appropriating eyes of an aspiring capitalist, thereby amalgamating empirical observation with poetic imagination, in keeping with other Early Modern world-making efforts.[92] He immediately (and imaginatively) sets about converting everything that he sees into material wealth. And so, this "secret kind of pleasure" that he derives from this "delicious vale" lies in his conditioned impulse to channel everything into a "commodity system." He imagines the inheritance to be gained through the conveyance of these natural resources / goods into the "circuit of capitalism," and, accordingly, he fancies himself transported back home to England as landed gentry. Upon first glance this fresh green scene – his first visit to the eastern side of the island – does not inspire any sort of understanding of world-ecology. To couch this in Moore's terms (as noted earlier), Crusoe does not "see how humans and other species have co-produced [this delicious vale] and how that 'bundled' [vale] simultaneously conditions and constrains capital."[93] Importantly, however, Defoe does cleverly insert a glimmer of such a world-ecological awakening into this scene, in so far as Crusoe remarks how it all "look'd like a planted garden" (80).

That is, not only does this passage complicate John Locke's hugely influential labor theory of property in that Crusoe imaginatively takes possession of this other side of the island without having invested any of his own labor in it (at this point, he has yet to pick a single piece of fruit or touch anything except with his appropriating eyes) – but that it "look'd like a planted garden" also suggests some prior human intervention in the island's ecosystem. This is reinforced by the fact that not one of the plants identified here is indigenous to the West Indies. Take, for example, the orange trees that Crusoe insists were "all wild." Sweet oranges are commonly grown today on coffee plantations in the Caribbean, but they are not, according to Herbert A. Raffaele and James W. Wiley, indigenous to the region; instead, they are "probably native to China, Vietnam, and other southeastern Asiatic regions," as are lemons.[94] Defoe also includes the citron tree here, which is particularly intriguing, as this large fragrant citrus fruit is believed to be one of the four original citrus fruits "native to the subtropical and tropical regions of Asia and the Malay Archipelago."[95]

In *The Citrus Industry*, Herbert John Webber observes that, the "history of the spread of citrus reads like a romance," as the "beautiful appearance of both tree and fruit attracted the attention of travelers and received mention in their written narratives."[96] However, the global spread of citrus, according to Webber, was slow. Alexander is supposed to have transported the fruit to the Mediterranean from Persia, where his botanists "found the citron or 'Persian Apple' extensively cultivated," though references to citrus fruits in India are found in texts that date back prior to 800 BC.[97] Pompeian mosaics are cited as evidence of the Romans' familiarity with the orange tree prior to the destruction of Pompeii in AD 70, yet it is "only after the period of the Crusades" that European historians explicitly refer to lemons, limes, and oranges, and not until the sixteenth century that the sweet orange would acquire any commercial significance in southern Europe. For our purposes, however, it is worth noting that Christopher Columbus likely first introduced citrus fruits to the Americas on his second voyage.[98] And, as the naturalist Oviedo y Valdéz notes:

> Orange trees from Castile were brought to this island of Hispaniola, and they have multiplied so abundantly that now they are past counting; the fruit is very good, both the sweet and the sour. They grow in this city of Santo Domingo and all over the islands wherever Christians have their estates and gardens. And what is true here is equally true in the other islands, and also on the main land where there are settlements of Spaniards ... There are many lemon trees and limes, and many citrons, and as I have already said great quantities of each.[99]

Similarly, Momsen and Richardson observe that cacao was also "introduced as a crop to the Caribbean by the Spanish who took it from Venezuela and planted it in Trinidad probably in 1525 and to Jamaica from 'Caracus [sic] and Guatemala.'"[100]

Webber's history offers some explanation for Crusoe's discovery of citrus on the other / eastern side of the island. The scenario outlined here is not only of a piece with widespread European efforts to redistribute the Earth's flora, as detailed in Schiebinger and Swan's collection, *Colonial Botany*,[101] but also reminiscent of the failed Spanish efforts to settle the Juan Fernández archipelago. Or, rather, the correspondence to Selkirk's experience reinforces the transoceanic – i.e. Pacific-Atlantic – nature of Defoe's novel. The non-native status of the plants mentioned here perhaps explains why Defoe opts *not* to construe this other side of the island in terms of wilderness, but a space resembling a "planted garden" (80). For what he describes here is precisely this – a former garden, or the feral remnants of what once was a Spanish plantation (possibly a citrus grove). What Crusoe discovers is *not* a pristine, but disturbed habitat co-produced by human-non-human activity. And, in this particular regard, Crusoe's narrative neatly resonates, again, with Alexander Selkirk's experience on Juan Fernández, as Lambert notes: "abandoned Spanish settlements left the islands packed with goats, turnips, cress, and other European crops to supplement the astonishing richness of marine life [craw-fish and sea lions], and the iconic cabbage trees."[102]

These passages are centrally important to the evolution of Crusoe's ecological consciousness, but they also beg the question (again) of Defoe's familiarity with the natural history of the West Indies. Had he read, for example, Richard Ligon's foundational text, *A True and Exact History of the Island of Barbados* (1657)? Or had he read the first volume of Hans Sloane's influential natural history of Jamaica – *Voyage to the Islands of Madera, Barbados, Nieves, S. Christophers and Jamaica, with the Natural History of the Trees, Four-footed Beasts, Fishes, Birds, Insects, Reptiles, etc. of the Last of those Islands* (1707)?[103] Not only do the citrus fruit trees that Crusoe encounters on this eastern side of the island figure in Ligon's Eden-like account of Barbados, but, like a true Englishman, Ligon's imagination is similarly preoccupied with enclosures, as he notes that "the Lime tree is like a thick Hollybush in *England*, and as full of prickles: if you make a hedge of them, about your house, 'tis sufficient proof against the *Negroes*; whose naked bodies cannot possibly enter it, and it is an extraordinary sure fence against Cattle."[104]

Ligon clearly understood the rhetorical-physiological appeal of citrus fruit, but his curious lumping of enslaved Africans together with cattle as bodies to safeguard one's house against calls into focus capitalism's reliance upon the appropriation of cheap work/energy, including the unpaid labor of human *and* extra-human natures. Ligon's lime tree hedge symbolically ties in neatly with Early Modern efforts, including scientific and technical strategies, to externalize and objectify nature alongside non-European peoples, whether as exchangeable commodities or simply things to be kept outside the grounds of one's house – i.e. separated from humanity.[105] And, of course, similarly racist-economic equivalencies punctuate Crusoe's early involvement in the transatlantic slave trade, the awful business that Defoe supported on economic grounds, as in his *A Plan of the English Commerce* (1728). Indeed, one is encouraged to view the cultural assimilation of Friday as part and parcel of Crusoe's overarching agricultural economy. The parallels that Defoe establishes between, say, Friday's so-called civilization and Crusoe's domestication of goats, calls into focus the yoking together of non-human animals and black bodies – i.e. the "black-animal subtext" that is, as Bénédict Boisseron suggests, "deeply ingrained in the cultural genetics of the global north, an inherited condition informed by a shared history of slavery and colonization."[106]

Furthermore, although one may be encouraged to interpret Crusoe's shipwreck as a gloss upon the immorality of the slave trade – that is, as God's punishment for his embarkation upon a slave ship bound for West Africa – the term Christian (and Christianity) frequently carries with it economic value in Crusoe's eyes. The term implies membership in capitalist civilization, and as such may be used to demarcate a unit of labor – i.e. some human body that may be exploited (low-cost labor), as opposed to either a human or extra-human nature that may be appropriated (unpaid labor). Crusoe's journal, in which he employs the following analogy to weigh the pros and cons of his situation upon the island – i.e. good = credit, whereas evil = debt – reinforces this yoking together of Christianity and capitalism, and, at one point, so too does Crusoe's rationalization for his sale of his African companion, Xury, to the Spanish ship captain for 60 pieces of eight. Crusoe's cultural assimilation of Friday, including his conversion of Friday to Christianity, similarly enhances his usefulness (or labor value):

> After *Friday* and I became more intimately acquainted . . . I let him into the mystery . . . of gunpowder, and bullet, and taught him how to shoot: I gave him a knife . . . I gave him a hatchet, which was not only as good a weapon in some cases, but much more *useful* upon other occasions. (Italics mine, 175)

And, interestingly, Crusoe construes cannibalism not as immoral, per se, but *unnatural* – i.e. without the boundaries of capitalist civilization – or simply wasteful, much as Defoe regards it as wasteful to let African land remain unimproved – that is, "left naked, and thrown up to the wilderness." In his *Serious Reflections During the Life and Surprising Adventures of Robinson Crusoe* (1720), for example, Defoe precisely refers to cannibalism as unnatural. And one of the first things that Crusoe must do to make Friday "useful, handy, and helpful" (166) is to "bring [him] off from his horrid way of feeding, and from the relish of a cannibal's stomach" (166). That he does so by teaching him to relish goat flesh, not only stresses the powerful biotic alliance of humans and goats (a partnership that, as noted earlier, was instrumental to the global spread of capitalism, in that remote oceanic islands were strategically populated with goats to provide seafaring Europeans with convenient points of resupply), but also the co-production of capitalism by human and extra-human natures.

Alternatively, the term "savage" repeatedly functions in the novel to identify both wild beasts and non-European bodies as separated from humanity, or simply (again) outside the boundaries of capitalist civilization. The aspiring, yet naive capitalist version of Crusoe, and his appraisal of West Africa (possibly near Gambia or Senegal) implies as much, similarly lumping Africans together with non-human – i.e. savage – beasts:

> who wou'd ha' suppos'd we were sail'd on to the southward to the truly *barbarian* coast, where whole nations of Negroes were sure to surround us with their canoes, and destroy us; where we could ne'er once go on shore but we should be devour'd by savage beasts, or more merciless savages of human kind. (21)

This early version of Crusoe (the naive, pre-shipwreck Crusoe who as yet fails to see how nature works for capitalism) seems to regard these extra-human natures (unlike the slaves or cattle in Ligon) as value-less, in keeping with Shiva's point about how capitalism regards the "labor of women and Third World farmers" as "nonlabor, mere biology, a natural resource; their products are thus akin to natural deposits."[107] Crusoe's initial outlook resonates with Defoe's appraisal of the as yet unappropriated Nature of West Africa in his *Plan of the English Commerce*:

> But all this while here is not the least Use made of the Land; the fruitful Soil lies waste, a vast extended Country, pleasant Vallies, the Banks of charming Rivers, spacious Plains, capable of Improvement and Cultivation, to infinite Advantage, lie waste and untouch'd, over-run with Shrubbery and useless Trees; as a Forrest trod under Foot with wild Creatures; and the yet wilder Negroes, who just plant their Maize, and a few Roots and Herbs, like as we do for our Garden-stuff, and all the rest is left naked, and thrown up to the Wilderness.[108]

Defoe not only acknowledges the potentially infinitely valuable work/energy inherent in such geographical features / conditions with terms like "fruitful" and "charming," but his *Plan* also calls for the improvement of such land, basically advocating for the capitalist appropriation of both human and extra-human natures. In this respect, at least, Defoe's novel invites readers to consider how, as Boisseron puts it, "the history of the animal and the black in the black Atlantic is *connected*, rather than simply comparable." Arguably, the novel is one of "various instances, in the cross-Atlantic history of the black diaspora, of intersectional encounters, analogies, and battles, that reveal the intextricability of the animal and the black."[109]

Furthermore, Ligon's seemingly innocuous comment upon the lime tree's potential as hedge resonates with *Crusoe*'s capitalism, in so far as he invites us to take into account Moore's analysis of the law of value, and its relationship to so-called cheap natures in the history of capitalism. Moore explains:

> The law of value represents a determination of socially necessary labor time, which occurs simultaneously through organization and technical innovation *and* through strategies of appropriating the unpaid work/energy of "women, nature, and colonies."[110]

Moore's point is that value (in a capitalist economy) depends not exclusively upon labor time – that is, the average amount of time required to produce the average commodity – but also various extra-economic efforts to "identify, secure, and channel unpaid work [including the unpaid work of extra-human natures] outside the commodity system into the circuit of capitalism."[111] He substitutes work/energy for labor here because of its capaciousness; work/energy includes photosynthesis, as well as the labor associated with childbearing.

Despite the considerable attention that gets paid to Crusoe's (and Friday's) labor, Defoe frequently glosses over the unpaid work/energy of extra-human natures. Yet both play integral roles in the spatial reorganization of the island. Consider, again, Crusoe's goats (L. *Capra hircus*). Crusoe relies upon these grazers to not only convert otherwise unusable plants into valuable protein, much as European plantation owners relied upon African slaves to convert a grass – i.e. sugar cane (L. *Saccharum officinarum*) – into similarly valuable substances / things: granulated sugar, molasses, and rum (See Chapters 2 and 3). Their work in clearing ground, or, in effect, deforesting the island becomes all the more critical as the human population of Crusoe's island increases:

> I begun now to consider, that having two mouths to feed, instead of one, I must provide more ground for my harvest, and plant a larger quantity of corn than I used to do; so I mark'd out a larger piece of land, and began the fence in the same manner as before, in which *Friday* not only work'd very willingly, and very hard; but did it very cheerfully, and I told him ... that it was for corn to make more bread, because he was now with me ... He appear'd very sensible of that part, and let me know that ... he would work the harder for me, if I would tell him what to do. (168)

And so begins "the pleasantest year of all the life I led in this place," says Crusoe – though not bothering to explain Friday's curious math and grammar here, which basically accounts for the production of surplus value. That is, why must Friday "work the *harder* for [Crusoe]" [italics mine], and not simply *as hard as* Crusoe? And precisely what sort of pleasure does Crusoe derive from Friday's willingness to work hard, and cheerfully for him? The answer to both of these questions lies in Friday's failure to consider the rate of exploitation, which, according to Moore, "increases when the average worker [Friday] procures a rising mass of value (often, a rising physical volume of commodities [corn]), so long as wages increase more slowly than productivity."[112] With only two mouths to feed, Friday has only to work equally hard as Crusoe to ensure that both men are fed. His working harder necessarily generates a surplus, and, of course, the additional space required to produce more corn renders Crusoe's goats all the more valuable as grazers / ecosystem engineers.

Another way in which Defoe's novel treats the invisibility of such unpaid work/energy lies in the general absence of women. There is only a brief mention of his mother's opposition to Crusoe's "going to sea" (5–8), and then slight reference to the "stark naked" (27) West African women. The novel is almost entirely homosocial, and thus obscures the unpaid labor of women as bearers of children (an issue that, as I point out in Chapter 3, gets highlighted in Leonora Sansay's *Secret History*), etc. – though it's worth noting here that Defoe compensates for this absence of women in his sequel, *The Farther Adventures of Robinson Crusoe* (1719), which carefully attends to this question of capitalism's appropriation of the unpaid work/energy of women. Notably, at one point Crusoe's compatriots – three Englishmen – are given the opportunity to each select one of five indigenous women, "well favour'd agreeable Persons, both in Shape and Features, only tawny"[113] – to serve as either servant or wife. The cheerful willingness of these women to "work for the Men who had brought them away" – "they all fell a Dancing; and presently one fell to taking up this, and another that, any Thing that lay next, to carry on their Shoulders, to intimate that they were willing to work" – corresponds with Friday's willingness to work hard, and cheerfully in *Robinson Crusoe*.[114] However, it is the Englishman's inclination to treat these women as *both* wives and servants that evidently dovetails with capitalism's routine relegation of women to the status of cheap nature:

> The Governour ... ask'd the three Men, what they intended to do with these Women, and how they intended to use them; whether as Servants, or as Women? One of the *English* Men answer'd

very boldly and readily, That they would <u>use</u> them as both.¹¹⁵ (Underscoring mine.)

The distinction that the Governor draws here between Women and Servants mirrors the Cartesian binary, in which humanity is separated from an externalized Nature. In the Governor's estimation, an indigenous servant is something other than human / woman – that is, merely a form of cheap nature, a quantifiable unit of work / energy / food. This idea recalls both Shiva's ecofeminist point about capitalism's mistreatment of women's labor as mere biology – an appropriated natural resource – and Gómez-Barris's work on the silver mining industry in Bolivia, in which "women provide labor to the extractive zone by supporting the heterosexual mining [or, in *Crusoe*'s case, farming] family at home."¹¹⁶ Consider Crusoe's prior assumption, that

> the Sight ... was something uncouth to our *Spaniards* ... to see two naked Men, and five naked Women, all together bound, and in the most miserable Circumstances that human Nature could be suppos'd to be, (*viz*), to be expecting every Moment to be dragg'd out and have their Brains knock'd out, and then to be eaten up like a Calf that is kill'd for a Dainty.¹¹⁷

Defoe's invocation of cannibalism here merely reinforces the racist equivalency of indigenous Americans with cheap nature, not unlike a "Calf that is kill'd for a Dainty." And so, that the Englishmen are apt to treat these women as *both* wives and servants suggests a peculiarly capitalistic acknowledgment of the unpaid labor of wives as bearers of children. Has the future author of *Moll Flanders* (1722) developed a newfound critical appreciation for capitalism's relentless appropriation of women's work/energy? Or might we link this new ecofeminist angle to the development of Crusoe's world-ecological outlook?

I am apt to think that both cases may be true – that Defoe saw a link between Moll's fertility and childbearing and Crusoe's fortunate turnover of agricultural produce. But, first, we must return to the question of the rhetorical appeal of citrus. Ligon explains that the purpose of these fruits – citrons, oranges, lemons, and limes – is "to whet our appetites."¹¹⁸ That is, Ligon's comment calls to our attention the rhetorical value of citrus as integral to the representation of Barbados as island Eden. Such fruitfulness often figures in the propaganda of American settlement as a lure, inviting readers to participate in the colonial enterprise. Deckard notes, for example, that as plantation money from the sales of sugar and molasses flowed from the Caribbean islands back across the Atlantic financing the building of stately homes with *ostentatious gardens* and giving rise to a cult of extravagance, paradise became increasingly defined in the secular terms of exclusivity and luxury, a consumer Eden which could be accessed not through religious piety, but through the accumulation of money and status. (Italics mine.)[119]

(Worth noting here is that prior to the shipwreck Crusoe had already established a successful plantation in Brazil, such that, at novel's end, he's able to return to England in possession of the sort of money and status that Deckard describes.) The propagandistic appeal of Ligon's citrus fruit ties in nicely with what Deckard describes as this discursive transformation of paradise, in which "the pursuit of mystical bliss was replaced by the craving for physical pleasures . . . the addictive stimulations of tea, coffee, tobacco, and sugar."[120] Isn't that precisely what happens to Crusoe when he stumbles upon them: is his appetite for material wealth not whetted by the appearance of lemons and limes? In fact, Crusoe claims that thoughts of the "fruitfulness of that valley, and the pleasantness of the situation" (81) ran long in his head, such that he felt compelled to choose this eastern side of the island as the site for his so-called country estate:

> I was so enamour'd of this place, that I spent much of my time there for the whole remaining part of the month of *July*; and . . . I built me a little kind of a bower, and surrounded it at a distance with a strong fence, being a double hedge, as high as I could reach, well stak'd, and fill'd between with *brushwood*; and here I lay very secure, sometimes two or three nights together, always going over it with a ladder, as before; so that I fancy'd now I had my country-house, and my sea-coast house. (81–2)

At the very least, Defoe's narrative partakes of what Webber describes as the romance of citrus, presumably to elicit his readers' interest in the Americas. Indeed, the emphasis that Ligon puts on Barbados's vegetable production seems perfectly in sync with the advertising of colonial real estate, as it were, that takes place in much empire writing, not unlike John Poyntz's *The Present Prospect of the Famous and Fertile Island of Tobago* (1683), which Richard Grove identifies as a likely source text for *Robinson Crusoe*.[121] That Poyntz too takes into account Tobago's abundance of oranges, lemons, limes, and citrons clearly reinforces this connection, or at least offers some explanation for the presence of these citrus fruits in Defoe's novel. Poyntz writes:

But of *Oranges* here are three sorts; The sower [*sic*] for sauce, and the Flowers for Essences, the sweet ones are eaten for Recreation. But the *China-Orange* that grows here in *America*, super-excels those in *Europe* beyond express.

Of *Lemons* also, here are two several sorts; the sower one, for *Lemonadoes*; and the sweet one for Delectation. So of *Limes* also, here are sweet and sower: with the last of which, they make Limeads and Punch.[122]

Given Grove's assessment of sixteenth- and seventeen-century travel literature – specifically, that many tropical islands were perceived as "sites of nurturing relief from arduous and disease-ridden sea journeys" – it seems obvious why both authors would choose to emphasize the islands' citrus fruits. The ascorbic in these fruits is precisely what the bodies of sailors suffering from scurvy would be craving (see, for example, Jonathan Lamb's work on scurvy and the scorbutic imagination).[123] But it does seem a bit odd that neither Ligon, nor Poyntz takes the trouble to consider the Asiatic origins of these fruit trees. Ligon also doesn't bother to explain the importation of animals that figure in his so-called exact, yet obviously limited history. Among the animals that Ligon takes into account, including cats, rats, oxen, bulls, cows, horses, hogs, sheep and goats, the Arabian camels (or dromedaries) seem the most glaringly obvious Old World creatures, and are prominently featured on his map of the island.

Another possible source of inspiration (and information) for Defoe would have been Hans Sloane. After receiving his degree in medicine, the soon-to-be "enormously active and successful" doctor, man of science, and collector of curiosities traveled to Jamaica in 1687 as physician to the 2nd Duke of Albermarle. The position afforded the young doctor an opportunity to explore the island's natural wonders: "he hired artists to record nature and wildlife, kept detailed notes and also wrote about his adventures to London friends."[124] The result of Sloane's investigations was an immense collection of curiosities, described by John Evelyn as "being an universal Collection of the natural productions of Jamaica consisting of Plants, Corralls, Minerals, Earth, shells, animals, Insects &c."[125] These explorations (and the resulting collection) would form the basis of Sloane's voluminous study of Jamaica's natural history, *A Voyage to the Islands of Madera, Barbados, Nieves, S. Christophers and Jamaica . . .* (1707), in which he carefully acknowledges – or at least does not ignore – humankind's geographical agency. That is, while he neglects to account for the Asiatic origins of certain plants – namely, the aforementioned citrus fruits – he does (unlike Ligon) link Spain's colonization of Jamaica to the introduction of both oranges and limes:

> I went to *Guanaboa*, where are large Settlements and Plantations, and observed that tract of Ground called the Red Hills between *Guanaboa* and the Town ...
> On these Red Hills, four Miles from Town, lived Mr. *Barnes* a Carpenter, who used to cut and bring Wood to the Town ... He carried me half a Mile up his Plantation, shew'd me the Woods, wherein the *Spaniards* had usually planted their *Cassada* for the Town, after felling of the Woods. The Trees were grown, from the time the *Spaniards* had quitted the Island, to the time I saw them, to be at least forty or fifty Foot high, long small, and straight. They often in those Woods meet with Palisadoes, Orange-Walks, Limes, and other marks of formerly planted Ground.[126]

Here Sloane draws his readers' attentions to the Spaniards' routine clearing of forests and planting of Cassada (or Cassava) trees (native to South America), but also notes their establishment of "Orange-Walks." Accordingly, this passage resonates with Crusoe's assessment of the eastern side of the island – namely, that it "looked like a planted garden." The presence of cocoa, orange, lemon, lime, and citron trees suggest that the island is not nearly as removed from the "ordinary course of the trade of mankind" (51) as Crusoe initially suspects. Or, rather, anyone who had read Sloane's natural history of Jamaica might have linked the vegetation that Crusoe describes here to Spanish settlement of the Americas.

However, this is not the first indication that Defoe provides us of the island's susceptibility to invasion by foreign (or introduced) species / human intervention. Ironically, just a few paragraphs prior to Crusoe's initial assessment of the island's location – again, "some hundreds of leagues out of the ordinary course of the trade of mankind" (51) – he mentions having "discover'd that there were goats on the island, which was a great satisfaction to me" (50). This is an especially curious feature because, as noted earlier, large mammals are typically not endemic to such oceanic islands. In his analysis of the fate of remote islands, for example, Charles Elton (a foundational figure in the study of ecology) observes that, on Easter Island, "the number of animal species that seem to be native is almost absurd ... a green lacewing, a fly, a weevil, a water beetle, and a land snail."[127] Even New Zealand – an island considerably larger than, say, the Juan Fernández archipelago – has no native mammals, except for bats.[128] And so, the presence of goats not only seriously undermines the remote, desert status of Crusoe's island, but may also help explain the barley's so-called miraculous growth, as "disturbed habitats are particularly susceptible to invasion."[129]

Evidently, the zoology of Crusoe's island was inspired by several potential source texts, including, most obviously, Woodes Rogers's account of Alexander Selkirk's nearly 4.5-year sojourn on Juan Fernández in *A Cruising Voyage Round the World* (1712), Richard Steele's treatment of the same in *The Englishman* (1713), and, last but not least, Robert Knox's *An Historical Relation of the Island of Ceylon* (1681). Notably, that these source texts engage animals, plants, peoples, and places that are situated not in the Atlantic, but Indian and Pacific oceans clearly invites us to read Defoe's novel in a transoceanic, global context, as it were, in keeping with Michelle Burnham's efforts to read American literature in a "maritime global context."[130] Knox's *Historical Relation . . . of Ceylon*, for example, offers some explanation for Crusoe's initial paranoia about ravenous beasts. Knox observes that, in addition to goats, Ceylon boasts a rich variety of large animals, including "Cowes, Buffaloes, Hogs, Goats, Deer, Hares, Dogs, Jacols, Apes, Tygers, Bears, Elephants, and other Wild Beasts."[131] But, as noted earlier, it was most likely Rogers's and/or Steele's account of Selkirk's animal husbandry upon Juan Fernández that figures in Defoe's decision to populate Crusoe's island with goats, in particular, though such animals and plants – i.e. creatures of empire – were routinely introduced to otherwise remote oceanic islands to provide sailors with a "food source to access during long voyages . . . Domestic goats (*Capra hircus*) were introduced to provide food for sailors on long voyages, but they quickly became a self-sufficient feral population."[132]

This is an interesting scenario because, of course, feral goat populations, such as those mentioned in Steele's treatment of Selkirk, "exert a tremendous amount of pressure on ecosystem processes through foraging and movement through vegetation."[133] Again, Elton observes that the introduction of red deer has had a profound impact upon New Zealand's native forests:

> it is likely that on many watersheds the deer, helped by [similarly introduced] domestic stock [including sheep], have tipped the scale towards a cycle of catastrophic soil erosion, which is felt not only in the mountains but also in those parts of the lowland valleys that receive the extra load of silt washed from above.[134]

The deforestation of Easter Island too, explains Elton, was likely owing to the co-production of humans (removal of timber) and "grazing sheep and cattle."[135] Tiny by comparison to goats, European rabbits have similarly "devastated vegetation" on many of the 800 islands to which they have been introduced, including the continent-sized island of Australia. Simberloff notes: "On Australia ... their [the rabbits'] biggest ecological impact is stripping and killing seedling trees and perennial shrubs, especially acacias, thereby contributing substantially to deforestation and desertification."[136]

Of course, it's possible that Defoe included these goats to showcase how species collaborate in empire building, as Crusoe's long-term survival and dominance over the island in part hinges upon his re-domestication of them. Crusoe notes, for example, that, "I had no want of food, and of that which was very good too; especially these three sorts, *viz.* goats, pidgeons, and turtle or tortoise" (87–8). And, later, after several failed attempts, and, most importantly, with his ammunition running low, he finally figures a way to "maintain as many [goats] as I should have in any reasonable time." For starters, it dawns on Crusoe that he must build an enclosure to separate out the tame goats:

> it presently occurr'd to me, that I must keep the tame from the wild, or else they would always run wild when they grew up, and the only way for this was to have some enclosed piece of ground, well fenc'd either with hedge or pale, to keep them in so effectually, that those within might not break out, or those without break in. (116)

And then Defoe takes us step by step through Crusoe's process of domestication beginning with his selection of a suitable location:

> Those who understand such enclosures will think I had very little contrivance, when I pitch'd upon a place very proper for all these, being a plain open piece of meadow-land or *savanna,* (as our people call it in the western colonies,) which had two or three little drills of fresh water in it, and at one end was very woody ...
>
> I was about three months hedging in the first piece [of meadowland], and till I had done it I tether'd the three kids in the best part of it, and us'd them to feed as near me as possible to make them familiar; and very often I would go and carry them some ears of barley, or a handful of rice, and feed them out of my hand; so that after my enclosure was finished, and I let them loose, they would follow me up and down, bleating after me for a handful of corn.
>
> This answer'd my end, and in about a year and half I had a flock of about twelve goats, kids and all; and in two years more I had three and forty, besides several that I took and killed for my food ...

But this was not all, for now I not only had goats flesh to feed on when I pleas'd, but milk too ... (117)[137]

This passage squarely situates Crusoe in the web of life. Worth noting here is how the barley, rice, and corn figure in Crusoe's formation of a biotic alliance with these goats. Were it not for the accidental introduction and so-called providential growth of such cereal grasses, Crusoe might never have been able to re-domesticate these grazing mammals. That is, Crusoe's thriving existence upon the island (the history of his capitalism, as it were) depends not merely, as Cole suggests, upon the rats' mysterious disappearance,[138] but upon the succession of other historical natures: the barley, rice, corn, cats, goats, and, of course, the geo- and climatological conditions of the island itself (the "meadow-land" boasting several sources of fresh water, and with one end "very woody" offering shade). Accordingly, Crusoe's story dovetails neatly with one of Moore's key points: "humans build empires on their own as much as beavers build dams on their own. Both are 'ecosystem engineers.' Neither exists in a vacuum."[139] As scholars like Alfred Crosby, Virginia Anderson, and Rebecca J. H. Woods have pointed out too, empires are not built by humans alone, but in collaboration with other species, including the livestock that continue to transform ecosystems throughout the world.[140]

Additionally, Crusoe's goats also figure as not-so-subtle reminders that, as Greg Dening puts it, "every species of tree, plant, and animal on an island has crossed the beach."[141] The coconut is a good example of this reality because its seeds "can float for months on salty ocean currents," which evidently "explains their prevalence on tropical coasts and oceanic islands around the world."[142] Poyntz's account of the "Cocur-Nut-tree [sic]" draws our attention to the remarkable utility of this fruit, a matter of fact that might have appealed to Defoe, as Crusoe tends to obsessively weigh every object's various use and exchange values. Poyntz writes:

> the *Cocur-Nut-tree*, and the fruit that hangs upon it, the *Indians* idolize it ... because to produce both meat, drink and Cloth: it's true beyond dispute, that the Nut ... is sweet beyond the sweetest *Almond* ... but the Shell serves for Cups, Spoons, and Dishes; and the Rind encompassing the Shell, serves the *Indians* for covering, and with the Leaves they thatch their Houses, and make Baskets, but some more ingenious make Ropes, and Lines for *Fishing*.[143]

This passage alerts us to the considerable work/energy embedded in the coconut palm tree. Accordingly, in his *Natural History of*

Barbados (1750), the Reverend Griffith Hughes invites his readers to regard the coconut palm as evidence that "Providence hath enriched every Climate with Blessings peculiar to itself, and adapted to the Necessities of its Inhabitants," a suggestion which neatly corresponds with Crusoe's initial, providential interpretation of the barley that takes root upon his island.[144] The coconut palm appears to have captured the interests of eighteenth-century natural historians because its fruit is so remarkably useful, not to mention widely distributed throughout the tropical regions of the world. Is it not surprising, then, that Defoe neglects to account for the presence of any coconuts on Crusoe's island? Although not indigenous to the Caribbean (the coconut palm is supposed to be native to Malaya or the Indo-Pacific region),[145] Crusoe's island would likely have been punctuated with coconut palm trees. And would Defoe's Crusoe not have recognized the coconut's manifold usefulness? Would Crusoe not have bothered to appropriate the unpaid work/energy of this extra-human nature, much as he does with the barley, rice, corn, and goats? Why doesn't the coconut appear in Crusoe's web of life?[146]

Although there does not seem to be any convenient explanation for Defoe's inattention to the coconut palm, which, according to Raffaele and Wiley, "commonly grows wild along sandy shores" throughout the Caribbean[147] (that is, not unless we subscribe to Cole's and Bender's assessment of the island's so-called metaphysical security), the continuous communication between land and sea that figures in the coconut's naturalization on tropical shores across the globe also plays a prominent role in the novel's climatic footprint scene. That is, perhaps Defoe's most compelling engagement with this *tidal dialectic* – that is, what Elizabeth DeLoughrey refers to as the "dynamic and shifting relationship between land and sea"[148] – occurs when Crusoe's sense of security (or isolation) is shattered by his discovery of an unknown / seemingly inexplicable footprint on the sandy shore of his island:

> It happen'd one day about noon going towards my boat, I was exceedingly supris'd with the print of a man's naked foot on the shore, which was very plain to be seen in the sand: I stood like one thunder-struck, or as if I had seen an apparition; I listen'd, I look'd round me, I could hear nothing, nor see any thing, I went up to a rising ground to look farther, I went up the shore and down the shore, but it was all one, I could see no other impression but that one, I went to it again to see if there were any more, and to observe if it might not be my fancy; but there was no room for that, for there was

exactly the very print of a foot, toes, heel, and every part of a foot; how it came thither, I knew not, nor could in the least imagine. (122)

Crusoe's most rational solution to the lingering question of the footprint's origins – "that it must be some savages of the main land over-against me, who had wander'd out to sea in their *canoes*, and either driven by the currents, or by contrary winds, had made the island" (123) – clearly challenges his initial assessment of the island's remoteness. In other words, the fact remains that islands are *not* removed from the rest of the world / nature – but (owing to the remarkable economy of ocean currents, wind, and weather patterns) supremely vulnerable to invasion. In *Out of Eden*, for example, Alan Burdick notes that "snails and frogs from Cuba and Central America, borne aloft on the winds of tropical hurricanes, land in Florida with sufficient regularity that they have established nascent colonies in the Everglades." He also explains that "ship captains have witnessed lush rafts of flotsam drifting far out at sea and harboring all manner of tagalongs: crabs, barnacles, field mice, boa constrictors, termites, geckos, squirrels, thirty-foot-tall palm trees."[149]

Moreover, Crusoe's initial reaction to this "print of a man's naked foot on the shore" enables us to see human history implicated within, or thoroughly confused with the histories of particular natures. He explains:

> I came home to my fortification, not feeling, as we say, the ground I went on, but terrify'd to the last degree, looking behind me at every two or three steps, mistaking every bush and tree, and fancying every stump at a distance to be a man; nor is it possible to describe how many . . . *wild ideas* were found every moment in my fancy, and what strange unaccountable whimsies came into my thoughts by the way. (Italics mine, 122)

Although this passage may first appear to be describing the ravings of someone who has been frightened out of his wits, there is definitely an underlying logic to Crusoe's "wild ideas." For, instead of merely "mistaking every bush and tree . . . for a man," I would argue that Crusoe is not only finally able to recognize the role of man in the island's present state, but he is also that much closer to grasping how the history of capitalism is, as Moore suggests, "one of successive historical natures."[150] That is, human and natural history are fused as Crusoe fancies "every stump at a distance to be a man" (122). Or what makes these ideas *wild* is precisely this elevation of Crusoe's ecological consciousness. The distance that is required for this confusion to take place suggests that Crusoe's failure to see this before stemmed from either a Cartesian separation of humanity and nature or some measure of near-sightedness – i.e. an inability to see beyond the present time to acknowledge the collaborative work/energy of preceding natures.

I would like to propose that we read this passage as an allegory for human history's implication in natural history – or, simply, the unification (not separation) of humanity and nature. The complexion of Defoe's early work – his book on the "Great Hurricane" of 1703 and "The Destruction of the Isle of St. Vincent," which "was written at the same time as he was completing *Robinson Crusoe*," suggests that he was preoccupied with environmental issues, including (as Grove notes) the possibility of extinction.[151] But whereas Defoe's work on St. Vincent takes into account the "immediate hand of Nature, directed by Providence," *Crusoe* not only takes God out of the equation, as was the case when Crusoe sorts through the barley's seemingly miraculous appearance upon the island: "my religious thankfulness to God's Providence began to abate too upon the discovering that all this was nothing but what was common" [or natural] (64). The novel also dispenses altogether with the tropical island Eden mythology, which, as Grove explains, played an integral role in the promotion of American settlement. Instead, Defoe obliges us to consider every island on this planet to be *not* a closed system (as Cole's and Bender's readings of the novel imply), but (rather) extremely susceptible to bio-invasion. Taken together, these works reveal Defoe's preoccupation with "amazing accidents" – whether natural or artificial, including (as noted earlier) Crusoe's accidental introduction of barley to the island. And, of course, as I suggested in the Introduction, I imagine that Defoe would be equally drawn to Trouvelot's amazing accident – his introduction of the European gypsy moth to America's hardwood forests, however tragic. Even his translation of Selkirk's Pacific island experience to the Atlantic can itself be interpreted as an allegory for the shrinking of the world vis-à-vis the global dispersion and confusion of Old and New World humans, animals, and plants. Notably, Defoe's transoceanic stitching together of Pacific and Caribbean island histories not only invites us to consider what (as noted earlier) Michelle Burnham has described as the "intertwined commercial, political, and literary developments that accompanied the explosion in global maritime travel and exploration" that took place in the late eighteenth and early nineteenth centuries, "as a host of scientific and commercial voyages mutually dedicated to discovery and profit [such as the voyages of Captain James Cook] forever connected the Pacific to the rest of the world's oceans, including the Atlantic."[152] Defoe's convenient translation of Pacific island source texts, including the story of Selkirk, to Crusoe's Caribbean island simultaneously invites us to reflect upon the very movement of water itself – the fact that, as Burnham puts it, "oceanic water only merges, melds, and mixes with more water – with bays and inlets, with rivers, gulfs and seas, but also with other oceans."[153] Fijian writer, Epeli Hau'ofa refers to how this sort of consciousness of the movement of water encourages Pacific island peoples to engage in a kind of "world enlargement ... that makes nonsense of all national and economic boundaries."[154] And, although I would not go so far as to describe *Robinson Crusoe* as similarly defiant of "all national and economic boundaries," Crusoe certainly develops a keen awareness of how oceanic water figures in the merging, melding, and mixture of cultures *and* natures, humans and non-humans. And it is a kind of transoceanic shrinking of the globe that Defoe acknowledges at the outset of his 1724 novel, *A New Voyage Round the World*, which Benjamin Pauley describes as "capitalist pornography."[155] He writes:

> I do not in this lessen the merit of those gentlemen who have made such a long voyage as that round the globe; but I must be allowed to say, as the way is now a *common road*, the reason of it thoroughly known, and the occasion of it more frequent than in former times, so the world has done wondering at it; we no more look upon it as a mighty thing, a strange and never-heard-of undertaking. This cannot be now expected of us, the thing is made familiar, every ordinary sailor is able to do it ... and he that can carry a ship to Lisbon, may with the same ease carry it round the world. (Italics mine.)[156]

That Defoe refers to the circumnavigation of the globe as "now a common [or heavily trafficked] road" clearly suggests that he understood the world to be shrinking in conjunction with the global spread of European commerce (capitalism), and in *Robinson Crusoe* he provides us with numerous opportunities to think about the resulting vulnerability of island ecosystems. That "every ordinary sailor is able to do it" speaks to the various ways in which Europeans equipped oceanic islands, such as Juan Fernández, to serve as convenient rest stops. Ultimately, this line, I argue, reflects not the "effects of an expanding world, transformed by the discovery of a new continent on the other side of the Atlantic,"[157] so much as the opening of new Atlantic-Pacific avenues of trade, and, as such, portends the corresponding shrinkage of global biodiversity through the biological approximation of one place to another (ongoing transportation of Crusoe's goats, rats, cats, etc.). Indeed, once Crusoe stumbles upon evidence of other human visitations to the island – specifically, at his "seeing the [S.W.] shore spread with skulls, hands, feet and other bones of human bodies" (130) – he becomes increasingly preoccupied with ocean currents, or the alternating ebb and flow of the ocean surrounding the island. This preoccupation increases dramatically in the "twenty third year of residence in this island," a point at which he claims he "was so naturaliz'd to the place, and to the manner of living, that *could I have* but enjoy'd the certainty that no savages would come to the place to disturb me, I *could have* been content to have capitulated for spending the rest of my time there, even to the last moment" (italics mine,142). That Defoe uses the term "naturalized" – that is, as opposed to, say, habituated – significantly showcases Crusoe's new mindset. Interestingly, invasion biologists use the term naturalized to "describe a population that was introduced long ago and perpetuates itself without human assistance, though not necessarily in pristine 'natural' environments."[158] Plus, the grammatical construction of this sentence implies that he is no longer unaware of the island's susceptibility to invasions. Crusoe explains the underlying circumstances for this raising of his tidal / oceanic consciousness as follows:

> It was now the month of *December* ... in my twenty third year; and this being the *southern* Solstice ... was the particular time of my harvest, and requir'd my being pretty much abroad in the fields, when going out pretty early in the morning ... I was surpris'd with seeing a light of some fire upon the shore ... where I had observ'd some savages had been, as before; but not on the other side; but to my great affliction, it was on my side of the island. (143–4)

And, aptly, he proceeds to carefully note how the tidal currents direct the course of the mainlanders' canoes:

> They had two *canoes* with them, which they had haled up upon the shore; and as it was then tide of ebb, they seem'd to me to wait for the return of the flood, to go away again; it is not easy to imagine what confusion this sight put me into, especially seeing them come on my side the island, and so near me too; but when I observ'd their coming must be always with the current of the ebb, I began afterwards to be more sedate in my mind, being satisfy'd that I might go abroad with safety all the time of the tide of flood, if they were not on shore before ... (144–5)

This is a most interesting passage because it completely contradicts Crusoe's prior assessment of the island's remoteness. The explanation that he offers of how the so-called savages rely upon tidal currents – the ocean's ebb and flow – to travel to and from the island not only provides us with a precise idea of how oceanic islands communicate with the rest of the world, but also (as noted previously in this chapter) with a world-ecological view of the conditions and constraints that particular natures (in this case, oceanic water) levy upon human agency. I refer to this ongoing relationship between land and sea repeatedly in this study (see especially Chapter 4), in no small part because (as I've noted earlier) the British Empire was built upon the transportation of human and extra-human natures overseas (the overseas trade that Defoe promoted throughout his career), and, of course, our present-day global capitalism continues to rely very heavily upon the transoceanic delivery of resources and commodities aboard massive cargo ships. Most importantly, Crusoe's island, which figures not as a pristine wilderness, or Eden-like tropical setting, but a notably disturbed habitat (as evidenced by the barley's miraculous taking root and speedy growth) offers some allegorical notion of the ecological footprint of this transoceanic, global economy. In particular, I'm thinking here of the role that overseas shipping has played in the spread of invasive species – the accidental tourists (animals and plants) who, as a consequence of this transshipment of goods overseas, have settled into bioregions that may or may not welcome their input. Simberloff observes, for example, "after the American Civil War, steamships greatly sped up the ocean crossing, and nursery stock imported into the United States, especially from Europe, drastically increased the number of introduced insect species."[159] As well, the spotted lanternfly's most recent invasion of Pennsylvania is supposed to be the result of eggs that hitched a ride on (or in) a shipping container, like those carried aboard the huge cargo ships that routinely sail from China to the United States.[160]

Crusoe's consciousness of this ecological reality – that islands do not exist in isolation, but consistently interact with the rest of the world – increases further still with the discovery of the "wreck of a [Spanish] ship cast away in the night" (147). The scene that I have in mind is one in which Crusoe contemplates venturing out to the shipwreck to search for survivors and scavenge for both useful and not so useful (exchange value) objects. Crusoe debates whether and how he might

> venture out in [his] boat, to this wreck; not doubting but I might find something on board, that might be useful to me; but that did not

> altogether press me so much, as the possibility that there might be yet some living creature on board, whose life I might not only save, but might by saving that life, comfort my own to the last degree. (149)

It is at this point that Crusoe positions himself at an elevated point on the island, where he can see clearly "how the sets of the tide, or currents lay" (150):

> And now I was to launch out into the ocean, and either to venture, or not to venture. I look'd on the rapid currents which ran constantly on both sides of the island, at a distance, and which were very terrible to me ... for I foresaw that if I was driven into either of those currents, I should be carry'd a vast way out to sea, and perhaps out of my reach, or sight of the island again ...
>
> These thoughts so oppress'd my mind, that I began to give over my enterprise, and having haled my boat into a little creek on the shore, I stept out, and sat me down upon a little rising bit of ground, very pensive and anxious ... when as I was musing, I could perceive that the tide was turn'd, and the flood came on, upon which my going was for so many hours impracticable; upon this presently it occurr'd to me, that I should go up to the highest piece of ground I could find, and observe, if I could, how the sets of the tide, or currents lay, when the flood came in, that I might judge whether if I was driven one way out, I might not expect to be driven another way home, with the same rapidness of the currents: This thought was no sooner in my head, but I cast my eye upon a little hill, which sufficiently over-look'd the sea both ways, and from whence I had a clear view of the currents, or sets of the tide, and which way I was to guide my self in my return; here I found, that as the current of the ebb set out close by the south point of the island, so the current of the flood set in close by the shore of the north side, and that I had nothing to do but to keep to the north of the island in my return, and I should do well enough.
>
> Encourag'd with this observation, I resolv'd the next morning to set out with the first of the tide ... (150–1)

I quote this passage at length because it reflects Crusoe's realization that his island – the island upon which not merely his English barley, but capitalist ideals have taken root – does not exist in a vacuum, per se, but communicates with the "rest of nature in a flow of flows."[161] Crusoe's new view of the ocean shares something with the "printed News Papers" that Defoe champions in his *Journal of the Plague Year* – for it is a medium through which information travels.[162] Albeit, the ocean serves not only to spread "Rumours and Reports of Things," but also functions as a channel through which actual organisms travel, whether purposefully or accidentally. Indeed, what frightens Crusoe most as he contemplates the question – to venture or not to venture – is precisely the possibility of his being accidentally "carry'd a vast way out to sea, and perhaps out of my reach, or sight of the island again" (150). Of course, chances are that, were he carried out to sea, he would eventually make landfall at another island or landmass, much like the flotsam or jetsam (the marine debris) that tends to accumulate on coastlines across the world (especially as a result of today's globalized economy, which is very much the sort of economy that, as noted earlier, Defoe doggedly promoted in his *Weekly Review*).[163] The beaches of Henderson Island, which is situated in the Pacific Ocean some 3,100 miles from the nearest human settlement, for example, continue to get piled up with plastic pollution – approximately "37.7 million pieces of plastic debris," to be precise: "turtles get tangled in fishing wire. Land crabs make their homes in toxic plastic."[164]

So, despite the emphasis that Defoe scholars have placed on the island's so-called remoteness or apparent metaphysical security, what I find most striking about *Robinson Crusoe* is the degree to which Defoe gradually (and subtly) debunks this remarkably alluring and persistent myth of isolated island space. Crusoe's island may appear at first to be a paradise – a "utopia disengaged from the rest of the world"[165] – but, through Crusoe's growing awareness of the island's accessibility to visitors and/or invaders, Defoe encourages us to read this space like every other island in the world as *not* entirely separated from, but inextricably linked to other geographical spaces by virtue of "how the sets of the tide, or currents lay" (150). As well, Defoe encourages us to view Crusoe's capitalism as not separated from Nature – not a project, per se, or something that is done to an otherwise externalized Nature – but a historical *process*, in which human and extra-human natures collaborate in the accumulation of capital. This point is reinforced in *The Farther Adventures of Robinson Crusoe*, where, as Jason H. Pearl puts it, "the island pulls toward itself every passing vessel and serves as a home to a diverse and contentious populace."[166] Of course, Defoe makes it clear in *Robinson Crusoe* that islands don't necessarily pull things toward them; they're not magnetic centers of attraction. But he does teach us what numerous contemporary ecologists have duly noted, that islands are supremely vulnerable to biological invasions, and, again, that capitalism is co-produced by manifold species.

Notes

1. Woodes Rogers, *A Cruising Voyage Round the World: First to the South-Seas, thence to the East-Indies, and homewards by the Cape of Good Hope* . . . (1712) (Amsterdam: N. Israel, 1969), 124.
2. Rogers, *Cruising*, 124–5.
3. Rogers, *Cruising*, 130.
4. William Dampier, *A New Voyage Round the World, Describing particularly the Isthmus of America, several Coasts and Islands in the West Indies, the isles of Cape Verde, the Passage by Terra del Fuego, the South-Sea Coasts of Chili, Peru, and Mexico* . . . (1697) (New York: Dover, 1968), 66.
5. See Sir Albert Gray, "Introduction," William Dampier, *New Voyage*, p. xl, n.3.
6. Rajani Sudan, *The Alchemy of Empire: Abject Materials and the Technologies of Colonialism* (New York: Fordham University Press, 2016), 6.
7. Carney, "Out of Africa," 206.
8. Dampier, *New Voyage*, 67.
9. Daniel Defoe, *The Farther Adventures of Robinson Crusoe; Being the Second and Last Part of his Life, and the Strange Surprizing Accounts of his Travels Round Three Parts of the Globe* (London: W. Taylor, 1719), 40.
10. Rogers, *Cruising*, 130.
11. Rogers, *Cruising*, 131.
12. Richard Steele, "The Story of Alexander Selkirk," *The Englishman* (1713), *The Commerce of Everyday Life: Selections from* The Tatler *and* The Spectator, edited by Erin Mackie (New York: Bedford/St. Martin's, 1998), 441.
13. Rogers, *Cruising*, 130.
14. Portuondo, *Secret Science*, 7.
15. Rogers, *Cruising*, ix.
16. Rogers, *Cruising*, x.
17. Rogers, *Cruising*, xi.
18. Rogers, *Cruising*, 137.
19. Michelle Burnham, *Transoceanic America: Risk, Writing, and Revolution in the Global Pacific* (Oxford: Oxford University Press, 2019), 3.
20. Jason Moore, *Capitalism in the Web of Life: Ecology and the Accumulation of Capital* (London: Verso, 2015), 16.
21. Andrew Lambert, *Crusoe's Island: A Rich and Curious History of Pirates, Castaways and Madness* (London: Faber & Faber, 2016), 29.
22. Solving the problem of scurvy was integral to the development of a transoceanic, global economy. And had Captain Pickering not died from scurvy aboard the Cinque Ports, Selkirk might never have been

stranded on the Juan Fernández archipelago. For more on scurvy, see Jonathan Lamb, *Scurvy: The Disease of Discovery* (Princeton: Princeton University Press, 2016).
23. Vandana Shiva, *Biopiracy: The Plunder of Nature and Knowledge* (Boston: South End Press, 1997), 32.
24. Dampier, *New Voyage*, 68.
25. Dampier, *New Voyage*, 68.
26. Ayesha Ramachandran, *The Worldmakers: Global Imagining in Early Modern Europe* (Chicago: The University Press of Chicago, 2015).
27. Lambert, *Crusoe's Island*, 20.
28. Dampier, *New Voyage*, 67.
29. Lambert, *Crusoe's Island*, 20.
30. John Locke, *Two Treatises of Government* (London: Everyman, 2000), 128.
31. Lambert, *Crusoe's Island*, 21.
32. Rogers, *Cruising*, 133.
33. Rogers, *Cruising*, 127–9.
34. Rogers, *Cruising*, 131.
35. Rogers, *Cruising*, 135.
36. Rogers, *Cruising*, 132.
37. Rogers, *Cruising*, 132.
38. Rogers, *Cruising*, 135.
39. Rogers, *Cruising*, 132.
40. Lucinda Cole, *Imperfect Creatures: Vermin, Literature, and the Sciences of Life, 1600–1740* (Ann Arbor: University of Michigan Press, 2016).
41. Rogers, *Cruising*, 128.
42. Steele, *The Englishman*, 440.
43. Cole, *Imperfect Creatures*, 146–7.
44. Loss, et al. estimate that in the United States alone, free-ranging domesticated cats "kill 1.3 – 4.0 billion birds and 6.3 – 22.3 billion mammals annually ... and are likely the single greatest source of anthropogenic mortality for US birds and mammals." Noting that cats are "among the 100 worst non-native invasive species in the world," they point out that "free-ranging cats on islands have caused or contributed to 33 (14%) of the modern bird, mammal, and reptile extinctions recorded by the International Union for Conservation of Nature (IUCN) Red List." See Scott R. Loss, Tom Will, and Peter P. Marra, "The impact of free-ranging domestic cats on wildlife in the United States," *Nature Communications* 4, no. 1396 (29 January 2013), 1–2. Similarly, Daniel Simberloff observes: "on subantarctic Marion Island in the southern Indian Ocean, cats were introduced in 1949 and are now estimated to kill over 400,000 birds per year, mostly ground-nesting petrels." Daniel Simberloff, *Invasive Species:*

What Everyone Needs to Know (Oxford: Oxford University Press, 2013), 43.
45. Cole, *Imperfect Creatures*, 146.
46. Steele's erasure of this detail may have something to do with the supposed bestiality that took place between Selkirk and his goats. See Diana Souhami, *Selkirk's Island: The true and strange adventures of the real Robinson Crusoe* (New York: Harcourt, 2001).
47. Simberloff, *Invasive Species*, 41.
48. The Swedish expedition led by botanist, Carl Skottsberg, and resulting publication, *The Natural history of Juan Fernández and Easter Island* (Uppsala: Almqvist & Wiksells Boktryckeri, 1920), remains the standard biological resource for information about the island's indigenous (and introduced) plant and animal species.
49. Rogers, *Cruising*, 129.
50. Rogers, *Cruising*, 137.
51. Regarding biotic resistance theory, see Charles Elton, *The Ecology of Invasions by Animals and Plants* (1958), with a new forward by Daniel Simberloff (Chicago: University of Chicago Press, 2000).
52. Simberloff, *Invasive Species*, 47–8.
53. Simberloff, *Invasive Species*, 43. For more about native (versus invasive) rats, see Elton, *Ecology of Invasions*, 92.
54. Elton, *Ecology of Invasions*, 89.
55. *The Natural History of Juan Fernández and Easter Island*, Volume II, "Botany," edited by Carl Skottsberg (Uppsala: Almquist & Wiksells, 1920), 213.
56. Margaret Cohen, "Literary Studies on the Terraqueous Globe," *PMLA*, 125.3 (2010), 658.
57. Moore, *Capitalism*, 2.
58. Moore, *Capitalism*, 18.
59. See Sharae Deckard, *Paradise Discourse, Imperialism, and Globalization: Exploiting Eden* (New York and London: Routledge, 2010).
60. Rogers, *Cruising*, 129.
61. Rogers, *Cruising*, 127.
62. Robert Louis Stevenson, *Kidnapped* (1886) (New York: Penguin Books, 1994), 154.
63. Cole, *Imperfect Creatures*, 9. See also Bruno Latour, *Politics of Nature: How to Bring the Sciences into Democracy*, translated by Catherine Porter (Cambridge, MA: Harvard University Press, 2004), 75.
64. Daniel Defoe, *The Life and Strange Suprizing Adventures of Robinson Crusoe of York, Mariner*, etc. (London: W. Taylor, 1719), edited by John Richetti (New York: Penguin Books, 2001), 39. Further citations will be parenthetical.
65. Simberloff, *Invasive Species*, 47.

66. Columbus, *Diario*, quoted in Antonello Gerbi, *Nature in the New World: From Christopher Columbus to Gonzalo Fernández de Oviedo* (Pittsburgh: University of Pittsburgh Press, 1985), 14–15.
67. Alan Burdick, *Out of Eden: An Odyssey of Ecological Invasion* (New York: Farrar, Straus, and Giroux, 2005), 99.
68. Charles Elton, *The Ecology of Invasions by Animals and Plants* (1958), quoted in Burdick, *Out of Eden*, 99.
69. Josep Greimler, Patricio Lopez S., Tod F. Stuessy, and Thomas Dirnböck, "The Vegetation of Robinson Crusoe Island (Isla Masatierra) Juan Fernández Archipelago, Chile," *Pacific Science* 56, no. 3 (2002), 263.
70. Regarding tropical island Edens, see Richard H. Grove, *Green Imperialism: Colonial expansion, Tropical Island Edens and the Origins of Environmentalism, 1600–1860* (Cambridge: Cambridge University Press, 1995). See also Elizabeth DeLoughrey's debunking of the myth of isolated island space in *Routes and Roots: Navigating Caribbean and Pacific Island Literatures* (Honolulu: University of Hawaii Press, 2007).
71. Simberloff, *Invasive Species*, 48–9.
72. Elton, *Ecology of Invasions*, 147.
73. Quoted in John Richetti, *The Life of Daniel Defoe* (Malden, MA: Blackwell Publishing, 2005), 190.
74. Jason H. Pearl, "Desert Islands and Urban Solitudes in the *Crusoe* Trilogy," *Studies in the Novel* 44, no. 2 (Summer 2012), 125. See also Bruce McLeod, *The Geography of Empire in English Literature, 1580–1745* (New York: Cambridge University Press, 1992).
75. Robert P. Marzec, "Enclosures, Colonization, and the *Robinson Crusoe* Syndrome: A Genealogy of Land in a Global Context," *Boundary 2* (Summer 2002), 129–56.
76. Patricia Seed, *Ceremonies of Possession in Europe's Conquest of the New World, 1492–1640* (Cambridge: Cambridge University Press, 1995), 16–40.
77. Jill Casid, *Sowing Empire: Landscape and Colonization* (Minneapolis: University of Minnesota Press, 2005), 103.
78. See, in particular, Richard H. Grove's discussion of the King's Hill Forest Act in *Green Imperialism*, 266.
79. See William Cronon, "The Trouble with Wilderness; or, Getting Back to the Wrong Nature," *Uncommon Ground: Rethinking the Human Place in Nature*, edited by William Cronon (New York: W. W. Norton, 1995), 70.
80. Bill McKibben, *The End of Nature* (1989), Reissue (New York: Random House Trade Paperback, 2006).
81. Moore, *Capitalism*, 12.
82. Defoe, *Farther Adventures*, 1–2.
83. This phrase derives from *Uncommon Ground: Rethinking the Human Place in Nature*, edited by William Cronon (New York: W. W. Norton, 1995).

84. See John Richetti, "Introduction," *Robinson Crusoe* (London: Penguin, 2001).
85. Richetti, *Life of Daniel Defoe*, 193.
86. For a concise and useful survey of such critical approaches, see Jason H. Pearl's insightful essay, "Desert Islands and Urban Solitudes in the *Crusoe* Trilogy," 126.
87. Cole, *Imperfect Creatures*, 147. See also John Bender, *Ends of Enlightenment* (Palo Alto, CA: Stanford University Press, 2012).
88. Rachel Carson, *The Sea Around Us* (1951), Special Edition (Oxford: Oxford University Press, 1991), 112.
89. Portuondo, *Secret Science*, 7.
90. Moore, *Capitalism*, 14.
91. In his *Second Treatise of Government*, Locke champions agricultural improvement. He writes: "For I ask whether in the wild woods and uncultivated waste of America left to nature, without any improvement, tillage or husbandry, a thousand acres [will] yield the needy and wretched inhabitants as many conveniences of life as ten acres of equally fertile land do in Devonshire where they are well cultivated?" Locke, *Two Treatises of Government*, 133.
92. Ramachandran, *Worldmakers*, 15.
93. Moore, *Capitalism*, 51.
94. Herbert A. Raffaele and James W. Wiley, *Wildlife of the Caribbean* (Princeton: Princeton University Press, 2014), 63.
95. G. S. Wratt and H. C. Smith, *Plant Breeding in New Zealand* (Wellington: Butterworths, 1983), 117.
96. Herbert John Webber, "History and Development of the Citrus Industry," *The Citrus Industry*, edited by Walter Reuther, Herbert John Webber, and Leon Dexter Batchelor, Revised Edition (Berkeley: University of California Press, 1967), 1.
97. Webber, "History," 3–4.
98. Webber, "History," 14–15.
99. Quoted in Webber, "History," 16.
100. Janet Henshall Momsen and Pamela Richardson, "Caribbean Cocoa: Planting and Production," *Chocolate: History, Culture, and Heritage*, edited by Louis E. Grivetti and Howard-Yana Shapiro (Hoboken: Wiley, 2009), 484.
101. See Londa Schiebinger and Claudia Swan, eds, *Colonial Botany: Science, Commerce, and Politics in the Early Modern World* (Philadelphia: University of Pennsylvania Press, 2005), 1–16.
102. Lambert, *Crusoe's Island*, 21.
103. The first volume of Sloane's *Voyages* is concerned mainly with plants, while the second volume – which focuses on Jamaican zoology – wasn't published until 1725, or six years after the publication of *Robinson Crusoe*.

104. Richard Ligon, *A True and Exact History of the Island of Barbados* (1657) (Indianapolis: Hackett Publishing, 2011), 125.
105. See Moore, *Capitalism*, 18.
106. Bénédict Boisseron, *Afro-Dog: Blackness and the Animal Question* (New York: Columbia University Press, 2018), ix.
107. Shiva, *Biopiracy*, 61. See also Claudia Von Werlhof, "Women and Nature in Capitalism," *Women: The Last Colony*, edited by Maria Mies (London: Zed Books, 1989).
108. Daniel Defoe, *A Plan of the English Commerce. Being a Compleat Prospect of The Trade of this Nation, as well the Home Trade as the Foreign* (London: Charles Rivington, 1728), 330.
109. Boisseron, *Afro-Dog*, xx.
110. Moore, *Capitalism*, 54.
111. Moore, *Capitalism*, 17.
112. Moore, *Capitalism*, 15.
113. Defoe, *Farther Adventures*, 86.
114. Defoe, *Farther Adventures*, 87.
115. Defoe, *Farther Adventures*, 88.
116. Shiva, *Biopiracy*, 61; and Macarena Gómez-Barris, *The Extractive Zone: Social Ecologies and Decolonial Perspectives* (Durham, NC: Duke University Press, 2017), 114.
117. Defoe, *Farther Adventures*, 86–7.
118. Ligon, *True and Exact History*, 124.
119. Deckard, *Paradise Discourse*, 12.
120. Deckard, *Paradise Discourse*, 12.
121. Grove, *Green Imperialism*, 228.
122. John Poyntz, *The Present Prospect of the Famous and Fertile Island of Tobago: With a Description of the Situation, Growth, Fertility, and Manufacture of the said Island* (London: George Larkin, 1683), 8.
123. See Jonathan Lamb, *Scurvy: The Disease of Discovery* (Princeton: Princeton University Press, 2016). See also Jonathan Lamb, "'The Rime of the Ancient Mariner,' A Ballad of Scurvy," *Pathologies of Travel*, edited by Richard Wrigley and George Revill (Amsterdam: Editions Rodolpi B.V., 2000); *Preserving The Self in the South Seas, 1680–1840* (Chicago: University of Chicago Press, 2001); and, with Margaret S. Ward, James M. May, and Fiona E. Harrison, "Behavioral and monoamine changes following severe Vitamin C deficiency," *Journal of Neurochemistry* 124 (2013), 363–75.
124. Philip Blom, *To Have and to Hold: An Intimate History of Collectors and Collecting* (Woodstock: The Overlook Press, 2003), 79. See also Susan Scott Parrish, *American Curiosity: Cultures of Natural History in the Colonial British Atlantic World* (Chapel Hill: University of North Carolina Press, 2006).
125. Quoted in Blom, *To Have and To Hold*, 81.

126. Hans Sloane, *A Voyage to the Islands of Madera, Barbados, Nieves, S. Christophers and Jamaica, with the Natural history of the Trees, Four-footed Beasts, Fishes, Birds, Insects, Reptiles, etc. of the Last of those Islands* (London: Printed by B. M. for the Author, 1707), lxx.
127. Elton, *Ecology of Invasions*, 78.
128. Elton, *Ecology of Invasions*, 89.
129. Simberloff, *Invasive Species*, 48–9.
130. Burnham, *Transoceanic*, 4.
131. Robert Knox, *An Historical Relation of the Island of Ceylon in the East-Indies: Together with an Account of the Detaining in Captivity the Author and divers other* Englishmen *now Living there, and of the Author's Miraculous ESCAPE* (London: Printed by Richard Chiswell, 1681), Chapter VI, p. 21.
132. March Chynoweth, Christopher Lepczyk, and Creighton M. Litton, "Feral Goats in the Hawaiian Islands: Understanding the Behavioral Ecology of Nonnative Ungulates with GPS and Remote Sensing Technology," *Proceedings 24th Vertebrate Pest Conference*, edited by R. M. Timm and K. A. Fagerstone (Davis: University of California, Davis, 2010), 41. See also K. Campbell and C. J. Donlan, "Feral Goat Eradiction on Islands," *Conservation Biology* 19, no. 5 (2005), 1362–74; and C. F. Yocum, "Ecology of Feral Goats in Haleakala National Park, Maui, Hawaii," *American Midland Naturalist* 77 (1967), 418–51. It might be worth noting too that recent mitochondrial DNA analysis has identified the wild Bexoar Ibex of the Zagros Mountains in Iran as the most likely progenitor of all domestic goats.
133. Chynoweth et al., "Feral Goats," 43.
134. Elton, *Ecology of Invasions*, 89.
135. Elton, *Ecology of Invasions*, 78.
136. Simberloff, *Invasive Species*, 48.
137. The complete account of Crusoe's domestication of goats unfolds over pages 115–17.
138. Cole, *Imperfect Creatures*, 146–7.
139. Moore, *Capitalism*, 7.
140. See Alfred Crosby, *Ecological Imperialism: The Biological Expansion of Europe, 900–1900*, New Edition (Cambridge: Cambridge University Press, 2004); Virginia DeJohn Anderson, *Creatures of Empire: How Domestic Animals Transformed Early America* (Oxford: Oxford University Press, 2006); and Rebecca J. H. Woods, *The Herds Shot Round the World: Native Breeds and the British Empire, 1800–1900* (Chapel Hill: University of North Carolina Press, 2017).
141. Quoted in DeLoughrey, *Routes and Roots*, 8.
142. Burdick, *Out of Eden*, 49.
143. Poyntz, *Present Prospect*, 10.
144. Griffith Hughes, *The Natural History of Barbados* (London: Printed for the Author, 1750), 102.

145. Raffaele and Wiley, *Wildlife*, 66.
146. In her presentation at the International Society for Eighteenth-Century Studies' 15th International Congress on the Enlightenment (University of Edinburgh, July 15 – 19, 2019), Elizabeth Kowaleski Wallace similarly noted the curious absence of any insects in *Robinson Crusoe*.
147. Raffaele and Wiley, *Wildlife*, 66.
148. DeLoughrey, *Routes and Roots*, 3.
149. Burdick, *Out of Eden*, 49.
150. Moore, *Capitalism*, 19.
151. Cited in Grove, *Green Imperialism*, 228. See also Daniel Defoe, *The Storm: Or, A Collection of the Most Remarkable Casualties and Disasters Which happen'd in the Late Dreadful Tempest Both By Sea and Land* (London: G. Sawbridge, 1704).
152. Burnham, *Transoceanic*, 3.
153. Burnham, *Transoceanic*, 8.
154. Quoted in Burnham, *Transoceanic*, 9.
155. Benjamin Pauley, "On Teaching Another Defoe," *Digital Defoe: Studies in Defoe and His Contemporaries,* no. 1 (Spring 2009), 115, n.4. Available at <http://english.illinoisstate.edu/digitaldefoe/archive/spring09/teaching/pauleynotes.shtml>. Accessed 29 May 2023.
156. Daniel Defoe, *A New Voyage Round the World* (1724), collected in *The Works of Daniel Defoe*, Vol. 7 (Philadelphia: John D. Morris & Company, 1903), 1–2.
157. Ramachandran, *Worldmakers*, 5.
158. See Simberloff, *Invasive Species*, 311.
159. Simberloff, *Invasive Species*, 39.
160. See Dan Charles, "Vineyards Facing an Insect Invasion May Turn to Aliens for Help," National Public Radio, 16 September 2019. Available at <https://www.npr.org/sections/thesalt/2019/09/16/760147903/vineyards-facing-an-insect-invasion-may-turn-to-aliens-for-help>. Accessed 19 January 2022.
161. Moore, *Capitalism*, 12.
162. Daniel Defoe, *A Journal of the Plague Year* (1722) (Oxford: Oxford World's Classics, 1990), 1.
163. Pearl, "Desert Islands," 125.
164. Nsikan Akpan, "This tiny island with no humans is getting buried in plastic trash," *PBS News Hour*, 15 May 2017. Available at <https://www.pbs.org/newshour/science/remote-south-pacific-island-buried-worlds-plastic>. Accessed 17 October 2020.
165. Pearl, "Desert Islands," 126.
166. Pearl, "Desert Islands," 126.

Chapter 2

The Poetics of Biological Invasion and Crop Monoculture in Early Caribbean Literature

In the "Preface" to his West Indian georgic, *The Sugar Cane* (1764), Scottish poet and physician, James Grainger predictably emphasizes the novelty of his Caribbean environs, the artless representation of which he humbly suggests, "however rude, could not fail to enrich" British poetry:

> Soon after my arrival in the West-Indies, I conceived the design of writing a poem on the cultivation of the Sugar-Cane. My inducements to this arduous undertaking were, not only the importance and novelty of the subject, but more especially this consideration; that, as the face of this country was wholly different from that of Europe, so whatever hand copied its appearances, however rude, could not fail to enrich poetry with many new and picturesque images.[1]

Interestingly, Grainger's choice of the term, "enrich," clearly alludes to the enormous wealth that could be accrued on Caribbean sugar plantations, such as the one held by William Beckford in Jamaica and which generated roughly £50,000 per annum.[2] Indeed, Nuala Zahedieh observes, that, "between 1768 and 1772, Britain's sugar imports from the West Indies were worth over twice as much as total commodity imports from North America, and four times as much as tobacco which was North America's leading commodity."[3] And, as T. M. Devine points out, even Adam Smith, "the most eminent contemporary critic of the colonial system, waxed eloquent about their immense value: the profits of a sugar plantation in the Caribbean, he noted, 'were generally much greater than those of any cultivation that is known in either Europe or America.'"[4] In fact, by 1815, the British-controlled Caribbean islands, including Barbados, the Leeward Islands (Antigua, St. Kitts, Nevis, and Montserrat),

Jamaica, Grenada, Dominica, Saint Vincent, Tobago, Trinidad, Demerara, and Saint Lucia, accounted for some 60 percent of the transatlantic sugar trade – that is, following the Haitian Revolution and the cessation of the Napoleonic Wars. Again, Devine offers the following useful assessment:

> At the end of the eighteenth century the Caribbean colonies employed, directly or indirectly, half the nation's long-distance shipping, their fixed and moveable wealth was reckoned at more than £30 million sterling, duties on West Indian produce account for an eighth of the Exchequer revenues and the credit structures linked to the plantation economy were crucial elements in UK financial markets.[5]

In short, Britain's imperial economy was very much built on sugar cane.[6] Sugar was so profitable that British West Indian planters left little room to grow staple produce. And so, not surprisingly, early Caribbean newspapers, such as the *Daily Advertiser*, a Kingston, Jamaica-based newspaper printed by Strupar, Bennett, and Doddington on Harbour-Street, are laden with advertisements of imported items – "Yorkshire hams, Split peas, Dried tongues,"[7] etc., etc. – which sold at "very deare rates."[8]

According to Matthew Parker, by 1686, some 700 merchants "sent cargoes of foodstuffs, and increasingly, luxury items, to the islands, where the whites, on average, consumed three times more by value than their cousins in the mainland North American colonies."[9] The foreign letter books (1776-8) of Alexander Houston & Co., a syndicate that was born out of the War of the Spanish Succession (the ceding of St. Kitts to Britain in 1713) and which Devine describes as Scotland's "most powerful West Indian house,"[10] suggest that captains were regularly instructed to load their ships as full as possible with herrings, beef, biscuits, butter, and staves in "commerce for the West Indies."[11] An archival manuscript like Houston & Co.'s foreign letter books may seem relatively unimportant compared with Grainger's georgic, *The Sugar-Cane*, which formalizes the process of environmental engineering in readers' minds. However, as Michelle Burnham points out, "global commerce took place amidst tremendous risks," and "number-laden genres" not unlike Houston & Co.'s foreign letter books, etc., were integral to the success of such transoceanic ventures. "Such calculations," observes Burnham, "were designed to make it increasingly possible to reduce the risks of transoceanic travel and commerce necessary to achieve the pleasures and rewards of profit."[12]

Additionally, one also encounters numerous advertisements for lumber, "Pitch Pine" and "Ranging Timber" in boards, plank, and shingles of various dimensions, which was doubtless an effect of the islands' gradual deforestation.[13] Although the forests on Saint Vincent and Tobago remained relatively untouched by Europeans until the early 1780s, as Richard Grove explains, islands like Jamaica and Barbados had been cleared for sugar production as early as 1700, and the clearing of St. Christopher, the island upon which Grainger resided, was evidently "well underway" by the middle of the seventeenth century.[14] Towards the end of the eighteenth century, islands such as Barbados would provide colonists with an object lesson in the ecological significance of forests, but, in the meanwhile, as Bonham C. Richardson notes, "the conversion of the insular forest ecosystems to open cropland had ... been accomplished by expending a nearly inexhaustible supply of human energy – human life – imported from Africa."[15]

This transoceanic codependence of British colonies clearly suggests the global scope of the sugar revolution. Virginia Anderson points out the sugar revolution proved to be the 'greatest bonanza" for the New England meat and livestock trade,[16] whereas Sidney W. Mintz notes the British East India Company's monopoly of tea growing in India also played a significant role in sugar's rising economic and cultural significance. "The success of tea," writes Mintz, "like the less resounding successes of coffee and chocolate, was also the success of sugar. In the view of the West Indian interest, increasing consumption of any of these exotic liquid stimulants was highly desirable, for sugar went with them all."[17] But even more interesting than the economic discourse of enrichment that Grainger employs in his Preface to *The Sugar-Cane* is that, despite the emphasis that he places on the *novelty* of his Caribbean surroundings, the lengthy annotations that accompany his poetry (a sort of imperialist landscaping) frequently focus on *not* merely indigenous (or *New* World) organisms, but, rather, invasive species: Old World people, animals, and plants. The New World discourse that Grainger marshals in his "Preface" effectively serves to preserve an antiquated notion of the Atlantic Ocean as boundary (a line separating Old and New Worlds), while his annotations throughout register the ecological (and entropical) realities of the greater Caribbean's transoceanic agricultural economy.

I combine the terms *entropy* and *tropical* to account for the irreversibility of the island's ecological transformation through Europeans' deliberate (and accidental) introduction of Old World species. However, instead of a "closed system" – language that earthwork artist, Robert Smithson, employs in his definition of entropy, and, of course, language that resonates with both Cole's and Bender's readings of Crusoe's island as metaphysically secure (i.e. a "closed, zoomorphic world in which Crusoe hunts, gathers, farms, and stores under metaphysically secured conditions")[18] – the Caribbean islands are not closed, nor isolated from the rest of the world, per se, but greatly subject to trade winds and ocean currents, not to mention damaging hurricanes.[19] "Plants and animals have managed to not only reach [many of the world's most] remote archipelagos and islands without the help of man," according to Charles S. Elton, "but in some have evolved luxuriant tropical vegetation."[20] These sorts of so-called naturally occurring plant and animal migrations are as much a part of the fate of remote islands as Juan Fernández's (and/or Selkirk's goats), and, accordingly, they invite us to think in tidal dialectical terms about shared human-non-human histories that exceed or transcend, as Elizabeth DeLoughrey puts it, "national, colonial, and regional frameworks."[21]

And so, despite the truths outlined in this growing body of scholarship and scientific research about oceanic islands' susceptibility to environmental change, including Stuart McCook's observation, in "The Neo-Columbian Exchange," that "the demographic and epidemiological advantages enjoyed by Old World people, animals, and plants in the sixteenth and seventeenth centuries had largely disappeared by the eighteenth century," Grainger's "Preface" obscures the considerable extent to which, by 1764 (the year that R. and J. Dodsley published *The Sugar Cane* in London), the formerly "virgin soil" of the greater Caribbean had already become irreversibly transformed through a series of global biological transfers (or invasions).[22] Or, rather, Grainger's preliminary claims about the novelty of St. Christopher's geographical face effectively gloss over the tidal dialectical realities of Caribbean history.

Accordingly, in this chapter I propose to explore the imaginative, psycho-geographical and actual confusion of Old and New World ecologies in Caribbean empire writing – including local newspapers and magazines, such as the *Daily Advertiser* and *The Jamaica Magazine*, that, on a very practical level, made it possible for the sugar islands to cohere and flourish. Such confusion, I argue, not only functions as a form of *translatio imperii* or "colonial quotation" – a conventional rhetorical maneuver that, according to Barbara Fuchs, assimilates the "unknown by equating it with the already-known" – but also serves to measure the environmental impacts of the sugar revolution.[23] Essays that appeared in *The Jamaica Magazine* (Kingston, 1812–13) – works such as "An Account of Some Trees of

Prodigious Dimensions in Scotland" – beg to be read in light of widespread deforestation and the "yearning for lost landscapes" that later figures in much postcolonial Caribbean literature.[24] The publication of this account reflects, I argue, the considerable degree to which late eighteenth- and early nineteenth-century colonialists not only waxed nostalgic for their homeland, but also felt obliged to think about forest conservation, having learned the lesson of Barbados, an island which, as noted earlier, had been converted into an unsustainable sea of cane plants by 1700. Grove notes, for example, that colonial administrators, such as the Scotsman, General Robert Melville, took heed of the environmental history of Barbados and "sought to set aside land for forest reserves when . . . Tobago was converted into a sugar colony in 1764."[25] The *Jamaica Magazine*'s imaginative linking of Scotland and Jamaica, thus, merits consideration as an environmental measure, much as Grainger's similarly confusing *double vision* recalls that, at this early juncture, the British Empire was very much an entire interactive, transoceanic system tenuously built on West Indian sugar and East Indian tea.

It is partly the purpose of this chapter, then, to showcase the world-ecological orientation of early British West Indian authors, including John Singleton, whose poem, *General Description of the West-Indian Islands* (1767), treats, in sublime detail, the fragility of island ecosystems and the potentially devastating environmental impacts of crop monoculture (the agricultural practice of cultivating a single crop over a large tract of land year after year). One might be tempted to regard our current environmental crisis as owing in part to human disconnection from the earth – i.e. the Cartesian binary that treats Nature as some*thing* separated from humanity (see Introduction).[26] However, a close investigation of early Caribbean literature reveals that the initial cultivation of sugar cane was such a challenging enterprise that Europeans' troubling exploitation of the region did not begin with alienation from nature, but, rather, with their close attention to climate, meteorological patterns, animal and plant behavior, and local and world history (all subjects dealt with by Grainger in *The Sugar Cane*).[27] Indeed, Grainger's *The Sugar Cane* is not simply about the cultivation of sugar. The poem certainly serves as a veritable encyclopedia of useful local knowledge, and, as such, merits comparison to other efforts – scientific, cartographic, and botanical, etc. – to not merely redistribute the earth's flora, as outlined in Schiebinger and Swan's *Colonial Botany*,[28] but, specifically, to appropriate so-called cheap nature(s). That is, *The Sugar-Cane* begs to be read in light of "those extra-economic processes that identify, secure, and channel unpaid work" – including the unpaid work / energy of human and extra-human natures – "outside the commodity system into the circuit of capital."[29] Clearly designed to perfect the monoculture of sugar in St. Christopher, Grainger's poem is of a piece with the sorts of "technological transformation[s] of biodiversity" favored by what Vandana Shiva characterizes as a global economic system dominated by transnational corporations.[30] Grainger's claim to enrich poetry deserves mention again here, as the very gesture that he humbly relies on to do so – his careful representation of novel Caribbean details (plants, animals, etc.), "however rude" – directly parallels the extra-economic processes described by Moore. However, perhaps the most striking thing is that Grainger simultaneously adopts a world-ecological approach, in so far as the poem is not only engaged in capitalist appropriation, but also offers opportunities for thinking about the interaction of organisms within a transoceanic, global economy. The irony that monocultures are "ecologically unstable," as Shiva notes, "inviting disease and pests,"[31] actually renders Grainger's work in advising planters on pest control all the more necessary. (It would seem Grainger discovered a most lucrative, self-sustaining poetic enterprise here, in so far as the poem promotes the very monoculture that renders his recommendations on dealing with pests all the more necessary.)

This is but one of numerous complications attending the poem, as local knowledge often gets construed as the very basis of humanity's unification with nature: the cultivation of a sustainable, non-exploitative, non-anthropocentric, and non-imperialist relationship to the earth. Jonathan Bates, for example, insists that, "to come to know the earth, fully, and honestly, the crucial and perhaps only all-encompassing task is to understand the place, the immediate specific, place, where we live":

> We must somehow live as close to it as possible, be in touch with its particular soils, its waters, its winds; we must learn its ways, its capacities, its limits; we must make its rhythms our patterns, its laws our guide, its fruit our bounty. That. In essence, is bioregionalism.[32]

Thus, what makes a work like Grainger's *Sugar Cane* so very intriguing is that it simultaneously supports the industry responsible for the wholesale ecological transformation of the Caribbean *and* greatly contributes to the advancement of that local knowledge which Bates regards as fundamental to the development of a bio-regionalist ethic. Indeed, Grainger writes from the perspective of a dweller in the land. On the one hand, Grainger's work draws upon local knowledge to support the agribusiness of sugar, a gesture which remains a definitive characteristic of empire writing, as it were, akin to the sublimation of Indian techne by members of the British East India Company, a process which Rajani Sudan refers to as the "alchemy of empire."[33] This is a poem that not only remembers the "world of things," to quote from Michel Serres's *The Natural Contract*, but also thoroughly acknowledges the confusing and sometimes devastating interactivity of organisms in the Atlantic World, including the rats that Samuel Johnson, in his ridicule of *The Sugar Cane*, insisted were unpoetical by nature.[34] In this way, the poem challenges the Cartesian dualism that accords thing-like status to Nature out there, instead prioritizing the co-production of manifold species, or natures.

Consider, for example, the Old World dogs that were proliferating in Kingston at such an extraordinary rate that proposals were published in Jamaican newspapers about how to address this nuisance (biological invasion). The following appeared in the Kingston *Daily Advertiser*, 5 September 1791:

> A Correspondent observes, that, a tax upon Dogs would not only be a productive, but a very beneficial branch of the Revenue of this country. The numbers of these animals have so increased of late as to become a real nuisance. They are suffered to parade the streets at night, where, hunting as it were in packs, they become dangerous to any foot passenger that is so unfortunate as to fall in their way . . .

In addition to conveying what might be described as the Gothic horror of imperial excess, this passage begs us to ponder the ecological impacts of such dogs. Aside from merely posing a threat to colonists parading along Kingston's streets at night, dogs that are permitted to go feral, observes biologist Daniel Simberloff, "can also be enormously destructive": "roaming dogs threaten native mammal and reptile populations."[35] Many of humankind's four-legged "biotic allies" – from cats and dogs to cattle and goats – have been known to wreak considerable havoc on delicately balanced island ecosystems, as the Governor of St. Helena, Colonel Alexander Beatson sought to make perfectly clear in his 1810 publication arguing for the extermination of goats on that island, *Papers Relating to the Devastation Committed by Goats on the Island of St. Helena*.

Furthermore, it goes without saying that the unprecedented increase in the Caribbean's human population, especially including the enormous number of enslaved Africans, would also have a huge impact too. Alan Taylor observes, for example, that, "despite its small scale, by 1660 Barbados had 53,000 inhabitants – a density of 250 persons per square mile, which rose to 400 by the end of the century. In 1700 the human concentration on Barbados was four times greater than in England."[36] Given these statistics, it is difficult to see how any visitor to the West Indies, including Henrietta Marchant Liston, could ever use the term "picturesque" to account for a sugar plantation, except, of course, to propagandize British interests.[37] The pollution must have been revolting, as J. S. Handler notes: "poor sanitation formed an extremely significant dimension of the Barbadian disease environment."[38]

Taken together these details suggest that planters were not alienated from nature so much as constantly reminded of its (at times) brutal economy. Thus, I argue, that, in order to grasp the historical (and literary) legacy of present-day crises of ecological mismanagement, we must first understand that environmental change / degradation in the Caribbean took place *not* as a result of an ideological, Cartesian divorce between humans and their surroundings, or between humanity and nature, per se – but from relations of power particular to the plantation economy.

Thus, on one level, this chapter addresses an early tendency to conflate disparate landscapes through what Patricia Yaeger refers to as a "biotic reading" of relevant literature, including newspapers, one somewhat obscure travel journal, several contrasting works that I categorize as natural histories, and poetry, including Grainger's georgic and Singleton's *General Description*.[39] To some this may seem like a strange assortment of texts, but the overall point (as noted in the Introduction) is to highlight both the wide range of empire writing and the various ways in which this literature engages in (or with) specific "environment-making processes." Indeed, as Michael Niblett suggests: "Cultural practice is itself an ecological force, an integral pivot in humanity's capacity to rework life, land, and the body."[40] What makes this a biotic study is that I marshal facts (scientific truths) about animals and plants to outline the limitations or foresights of this literature. But, on another level, what I offer here is not only an ecocritical investigation of literature's implications for the non-human world.[41] The approach that I have adopted might also be described as echo-critical, a term that Yaeger coins in her insightful essay, "Sea Trash, Dark Pools, and the Tragedy of the Commons." Echo-criticism, writes Yaeger, invites "stories, novels, and other imaginative works about the sea to provide echo chambers, sites of wild or sober echolalia, for the most pressing questions about the ocean's and oceanic creatures' survival."[42] It is a carefully conceived, anachronistic reading practice that serves to highlight resonances between the past and present, much as this particular chapter seeks to flesh out the historical legacy of contemporary ecological crises, from Grainger's thoughts on pest control to the introduction of the mongoose to Jamaica in 1872.

Moreover, this chapter, in effect, responds to Margaret Cohen's vital prompt, that we must strive to remember how oceans knit together both geographical spaces and timelines.[43] The imaginative leaping across the Atlantic Ocean that this literature encourages – the commonplace psycho-geographical confusion of disparate environments, such as the British Isles, West Africa, South Asia, and the Caribbean – provides a constant reminder of the significance of transoceanic travel to capitalist development. From both an economic and ecological standpoint, we are still very much living in the shadows of the sugar revolution, and this is clearly reinforced by the fact that, as Cohen points out, "ships continue to convey over ninety percent of the world's freight."[44]

One of the challenges will be to tease out the real ecological consequences of an imaginative, literary tendency to confuse Old and New Worlds. Perhaps it was the intention of the *Jamaica Magazine* editors to appeal to Scottish-born readers' homesickness with picturesque descriptions of Scotland. Were they attempting to coordinate the interests of transplanted Scots, much as Jake Kosek insists that "Norteños (northern New Mexicans) have become a community united not so much by their ties to the land and shared practices of production, but by their shared memories of loss and longing for the land"?[45] Or were the editors so forward thinking as to consider that a close examination of the Scottish Highlands' natural history – a history that includes significant deforestation – might actually improve readers' understandings of Jamaica's ecology? Publishing an article on "some trees of prodigious dimension in Scotland" in *The Jamaica Magazine* imaginatively links these two colonial / environmental histories, and thereby prompts readers to deliberate upon relevant questions of forest conversation.

Transoceanic Confusion

In *The Journal of John Ker, Surgeon's Mate in the Royal Navy – a manuscript account describing his service in the West Indies, 1778–1782* – one discovers an emphatically transoceanic, global imagination at work. For most scholars the historical value of Ker's journal may lie in his careful documentation of several naval

The Poetics of Bio Invasion and Crop Monoculture 119

Figure 2.1 "St Christophers 1779," from *The Journal of John Ker, Surgeon's Mate in the Royal Navy* – *a manuscript account describing his service in the West Indies, 1778–1782*. (Courtesy of the Special Collections, National Library of Scotland, Edinburgh).

skirmishes that took place between Britain and France off the coast of Grenada. And Ker, who clearly had an impressive knack for visual illustration (see Figure 2.1), seizes this opportunity to diagram what would appear to be an otherwise relatively routine conflict between British and French ships in this highly lucrative and, thus, hotly contested region. Indeed, Ker's journal provides us with a valuable glimpse of two European nations vying for dominance of the Caribbean sugar trade, a hugely profitable industry that, arguably, laid the "foundations of the modern globalised world."[46] However, what renders Ker's journal remarkably relevant to this study is the degree to which he utilizes his dynamic imagination to confuse and remix disparate geographical locations.

For example, Ker, who evidently served in India immediately prior to his four-year stretch in the West Indies, claims that, "Calcutta still haunts my Fancy":

> Last night I dreamed I was on the Banks of the Ganges. I saw my Fair one. I saw her in Tears, still constant, still kind, still charming, I found her. But what was my Pain when waking I found it only – a Dream. I see no harm however in dreaming of the dear girl whether asleep or awake. It is a kind of Pleasure I would not willingly forego. It is all the Possession of her I have now to expect. The whole Life of Man is indeed little better than a Dream . . .

> Why was I ever so foolish as [to] let a serious attachment enter my Head? I who never thought of settling, whose Fancy even at home, was always in other Climes . . .[47]

Obviously, this is a romantic passage about heartbreak, a sailor's lost love in India. But I humbly suggest, there is more to this story. Ayesha Ramachandra notes that Early Modern world-makers had to grapple with the "effects of an expanding world, transformed by the discovery of a new continent on the other side of the Atlantic" – a world riddled with incredible diversity, such that it appeared to Andrew Marvel in 1651, "but a rude heap together hurled."[48] However, that's clearly not the case in Ker's journal, in which the world appears *not* to be expanding, but shrinking through the close approximation of the East and West Indies. Marie-Noëlle Bourguet points out that for some eighteenth-century Frenchmen (amateur meteorologists like Charles Mozard) the "politics of plant transfer and acclimatization" was very much founded on thermometric efforts to establish a correspondence between "the colonies of the eastern and western parts of the Torrid Zone."[49] Indeed, as I see it, the phrase "Calcutta still haunts my Fancy" represents a psychological mashing together of climes that implicitly speaks to the environmental impacts of the sugar revolution. This is not merely absentmindedness. Ker's tendency to be "always in other Climes," his penchant for the conflation of disparate environments, and/or the near simultaneous situation of his imagination on the shores of Grenada *and* on the banks of the River Ganges speaks to the transoceanic nature of this enfolding of colonial landscapes in the British psyche. However, such mash-ups also provide us with a figurative measure of the literal confusion of Old and New World ecologies, as many of the plants that were introduced to the Caribbean derive from South and Southeast Asia. The East and West Indies were not merely ideologically incorporated into an increasingly mobile and fluid British national-imperial consciousness, but literally confused. Consider, for example, Janet Schaw's account of Arthur Freeman's plantation in Antigua, which appears in the posthumously published *Journal of a Lady of Quality; Being a Narrative of a Journey from Scotland to the West Indies, North Carolina, and Portugal, in the years 1774–1776* (1923). "His plantation, which is laid out with the greatest taste," observes Schaw, "has a mixture of the Indian and the European":

> If your eye is hurt by the stiff uniformity of the tall Palmetto, it is instantly relieved by the waving branches of the spreading

Tammerand, or the Sand-box tree. The flowering cyder is a beautiful tree, covered with flowers, and along Mr. Freeman's avenue these were alternately intermixed with Orange trees, limes, Cocoa Nuts, Palmettoes, Myrtles and citrons, with many more which afforded a most delightful shade, which continued till we arrived at the bottom of a green hill, on which the house stands.[50]

This passage provides us with an idea of the plantation economy's landscape architecture, and, in particular, the efforts taken by planters like Freeman to remodel the Caribbean islands (in this case, Antigua) using introduced Asian and European species of fruit trees, etc. In other words, the Empire was built on the transportation of animals and plants, and often with devastating environmental consequences. Sugarcane, for example, the intensive, systematic cultivation of which, according to J. R. McNeil (and others) drove the wholesale ecological transformation of the Caribbean, "figured in the diets of Indian and Chinese peasants from perhaps 500 B.C."[51] And Christopher Columbus, who brought it over from the Canary Islands on his second voyage in 1493, first introduced it to the Americas. As Sidney W. Mintz explains, in his remarkable study of sugar in modern history, *Sweetness and Power*, "cane was first grown in the New World in Spanish Santo Domingo; it was from that point that sugar was first shipped back to Europe, beginning around 1516": "Santo Domingo's pristine sugar industry was worked by enslaved Africans, the first slaves having been imported there soon after the sugar cane. Hence it was Spain that pioneered sugar cane, sugar making, African slave labor, and the plantation form in the Americas," which, notably, as Mintz points out, some scholars continue to regard as the "'the favored child of capitalism.'"[52]

Ker's version of psycho-geography, which, much like "colonial quotation," involves the imaginative mashing together of disparate environments, is not exactly uncommon.[53] Such juxtapositions repeatedly occur in the *Jamaica Magazine*, a short-lived Kingston periodical that was published in 1812–13 in an effort to not simply "amuse" Jamaican readers, but "rectify many obvious evils," including "those fits of languor and idleness, to which the inhabitants of a tropical climate are too often exposed."[54] The very first issue of the magazine contains, among other things, a "Fragment of a Tour in Silesia," and two pieces of natural history focusing upon the Highlands of Scotland. The first, "A Picturesque Description of Part of the Highlands of Scotland," provides us with a panorama of the Highlands, presumably because, as the author insists, "it cannot be unsuitable to the feelings of man, that the sight of impressively magnificent natural objects should lead him to reflect with the sublimest [sic] sentiments of veneration, on the power and wisdom which gave them existence, and which preside over all the stupendous operations of nature."[55] The second offers an "Account of A Sea-Snake, Seen, in 1808, by the Reverend Mr. Maclean, And Others."

On one hand, the value of these latter two articles lies in their nostalgic appeal. As noted earlier, the editors might have chosen these excerpts to appeal to readers' "shared memories of loss and longing for [Scotland]."[56] However, with the Blue Mountains rising to roughly 7402 ft. on the outskirts of Kingston, Jamaica (that's roughly three thousand feet taller than the tallest mountain in Scotland, Ben Nevis, which measures 4409 ft.), it is possible too that the editors intended this panorama of the Highlands to evoke comparatively sublime feelings for Jamaica's "impressively magnificent natural objects." On the other hand, perhaps they saw a profound, natural-historical connection between the two regions: Scotland and Jamaica. Although climatologically distinct, both regions figure as extractive zones, to borrow a phrase from Macarena Gómez-Barris; they share a history of capitalist appropriation and widespread deforestation.

In either case, the publication of such gleanings in the *Jamaica Magazine* suggests that Jamaican readers were not only encouraged to think globally, but also eager to digest natural histories. Consider, again, Ker's *Journal*. In the following passage written from the Bay of St. Lucia, 13 February 1779, he lists the typical produce of a Barbadian plantation, and, most interestingly, he meditates upon the elusive origins of the coconut tree:

> We proceeded up the Rivulet where we Water ... Coming down again We landed, walked up to a Plantation where We saw abundance of Cacao Trees, Cotton ... Melons, Pompions, Plantanes [sic], Sugar Canes ... &c. It is somewhat remarkable that I have met only with One Coconut Tree in my Walks on shore. I begin to think this Tree is not a Native of the West Indian Islands but imported from the Continent on account of its numerous Properties.[57]

Ker's contemplation of the coconut tree's evident mysterious origins calls to mind that fact that its seeds can float for months on salty ocean currents, which evidently explains their prevalence on tropical coasts and oceanic islands around the world.[58]

Coconuts also figure prominently in Reverent Griffith Hughes's *Natural History of the Island of Barbados*. Published for a transatlantic audience via subscription in London in 1750, Hughes lengthy study of the "Vegetable [and animal] Creation" in Barbados was at least partially intended to glorify "God's Goodness."[59] Accordingly, Hughes presents the coconut tree as a reminder that, "Providence hath enriched every Climate with Blessings peculiar to itself, and adapted to the Necessities of its Inhabitants."[60] This is an especially interesting statement for two reasons. First, it begs the question: given the obvious value that Defoe's novel accords to specific nature's usefulness, why are there no coconuts on Crusoe's island? Second, this idea – that coconuts are reminders of God's Providence – relates to the author's overarching sense of the moral economy of Nature. Indeed, for Hughes – who was the rector of St. Lucy's Parish in Barbados – the "untainted Pleasures" that derive from studying natural history are "not such as proceed from the Transports of a heated Imagination," but the "still and serene" joys achieved through "meditating upon the *exact Harmony* so visible in the Works of the Creation" (italics mine). His efforts to view the world in a sort of providential light may correspond with his ministerial position, but seems outdated, in keeping with the unenlightened version of Crusoe who sees God as responsible for the English barley's so-called miraculous growth. Hughes writes:

> By contemplating these Subjects, we are gradually led from Things visible, to the Knowledge of him who is invisible. Here we see innumerable Instances of Harmony, Beauty, and Order, not to be imitated by the most laborious Endeavours of any human Art or Contrivance.[61]

Hughes's objective in promoting the study of Barbadian natural history would seem to parallel the intent of the *Jamaica Magazine* editors: to engage readers in an activity that is at once aesthetically pleasing and morally beneficial. And similarly in this regard, Hughes's work, I think, merits consideration as a sort of paradise discourse, in as much as Sharae Deckard notes, that, "the rise of Linnaean classification dictated a further secularization of paradise discourse within the framework of natural history, as 'Edenic edifices' were forged in the writing of naturalists who moved through the 'gardens' of the natural world like Adam, 'innocently' naming and collecting specimens." "This systemizing of nature," observes Deckard, "gave rise to a 'planetary consciousness' which only increased the global mobility of paradise discourse in application to the other regions and continents increasingly drawn under the umbrella of European imperialism."[62]

However, despite the obvious links to polite society (gentlemanliness), not to mention British imperialism, Hughes also appears to be drawing an important equation between natural history and religious study. And, in this respect, his work shows signs of what Deckard describes as paradise endangered, as it were: "as these landscapes were colonized, scientifically categorized, and mined for their resources, Europeans were stricken by a fear of having exhausted nature."[63] For example, does Hughes's suggestion that "Providence hath enriched every Climate with Blessings peculiar to itself, and adapted to the Necessities of its Inhabitants," not implicitly frame Europeans' ecological transformation of the Caribbean as a troubling distortion of God's plan? That is, if Barbados was *exactly* harmonious to begin with, then the purposeful (and occasionally inadvertent) biological transfer of so many organisms to the island, including rats, hogs, dogs, cattle, camels, yucca, sugar, coffee, plantains, guinea grass, pasture, weeds, ticks, mosquitoes, and various pathogens, among others, would obviously represent a significant violation of the *natural order of things*. Of course, every species is in one way or another involved in ecosystem engineering. But for Hughes such human-oriented transformations might be viewed as threatening God's primal authority over the island. At least, how would a natural historian like Hughes even begin to decipher God's work in a Barbados so thoroughly modified by human activities (more thoroughly modified than Juan Fernández – Robinson Crusoe's island, which Elton describes as such)?[64] How many layers of environmental palimpsest would the natural historian have to imaginatively erase to discover a Barbados untouched by humans?

Not only (as noted earlier) was the density of the human population on Barbados, an island merely 166.4 square miles, in 1700 four times greater than in England, but by the time Europeans arrived, the Caribbean had already experienced significant alterations at the hands of Native Americans. In Cuba, according to Antonio Benítez-Rojo, the Tainos cleared forests to make room for the cultivation of a number of non-native species, including yucca.[65] So, despite the gradual reforestation that took place between 1500 and 1620 (an event that McNeil links to the decimation of the Amerindian population), the islands that were first encountered by Europeans had, to use John Locke's terminology again, already been "removed out of the state that nature hath provided."[66] At least, this would appear to be the logical outcome of Hughes's suggestion, since, as noted earlier, Britons' conversion of Barbados into a 'terraced sea of cane plants' rendered it practically impossible for the island to actually provide for the "Necessities of its Inhabitants."[67] Food had to be imported because, as the governor of the island in 1676 observed, regarding the cultivation of sugar cane, "there is not a foot of land in Barbados that is not employed, even to the very seaside."[68]

Moreover, from the standpoint of sustainability, it is fair to say that Barbados was clearly adapted to the *luxuries*, not the necessities of its minority of white inhabitants, as it were, in keeping with Deckard's point about paradise transformed into a secular, consumer Eden.[69] Accordingly, Hughes struggles at times to reconcile this ecological transformation with God's original blessings. However, he often glosses over these changes in the land, and, as a result, his so-called natural history reveals itself to be occasionally undermined by a colonial imagination that sees value and beauty in those parts of the island that are, first and foremost, useful. Indeed, rather than lament the island's deforestation – the loss of innumerable trees that were removed to make room for the cultivation of cane plants, not to mention fuel the carefully supervised boiling houses integral to the refinement of sugar – Hughes weirdly equates their absence with a healthy climate:

> It is likewise no small Advantage ... that we have neither Bogs nor Marshes, to stagnate our Waters, which, being exhaled into Vapours, might be pernicious; nor large Forests of Trees, which not only prevent the Winds in their Passage, but likewise generate moist Air, caused by the great Quantity of Vapours which perspire through their Leaves, as well as from the shaded moist Soil: By this means the Inhabitants are free from the Fever and Ague, so common to the Inhabitants of uncultivated Islands.[70]

Hughes was not alone in drawing connections between deforestation and climate change, but the conclusion that he draws regarding forest perspiration and ill health contradicts the efforts of green imperialist organizations such as the London Society for the Encouragement of the Arts, Manufactures, and Commerce. As Richard Grove notes, one of the earliest examples of forest conversation legislation – the King's Hill Forest Act "passed by the St Vincent Assembly in 1791" – sought (under Robert Melville's insightful guidance) to preserve the forests as a means to curb climate change, or prevent drought.[71] Hughes, on the other hand, equates moisture not with prosperity or agricultural growth, but ill health.

Furthermore, by juxtaposing Hughes's work with earlier Caribbean histories we can begin to map out some of these changes. Published roughly one hundred years earlier, in 1657, Richard

Ligon's *True and Exact History of the Island of Barbados*, for example, paints a rather different picture of the island's "high large and lofty trees."[72] Of course, many of the trees listed in Ligon's largely paradisiacal account of the island's natural history were, in fact, as McNeil points out, "recent artifacts – not, as was easily supposed, primeval."[73] However, for Hughes to summarily state that Barbados has no "large Forests of Trees" – and that he considers this "no small Advantage" – reveals not merely his colonialist mindset, but exactly how much has changed since the publication of Ligon's foundational text. As for the island's birds, Hughes states – "Neither this, nor any of our neighbouring Islands, is stored with any great Variety of Birds; and the few that we have are not remarkable for their Notes, nor (the Humming-Bird excepted) for the Beauty of their Feathers; and our tame-bred Fowls, except the *Guiney* Fowls, *Muscovy* Ducks, and rumpless Fowls, are much the same as those in *England*."[74] This passage not only starkly contrasts the idea of Barbados as 'island Eden' that works like Ligon's *True History* helped to create, but also raises questions about the island's environmental degradation. (Again, I can't help but wonder whether, in moments like these, Hughes may be encouraging his readers to regard the sugar revolution as an abuse of God's providence. Such a reading would tie in nicely, after all, with what Deckard describes as the "myth of corrupted paradise," as it were, an expression of "growing anxiety about the impact of colonialism" upon paradisal spaces, so-called island Edens, etc.)[75] Of course, Ligon's frequent allusions to the East Indies, along with his map that prominently features a variety of Old World creatures, including cattle and camels, hint at these ecological changes.

A third work of natural history that merits consideration would be Colonel and Governor of St. Helena (1808–13) Alexander Beatson's aforementioned 1810 publication, *Papers Relating to the Devastation Committed by Goats on the Island of St. Helena*. (It's worth noting here too, that, Beatson was also an officer in the East India Company's service, as well as an agriculturalist.) Published by authority of the Governor and Council of St. Helena, and printed there for S. Solomon by J. Coupland in 1810, this booklet is but one of a series of concise texts that Beatson published in the early nineteenth century seeking to not only forestall the environmental degradation of this otherwise remote island, but also to promote forms of agricultural improvement that might help restore it to a state of ecological harmony, so to speak. Indeed, as Grove notes, in *Green Imperialism*, Beatson's experimentation in conservation, reforestation, and artificially induced rainfall helped lay a foundation for environmentalism.[76]

Compared with Ligon and Hughes, Beatson offers a refreshingly precise understanding of environmental change. In his *Papers*, in particular, he presents us with *not* a static catalog of St. Helena's plant and animal life, or an encyclopedic record of discreet organisms with little discussion of how they cooperate. Rather, what to my mind makes Beatson's work so very insightful is his holistic approach to island life. That he endeavors to explain how the introduction of a single organism may alter the island's ability to provide for other species suggests a keen understanding of ecological balance. And, of course, the interesting thing is not that Beatson's views are necessarily anti-imperialist, but precisely the opposite: they're motivated by a Governor's desire to serve the interests of the "Honorable [East-India] Company" – hence, he figures as an ideal example of what Grove means by "Green Imperialism."

For example, in *Papers*, Beatson insists that St. Helena was at one point composed primarily of forest: "its interior was one entire forest – even some of the precipices, overhanging the sea, were covered with Gumwood Trees."[77] However, the goats that were introduced by the Spanish in 1513 – a common practice that was intended to convert the island into a convenient point of refreshment and resupply for European ships traveling to and from Asia and South Africa – evidently nibbled away at the young trees until nothing of these huge indigenous forests remained (a fate comparable to the similarly remote Juan Fernández islands that I discuss in Chapter 1). I quote at length Beatson's account of this gradual deforestation:

> We have . . . a series of clear and satisfactory evidence that St. Helena, when first discovered, and for many years afterwards, abounded with trees; but of those "huge Forests," how few vestiges are now to be seen?
> The cause of this sad reverse, in the aspect of the Island is readily ascertained by what is daily passing before us. Ebony, Red-wood, White Cedar (or Gum-wood Tree), are all indigenous. They shed great quantities of seed; and numerous plants are seen annually to spring up, where the trees are secured from the trespass of Goats and Black Cattle . . . Does not this prove what would naturally take place if the young trees remained undisturbed; and that many parts of the Island would, in the course of a few years, be again covered with wood? Those young plants are preferred, by the Goats, to the finest pastures; they are consequently when exposed to their depredations,

> greedily devoured ... since the period of the introduction of Goats, this formerly woody Island has been wholly denuded ...
>
> To the Goats, therefore, is solely to be ascribed the total ruin of the forests, an evil which is now severely felt by every individual ... The mischief occasioned by the Goats, added to the neglect of fencing, and planting trees, have greatly increased the demand for imported fuel; and the loss to the Company upon the article of Coals, in 1808, amounted to no less a sum than £2729.7.8.[78]

Though the introduction of goats was certainly an unhappy occasion for the island, as Beatson suggests, from an environmentalist standpoint this passage is actually quite hopeful because it explicitly alludes to the possibility, if not likelihood of reforestation, providing, of course, that adequate steps are taken to contain the ravenous animals. Although St. Helena lies off the coast of West Africa and, thus, perhaps follows a different natural-historical trajectory than either the Caribbean or Pacific islands discussed earlier, parallels exist in terms of deforestation. Transoceanic comparisons may be drawn between Beatson's goats and either the goats that deforested Juan Fernández, or, indeed, the planters who deforested the Caribbean islands to feed and fuel the sugar industry. Is the Barbadian planters' clearing of a forest to cultivate sugar not a similarly evil consequence? Or would Beatson overlook such behavior because of its contribution to the wealth of the nation?

Moreover, that Beatson links the introduction of goats in 1513 to coal imports in 1810 suggests not only the considerable historical breadth of his environmental imagination, but also how he views the island as a community of cooperative organisms. This is true too in his recommendation that, as an alternative to goats, every farm ought to be outfitted with a large stock of hogs. For hogs, suggests Beatson, are "preferable to Goats on account of the great quantities of valuable manure they would produce for meliorating the Lands":

> There is indeed no species of husbandry so well adapted to St. Helena as that of Hoggeries. – By their means the most extensive produce in Yams, Potatoes, Mangel Wurzul, &c. might be consumed on the farm; which it would be impossible, in this mountainous country, to carry to market, even if it were in demand. For Hogs, there would also be a ready sale to the Company (at the English price of Pork), for the use of the Garrison; and in supplying to the other inhabitants: and the Planters might feed themselves and family at home without purchasing and sending for every sort of meat from James's Valley. – Moreover, if the Island price were lowered, there would be a very considerable sale to the Shipping.[79]

Although one might accuse Beatson of species-ism because of his obvious bias against goats, there is certainly something commendable in his world-ecological assessment of the ways in which hogs might help make the island a self-sustaining biotic community, or, more importantly, one less reliant upon imported goods. Beatson displays a refreshing awareness of each species' contribution here. And, again, I am reminded of Jason Moore's point about co-production:

> A capitalist looks at a forest and sees dollar signs; an environmentalist sees trees and birds and soils; a world-ecologist sees how humans and other species have co-produced the forest, and how that "bundled" forest simultaneously conditions and constrains capital today.[80]

That is, even though Beatson displays a certain mindfulness about how species collaborate to produce a healthy bio-region, the bottom line for him remains the same as for Crusoe (and Defoe): the promotion of overseas trade / further accumulation of capital. Moreover, there is a troubling degree of anthropocentrism that informs Beatson's ideas about agricultural improvement. It appears, for example, that the very principle of biological invasion does not bother Beatson so much as the specific *nature* of goats. Despite his obvious interest in restoring the island's indigenous forests, and despite the novelty of his ideas about human-non-human collaboration (if not co-production), this is no celebration of nature as is – but, rather, it is an anthropocentric tract composed with the same bottom line in mind as, say, Grainger's *Sugar Cane*: namely, enrichment. Not surprisingly, the plants he identifies as likely to thrive if the goats were exterminated are all non-native cash crops:

> If the Goats and Sheep were removed, many valuable Orchards and Gardens might easily be established in those well watered ravines or valleys which, on account of their depredations, have hitherto been unproductive. Fruit trees of every sort, Vines, Sugar Canes, Coffee, and Cotton, would all thrive luxuriantly in those warm and well sheltered situations.[81]

Beatson's vision for the island here noticeably shifts from Eden to Plantation – from biblical symbols of paradise, "Orchards and Gardens," to vegetal symbols of imperial wealth: "Sugar Canes, Coffee, and Cotton." (Here again, Beatson's vision corresponds with Deckard's assertion, that, the wealth generated by the West Indian sugar plantations in the eighteenth century transformed paradise into a consumer Eden.)[82] And so, one can't help but wonder how Beatson would have felt about the deforestation of the Caribbean sugar islands. Would he have sought to have the planters removed, much as he argues for the extermination of goats in St. Helena? Or would he have excused this geographical agency of the planters as a necessary sacrifice integral to the advancement of British interests? Would he not have welcomed this new installment in the myth of paradise, in which, as Deckard explains, "paradise became increasingly defined in the secular terms of exclusivity and luxury, a consumer Eden which could be accessed not through religious piety, but through the accumulation of money and status"?[83]

A quick glance at still another one of Beatson's publications – *Flora Sta. Helenica* (1825) – suggests that he was not diametrically opposed to the introduction of non-native species, but, rather, that he actually regarded St. Helena as ideally suited to serve as a sort of botanical melting pot. First, Beatson offers an explanation for the publication of this concise catalog of St. Helena's flora as not merely to demonstrate what the island can offer to the rest of the world, but "what it still remains in want of."[84] That he regards the island as *wanting* (or incomplete) suggests a curious reversal from the perspective he adopts when he's arguing for restoration of the island's magnificent forests and, thereby, advocating for the extermination of goats. Next, he proceeds to describe the island as an ideal rest stop in the transoceanic, global intercourse of plants:

> St. Helena being an Island of considerable elevation, and having its situation within the Tropics, possesses varieties of climate appropriate to very different kinds of plants. From these circumstances, and from its situation connecting it with the four quarters of the world, it is admirably adapted for being the resting place of such plants as are journeying from one of these regions to the other; where the sickly may regain in a congenial climate their natural vigour, and where almost every description of plants may by change of elevation in their site, and consequently of climate, acquire those habits which would enable them to survive and flourish in the Countries to which they are ultimately destined.[85]

Clearly this is someone who values humankind's geographical agency, in as much as he envisions St. Helena playing an integral role in the transportation of plants from Asia to Europe. Beatson regards St. Helena as a necessary stopover in the global diaspora of so-called exotic, or Asiatic plant species. In fact, to facilitate this process, he takes care to include key excerpts from Calcutta resident, Dr. W. Roxburgh's "Directions for taking care of growing Plants at Sea," and he explains that the "best way to introduce plants from abroad into our country is by seeds."[86] Of course, Beatson's vision – his longing to see St. Helena play a central role in the global distribution of plants – was by no means unique, but, as Schiebinger and Swan's collection, *Colonial Botany*, suggests (not to mention the citation of Roxburgh's "Directions"), resonant with the "large-scale alteration of nature by European global botanical, economic, and military operations."[87] As Marie-Noëlle Bourguet's work, in particular, makes clear, the commonplace usage of meteorological instruments suggests that Europeans, like Beatson, understood the importance of approximating climates to facilitate the process of plant transfer. "Thermometers and barometers," notes Bourguet, "were used as mediating devices, the function of which was to translate the singularity of a local climate into calibrated, portable, and comparable information."[88] Grove also points out that plant transfers were a top priority for organizations like the Society of Arts, which was "especially keen ... to promote the development of plant transfers between the Pacific, the East Indies and the West Indies" – so much so that, in 1760, "prizes were offered specifically for the successful introduction of cinnamon trees in the West Indies":

> In the same year, in one of its premium lists the Society suggested that land should be reserved in the colonies for gardens or nurseries for "experiments in raising such rare and useful plants as are not the spontaneous growth of the kingdom or of the said colonies."[89]

Thus, while Beatson's wish to see the island's forests restored to their former glory suggests someone with a robust and prescient environmental consciousness, that he regards agricultural improvement (especially the introduction of corn) and the transplantation of Asian plants to Europe as instrumental to St. Helena's future makes Hughes seem the far more radical of the two natural historians. For, although Hughes neglects to properly account for environmental change in Barbados, he at least seems inclined to appreciate nature as is, whereas Beatson not only laments, but also (mostly) lauds humankind's geographical agency for better and worse.

Indeed, Beatson's treatment of St. Helena as a potential site for agricultural-botanical experimentation not only corresponds to the history of the Saint Vincent Botanic Gardens, but also reflects what might be described as a rather more widespread tendency to regard the Caribbean islands as a sort of gardener's "paradise," if you will. At least Henrietta Marchant Liston uses these terms in her journals of travel from the United States to the West Indies in 1801. Of course, as Defoe's *Robinson Crusoe* eventually discovers, gardens reflect the presence, or ecological footprint of humans *in* nature; they are emblems of precisely the sort of experimentation that Beatson heralds in *Flora Sta. Helenica*. Yet, while Liston's reliance upon the aesthetics of the picturesque to describe plantation life in the West Indies may serve as an apt reminder of this fact, that she occasionally (and seemingly interchangeably) mixes her key terms – garden and wilderness – reflects a development in English garden design in the late eighteenth century that consisted of obscuring the gardener's work of landscaping. The gardens at Stowe would be a fine example of eighteenth-century efforts to make a carefully manipulated landscape appear as though it were naturally so.[90]

Liston, the Antiguan-born, or Creole, daughter of plantation owner Nathaniel Marchant and his first wife Sarah Nanton (North), was both an avid gardener and diarist, and she claims in her travel journals that, "to an ardent lover of Plants, the West Indies is a Paradise – what in a Hot House in England may be a beautiful shrub is here a Superb flowering Tree."[91] Liston's representation of the West Indies follows suit with a widespread British tendency to view the Caribbean as a sort of gardener's paradise. Accordingly, aside from visiting old family haunts (the aspects of which I pay closer attention to in Chapter 3), the real highlight of Liston's travels in the West Indies would have been the visit she paid to the St. Vincent Botanic Gardens, which was established by the Governor of the Windward Islands, General Robert Melville in 1765 for "the cultivation and improvement of many plants now growing wild and the import of others from similar climates [that] would be of great utility to the public and vastly improve the resources of the island."[92] Utility is the key term here, as the Botanic Gardens' greatest claim to fame may be its serving as the primary site for the cultivation of the breadfruit seeds that were introduced to the Caribbean by the infamous Captain William Bligh in 1793; evidently, "all of the breadfruit trees in St Vincent are derived from suckers of these original introductions."[93] The curator responsible for this considerable botanical achievement (and for numerous other introductions to the island, including plum rose and star fruit) was a Scotsman and University of Edinburgh graduate named Dr. Alexander Anderson, who took over the general management of the St. Vincent Botanic Gardens in 1783. D. J. Mabberley observes, that, "Anderson was the first in a long line of Scottish colonial experts concerned with the relationship between deforestation (resumed in St. Vincent during the French revolution), climate change, and extinction."[94] Notably, according to Richard Grove, the "principal piece of environmental legislation with which Anderson was connected was the King's Hill Forest Act of 1791" – legal action that "constituted one of the very earliest attempts at forest legislation in the English-speaking world based on climatic theory."[95]

Interestingly, it was the tour of Anderson's "collection" that prompted Liston to enthusiastically claim, that, as noted earlier, "to an ardent lover of Plants, the West Indies is a Paradise – what in a Hot House in England may be a beautiful shrub is here a Superb flowering Tree."[96] There are definitely echoes of Thomas Jefferson's *Notes on the State of Virginia* (1785) here, in that such a claim might have been marshaled to reject Georges-Louis Leclerc, Comte de Buffon's dubious claims about American degeneracy.[97] That said, Liston's attention to the non-human world, and to climate and plant growth suggests someone who is clearly not alienated from nature. It would seem that she intended her use of the picturesque as an apt reminder that what she is describing here is a very carefully planned environment. Indeed, drawing on Grove's work, Beth Mills suggests that, "the garden provided not only an opportunity for botanical study and experimentation, but in a metaphorical sense, a way for Europeans to gain control within a confined space of an unfamiliar physical environment."[98] However, the Garden did more than just "organize the unfamiliar," as Mills claims; it played a significant role in the *naturalization* of non-native species. Howard notes, for example, that, in his *Catalogue of Plants in His Majesty's Garden on the Island of St. Vincent*, Anderson lists "at least 348 different kinds of plants," a large percentage of which were introduced to the island. Thus, to say that the St. Vincent Botanic Gardens organized the unfamiliar neglects to account for the familiar Old World origins of many of the plants growing there, including the following medicinal plants: bergamot orange, *Italian* senna, aloe vera, and China root; and edibles: cinnamon, *East India* mango, rhubarb, coriander, sesame, and dates. (Beatson's *Flora Sta. Helenica* similarly catalogs all the known plants on that island, including many non-native species.)[99]

But perhaps the most curious thing about Liston's recollection of this episode is that she refers to Dr. Anderson's Botanic Garden as both a "wilderness" and a "collection." Liston's application of the term "wilderness" to such an artificial environment perhaps represents a new habit of thinking – one that presciently alludes to the fact that what we now call a wilderness is really, as William Cronon suggests, a "complex cultural construction."[100] And yet another way of thinking about her application of the term would be to take into account the biology of invasions. Grove notes, for example, that botanical gardens often acted as stimuli to a "whole set of metaphorical and botanical agendas," in which case it would be easy to read Anderson's efforts to incorporate so many *exotic* and useful plants into the St. Vincent Botanic Gardens as the botanical equivalent of the cultural work of the British Empire.[101] Indeed, Liston's use of the term "wilderness" to describe a botanical garden curiously invites us to consider those cases in which non-native species have become so thoroughly established in their new environments as to be frequently mistaken for indigenous species. (Invasion biologists use the term "naturalized" to "describe a population that was introduced long ago and perpetuates itself without human assistance, though not necessarily in pristine 'natural' environments.")[102] And yet, as I explain later, Liston's preoccupation with the manchineel tree may be of particular significance, since its appearance in the diary offers a convenient way to think about the nature of empire writing, including her own West Indian travel diary.

Geographical Agency in *The Sugar Cane*

Through his insistence, that in Nature "we see innumerable Instances of Harmony, Beauty, and Order, not to be imitated by ... any human Art or Contrivance," Hughes offers his readers an alternative to the imperialist rhetoric of agricultural improvement that one encounters in much literature of American settlement. For example, John Smith's bold claim, in his 1616 *A Description of New England*, "I made a Garden upon the top of a Rockie Isle in 43 ½, 4 leagues from the Main, in May, that grew so well, as it served us for sallets in June and July," presents human intervention as necessary to convert North America into a paradise on earth.[103] Indeed, Smith regards human labor as integral to the establishment of "Harmony, Beauty, and Order." For Smith, man is a "geographical agent," and New England, though not an Eden in and of itself, may be converted into a commercial paradise of sorts through rigorous human intervention, or geographical agency.[104] Accordingly, as noted in Chapter 1, throughout the seventeenth and eighteenth centuries, the term "wilderness" was invested with biblical overtones signifying desolation, barrenness, savagery, waste, bewilderment, and moral confusion.[105] For example, Locke, in his *Second Treatise of Government*, refers to America as an "uncultivated waste."[106] So, it seems revolutionary for Hughes to suggest in 1750 that Nature is harmonious as is. And yet, as noted earlier, he frequently undermines his own message through his failure to explicitly acknowledge changes in the land resulting from human intervention. He neglects to measure his survey of the island's vegetable [and animal] creations against Ligon's *True and Exact History*. As well, his equation of "Fever and Ague" with uncultivated islands seems to contradict his earlier assessment of the peculiar blessings God bestows upon every climate.

Of course, complications abound in eighteenth-century Caribbean literature, but perhaps two of the most intriguing, thoroughly complicated, and, I argue, ecologically oriented texts would be James Grainger's West-Indian georgic, *The Sugar-Cane: A Poem in Four Books* (1764), and John Singleton's topographical poem, *A General Description of the West-Indian Islands* (1767). Both of these poems explicitly acknowledge the geographical agency of humans, whether through Grainger's careful attention to the introduction of new species of animals and plants to the tiny island of St. Christopher or through Singleton's sublime rendering of soil erosion – i.e. "Runaway grounds, and astonishing gullies" – in Barbados.

Let us begin with Grainger's *The Sugar Cane*. In her Introduction to Virgil's *Georgics*, Kristina Chew explains that the "Georgics' subject is farming ... It is about things – the production of food, the raw materials of sheeps' fleeces and honey – that touch all of us as humans on this earth." Grainger's work seems no less concerned with *things*. Indeed, the poem is first and foremost concerned with those so-called things, or, rather, particular *unruly natures*, that figure in the maintenance of a successful sugar plantation: that is, Grainger treats a variety of relevant subjects, from composting to dealing with the "ills" that "await the ripening Cane," including hurricanes, weeds, the "imperfect creatures" (rats) that are the subject of Lucinda Cole's critical analysis of *Robinson Crusoe*,[107] monkeys, and, in Book IV (the most widely anthologized and very disturbing section of the poem), the looming threat of slave revolts. However, as is evident in Book I – the section of the poem that treats the richness of St. Christopher's soil, as well as the island's climate, meteorology, and topography – it is art's transformation of the "savage face of things" that, first and foremost, preoccupies Grainger's poetic imagination. And, in this respect at least, Grainger's *Sugar-Cane* merits consideration as a form of capitalist appropriation, which, as noted earlier, Moore defines as "those extra-economic processes that identify, secure, and channel unpaid work" – including the unpaid work / energy of human and extra-human natures – "outside the commodity system into the circuit of capital."[108] Grainger writes:

> As art transforms the savage face of things,
> And order captivates the harmonious mind;
> Let not thy Blacks irregularly hoe:
> But, aided by the line, consult the site
> Of thy demesnes, and beautify the whole. (182)

Although (as noted earlier) Grainger claims that his motivations for this undertaking were primarily literary – that is, to "enrich poetry" – clearly the poem was also intended to have tremendous practical value as a sort of how-to-manual for planters interested in the cultivation of sugar cane. It is a georgic, after all, and this stanza is on par with most others, in that it clearly contains useful advice about the organization of one's cane fields: "Let not thy Blacks irregularly hoe." And so, the transformation described here partly entails the civilization of so-called wild natures – e.g. the conversion of a tropical rainforest into a productive, neatly organized field of cane plants. Of course, there is the awful, disturbing human element to consider here too: the forcible appropriation / conversion of so many West African peoples (some 5 million over the course of the entire eighteenth century) into low-cost units of labor.[109] The plantation economy as such dovetails with Shiva's point (again) about how capitalism regards "the labor of women and Third World farmers" as "nonlabor, mere biology, a natural resource."[110]

Evidently, planters who lived in the West Indies did value the poem for its practical information, as one of Grainger's colleagues, Dr. Tailour, notes, in his unpublished elegiac poem, "On the Death of Dr. Grainger," that "their precepts often practic'd on your plains."[111] As well, if we consider that the term georgic derives from the Greek word earth, then I think we can read Grainger's opening assertion here – that "art transforms the savage face of things" – as a likely metaphor for the extractive *work* of the poem itself. Contrary to Hughes's glorification of nature as is, Grainger adopts what Gómez-Barris would likely describe as an extractive perspective, in that *The Sugar-Cane* not only celebrates, but also actively participates in the transformation of the island's savage face into a "terraced sea of cane plants."[112] The extractive view, according to Gómez-Barris, "facilitates the reorganization of territories, populations, and plant and animal life into extractible data and natural resources for material and immaterial accumulation."[113] At least, this is the primary function of the poetry, which figures as the superstructure of *The Sugar-Cane*.

However, Grainger's inordinately long annotations tell a slightly different story. Consider, for example, the following line celebrating the fertility of St. Christopher's soil: "Such, green St. Christopher,* thy happy soil!" (173). The footnote linked to this line provides a detailed account of the island's violent colonial history, from Columbus's so-called discovery, in his second voyage, 1493, to the "English, repulsing the few natives and Spaniards, who opposed them," and the subsequent struggles that took place between the English, Spanish, and French for possession of the island. This lengthy footnote represents the soil of St. Christopher as thoroughly saturated with blood – i.e. much less happy than as depicted in the poetry. What's more, a close inspection of these expansive notes reveals someone who is particularly attuned to the island's vulnerability to biological invasion. In Book II, for example, Grainger focuses upon particular environmental mishaps – namely, Europeans' inadvertent introduction of monkeys, rats, and other so-called vermin.

First, the monkeys:

Destructive, on the upland sugar-groves
The monkey-nation preys: from rocky heights,
In silent parties, they descend by night,
And posting watchful sentinels, to warn
When hostile steps approach; with gambols, they
Pour o'er the Cane-grove. Luckless he to whom
That land pertains! In evil hour, perhaps,
And thoughtless of to-morrow, on a die
He hazards millions; or, perhaps, reclines
On Luxury's soft lap, the pest of wealth;
And, inconsiderate, deems, his Indian crops
Will amply her insatiate wants supply.

Grainger suggests a remedy to these monkey infestations:

From these insidious droles (peculiar pest*
Of Liamuiga's hills) would'st thou defend
Thy waving wealth; in traps put not thy trust,
However baited: Treble every watch,
And well with arms provide them; faithful dogs,
Of nose sagacious, on their footsteps wait.
With these attack the predatory bands;
Quickly the unequal conflict they decline,
And, chattering, fling their ill-got spoils away.
So when, of late, innumerous Gallic hosts
Fierce, wanton, cruel, did by stealth invade
The peaceable American's domains,
While desolation mark'd their faithless rout;
No sooner Albion's martial sons advanc'd,

> Than the gay dastards to their forests fled,
> And left their spoils and tomahawks behind.

And then he proceeds to sing about rats:

> Nor with less waste the whisker'd vermine-race,
> A countless clan, despoil the low-land Cane.
>
> These to destroy,* while commerce hoists the sail,
> Loose rocks abound, or tangling bushes bloom,
> What Planter knows? – Yet prudence may reduce.
> Encourage then the breed of savage cats,
> Nor kill the winding snake, thy foes they eat.
> Thus, on the mangrove-banks of Guayaquil,
> Child of the rocky-desert, sea-like stream,
> With studious care, the American preserves
> The gallinazo, else that sea-like stream
> (Whence traffic pours her bounties on mankind)
> Dread alligators would alone possess. (199–200)

Notably, Grainger invokes the Seven Years War in the advice that he offers to planters about how to control these *peculiar* pests – namely, the monkeys that descend from the hills by night to "Pour o'er the Cane-grove." In doing so, he encourages us to read these animals as symbols of anyone (any human or extra-human nature) that threatens Britain's prosperity. His anthropomorphism supports this reading, as it is a "monkey-nation that preys" upon the canegroves, and it is a "countless clan" of rats that seeks to "despoil the low-land Cane." As I have argued previously, "Grainger's poetic description of a 'countless clan's' unwavering determination to 'spoil' the Empire's produce resonates with the Jacobite's nearly successful rebellion against the Hanoverian dynasty in 1745."[114] Grainger's military service in the Battle of Culloden reinforces this, as W. M. Speck notes, "the process of dehumanizing the rebels by calling them 'animals' and 'vermin,' which started when their pursuit through England was compared with a chase, continued as Cumberland [aptly nicknamed, the Butcher] pursued them to the north of Scotland."[115]

However, if we consider the note attached to this line – "From these insidious droles (peculiar pest / Of Liamuiga's hills) would'st thou defend / Thy waving wealth" (199)[116] – then we suddenly realize that what makes these monkeys *peculiar* is not merely their symbolic value, but precisely their status as non-native, or invasive species:

> The monkeys which are now so numerous in the mountainous parts of St. Christopher, were brought thither by the French when they possessed half that island. This circumstance we learn from *Pere Labat*, who farther tells us that they are a most delicate food. The English-Negroes are very fond of them, but the White-inhabitants do not eat them. They do a great deal of mischief in St. Kitts, destroying many thousand pounds *Sterling's* worth of Canes every year. (199)

And the annotation linked to Grainger's stanza on rats, similarly focuses on their accidental introduction to the island:

> Rats, &c., are not natives of America, but came by shipping from Europe. They breed in the ground, under loose rocks and bushes. *Durante*, a Roman, who was physician to Pope Sixtus Quintus, and who wrote a Latin poem on the preservation of health, enumerates domestic rats among animals that may be eaten with safety. But if these are wholesome, cane-rats must be much more delicate, as well as more nourishing. Accordingly we find most field Negroes fond of them, and I have heard that straps of cane-rats are publicly sold in the markets of Jamaica. (200)

The reader who digests Grainger's numerous annotations suddenly realizes that they are at once confronted *not* with New World species, but with familiar, Old World faces. In keeping with Stuart McCook's concept of the "Neo-Columbian Exchange," the face of this country in 1764 was no longer wholly different from that of Europe, contrary to Grainger's insistence in the Preface. (Of course, it is important that only in the annotations does Grainger acknowledge this troubling natural history. The poetry itself obscures these important details.) Despite Samuel Johnson's insistence that rats were unfit subjects for poetry – Grainger clearly understood the significance of these whiskered vermin that were thriving in this sea of cane fields. Not unlike Daniel Defoe's capitalist role model, Robinson Crusoe, or, for that matter, "the millions in Europe who," as Cole observes, "tried desperately to protect grain supplies from vermin," Grainger clearly regarded pest control as key to the success of St. Christopher's agricultural economy / sugar industry.[117] And, indeed, the seriousness of this topic would soon be reinforced by the publication of a book devoted to the subject of rat catching, as advertised in a Jamaican newspaper, the *Royal Gazette*, 21–8 October 1780: "Jones's Composition for Catching, and his Ingredients for Destroying Rats and Mice, are sold, with printed Directions, at this Office, at a Dollar each packet." Accordingly, Grainger seizes this opportunity to propose a few of his own, notably *co-productive* solutions to any potential infestations of rats on St. Christopher's sugar plantations.

First, whereas he recommends that planters employ "faithful dogs" to "attack the predatory bands" of upland monkeys – a solution that troublingly resonates with the article I cited earlier regarding the overabundance of dogs in Kingston, Jamaica – his initial solution to the rat problem is one that not only resonates with the story of Alexander Selkirk (Chapter 1), but would also further confuse Old and New World ecologies: he encourages the "breed of savage cats." Unfortunately, this idea – introducing one invasive species to eradicate another – represents a relatively common approach to the problem of bio-invasion. And, to make matters worse, Grainger must clearly have understood the biological-mathematical impossibility of the cat solution, as it were, in keeping with Cole's valuable observation, that rats reproduce at a rate far greater than that of cats (see Chapter 1).[118] Furthermore, in an annotation linked to line 95, he also proposes the introduction of the mongoose as a possible solution to St. Kitts' rat problem. And, in this regard, Grainger neatly anticipates the historic, and thoroughly tragic introduction of the mongoose to Jamaica in 1872:

> There is a species of East-Indian animal, called a Mungoes [i.e. mongoose], which bears a natural antipathy to rats. Its introduction into the Sugar-Islands would, probably, effectuate the extirpation of this destructive vermin. (201)

Clearly symptomatic of Britons' overall tendency to confuse Old and New Worlds, this particular annotation is especially ominous because, as McCook explains, mongooses would become a major problem in Jamaica, increasing in population "until they spread over the whole island and became a greater pest than the rats on account of their wholesale destruction of poultry, game, ground-nesting birds of various kinds, reptiles, and even fruits ... the decrease in birds was followed by a marked increase in certain insect pests," especially ticks.[119] Biologists regard the deliberate introduction of the mongoose to the Caribbean as one of the greatest environmental disasters of its kind in human history – responsible for the endangerment or extermination of "more species of mammals, birds and reptiles within a limited area than any other animal deliberately introduced by man anywhere in the world."[120] And, highlighting the transoceanic nature of this particular ecological crisis, in Chapter 4 I make a point of sharing late nineteenth-century Hawaii-based naturalist, Robert Cyril Lawton Perkins's observations regarding the extinction of indigenous bird species on the island of Oahu, a circumstance which he links to the introduction of the mongoose, "which swarms there," and other species, specifically cats and mynah birds.[121] None of these deliberate introductions – whether dogs, cats, or mongooses – would serve as an effective means of pest control on Caribbean (or Pacific) islands. And some, like the mongoose, would prove to be an even greater problem than the invaders they were supposed to control. Consider, again, the newspapers that were filled with complaints about the feral dogs roaming Kingston's streets: "the numbers of these animals have so increased of late as to become a real nuisance. They are suffered to parade the streets at night, where, hunting as it were in packs, they become dangerous to any foot passenger that is so unfortunate as to fall in their way . . ." (Kingston *Daily Advertiser*, 5 September 1791).

Embedded in Grainger's thoughtful annotations, however, one also discovers a truly novel solution to the rat's biological invasion of St. Christopher. Upon closer inspection, Grainger seems to be suggesting that perhaps the most effective pest control would be for planters to incorporate these animals into their diets. That is, much as innovative twenty-first-century biologists now propose that we begin fighting invasive species "one bite at a time," as it were, these annotations reveal Grainger to be remarkably forward thinking in his implicit advocacy of consuming invasive species. He cites Père Labat, who "tells us that [monkeys] are a most delicate food," and that the "English-Negroes are very fond of them" (199). And (again) he writes:

> *Durante* . . . enumerates domestic rats among animals that may be eaten with safety. But if these are wholesome, cane-rats must be much more delicate, as well as more nourishing. Accordingly we find most field Negroes fond of them, and I have heard that straps of cane-rats are publicly sold in the markets of Jamaica. (200)

It is possible that Grainger intended these observations to draw a behavioral and gastronomical line between so-called savage Africans and civilized Europeans (that he stereotypes Ibos as barbarous and animal-like in their habits and customs in the same stanza reinforces this reading).[122] But then why should he bother to claim that the Roman physician-poet, Durante, "enumerated rats among animals that may be eaten with safety"? Indeed, the popularity of georgic poetry at this historical juncture suggests that Britons were apt to regard the Roman Empire as a sort of aspirational peer, and *The Sugar Cane* certainly invites comparisons between the two empires.

And so, I argue that what Grainger (also a physician-poet) seems to be implicitly acknowledging here is the dual economic and ecological advantages of converting these invaders into foodstuff. For doing so would not only help preserve the cane fields, but also reduce the island's reliance upon imports to feed its growing population. (John Gilmore notes that, in 1756, St. Christopher – an island approximately 65 square miles – was "reported to have 21,891 slaves and 2,713 white inhabitants.")[123]

In this particular respect, Grainger appears to be attempting to work *through* or with (not against) nature to solve the island's rat problem. *The Sugar-Cane*, as such, stands in stark contrast to the U.S. Department of Agriculture's Plant Pest Control Division's efforts to remedy Etienne Trouvelot's failed gypsy moth experiment through indiscriminate usage of DDT (see Introduction). Indeed, *The Sugar-Cane* offers one of the most progressive takes upon the ecological transformation of the Caribbean, in so far as Grainger's implicit solution to the rat problem has since proved to be a very effective means of controlling invasive species. Consider, for example, the case of the lionfish, which has been wreaking ecological havoc in the fragile reefs of the Caribbean, Gulf Coast, and coastal waters of Florida since the early 1990s. Native to the Indian and Pacific Oceans, the lionfish was likely first introduced to the Atlantic through the pet trade (it is rumored that only six or eight specimens were released into the local ecosystem when Hurricane Andrew destroyed a Florida aquarium in 1992). And with its monstrous appetite and poisonous barbs, its habituation to both shallow and deep waters, and, of course, its ability to spawn "multiple times in a season," the lionfish has now become the "most numerous marine nonnative species in the world."[124] Scientists readily admit the impossibility of wiping out these invaders, but recent efforts by Jamaica's National Environmental and Planning Agency (NEPA) to teach local fisherman how to harvest the fish has evidently resulted in a 66 percent drop in lionfish sightings there. And the National Oceanic and Atmospheric Administration has recently launched a similar campaign based on the principle that "creating a consumer market for invasive species is one of the most successful ways of combating them."[125] What's more, the conservation biologist, Joe Roman, has established a website devoted to the consumption of invasive species,[126] which features a recipe for "Beer-Battered Lionfish with Dill Tartar Sauce."

And so, I argue that this is exactly the sort of scenario that Grainger obliges us to consider when he acknowledges that, if domestic rats are wholesome, then "cane-rats must be much more delicate, as well as more nourishing." The economics of such a proposal would resonate with Beatson's green imperialism, especially his suggestion that on St. Helena,

> the feeding of a population was not only baneful in its effect upon industry and cultivation, but the scanty produce which so small a portion of the lands afforded, aided by a combination to keep up the prices, had enhanced every article of farm produce to such a degree, that the object of maintaining the island, at so great an expense, was almost entirely defeated.[127]

Which is to say, in spite of their ecological concerns and environmental imaginations, for both Grainger and Beatson the bottom line appears to have been to increase the Empire's wealth.

Unnatural Disasters

Grainger's voluminous and illuminating annotations are certainly unusual, in that they appear, at times, to offer a counter-narrative to the sort of imperial landscaping that unfolds in his poetry. St. Christopher's soil is not nearly as happy as the poet suggests in Book 1, for example. And, curiously, it is always the annotations that reveal to us a man of science who is neither alienated from nature nor inattentive to history. (Most interestingly, the annotations occasionally take up more space on the page than the poetry.) However, the formal, subtextual status of Grainger's natural history ultimately leaves us with little doubt about his overarching attitude towards man's geographical agency in the Caribbean. It is art, first and foremost, that Grainger regards as capable of transforming the so-called "savage face of *things*" (italics mine). And, of course, this is a georgic poem whose final stanza not only predicts American independence, but also explicitly celebrates the increasing mobility and transoceanic, maritime strength that would distinguish Britain's vast, global "empire of the sea" in the nineteenth century.[128]

In Singleton's *A General Description of the West-Indian Islands* – a topographical poem that was actually inspired by Grainger's work – the case is a bit more ambiguous. In this poem, Singleton frequently prefers a bird's-eye view to the groundwork that one encounters in Grainger's *Sugar Cane*. Singleton paints mainly in sweeping broad strokes. He takes us, as Thomas Krise suggests, on a blank verse aerial tour of several islands, and – perhaps most importantly – with stanzas such as the one below, he leads us to believe that this is going to be a poem about the Caribbean's peculiar blessings:

> The pleasing subject, grateful muse, inspire,
> Whether thou most delight'st to court the breeze,
> That, sweeping o'er the spacious plain, salutes
> Thy rosy cheek with a soft-temper'd kiss;
> To wander pensive through the shady wood,
> Or climb the summit of the topmost hill;
> Alike each scene diversified attracts
> The feasted eye. – Not fam'd Hesperian lands,
> Nor gardens of Alcinous, could afford
> Theme more delightful to the poet's pen.[129]

However, a close reading of Singleton's work reveals *not* the usual representations of a sublime Nature, but one that is both frightened and vexed by particular human interventions, such as deforestation. This is perhaps why Singleton invokes the Greek mythological story of Atalanta's footrace with Hippomenes – namely, to clue us into the poem's real subject: mankind's cunning manipulation of nature.

For example, as one digs deeper into Singleton's tour of the West Indian islands, it gradually becomes clear that one is surrounded by the produce of man's geographical agency – citrus fruits, tamarind trees, "fat pastures" (284), and spacious, "level plains" (284). Indeed, the lofty tamarind to which Singleton's poetic imagination is repeatedly drawn derives *not* from the Americas, but tropical Africa. And, of course, the "level plains" which figure in his account of St. Croix were similarly man-made so that the island's "Rich canes" might "wave their tall blades o'er ev'ry hill" (284). Singleton's attention to the monoculture of the island – that he seizes this opportunity to highlight the numerous times the island's "teeming soil" has been planted (and replanted) with one single crop (284) – encourages us to make a connection between this and several other passages that detail the so-called "new horrors of the land" (292).

First, in Book 1, Singleton provides the following account of a mudslide:

> Sometimes in gentle drops they kindly fall
> Delightful o'er the plain; sometimes in puffs
> The dang'rous flurries* break (with storm surgcharg'd)
> From forth the hollow of contiguous hills;
> Then, with a rapid violence, they rush
> O'er frighted Nature's face in whirlwinds dire,
> And to the azure deep new horrors give.

*These land-flurries are oftentimes very fatal to vessels, if the mariners are not exceedingly watchful to shorten sail on their first appearance; many having been overset and lost within a musquet-shot of the shore, especially off Montserrat.

Or, consider Singleton's description of a hurricane:

> Whilst the new horrors of the land he views,
> Sorely, with perils imminent beset,
> For not less vex'd th' ruinous earth appears.
> O'er nature's face the desolation spreads,
> And thro' the gloom the tempest rushes wild;
> The mountains from their firm foundations shake,
> And rolling o'er their heads loud thunders crash;
> The vallies tremble, whilst the frightful gust
> With fatal blast destroys the hopeful field.
> High over head, from sable clouds surcharg'd,
> The streaming rains descend, and the huge floods
> In wide extended sheets of waters rise,
> O'er land dispreading vast extensive seas;
> The furious whirl-winds gather in the vales,
> And with destructive force uprend the earth;
> Whilst torrents in collected bodies rush
> With course impetuous from the mountain's height
> Down the steep slopes, and deluge all the plain.
> Rocks, stumps, and stones, and bulky trees they whirl
> Adown their channels vast, with rumbling noise;
> As once they say the furious gushing flood
> Bore headlong with it from adjacent hills
> The solid earth . . . (292–3)

At first glance, one may assume Singleton's purpose here is to account for a sublime and tempestuous Nature. But, since Nature is overwhelmed in these passages with sudden, intense fear – i.e. "frighted" – Singleton may be obliging us to acknowledge that such mudslides and flash floods are not necessarily naturally occurring, but man-made disasters – i.e. the effects of deforestation and the crop monoculture that he describes in the passage I cited above. Indeed, as J. R. McNeil points out, in *Mosquito Empires*, the

> removal of forests on Barbados set in motion other ecological changes. Weeds flourished on cleared ground and in strong sunshine, many of them invaders from across the Atlantic . . . the island's birds and tree-dwelling monkeys disappeared . . . soil erosion and nutrient loss quickly lowered sugar yields, requiring planters to deploy more

slaves (some of whom were employed in carrying eroded soil back uphill in baskets on their heads, a true labor of Sisyphus).

And – most importantly for Singleton – "gullies grew numerous and steep, so much so that horses had difficulty on the terrain and planters resorted to donkeys, and, briefly, camels."[130] Again, one is reminded of Bonham C. Richardson's observation, that "the conversion of the insular forest ecosystems to open cropland had ... been accomplished by expending a nearly inexhaustible supply of human energy – human life – imported from Africa." However, the gullies that arose as a consequence of deforestation necessitated the importation of additional help (other destructive mammals, including the camels that, as noted in Chapter 1, are prominently featured in Ligon's map of Barbados).[131] (It may be worth noting here that camels imported to Australia from British India and Afghanistan in the nineteenth century to support colonization efforts have become a real, invasive nuisance. Feral camels numbering in the hundreds of thousands are now "wreaking havoc on outback [notably, aboriginal] communities and the grazing lands of native wildlife.")[132] McNeil even cites one historical instance, in which "one downpour in November 1669 opened a gully in the churchyard of Christ Church parish that carried 1,500 coffins and their contents out to sea."[133] And, last but not least, he explains that the "soil and silt carried to coastlands formed new marshes" that would serve as breeding grounds for accidentally introduced mosquitoes.[134]

The gullies and flashfloods that we encounter in Singleton's work are not symptomatic of nature's power. Nor is it simply a matter of man's sublime geographical agency, however contrary to Grainger's assertion that "art transforms the savage face of things." It is not only that Singleton reveals to us the truly savage and sublime power of man's artistic (i.e. agricultural) cunning, as it were, in keeping with Deckard's point about how paradise discourse turns further east to focus on the Pacific (to Ceylon and the Oceanic and Polynesian islands) as Europeans in the Caribbean were "stricken by a fear of having exhausted nature."[135] But, rather, Singleton also anticipates Moore's point, that, "everything that humans do is a flow of flows, in which the rest of nature is always moving through us" (underscoring mine).[136] And nowhere is this more apparent than in the following description of Barbados's so-called "Run-away grounds, and astonishing gullies":

Whilst weeping hills their barrenness bewail,
Robb'd* of their native soil, which slides in flakes

With rapid force down their smooth slimy sides.
What time rough Boreas, with tempestuous blasts,
Rends up the solid earth, and torrents broad
Of thick descending rains rush from the heads
Of sloping hills, and sweep their sides away,
From the steep clift swift move the loosen'd canes,
And Devastation with her iron hand
Smites the afflicted earth; his sanguine hopes
Then oft the hapless planter sees destroy'd,
And where the canes their verdant blades uprear'd,
Gracing their gen'rous parent's teeming breast,
The face of Nature's chang'd, and nought but stones,
Or solid rocks, or barren sands appear.
More wonders yet! Still more tremendous sights!
Thy curious search shall lead thee to explore:
And the dark melancholy gullies view,
Where dismal gloom and silence stilly reigns;
Save when the torrents with impetuous rush
Roll down the steeps and tear their entrails up,
Forcing a dreary pass thro' all they meet,
To mix their waters with parental seas. (301)

Perhaps what renders this passage so absolutely horrifying is the alliteration and internal rhyme that Singleton uses to approximate the slippage of an "afflicted earth": "From the steep *clift swift* move the loosen'd canes / And Devastation with her iron hand / Smites the afflicted earth" (italics mine). "Clift swift." To paraphrase Carole King, Singleton makes us feel the unstable earth move under our feet – the rush of soil and silt slipping into the sea. He introduces us to an earth that has been rendered unstable through deforestation and intensive crop monoculture. In such instances, Singleton offers no generic descriptions of an island Eden, but (as noted in the Introduction) something more along the lines of the ironic paradises that, according to Deckard, crop up in postcolonial literatures such as Hervé Guibert's *Paradise*, which utilizes an "aesthetic of degradation."[137] Furthermore, the past tense that Singleton uses here reinforces McNeil's chronology of ecological change, as it suggests that a prior affliction took place on the island that merely prepared the earth to be smote by the rain's devastation. Indeed, the removal of trees, whose roots lend stability to the soil, is one of the leading causes for widespread erosion in the Caribbean. As Lugo, Schmidt, and Brown observe, "with the establishment of intensive monocultures [in the Caribbean], made possible in part by imported slave labor, forest lands were exploited extensively, causing soil erosion, sedimentation, and changes in water quality and quantity."[138] That planters blamed themselves for this gullying is evident; as Grove notes, limited soil-conservation measures were undertaken in St. Kitts, Nevis, and Jamaica due to soil erosion caused by extensive uninterrupted sugar production. "Detailed discussions took place," observes Grove,

> in the St Vincent Assembly in January 1790 on the subject of soil erosion and the causes of gullying. Particular mention was made by members of the size of the new gullies, which were so wide that even fully harnessed ox teams could not cross without the aid of specially constructed wooden bridges.[139]

Singleton, therefore, would not have been alone in recognizing these gullies as symptomatic of European planters' geographical agency, nor would it be so far-fetched to suggest that he (and others) regarded the resulting endemic mudslides and floods as *unnatural* disasters.

But, most importantly, through his usage of terms such as "dark melancholy," "dismal gloom," and still silence in his description of one the island's tremendous (and I might add man-made) gullies, Singleton reveals to us a truly postlapsarian Nature, utterly deprived of those blessings that figure in Ligon's *True and Exact History of the Island of Barbados*. "Silence stilly reigns": these are terms one might use to describe such *unnatural* disasters as, say, a Love Canal or Chernobyl (Mark Twain, for example, uses the phrase – "Sabbath stillness" – to account for the environmental after-effects of California's gold rush, and, as I detail in Chapter 4, Robert Louis Stevenson uses similar terms to describe the effects of crop monoculture, specifically the coconut plantations in Samoa).[140] Singleton's *General Description*, then, is not a celebration of tropical nature as is, but an ominous account of a nature that has been entropic-ally altered by man's agricultural cunning. Seemingly preoccupied with images of a Nature that is not sublime, but "frighted" (264), and an earth that is at once "vex'd" (292), "ruinous" (292), and "afflicted" (293), Singleton obliges us to think through a number of relevant, peculiarly transoceanic ecological crises.

In short, poems like Grainger's *The Sugar-Cane* and Singleton's *General Description* display a keen knowledge of natural history and environmental change, and they offer readers a veritable encyclopedia of local information. As Richard Grove observes, some of the earliest forest conservation legislation emerged out of the Caribbean experience, or plantation economy in the eighteenth century – that is, in the wake of wholesale deforestation of the islands of Barbados and Jamaica. And so, on the one hand, as an example of early Caribbean empire writing, Grainger's *Sugar-Cane* may be fraught with numerous complications, especially with regard to its racism, species-ism, and the overall propagandizing of British investment in the sugar revolution. Grainger's georgic not only partakes of capitalism's appropriation of so-called cheap natures – that is, it aims to help the sugar planter gain control over particular *unruly natures* (from tropical storms, weeds, rats, monkeys, etc., to the potentially rebellious human population of imported African slaves) – and, as Tobias Meneley's most recent work on geo-poetics, *Climate and the Making of Worlds* (2021), suggests, the poem, a georgic, formalizes the process of environmental engineering.[141] On the other hand, it also simultaneously affords us a valuable opportunity to think through particular ecological crises, especially biological invasion. In addition, works like Singleton's *General Description* reflect a growing fear of having exhausted nature. Such poems rely upon an "aesthetic of [environmental] degradation"[142] through their inviting readers to think about deforestation, crop monoculture, soil erosion, and species extinction – i.e. problems that continue to haunt and press upon us with increasing urgency in the twenty-first century.

Notes

1. James Grainger, *The Sugar Cane: A Poem in Four Books, With Notes* (1764), *Caribbeana: An Anthology of English Literature of the West Indies, 1657–1777*, edited by Thomas W. Krise (Chicago: University of Chicago Press, 1999), 167. Further citations will be parenthetical.
2. See Amy Frost, "Big Spenders: The Beckford's and Slavery." 30 October 2014. Available at <http://www.bbc.co.uk/wiltshire/content/articles/2007/03/06/abolition_fonthill_abbey_feature.shtml>. Accessed 4 June 2023.
3. Nuala Zahedieh, "Economy," *The British Atlantic World, 1500–1800*, edited by David Armitage and Michael J. Braddick (Houndmills: Palgrave Macmillan, 2002), 58.
4. T. M. Devine, *Scotland's Empire: The Origins of the Global Diaspora* (London: Penguin, 2003), 221.
5. Devine, *Scotland's Empire*, 221.
6. See also *The Oxford History of the British Empire*, Volumes I–V, Wm. Roger Louis, Editor-in-Chief (Oxford: Oxford University Press, 1998).
7. The Kingston *Daily Advertiser*, 3 January 1791. Printed by Strupar, Bennett, & Doddington, in Harbour-street, Kingston, Jamaica.

8. Richard Vines to John Winthrop, July 1647. Quoted in Matthew Parker, *The Sugar Barons: Family, Corruption, Empire, and War in the West Indies* (New York: Walker & Company, 2011), 35.
9. Parker, *Sugar Barons*, 127.
10. Devine, *Scotland's Empire*, 229.
11. Alexander Houston and Company's Foreign Letter Book No E, Commencing at Glasgow the 4th March 1776 and Ending the 24 April 1778, Special Collections, National Library of Scotland, p. 47.
12. Michelle Burnham, *Transoceanic America: Risk, Writing, and Revolution in the Global Pacific* (Oxford: Oxford University Pres, 2019), 10.
13. Kingston *Daily Advertiser*, 3 January 1791.
14. Bonham C. Richardson, *Caribbean Migrants: Environment and Human Survival on St. Kitts and Nevis* (Knoxville: University of Tennessee Press, 1983), 61.
15. Richardson, *Caribbean Migrants*, 62.
16. Virginia DeJohn Anderson, *Creatures of Empire: How Domestic Animals Transformed Early America* (Oxford: Oxford University Press, 2006), 151.
17. Sidney W. Mintz, *Sweetness and Power: The Place of Sugar in Modern History* (New York: Penguin, 1986), 114.
18. Lucinda Cole, *Imperfect Creatures: Vermin, Literature, and the Sciences of Life, 1600–1740* (Ann Arbor: University of Michigan Press, 2016), 147. See also John Bender, *Ends of Enlightenment* (Palo Alto, CA: Stanford University Press, 2012).
19. Robert Smithson, "Entropy Made Visible" (1973), *Robert Smithson: The Collected Writings*, edited by Jack Flam (Berkeley: University of California Press, 1996), 301.
20. Charles S. Elton, *The Ecology of Invasions by Animals and Plants* (1958), with a new forward by Daniel Simberloff (Chicago: University of Chicago Press, 2000), 77.
21. Elizabeth DeLoughrey, *Routes and Roots: Navigating Caribbean and Pacific Island Literatures* (Honolulu: University of Hawaii Press, 2007), 3.
22. Stuart McCook, "The Neo-Columbian Exchange: The Second Conquest of the Greater Caribbean, 1720–1930," *Latin American Research Review* 46, Special Issue (2011), 13. The publication of Charles Elton's *The Ecology of Invasions by Animals and Plants* in 1958 marks the formal beginnings of invasion biology.
23. Barbara Fuchs, "Conquering Islands: Contextualizing *The Tempest*," *Shakespeare Quarterly* 48, no. 1 (Spring 1997), 47.
24. Lizabeth Paravisini-Gerbert, "Deforestation and the Yearning for Lost Landscapes in Caribbean Literatures," *Postcolonial Ecologies: Literatures of the Environment*, edited by Elizabeth DeLoughrey and George B. Handley (Oxford: Oxford University Press, 2011), 99.

25. Richard Grove, *Green Imperialism: Colonial Expansion, Tropical Island Edens, and the Origins of Environmentalism, 1600–1860* (Cambridge: Cambridge University Press, 1995), 283.
26. Jason W. Moore, *Capitalism in the Web of Life: Ecology and the Accumulation of Capital* (London: Verso, 2015), 18–21.
27. Quoted in Elizabeth DeLoughrey, Renée K. Gosson, and George B. Handley, "Introduction," *Caribbean Literature and the Environment: Between Nature and Culture* (Charlottesville: University of Virginia Press, 2005), 4.
28. See Schiebinger and Swan, eds, *Colonial Botany: Science, Commerce, and Politics in the Early Modern World* (Philadelphia: University of Pennsylvania Press, 2005).
29. Moore, *Capitalism*, 17.
30. Vandana Shiva, *Biopiracy: The Plunder of Nature and Knowledge* (Boston: South End Press, 1997), 88–90.
31. Shiva, *Biopiracy*, 89.
32. Quoted in Louisa Gairn, *Ecology and Modern Scottish Literature* (Edinburgh: Edinburgh University Press, 2008), 49.
33. Rajani Sudan, *The Alchemy of Empire: Abject Materials and the Technologies of Colonialism* (New York: Fordham University Press, 2016), 5–15.
34. Michel Serres, *The Natural Contract*, translated by Elizabeth MacArthur and William Paulson (Ann Arbor: University of Michigan Press, 1995), 2.
35. Daniel Simberloff, *Invasive Species: What Everyone Needs to Know* (Oxford: Oxford University Press, 2013), 133.
36. Alan Taylor, *American Colonies: The Settling of North America* (New York: Viking Penguin, 2001), 210.
37. See the 1801 Caribbean travel diary of Henrietta Marchant Liston, Special Collections, National Library of Scotland, pp. 13–14.
38. See Jerome S. Handler, "Diseases and Medical Disabilities of Enslaved Barbadians From the Seventeenth Century to around 1838," *The Journal of Caribbean History* 40, no. 1 (2006), 1–38.
39. Patricia Yaeger, "Editor's Column: Sea Trash, Dark Pools, and The Tragedy of the Commons," *Publications of the Modern Language Association (PMLA)* 125, no. 3 (2010), 523–42.
40. Michael Niblett, *World Literature and Ecology: The Aesthetics of Commodity Frontiers, 1890–1950* (Cham: Palgrave Macmillan, 2020), 3.
41. See Michael P. Branch and Scott Slovic, "Surveying the Emergence of Ecocriticism," *The ISLE Reader: Ecocriticism 1993–2003*, edited by Branch and Slovic (Athens: University of Georgia Press, 2003), xiv–xv.
42. Yaeger, "Editor's Column," 538.
43. See Margaret Cohen, "Literary Studies on the Terraqueous Globe," *PMLA* 125, no. 3 (2010), 657–62.

44. Cohen, "Literary Studies," 658.
45. Jake Kosek, *Understories: The Political Life of Forests in Northern New Mexico* (Durham, NC: Duke University Press, 2006), 32.
46. Review of Matthew Parker's *The Sugar Barons*, "The Sugar Trade: Sweet and Rich," *The Economist*, 31 August 2011. Available at <http://www.economist.com/node/21525808>. Accessed 4 June 2023.
47. *The Journal of John Ker, Surgeon's Mate in the Royal Navy – a manuscript account describing his service in the West Indies, 1778–1782*, Special Collections, National Library of Scotland, Edinburgh, p. 9.
48. Ayesha Ramachandra, *The Worldmakers: Global Imagining in Early Modern Europe* (Chicago: The University Press of Chicago, 2015), 5.
49. Marie-Noëlle Bourguet, "Measurable Difference: Botany, Climate, and the Gardener's Thermometer in Eighteenth-Century France," in *Colonial Botany: Science, Commerce, and Politics in the Early Modern World*, edited by Londa Schiebinger and Claudia Swan (Philadelphia: University of Pennsylvania Press, 2005), 280.
50. Janet Schaw, *Journal of a Lady of Quality; Being a Narrative of a Journey from Scotland to the West Indies, North Carolina, and Portugal, in the years 1774 to 1776*, edited by Evangeline Walker Andrews, in collaboration with Charles McLean Andrews (New Haven: Yale University Press, 1923), 101.
51. J. R. McNeil, *Mosquito Empires: Ecology and War in the Greater Caribbean, 1620–1914* (Cambridge: Cambridge University Press, 2010), 23.
52. Mintz, *Sweetness and Power*, 32.
53. For a concise history of psychogeography, see Merlin Coverley, *Psychogeography* (Harpenden: Pocket Essentials, 2010). See also Michel De Certeau, *The Practice of Everyday Life* (Berkeley: University of California Press, 1988).
54. *The Jamaica Magazine; Containing Original Essays, Moral Philosophical, and Literary: Together with Interesting Sketches, Biographical and Political, From the Latest European Publications . . . Collected by a Gentleman of General and Extensive Readings . . .* (Kingston: Jamaica, 1812), Issue 1, 17–18.
55. *The Jamaica Magazine*, Issue 1, 22.
56. Kosek, *Understories*, 32.
57. Ker, *Journal*, 25.
58. Alan Burdick, *Out of Eden: An Odyssey of Ecological Invasion* (New York: Farrar, Straus, and Giraux, 2005), 49.
59. Griffith Hughes, *The Natural History of Barbados* (London: Printed for the Author, 1750), iv.
60. Hughes, *Natural History of Barbados*, 102.
61. Hughes, *Natural History of Barbados*, iii–iv.

62. Sharae Deckard, *Paradise Discourse, Imperialism, and Globalization: Exploiting Eden* (New York and London: Routledge, 2010), 11.
63. Deckard, *Paradise Discourse*, 12.
64. Elton, *Ecology of Invasions*, 78.
65. "In addition to yucca," notes Antonio Benítez-Rojo, "the Tainos introduced – either the species or its cultivation – cotton, sweet potatoes, the root vegetable called *malanga*, pineapples, tobacco, peanuts, maize, peppers, beans, and squash." See Benítez-Rojo, translated by James Maraniss, *Caribbean Literature and the Environment: Between Nature and Culture*, edited by Elizabeth DeLoughrey, Renée K. Gosson, and George B. Handley (Charlottesville: University of Virginia Press, 2005), 35.
66. See McNeil, *Mosquito Empires*, 23. See also John Locke, *Two Treatises of Government*, ed. Mark Goldie (London: Everyman, 1993), 128.
67. Taylor, *American Colonies*, 210.
68. Quoted in Taylor, *American Colonies*, 210.
69. Deckard, *Paradise Discourse*, 12.
70. Hughes, *Natural History of Barbados*, 3.
71. Grove, *Green Imperialism*, 266.
72. Richard Ligon, *A True and Exact History of the Island of Barbados* (1657) (Indianapolis: Hackett Publishing, 2011), 64.
73. McNeil, *Mosquito Empires*, 23.
74. Hughes, *Natural History of Barbados*, 69.
75. Deckard, *Paradise Discourse*, 12.
76. See Grove, *Green Imperialism*.
77. Alexander Beatson, *Papers Relating to the Devastation Committed by Goats on the Island of St. Helena, From the period of their Introduction to the Present Time; Comprising Experiments, Observations & Hints, Connected with Agricultural Improvement And Planting, &c. &c. &c.* (St. Helena: J. Coupland, 1810), 12.
78. Beatson, *Papers*, 13–14.
79. Beatson, *Papers*, 17.
80. Moore, *Capitalism*, 51.
81. Beatson, *Papers*, 19.
82. Deckard, *Paradise Discourse*, 12.
83. Deckard, *Paradise Discourse*, 12.
84. Alexander Beatson, *Flora Sta. Helenica* (St. Helena: Printed by J. Boyd, 1825), i.
85. Beatson, *Flora*, i–ii.
86. Beatson, *Flora*, iii–v. See also Dr. W. Roxburgh, "Directions for taking care of growing Plants at Sea," *The Annual Register, or A View of the History, Politics, and Literature for the Year 1810*, Second Edition (London: Baldwin, Cradock, and Joy, 1825), 619.
87. Schiebinger and Swan, *Colonial Botany*, 8.

88. Bourguet, "Measurable Difference," in *Colonial Botany*, 271.
89. Grove, *Green Imperialism*, 268.
90. See John Dixon Hunt and Peter Willis, eds, *The Genius of Place: The English Landscape Garden, 1620–1820* (Cambridge, MA: MIT Press, 1988).
91. Liston, Caribbean Travel Diary, 39.
92. Quoted in Edward Smith, *The Life of Sir Joseph Banks* (Cambridge: Cambridge University Press, 2011), 120. For an early history of the St. Vincent Botanic Gardens, see Rev. Lansdown Guilding, *An Account of the Botanic Gardens in the Island of St. Vincent, From Its Establishment to the Present Time* (Glasgow: Richard Griffin & Company, 1825).
93. See <http://www.bgci.org/garden.php?id=314>. Accessed 31 May 2023. See also D. J. Mabberley, "Anderson, Alexander (1748?–1811)," *Oxford Dictionary of National Biography* (Oxford University Press, 2004). Available at <http://www.oxforddnb.com/view/article/465>. Accessed 19 October 2016.
94. Mabberley, "Anderson." Available at <http://www.oxforddnb.com/view/article/465>. Accessed 19 October 2016. See also *Alexander Anderson's The St Vincent botanic garden*, edited by R. A. Howard and E. S. Howard (Cambridge, MA: Harvard University Press, 1983).
95. Grove, *Green Imperialism*, 293; and Richard Grove, "The Island and History of Environmentalism," *Nature and Society in Historical Context*, edited by Mikaláš Teich, Roy Porter, and Bo Gustaffson (Cambridge: Cambridge University Press, 1997), 160.
96. Liston, Caribbean Travel Diary, 39.
97. See Lee Alan Dugatkin, *Mr. Jefferson and the Giant Moose: Natural History in Early America* (Chicago: University of Chicago Press, 2009), 10–30.
98. Beth Mills, "'The Bad Old Days Look Better': Enlightened Colonial Land Management Practices and Land Reform in the British Windward Islands," *Environmental Planning in the Caribbean*, edited by Jonathan Pugh and Janet Henshall Momsen (Aldershot: Ashgate, 2006), 22. See also Grove, *Green Imperialism*.
99. Beatson, *Flora*.
100. William Cronon, "The Trouble with Wilderness; or, Getting Back to the Wrong Nature," *Uncommon Ground: Rethinking the Human Place in Nature*, edited by William Cronon (New York: W. W. Norton, 1995), 81.
101. Grove, *Green Imperialism*, 281.
102. See Simberloff, *Invasive Species*, 311.
103. John Smith, *A Description of New England* (1616), *Captain John Smith: Writings, With Other Narratives of Roanoke, Jamestown, and the First English Settlement of America* (New York: The Library of America, 2007), 143.

104. Grove, *Green Imperialism*, 24.
105. See Cronon, "The Trouble with Wilderness," 70–1.
106. See Locke, *Two Treatises*, 133.
107. Cole, *Imperfect Creatures*.
108. Moore, *Capitalism*, 17.
109. Alan Taylor notes, in *American Colonies*, that, "the slave trade diminished the inhabitants of West Africa, who declined from 25 million in 1700 to 20 million in 1820." Taylor, *American Colonies*, 323.
110. Shiva, *Biopiracy*, 61.
111. Dr. Tailour, "On the Death of James Grainger," unpublished manuscript, located inside an original copy of James Grainger's *The Sugar Cane* held in the Library & Archives at the Royal Botanical Garden Edinburgh.
112. Taylor, *American Colonies*, 210.
113. Gómez-Barris, *Extractive Zone*, 5.
114. Louis Kirk McAuley, "'Art Transforms the Savage Face of Things': Scottish Identity & the '45 Jacobite Rebellion in James Grainger's West-Indian Georgic, *The Sugar Cane*," *Symbiosis: A Journal of Anglo-American Literary Relations* 16, no. 1 (April 2012), 102.
115. W. M. Speck, *The Butcher: The Duke of Cumberland and the Suppression of the '45* (Caernarfon Gwynedd, Cymru: Welsh Academic Press, 1995), 147.
116. It is notable that Grainger uses the indigenous name, Liamuiga, for St. Christopher here.
117. Cole, *Imperfect Creatures*, 22.
118. Cole, *Imperfect Creatures*, 146–7.
119. Although the introduction of the mongoose did have some initial impact upon the rats, McCook explains that, "over the longer term, the rat population adapted to the mongoose by shifting their habitat up into trees, where the mongooses did not climb." See McCook, "Neo-Columbian Exchange," 26–7.
120. Christopher Lever, *Naturalized Animals: The Ecology of Successfully Introduced Species* (London: T. & A. D. Poyser, 1994), quoted in McCook, "Neo-Columbian Exchange," 27.
121. Robert Cyril Lawton Perkins, *Barefoot on Lava: The Journals and Correspondence of Naturalist R. C. L. Perkins in Hawai'i, 1892–1901*, edited by Neal L. Evenhuis (Honolulu: Bishop Museum Press, 2007), 306.
122. Grainger claims that many of the Ibos "have their teeth filed, and blackened in an extraordinary manner. They make good slaves when bought young; but are, in general foul feeders, many of them greedily devouring the raw guts of fowls: They also feed on dead mules and horses ..." (200).
123. John Gilmore, *The Poetics of Empire: A Study of James Grainger's The Sugar-Cane* (London: Athlone Press, 2000), 14.

124. See Casey N. Cep, "An App to Find Nemo," *The New Yorker*, 22 July 2014. Available at <http://www.newyorker.com/tech/elements/app-hunts-fish-2>. Accessed 7 November 2014. See also Lizette Alvarez, "A Call to Action Against a Predator Fish With an Important Ban, an App and Even Rodeos," *The New York Times*, 25 September 2014. Available at <http://www.nytimes.com/2014/09/26/us/a-call-to-action-against-a-predator-fish.html>. Accessed 7 November 2014; David McFadden, "Invasive Lionfish on the Decline in Jamaica after National Campaign to Save Reefs," *Huffington Post*, 13 April 2014. Available at <http://www.huffingtonpost.com/2014/04/14/lionfish-jamaica-invasive-species_n_5143460.html>. Accessed 7 November 2014.
125. Cep, "An App to Find Nemo," *The New Yorker*. Available at <http://www.newyorker.com/tech/elements/app-hunts-fish-2>. Accessed 7 November 2014.
126. Available at <http://eattheinvaders.org/>. Accessed 4 June 2023.
127. Alexander Beatson, *Tracts relative to the island of St Helena, Written during a residence of five years* (London: W. Bulmer & Co., 1816), lxiii.
128. P. J. Marshall, "Introduction," *The Oxford History of the British Empire, Volume II, The Eighteenth Century* (Oxford: Oxford University Press, 1998), 5.
129. John Singleton, *A General Description of the West-Indian Islands, As far as relates to the British, Dutch, and Danish Governments, from Barbados to Saint Croix* (1767), in *Caribbeana: An Anthology of English Literature of the West Indies, 1657–1777*, edited by Thomas W. Krise (Chicago: University of Chicago Press, 1999), 263. Further citations will be parenthetical.
130. McNeil, *Mosquito Empires*, 28.
131. Richardson, *Caribbean Migrants*, 62.
132. Ben Lerwill, "The Strange Story of Australia's Wild Camel," BBC, 11 April 2018. Available at <https://www.bbc.com/travel/article/20180410-the-strange-story-of-australias-wild-camel>. Accessed 20 January 2022.
133. McNeil, *Mosquito Empires*, 28.
134. McNeil, *Mosquito Empires*, 28–9.
135. Deckard, *Paradise Discourse*, 12.
136. Moore, *Capitalism*, 7.
137. Deckard, *Paradise Discourse*, 17.
138. Ariel E. Lugo, Ralph Schmidt, and Sandra Brown, "Tropical Forests in the Caribbean," *Ambio* 10, no. 6 (1981), 320. See also J. S. Beard, *The Natural Vegetation of the Windward and Leeward Islands* (Oxford: Clarendon Press, 1949).
139. Grove, *Green Imperialism*, 294.
140. Mark Twain, *Roughing It* (1872) (New York: Penguin Books, 1985), 413.

141. Menely astutely observes, that, "poetry offers an archive of geohistory because poems formalize the activity of making as a transformative redirection of planetary energy." Tobias Menely, *Climate and the Making of Worlds: Toward a Geohistorical Poetics* (Chicago: University of Chicago Press, 2021), 15.
142. Again, Sharae Deckard employs this key phrase in reference to the ironic Edens that figure in postcolonial literatures such as Hervé Guibert's *Paradise*. See Deckard, *Paradise Discourse*, 17.

Chapter 3

Capitalism, Domestic Violence, and the "Botany of Desire" in Leonora Sansay's *Secret History; Or, the Horrors of St. Domingo*

A "Gardener's Paradise"

In her journals of travel from the United States to the West Indies (1796–1801), Henrietta Marchant Liston, the Antiguan-born Creole wife of Scottish diplomat, Robert Liston, claims that, "to an ardent lover of Plants, the West Indies is a Paradise – what in a Hot House in England may be a beautiful shrub is here a Superb flowering Tree."[1] Liston's representation of the West Indies follows suit with a widespread British tendency to view the Caribbean as a sort of gardener's paradise – a landscape whose wildness may be transformed into an immensely valuable Eden, much as John Smith celebrates humankind's geographical agency with his claim (as noted earlier), "I made a Garden upon the top of a Rockie Isle in 43 ½, 4 leagues from the Main, in May, that grew so well, as it served us for sallets in June and July."[2] That it is no arbitrary patch of leafy greens that Smith claims to have cultivated on this rocky isle, but properly "a Garden" (a potent symbol of Britishness) serves to not only familiarize the unfamiliar, or effectively anglicize the land, but also (and perhaps most importantly) to *implant* ideas of vegetal abundance in the minds of his English readers.[3] Furthermore, as Jonathan Lamb's valuable research on scurvy indicates, this image also would have had considerable appeal to the scorbutic imaginations of English sailors. Indeed, as Woodes Rogers's account of Juan Fernández, in *A Cruising Voyage Round the World* (1712), suggests, locating suitable refreshment for scorbutic sailors was integral to the establishment of a truly transoceanic economy – hence, the emphasis that Rogers (vis-à-vis Selkirk) places upon the island's capacity to support additional agriculture (see Chapter 1).[4]

Similar garden imagery repeatedly crops up in early Caribbean literature, from Richard Ligon's *True and Exact History of the Island of Barbados* (1657),[5] a propagandistic work extolling the island's natural beauty and commercial value, to A. C. Carmichael's so-called proto-ethnographic account of the *Domestic Manners and Social Conditions of the White, Coloured, and Negroe Population of the West Indies* (1833).[6] Showcased in Beth Fowkes Tobin's *Colonizing Nature*, Carmichael's work represents the slave garden as a site of agricultural abundance, very much in keeping with Liston's idea of a gardener's paradise; as Tobin puts it, the false impression that Carmichael (a plantation owner's wife) "gives is that growing vegetables is easy, and harvesting them is even easier," concealing, as it were, the extensive agricultural knowledge required to grow food in the tropics: "She employs the pastoral trope of nature's bounty without human labor to underscore the ease with which plants grow in the West Indies, a trope suggesting that the enslaved, like those living in the golden age, do no labor in their gardens but merely reap what nature generously bestows."[7] Similarly, in her posthumously published *Journal of a Lady of Quality; Being the Narrative of a Journey from Scotland to the West Indies, North Carolina, and Portugal; in the years 1774 to 1776* (1921), Janet Schaw describes the Eleanora plantation in Antigua as a "delightful vision, a fairy Scene or a peep into Elysium . . . surely the first poets that painted those retreats of the blessed and the good, must have made some West India Island sit for the picture."[8] And Lady Mary Nugent, the wife of Jamaica's Lieutenant Governor (1801–15), describes the plantations surrounding Kingston, Jamaica, as a "blissful garden," the center of which is the "indescribably lovely" Clifton estate.[9] Journals like Schaw's and Nugent's are especially notable because they were never intended for publication. Like Liston's West Indian travel diary, a highly selective aide memoire that remembers, however disturbingly, the plantation economy in picturesque terms, the garden imagery that one encounters in Nugent's journal was not calculated for rhetorical effect, but accurately conveys how very widespread and deeply personal was this misperception of the Caribbean as (to quote Liston again) a "gardener's paradise." Even Mary, the principal narrator of Leonora Sansay's Gothic novel set during the Haitian Revolution, *Secret History; Or, the Horrors of St. Domingo* (1808), claims, that, "St. Domingo was formerly a garden."[10] Of course, the operative term here is "formerly," and (as we shall soon see) Sansay has quite a different idea of a garden in mind than that which appears in the propaganda of American settlement.

In evolutionary biology too, the garden plays a significant role as artifact – that is, to quote Michael Pollan, as a "relatively small arena of artificial selection."[11] In *On The Origin of Species* (1859), for example, Charles Darwin takes advantage of this powerful cultural icon – the kitchen garden – to articulate how artificial selection figures in the broad scheme of evolutionary biology. Gardens are filled with particular plant species (or varieties) selected on the basis of their possessing characteristics especially well suited to satisfying some human interest or desire – say, for example, as Pollan indicates, the apple's capacity to satisfy the human liking for sweet things and intoxication. The key thing is that Darwin treats artificial selection as part of a "gradual process of improvement."[12] "The most important point of all this," writes Darwin, "is that the animal or plant should be so highly *useful* to man, or *so much valued by him*, that the closest attention should be paid to even the slightest deviation in the qualities or structure of each individual" (italics mine).[13] For Darwin, the garden is an important emblem of humankind's progressive power of selection. His reliance upon the term "improvement" implies as much (the term was frequently used during the Enlightenment to herald the conversion of commonly held tenant farms into large-scale agribusinesses), while his highlighting the role that utility plays in determining the prosperity of particular variations gives root to Pollan's premise, that, "human desires form as much a part of natural history as the hummingbird's love of red."[14]

Contrary to Darwin's overwhelmingly positive valuation of domestication, however, Sansay's Gothic novel encourages us to adopt a more cynical, and distinctly gendered outlook, in which case artificial selection becomes a form of domestic abuse. Citing the careful efforts of florists to weed out the rogue plants that deviate from a particular standard of beauty, Darwin sees astonishing improvement "when the flowers of the present day are compared with drawings made only twenty or thirty years ago."[15] Sansay's novel, on the other hand, implicitly asserts a horrifying connection between horticultural standards of beauty and those applied by European men to the Creole, African, and mulatto women residing within the plantation economy. She laments the role that artificial selection plays in determining the fate of so many women. In this particular respect, Sansay's work builds upon J. Hector St. John de Crevecoeur's provocative assertion, that, "men are like plants" – yet, as for the future of Euro-American agribusiness, she lacks the optimism conveyed by Crevecoeur's narrator. In other words, is the secret history that Sansay's novel reveals not akin to that which Darwin details in his *Origin of Species*?

Sweetness, Capitalism, and Misogyny

In *Capitalism in the Web of Life*, Jason Moore challenges us to view capitalism as both project and *process*, and so contingent upon particular biological and geological conditions. "Nature matters," writes Moore, "to the whole of [this] historical process, not merely as its context, or its unsavory consequences."[16] The underlying point here, that nature lies not outside of culture, a passive thing upon which capitalist forces go to work, but, rather, actively works for capitalism, in as much as capitalism works for nature, corresponds, I argue, to the confusion of nature-culture that figures in Sansay's novel. A large-scale sugar plantation not unlike Grand Rivière on the Cul de Sac, a fertile plain near Port-au-Prince, had the potential to generate huge profits, as Paul Cheney observes, but the risk of failure was no less great, owing to a variety of environmental circumstances: soil depletion, hurricanes, drought, etc.[17] That is, while the advent of chemical fertilizers, large-scale irrigation systems, and heavy-duty synthetic pesticides has encouraged us to view nature as infinitely manipulatable, the West Indian sugar plantation owners and overseers in the 1700s would likely have had a serious appreciation for the work of nature, in keeping with Francis Bacon's insistence, in *Novuum Organum* (1620), that, "one must study Nature and follow her."[18] Indeed, as I've detailed in the preceding Chapter 2, much as James Grainger's *The Sugar-Cane* figures as a veritable encyclopedia of local / Caribbean knowledge, European planters were not alienated from Nature, but thoroughly familiar with various particular natures relevant to the accumulation of capital. On one level, that is, works like Grainger's beg to be read in light of capitalist appropriation – i.e. "those extra-economic processes that identify, secure, and channel unpaid work outside the commodity system into the circuit of capital."[19] Sansay's novel similarly engages this idea of appropriation; however, as the novel is most carefully focused upon neither the cultivation of sugar, nor the institution of slavery, but marriage instead, her work serves as a powerful reminder of how the plantation economy (or, more broadly speaking, global capitalism) similarly banks upon the unpaid labor of women. Indeed, the novel is precisely concerned with the situation of women's work/energy within the relations of power and reproduction. Or, rather, as Michelle Burnham explains, Sansay's work is "most explicitly aware of the ways in which circuits of desire are caught up in circuits of commerce and profit that, by 1808, are inescapably transoceanic and tragically destructive."[20]

However, it is not merely that, as Burnham suggests, women's bodies figure in the novel as "a kind of switch that exposes the dynamic interrelation between individual desire and capitalist drive,"[21] but, I argue, that the novel invites us to consider European men's violent sexual appetite (and the corresponding misogyny / dehumanization of women) as one of the primary, if not the driving force(s) behind global capitalism. It is not merely that women – planters' wives, mistresses, female servants, and enslaved African women – get entangled in the circuitry of capitalism, but that the exploitation of women's bodies lies at the heart of what Burnham describes as an "inescapably transoceanic and tragically destructive" global economy. Again, I am reminded here of Sharae Deckard's important point about how paradise gets reconceived during the Enlightenment as a "consumer Eden." She explains:

> as plantation money from the sales of sugar and molasses flowed from the Caribbean islands back across the Atlantic, financing the building of stately homes with ostentatious gardens and giving rise to a cult of extravagance, paradise became increasingly defined in the secular terms of exclusivity and luxury ... The pursuit of mystical bliss was replaced by the craving for physical pleasures: the addictive stimulations of tea, coffee, tobacco, and sugar.[22]

Here too, I think, Sansay's novel comes in handy as a critical reminder of how women's bodies figure in this paradise transformed. In a key passage of the novel, one in which two *fair fugitives* (an important phrase Ann Radcliffe employs in her foundational female Gothic novel, *A Sicilian Romance* (1790)) – i.e. two sisters determined to escape the horrors of the Haitian Revolution – conceal themselves among (or get confused with) sacks of coffee and sugar in an American merchant's storehouse, Sansay establishes a troubling parallel between the widespread consumption of such addictive stimulants as coffee, sugar, tea, and tobacco (commodities central to the Enlightenment's reimagining of paradise as consumer Eden) and the troubling objectification / exploitation of women's bodies / work / energy. That is, as I see it, the novel invites readers to consider this horrifying dehumanization of women as an integral feature, if not the primary objective of a transoceanic capitalist economy tailored to satisfy European men's cravings for physical pleasure.

****

Drawing (once again) upon Moore's concept of work/energy, and, in particular, his ideas about how the "capital-relation transforms the work/energy of *all* natures into a frankly weird crystallization of wealth and power: value"[23] – this chapter explores Leonora Sansay's treatment of the Haitian Revolution (1791–1803) in her Gothic novel, *Secret History; Or, the Horrors of St. Domingo* (1808). That Sansay chooses to *not* make the Haitian Revolution / Haitian independence – the most significant disruption to global sugar production in roughly five centuries[24] – her primary object of study, but, instead, focuses upon the horrifyingly misogynistic, amorous intrigues of Europeans, I argue, invites readers to reconsider the brutal nature of capitalism in the Caribbean. My approach is certainly sympathetic to Helen Hunt's and Michelle Burnham's distinct, but equally compelling analyses of Sansay's novel. Hunt, for instance, highlight's the novel's interweaving of the horrors of revolutionary war and domestic violence in her neat analysis of women's erotic dominance over other women,[25] whereas Burnham carefully considers the "interwoven forms of political, economic, and domestic violence in the novel,"[26] ultimately arguing that "revolutionaries and coquettes emerge in *Secret History* as unexpected products of the sexual-economic circuits of drive, risk-taking figures whose actions threaten to turn against those 'midwives' who, like Columbus at the birth of the New World, helped bring them into being."[27] However, while I certainly appreciate Hunt's close analysis of Mary's mastery over the narrative – a circumstance neatly juxtaposed with the routine pitting of women against one another in a such a hostile (i.e. misogynistic) environment as the plantation system – my work is most closely connected to Burnham's, not only because we are both interested in Sansay's yoking together of sexual and economic desire, but also because of her careful situation of the novel in not merely a transatlantic, but global – i.e. transoceanic – system of exchange. What distinguishes my work is an insistence upon the primacy of misogyny as a motivating force for the so-called triumph of capitalism, as well as my efforts to extend Sansay's analysis of gender politics into the realms of ecological imperialism and evolutionary biology.

Instead of simple avarice, the passion whose rehabilitation by Enlightenment philosophers neatly coincides with capitalism's rise,[28]

Sansay relies upon a series of extra-human metaphors to link European agribusiness (the sugar revolution) to gender injustices: domestic abuse of (and sexual violence towards) women that, not unlike the history of sugar cane (L. *Saccharum officinarum*) itself, knows no geopolitical, racial, ethnic, and/or religious boundaries. It is a distinctly gendered *botany of desire* (to use Pollan's terminology) that Sansay posits as the secret history of capitalist exploitation in the Caribbean. Not only does Sansay's narrator, Mary, compare her sister's sexual appeal to the sweetness of flora, anticipating Sidney W. Mintz's efforts to showcase the "special significance . . . of sugar in the growth of world capitalism,"[29] she also claims that, "St. Domingo was formerly a garden" (70), which is important because the garden referred to here is emphatically *not* one of the Edenic, island paradises featured in the propaganda of American settlement, but, rather, a garden distinguished by its gross immorality – an immorality characterized by libidinous excess and horrifying violence. I shall focus, in particular, upon Sansay's bookending of Mary's narrative with two important scenarios: the flight of "all the women" into the mountains to escape the horrors of war (62), and the spectacular migration of land crabs, "in countless multitudes from the mountain, in order to lay their eggs on the shore" (145). This narrative framework establishes a troubling connection between the brutality of capitalism and natural selection, as it were – between women's struggle for survival in a plantation economy designed to satisfy particular masculine desires and the arduous efforts of a particular *unruly nature* – the female red land crab (*Gecarcinus ruricola*) – to reproduce. In other words, the point of the land crab migration scene may be to inspire women to rise in multitudes against structures of oppression – the institutions of slavery and marriage, as well as the plantation that transforms the work/energy of all natures into value. Much as the source of patriarchal power, according to Vandana Shiva, lies in "separation and fragmentation" – i.e. "Nature is separated from and subjugated to culture; mind is separated from and elevated above matter; female is separated from male, and identified with nature and matter" – this scenario depicted in the novel invites readers to rebuild connections and to restore the very cycles of regeneration disrupted by man's efforts to engineer the world.[30] Or, rather, she may be encouraging women to embrace a sort of "communal feminism," in which, as Macarena Gómez-Barris describes it, "exchange with the other's life history" becomes a "source of political insight." In this respect, the novel prioritizes a distinctly female eye, or perspective that "moves beyond the cycloptic colonial view, envisioning theories, activities, solidarities that . . . extractive capitalist economies cannot fully capture."[31] However, Sansay's point in bookending the novel with these two critically important scenes may also be to situate cycles of capitalist exploitation (boom and bust) in the web of life (birth and death). This chapter will examine such problems / tensions in Sansay's intriguing novel.

"Mistaken Avarice"

Over the course of the seventeenth and eighteenth centuries, avarice (or greed) experiences a sort of rehabilitation in the eyes of numerous Enlightenment philosophers vis-à-vis what Albert O. Hirschman, in his influential study, *The Passions and the Interests*, describes as their "political arguments for capitalism before its triumph."[32] Based on the notion that "passions are opposed to passions and one may serve as a counterweight to another," avarice gets reimagined as not merely a "universal passion, which operates at all times, in all places, and upon all persons," according to David Hume,[33] but specifically a countervailing passion, one that "could be usefully employed to oppose and bridle such other passions as ambition, lust for power, or sexual lust."[34]

In his *Treatise of Human Nature*, for example, Hume highlights the awesome power of greed as a motivating force when he observes:

> 'Tis certain, that no affection of the human mind has both a sufficient force, and a proper direction to counter-balance the love of gain, and render men fit members of society, by making them abstain from the possession of others. Benevolence is too weak for this purpose; and as to the other passions, they rather inflame this avidity, when we observe, that the larger our possessions are, the more ability we have of gratifying all of our appetites. There is no passion, therefore, capable of controlling the *interested affection*, but the very affection itself, by an alteration of its direction.[35] (Italics mine.)

This idea – that greed cannot be controlled by any other passion except greed itself – should be familiar to anyone who has studied the transatlantic slave trade, as it plays a prominent role in several important abolitionist works. Quaker Anthony Benezet, in *Some Historical Account of Guinea* (1771), advocates for abolition on the basis that it would be more profitable for Britain to engage in fair trade with not merely the coastal, but also the interior districts of Africa:

> A farther considerable advantage might accrue to the British nation in general, if the slave trade was laid aside, by the cultivation of a fair, friendly, and humane commerce with the Africans, without which it is not possible the inland trade of that country should ever be extended to the degree it is capable of . . . the advantages of this trade would soon become so great, that it is evident this subject merits the regard and attention of the government.[36]

And, more famously, the former slave, Olaudah Equiano, offers a similar economic incentive for abolition of the transatlantic slave trade in his autobiography, *The Interesting Narrative of the Life of Olaudah Equiano, or Gustavus Vassa, The African* (1789):

> As the inhuman traffic of slavery is now taken into the consideration of the British legislature, I doubt not, if a system of commerce was established in Africa, the demand for manufactures would most rapidly augment, as the native inhabitants would insensibly adopt the British fashions, manners, customs, &c. In proportion to the civilization, so will be the consumption of British manufactures . . . it lays open an endless field of commerce to the British manufactures and merchant adventurers . . . The abolition of slavery would be in reality a universal good.[37]

Implicitly acknowledging the validity of Hume's assessment, Equiano (not unlike Benezet) clearly imagined the success of the abolitionist cause to be contingent upon his tapping into the interested affections of British readers. Members of Parliament, in particular, had to be sold on the idea that a continuation of the slave trade would mean a net loss in the nation's income.

However, the question of counteracting greed is rendered somewhat moot by virtue of Hume's wholesale revision of this passion. In "Of Interest," for example, Hume treats the love of gain as a potentially harmless employment of one's mind or body, if not an altogether beneficial force owing to its ability to circumvent the love of pleasure. Commerce, writes Hume:

> increases frugality, by giving occupation to men, and employing them in the arts of gain. Which soon engage their affection, and remove all relish for pleasure and expence. It is an infallible consequence of all industrious professions, to beget frugality, and make the love of gain prevail over the love of pleasure.[38]

Of course, not everyone was apt to regard greed as such a constructive force. Earlier in the century, the story of Inkle and Yarico appeared in Addison and Steele's *The Spectator* (3 March 1711).

The story concerns a young English trader, a Mr. Thomas Inkle, who – while traveling to the West Indies to "improve his Fortune" – narrowly escapes an Indian attack on the mainland of North America, and whose life is sustained through the "good Offices" of an indigenous American woman, Yarico.[39] The two young people become romantically involved, passing their time away as lovers until the appearance of an English vessel bound for Barbados gravely tests the strength of Inkle's sympathy / romantic attachment. Indeed, the version of this story that was published in *The Spectator* emphasizes how thoroughly did Inkle's father instill in his child a "Love of Gain":

> Our Adventurer was the third Son of an eminent Citizen, who had taken particular Care to instill into his Mind an early Love of Gain, by making him a perfect Master of Numbers, and consequently giving him a quick View of Loss and Advantage, and preventing the natural Impulses of his Passions, by Prepossession towards his Interests.[40]

And, accordingly, it is precisely this "Love of Gain" that returns with a vengeance when Inkle discovers himself in "*English* Territories" again:

> To be short, Mr. *Thomas Inkle*, now coming into *English* Territories, began seriously to reflect upon his loss of Time, and to weigh with himself how many Days Interest of his Mony he had lost during his Stay with *Yarico*. This thought made the Young Man very pensive, and careful what Account he should be able to give his Friends of his Voyage. Upon which Considerations, the prudent and frugal young Man sold *Yarico* to a *Barbadian* Merchant; notwithstanding that the poor Girl, to incline him to commiserate her Condition, told him that she was with Child by him. But he only made use of that Information, to rise in his Demands upon the Purchaser.[41]

Riddled with racist overtones, this utterly tragic, tear-jerking tale clearly cautions readers against such unbridled greed. That is, *The Story of Inkle and Yarico* depicts greed not as a counterweight to other base passions, but something far more diabolical: a force capable of circumventing the most innate of human sympathies – namely, the love that a parent experiences for his or her child.

However, as Equiano's most basic argument for abolition suggests, by century's end Hume's positive valuation of greed (a revaluation that resembles the alchemy of empire, in which, as Rajani Sudan describes it, base materials are converted into something infinitely more valuable)[42] appears to have held sway over the British imagination at large, an ideological shift that would help pave the way for the British Empire's (not to mention the United States') exponential growth throughout the nineteenth century.

But is greed truly the primary driving force behind capitalism's global spread?

****

It would seem an obvious truth that greed (avarice, the interested affection, etc.) fueled the rise of capitalism. Accordingly, in *The Making of Haiti*, Carolyn Fick claims, that, "the first and foremost aim of the planters was to make money, make more money, and as quickly as possible, then return to France to enjoy the luxuries that wealth afforded."[43] However, it may be merely a matter of emphasis, but I think it important to consider that the acquisition of money (the accumulation of capital) was for most planters not the end goal in itself, as it was, say, for Daniel Defoe's inveterate capitalist – the restless, and wanderlustfully acquisitive Robinson Crusoe who is hardwired to accumulate material wealth for its own sake (see Chapter 1). Rather, as Fick herself here observes, the average planter was ultimately motivated by a desire to *enjoy* the luxuries that wealth afforded – that is, to satisfy (as Deckard's work suggests) their cravings for physical pleasure.[44] This motivation explains, at least in part, why such extreme, "wasteful displays of wealth,"[45] including the grossly extravagant ball that Sansay details in her *Secret History*, were commonplace amongst the island's plantocracy. Not only were these extravagances designed to distinguish the French nobility in a plantation economy noted for its "promiscuous confusion of classes and races,"[46] they also, I argue, provide us with some indication of the primacy of the so-called Sugar Baron's carnal motivations, or sexual drive – i.e. that which propels their misogynous objectification of women's bodies.

Furthermore, it was not greed alone, but a coincidence of factors that led to capitalism's so-called triumph. First, as Hirschman's work so carefully details, the emergence of an ideology that saw greed as having the capacity to harness or curtail other base passions – say, for example, the love of pleasure. And, second, capitalism rises in conjunction with the emergence of a most lucrative sugar industry in the Caribbean – an industry squarely situated in not merely a transatlantic, but a transoceanic system of exchange, and one built upon a plantation economy blending the principles of field and factory.[47]

For only as such could the plantations produce enough sugar to satisfy Europeans' expanding (after 1650) taste for sweetness.

The considerable technical complexity, and the time-consciousness that renders the sugar plantation as much a factory as field deserves a bit more attention here not only because these elements helped, as Cheney insists, lay the foundation for the Industrial Revolution.[48] The situation of this industry upon an assortment of delicately balanced Caribbean islands, and the speed upon which the production of sugar itself depends, calls to our attention one of the most important, distinguishing features of our present-day ecological crisis – namely, our addiction *not* to sugar, but speed. And by speed I mean both our reliance upon the rapid transportation of goods, people, information, etc., as well as the development of technologies that better enable our various industries to harvest natural resources more quickly and with less labor invested to increase profitability – in short, the capitalist emphasis upon turnover time. If, as Sidney Mintz claims, the transformation of sugar from a luxury into a necessity not only accompanied the development of the West, but also epitomized the "productive thrust and emerging intent of world capitalism,"[49] (xxvii), it did so first and foremost by making speed a crucial, however unsustainable feature of our everyday existence. As I have already noted, Daniel Defoe's *The Farther Adventures of Robinson Crusoe*, perhaps even more so than *Robinson Crusoe* itself, does a fine job of instilling in readers this principle of speed by glossing over the passage of time, and, in particular, the amount of time required for the cultivation of staple crops: corn, barley, rice, etc. Reading either *Robinson Crusoe* or *The Farther Adventures* . . . is a bit like watching time-lapse photography, as plants grow to maturity seemingly instantaneously, and with little attention paid to what Beth Tobin describes as the difficulties of growing crops in a tropical climate.[50]

Sugar Production and the Global Economy / Ecology

This question of speed (or turnover time) looms ominously over the commercial extraction of sucrose from the sugar cane plant, though it is a particularly important factor during harvest. Sugar cane, or L. *Saccharum officinarum*, is a perennial true grass, a member of a family of flowering plants known as Poaceae that includes cereal grasses (wheat, barley, corn, millet, rye, rice, oats, and sorghum), and, thus, as a family, ranks as "the world's single most important source of food."[51] The sugar cane, notes Mintz, "was first domesticated in New Guinea, and very anciently," and then, perhaps two thousand years later, "carried to the Philippines and India."[52] Given its tropical origins, sugar cane requires a substantial amount of water (some 80–90 inches) during the growing period – hence, early efforts to conserve Jamaica's forests, such as the King's Hill Forest Act of 1791, were precisely designed to guard against climate change, and, specifically, drought. Furthermore, as Grainger clearly details in his georgic, *The Sugar-Cane* (see Chapter 2), the plant is also prone to a variety of diseases, weeds, and pests, and, as such, requires careful attendance as it grows to maturity in roughly eight to nine months, though this may take longer depending on environmental circumstances: e.g. in Hawaii a sugar cane plant may take from eighteen to twenty-two months to grow to maturity.

The cultivation of sugarcane requires considerable labor. However, that labor does not begin to compare in intensity to the rather more time-sensitive labor of milling and refinement.[53] Indeed, after the sugar cane plants are cut at their peak of ripeness, they must be ground in the mill to extract the juice within roughly three days to "prevent the stalks from becoming unworkably rigid, and also to stave off fermentation, which converts valuable crystallizable sugar into uncrystallizable sugar (molasses)."[54] Simply put, there is an extreme sense of urgency that overwhelms the plantation at harvest time with overseers ever mindful of the fact that good quality sugar depends upon their maintaining a tight schedule of cutting, milling, and refinement.

Accordingly, a central component of every sugar plantation in Saint Domingue was the animal or water-powered three-cylinder rolling mill. A significant but necessary expenditure, the mill's steady grinding motion clearly anticipates the factory work of the Industrial Revolution in terms of both labor intensity and risk of physical injury. That is, working the mill to extract the cane juice was not only exceptionally hard work, but also, given the long hours, very dangerous too. In his account of a plantation day on St. Kitts, for example, Rev. James Ramsay observes, in *An Essay on the Treatment and Conversion of African Slaves in the British Sugar Colonies* (1784), that, "some pretendedly industrious planters, men of much bustle, and no method, will, especially in moon-light, keep their people till ten o'clock at night, carrying wowra, the decayed leaves of the cane, to boil off the cane juice:

> a considerable number of slaves is kept to attend in turn the mill and boiling house all night. They sleep over their work; the sugar is ill

tempered, burnt in the boiler, and improperly struck; while the mill every now-and-then grinds off an hand, or an arm, of those drowsy worn down creatures that feed it.[55]

Ramsay's account corresponds with Lady Nugent's remarks about the manufacture of sugar. At New Hall, or Mr. Mitchell's Penn, Nugent received her first introduction to the "whole process of sugar making, which is indeed very curious and entertaining."[56] And, notably, so struck was she with the dreadful labor intensity of it all that she insists, "I would not have a sugar estate for the world!" She writes:

> I asked the overseer how often his people were relieved. He said every twelve hours; but how dreadful to think of their standing twelve hours over a boiling cauldron, and doing the same thing; and he owned to me that sometimes they did fall asleep, and get their poor fingers into the mill; and he shewed me a hatchet, that was always ready to sever the whole limb, as the only means of saving the poor sufferer's life! I would not have a sugar estate for the world![57]

Aside from reinforcing Ramsay's account of the awful brutality of harvest time, and especially millwork, this passage from Nugent's journal calls into focus the final, and undoubtedly most tricky step in the manufacture of sugar – namely, refinement. The conversion of cane juice into sugar granules represents a similarly all-consuming and time-sensitive activity, a process comprised of a carefully orchestrated sequence of boiling(s), in which the juice was/is heated, cooled, and separated over again in a series of large to small cauldrons commonly referred to as a Jamaica Train. More art than science, notes Cheney, "the distinct processes of sugar boiling – defecation, evaporation, and separation – took place in parallel, meaning that in a given cauldron one or more of these processes were taking place simultaneously, only with less volume and greater purity as the cane juice moved down the line."[58]

In short, the sugar plantation's "labor regimentation, heavy fixed-capital investment, and technical innovation"[59] laid the basis for the factory system that would define the European economy in the nineteenth century. Thomas Tyron's account of sugar production upon the island of Barbados in 1700 reveals precisely the factory-like atmosphere of the plantation during harvest, as he notes "'tis to live in perpetual Noise and Hurry, and the only way to render a person Angry, and Tyrannical, too; since the Climate is so hot, and the labor so constant."[60] Accordingly, Laurent Dubois and John D. Garrigus note too, that, "sugar was most profitable for the biggest planters and for those who could bend their workers to the industrial discipline that the crop imposed."[61]

To be sure, speed was of the essence. Any unnecessary delay between harvest, extraction, and refinement would likely result in lower quality sugar, if not spoilage. And so, in this respect, sugar production mirrors the extent to which humans have become victims of their own desire not merely for sweetness, but speed. Rev. James Ramsay's account of the drowsy slave's lost limb does more than just detail for us one horrifying aspect of the plantation economy; broadly speaking, that lost limb forecasts (in a metaphorical sense) the considerable adverse environmental consequences of capitalism's preoccupation with turnover time. (Correspondingly, in *Speed and Politics*, Paul Virilio treats speed – not class or wealth – as the "primary force shaping civilization.")[62]

****

Perhaps more importantly, the sugar revolution laid the foundation for our present-day global economy precisely because it was *not* limited to the triangular trade across the Atlantic Ocean. Mintz notes, for example, that the British East India Company's monopoly of tea growing in India played a significant role in sugar's rising economic and cultural significance. "The success of tea," writes Mintz, "like the less resounding successes of coffee and chocolate, was also the success of sugar. In the view of the West Indian interest, increasing consumption of any of these exotic liquid stimulants was highly desirable, for sugar went with them all."[63] Burnham's similar point – namely, that "the Caribbean at the start of the nineteenth century was part of a global and transoceanic system of exchange, contact, and exploitation that extended well beyond the Atlantic"[64] – is absolutely crucial to understanding the circuitry of global capitalism.

Janet Schaw, for example, insists that "London itself cannot boast of more elegant shops than you meet with at St John's,"[65] and that the stores in St. Kitts "are full of European commodities."[66] Schaw's remarks upon the Dutch-controlled, free port island of St. Eustatius, in particular – a "place of vast traffic from every part of the globe"[67] – highlight the Caribbean colonies' central role in the formation of a transoceanic, global economy:

> From one end of the town of Eustatia to the other is a continued mart, where goods of the most different uses and qualities are displayed before the shop-doors. Here hang rich embroideries, painted silks, flowered Muslins, with all the Manufactures of the Indies ...

French and English Millinary-wares ... But it were endless to enumerate the variety of merchandize in such a place, for in every store you find every thing.⁶⁸

"In every store you find every thing." Schaw's claim succinctly provides us with an idea of how the sugar boom transformed the West Indies into a bustling center of international trade.

The sugar revolution was not merely a transatlantic, but transoceanic historical unfolding, linking Europe, Africa, the Americas, *and* Asia in an immensely lucrative "system of exchange, contact, and commerce."⁶⁹ As such, sugar helped lay the foundation for our present-day global economy that is still so very heavily dependent upon transoceanic travel. That is, whether we care to admit it or not, we are all living in sugar's shadow. Perhaps, as Mintz's remarkable exploration of the place of sugar in modern history suggests, it was humankind's sweet tooth (supposedly a universal phenomenon), and not merely greed that laid the foundation for global capitalism. And yet, as the feminist perspective afforded by Sansay's *Secret History* suggests, perhaps it was neither greed nor sweetness alone, but these factors combined with the nearly equally widespread, and thoroughly disturbing practice of misogyny that drove the sugar revolution. That is, as I see it, Sansay's novel invites us to think about the unpaid labor of women in the West Indies (as wives, mothers, and mistresses) – a communal feminist approach, in so far as we're invited to draw parallels between the women laboring in Saint Domingue and other parts of the globe, including the Indigenous-Bolivian women and children who, as Gómez-Barris notes, "provide labor to the extractive zone by supporting the heterosexual 'mining family' at home."⁷⁰ In addition, *Secret History* encourages us to consider the misogynistic exploitation of such women as not merely a side effect of the sugar revolution, but comparable to, say, Crusoe's restless accumulation of capital, as an end goal in itself. Again, for planters the overarching point was not merely to accumulate money and status, but to *enjoy* the luxuries that wealth afforded – to satisfy one's cravings for physical pleasure in this newly imagined and, I might add, male-dominated, or distinctly patriarchal consumer Eden.

Women's Labor/Energy

If, as Moore claims, capitalism coheres by a law of cheap nature – that is, "cheap labor-power, food, energy, and raw materials"⁷¹ – then we must take a close look at women's contributions to the sugar revolution, in order to highlight just how heavily capitalism depends upon their exploitation / dehumanization. An obvious example of said contingency appears in the posthumously published *Lady Nugent's Journal* (1905), a journal recorded by the New Jersey-born Lieutenant Governor's wife of Jamaica, 1801–15. Née Mary Skinner, Lady Mary Nugent's encounter with a little mulatto girl – "a sickly delicate child, with straight light-brown hair, and very black eyes"[72] – upon Simon Taylor's plantation, Golden Grove, calls into focus the horrifying ways in which African women were forcibly channeled into the circuit of capital. In particular, this experience obliges Lady Nugent to confront the plantation economy's awful appropriation of the work/energy of female slaves in terms of their childbearing. Through conversation with the plantation's housekeeper, an Irish woman named Nelly Nugent (no relation), Lady Nugent is not only brought to bear in mind the awful hardships imposed upon pregnant female "field negroes" who "work in the fields till the last six weeks, and are at work there again in a fortnight after their confinement,"[73] but the explanation that Nelly offers Lady Nugent for the awkwardness of Mr. Taylor's dismissal of the sickly mulatto girl who had been "sent into the drawing-room to amuse me [Lady N]" also calls into focus the routine sexual abuse of female slaves by plantation owners such as Taylor.[74] Nugent explains that she is Taylor's "own daughter, and that he had a numerous family, some almost on every one of his estates."[75] Furthermore, Nelly's horrible stereotypical assessment of the efficiency with which black women bear children provides us with some indication of the considerable extent to which the West Indian plantation economy relied upon this sort of unpaid work/energy of black female slaves, in particular. Not only is Nelly supposed to have remarked "that it was astonishing how fast these black women recovered after lying-in"[76] – a comment that serves to justify Taylor's insistence upon their return to the cane fields two weeks after childbirth (and one that recalls capitalism's preoccupation with speed / turnover-time) – but she also implicitly acknowledges the value accorded to such women's labor in terms of supplying cheap labor-power: "the smallest children are employed in the field, weeding and picking the canes; for which purpose they are taken from their mothers at a very early age."[77] Indeed, if capitalism coheres by a law of cheap nature, then, as this horrifying episode from *Lady Nugent's Journal* suggests, the Jamaican sugar plantation's coherence similarly rested upon the unpaid labor of black women as veritable baby-making machines. In keeping with Sansay's

Secret History, Nugent's journal, thus, provides us with an idea of the horrors particular to women's experience of the plantation economy. Such horror represents a peculiar form of biopiracy, in which, as Shiva puts it, capital aims to invade and exploit the "interior spaces of the bodies of women, plants, and animals."[78]

Janet Schaw's posthumously published *Journal of a Lady of Quality* similarly attests to the plantation economy's disturbing appropriation of black women's work/energy. Hailing from a family of gentleman farmers near Edinburgh, Scotland, Schaw "sailed with her brother Alexander and other family members and servants on the Jamaica packet from Burntisland on the Firth of Forth bound for Antigua in October 1774" (some twenty-seven years prior to Henrietta Liston's return to the island in 1801).[79] The Schaws arrived in St. John's Island on 12 December 1774, before traveling on to St. Kitts, where, according to T. M. Devine, Alexander would take up his appointment as a customs official.[80] That is, they arrived at the height of the two islands' prosperity, "with the Hamiltons, Martins, and Paynes dispensing almost royal hospitality."[81] Schaw's journal is comprised of the letters that she regularly wrote home to Scotland, and, as they never were intended for publication, we can judge from these precisely how thoroughly she enjoyed hobnobbing with Antigua's planter society, including the likes of John Halliday, William Dunbar, Sir Ralph Payne, Patrick Malcolm, and Colonel Samuel Martin. As well, one can see how throughout she remains indifferent to the plight of said black women. Schaw's careful attention to the island's flora and the excessive luxury (elaborate feasts, the "very elegant and heartsome" balls, etc.) she enjoys as a guest of the island's planter elites stands in stark contrast to her refusal to admit the horrors of slavery. She insists, for example, that Col. Martin's plantations are "cultivated to the height by a large troop of healthy Negroes, who *cheerfully* perform the labour *imposed* on them by a kind and beneficent Master" (italics mine).[82] But, most disturbingly, she seizes this opportunity to extol the benefits of Martin's kindness *not* primarily in terms of ethics (as the right, or humane thing to do), but economics – that is, as the most profitable method available to planters:

> The effect of this kindness is a daily increase of riches by the slaves born to him on his own plantation. He told me he had not bought in a slave for upwards of twenty years, and that he had the morning of our arrival got the return of the state of his plantations, on which there then were no less than fifty two wenches who were pregnant.

> These slaves, born on the spot and used to the Climate, are by far the most valuable, and seldom take these disorders, by which such numbers are lost that many hundreds are forced yearly to be brought into the Island.[83]

Here, again, one is presented with a most disturbing idea of how capitalism coheres by a law of cheap nature, in which case black women figure as unpaid laborers / baby-making machines, sparing, as it were, Col. Martin the greater annual expense of having to import slaves from West Africa.

Of course, this question of capitalism's appropriation of women's labor extends beyond the institution of slavery. And this is precisely why, I argue, that Sansay chooses *not* to focus on the Haitian Revolution, but, rather, the amorous intrigues and, most importantly, the domestic abuse of women broadly speaking (French, Creole, mulatto and black women altogether). The opening scene, for example, consists of a crowd of unidentified ladies fleeing into the mountains outside Cape François / Cap-Français to escape the horrors of warfare: "The ladies, bearing their children in their arms, or supporting the trembling steps of their aged mothers, ascended in crowds the mountain which rises behind the town" (62). Or, consider that, in the *Constitution of the French Colony of Saint-Domingue* (1801), François Dominique Toussaint L'Ouverture – the former slave and military commander who would become Haiti's de facto ruler in the wake of the National Convention's abolition of slavery in 1794 – marshals the discourse of marriage and family in his reinforcement of the island's agrarian economy. That is, L'Ouverture intriguingly folds women's labor (vis-à-vis marriage) into the very constitution of Haiti. In Title IV – Of Morals, he insists the value of marriage lies in the purifying influence it has upon the public: "Article 9. The civil and religious institution of marriage encourages the purity of morals, and therefore those spouses who practice the virtues their status demands of them will always be distinguished and specially protected by the government."[84] Article 10 reinforces the Constitution's endorsement of marriage, as it plainly states, that, "divorce will not be allowed in the colony."[85] And, then, in Title VI – Of Cultivation and Commerce, the language that he employs implicitly links the patriarchal institution of marriage to the island's future economic stability. He writes: "Each plantation is a factory that requires the union of cultivators and workers; it is the peaceful refuge of an active and faithful *family*, where the owner of the property or his representative is of necessity the *father* (italics mine)."⁸⁶ (Of course, this planter-father figure recalls Lady Nugent's troubling realization at Golden Grove plantation of the horrifying ways in which European men forcibly channeled African women into the circuit of capital.)

Although the scenario that the Haitian Constitution describes here of the plantation as manufactory neglects to account for the interest that Creole women often took in business affairs (Cheney), the familial metaphor that L'Ouverture employs nonetheless alerts us to the important, though potentially less visible role played by Creole and/or European women in the plantation economy. "Families," explains Cheney, "provided essential connective tissue for long-distance trade networks."⁸⁷ Because marriage was instrumental to the formation of transatlantic trade relations, and especially so perhaps given the exclusive, commercial feedback loop that was (as noted earlier) created by French policy, marriages and, of course, married women were an essential ingredient.

But, on a very practical, daily basis, what precisely did Creole women such as those depicted in Sansay's novel do to support the plantation economy? And, more importantly, precisely how aware were these women of the horrors of that system upon which their lavish lifestyles depended? Some women obviously played very active roles in not merely the domestic, but plantation (or agricultural) economy. Whereas Schaw insists that Creole women make "excellent wives, fond attentive mothers and the best house wives I have ever met with . . . the domestick Economy is entirely left to them,"⁸⁸ Lady Nugent provides us with the example of Mrs. Sympson, a widow who managed the Money Musk estate – an estate of some twelve thousand a year – "entirely herself." Indeed, Nugent takes care to point out, that, "she [Mrs. Sympson] is an excellent planter, and understands the making of sugar, &c. to perfection."⁸⁹

However, it is interesting that L'Ouverture uses the language of purification to convey the significance of marriage in Haiti, because such a process – a boiling off of impurities – corresponds precisely with both the manufacture of sugar *and* Mrs. A. C. Carmichael's efforts to obscure the horrors of slavery in her so-called protoethnographic work, *Domestic Manners and Social Conditions of the White, Coloured, and Negro Populations of the West Indies* (1833). A planter's wife who, in the 1820s, sojourned for five years in St. Vincent and Trinidad, Carmichael carefully depicts planters as hard-working, industrious men, loath to excessive drink and "luxury of any description":

destitute of those common comforts, which every British farmer enjoys, but which no money can purchase in a tropical country, they are also without those luxuries which are to be found in the East Indies. Some few indeed have good houses; but the majority are contented with a very humble dwelling, furnished too in the simplest style imaginable.[90]

Despite Carmichael's constant disclaimer that, basically, times have a changed – "some fifty years ago, colonial society was upon a very different footing from what it now is"[91] – her assertions frequently fail the test of truth. As noted earlier, it was considered a strict necessity that the planters in Haiti engage in various forms of conspicuous consumption.[92] And Lady Nugent's journal, which was never intended for publication, and so lacking in the sort of rhetorical sleight of hand that figures in published works designed to reinforce the plantation system, proves useful on this point too. Nugent describes in greater or lesser detail one lavish social event after another, including grand balls (tremendous displays of wealth, pomp, and circumstance, in which she dresses the part, at one point outfitted with a "gold tiara, and white feathers,"[93] and "profuse dinners," including those at the Bushy Park estate, in particular, that make her "sick of so much eating and fatigue":

> I don't wonder now at the fever the people suffer from here – such eating and drinking I never saw! Such loads of all sorts of high, rich, and seasoned things, and really gallons of wine and mixed liquors as they drink! I observed some of the party, to-day, eat of late breakfasts, as if they had never eaten before – a dish of tea, another of coffee, a bumper of claret, another large one of hock-negus; then Madeira, sangaree, hot and cold meat, stew and fries, hot and cold fish pickled and plain, peppers, ginger sweetmeats, acid fruit, sweet jellies – in short, it was all as astonishing as it was disgusting.[94]

This passage recalls Deckard's point about paradise transformed into a consumer Eden.[95] Nugent clearly raises questions about the veracity of Carmichael's claims of planter modesty, as does Schaw, who similarly records in minute detail the extravagant feasts she enjoys during her stopover in Antigua. Indeed, Schaw claims that upon Mr. Halliday's plantation, "we had a family dinner, which in England might figure away in a newspaper, had it been given by a Lord Mayor, or the first Duke in the Kingdom."[96] And, before providing her family back home with a comprehensive account of each course, the "method of placing the meal," etc., she proceeds to defend the planter elite's gross indulgence as only natural: "Why should we blame these people for their luxury? Since nature holds out her lap, filled with every thing that is in her power to bestow, it were sinful in them not to be luxurious."[97] Or, as Beth Fowkes Tobin explains, "one needs to read only a few pages of *The History of Mary Prince, A West Indian Slave* (1831) – her account of being flogged, beaten, starved, overworked, and berated even when ill – to realize that Carmichael's soft-focus version of slavery is questionable, if not grossly inaccurate."[98] (Of course, this soft focus that Tobin attributes to Carmichael's work may have something to do with its publication history, whereas Schaw's biases are peculiarly her own.)

However, while Carmichael's account of the "duties of a planter's wife" must be read with a healthy measure of skepticism, the image that one receives of a woman who is not exactly sheltered from, but intimately acquainted with the management of slaves corresponds with the history of Mary Prince. That is, while Carmichael maintains her unbelievably soft focus in depicting the dutiful planter's wife as a caring "mother" to all, and Prince is apt to draw our attention to the savagery of various of her mistresses, including Mrs. I---- – who "caused [Prince] to know the exact difference between the smart of the rope, the cart-whip, and the cow-skin, when applied to my naked body by her own cruel hand"[99] – taken together (and read in conjunction with Lady Nugent's journal) we get a glimpse of how actively women participated in the plantation economy, and not merely in terms of fostering trade relations through marriage.

While Henrietta Liston's Caribbean travel diary, cited earlier for its representation of the West Indies as a gardener's paradise, would seem to imply that Creole women born into the wealth and luxury typical of the planter class had little practical knowledge of the horrors of slavery, the examples given here contradict this notion. (Nugent appears to be sympathetic to the cause of abolition; at least, she claims to be studying the words of leading parliamentary abolitionist, William Wilberforce. However, one is hard-pressed to find examples of anything other than humane management of the enslaved, including those whom she takes pains to carefully convert to Christianity.) And so, would it not make sense for us to consider Liston's omission of certain details in her work as not a genuine, but a willful sort of ignorance – a convenient denial of unpleasant sociopolitical realities? Or, rather, would it not be fair to describe the planter's / governor's / ambassador's wife's greatest contribution to the plantation economy as akin to the refinement of sugar cane – a filtering out of the most vicious and horrifying elements of slavery – in keeping with the language that L'Ouverture employs in the Haitian Constitution of 1801? Was it not the planter's wife's duty to not only conspicuously consume the fruits of her husband's labor, a gesture that was in Saint Domingue regarded as necessary to distinguish the planter elites from an otherwise confusing mixture of social classes and races, but also to practice the art of distraction to conceal the real horrors of that plantation economy upon which their wealth (and the wealth of European nations) depended? (Of course, the conspicuous, dazzling display of the planter's wealth may itself serve as an enticing distraction – a beautiful enticement that may cause one to overlook the horrors of slavery, etc.)

That said, in her potentially misleading account of the "duties of the planter's wife," Carmichael does something else deserving of our attention here. She claims it was the wife's job to "superintend pigs, poultry, &c. with sundry other occupations of the same nature, she must attend also to the garden, and that most minutely; otherwise, she would reap little from it."[100] This is an interesting set of claims because it extends the planter's wife's sphere of influence beyond the boundaries of the household to spaces where she would likely have observed the brutal management of field slaves. The figure of Lady Nugent's Mrs. Sympson comes to mind here. It is interesting too because such minute attention to the cultivation of staple crops would seem to have informed Henrietta Liston's lifelong passion for gardening and, to couch this in Beth Tobin's terminology, for the colonizing of nature. And so too, women like Liston and Nugent, in the attention that they both give to landscaping, reveal to us how very deeply ingrained in the Anglo-American mindset was the image of the West Indian plantation as Edenic garden.

Baptized on 17 March 1752 at St. Paul's Church in Falmouth, Antigua, Henrietta Marchant Liston "was the daughter of plantation owner Nathaniel Marchant and his first wife Sarah Nanton." According to Louise V. North, she "grew up in comfortable circumstances, was well educated, and seems to have traveled to Great Britain and France."[101] And on 27 February 1796 – after a rather lengthy and complicated long-distance courtship – she married a Scottish diplomat, Robert Liston at St. Andrew's Episcopal Church in Glasgow. Less than one month later, the newly-weds traveled to America, where they would not only befriend notable U.S. icons (and, of course, slave-owning Virginian plantocrats), George and Martha Washington at Mount Vernon, but also (in subsequent years) proceed to explore the eastern seaboard from Philadelphia, Pennsylvania to Charleston, South Carolina.[102] It was at this point that Henrietta would prove to be a careful, yet biased observer of human affairs through the journals she kept of their travels, including a trip to the West Indies in 1801. Although this particular journal, through its denial of the harsher realities of plantation life, clearly suggests that Liston had a sheltered childhood in Antigua, it also contains some rather interesting observations about the extra-human world, for (in addition to being a diarist and travel writer) she evidently was an avid gardener, whose "American garden" was supplied with seeds and botanical specimens from the Caribbean and North America. At the very least, she clearly had an eye for plants. Indeed, Liston's journal paints plantation life as a picturesque scene of botanical wonderment.

Because she was born in Antigua, I suppose one can excuse Liston's romantic views. This was first and foremost a homecoming journey – a carriage ride down memory lane, as it were, in which she revisited Antiguan plantations familiar to her in her childhood, as well as paid a visit to her mother's "little cottage." However, her attribution of "cheerfulness" to "Crop time," or the sugar cane harvest – a period in which (as noted earlier vis-à-vis Ramsay's account of a plantation day) some slaves labored exceedingly long hours in the boiling houses and sugar mills – reveals her privileged divorce from (or perhaps unwillingness to confront) the horrifying realities of the sugar revolution. For example, in the following passage – "Cherry Hill, 4th January 1801" – she relies on the aesthetics of the picturesque to describe a sugar plantation:

> After a succession of dinners for more than ten days, we set all out yesterday in our little Summer Wagon ... Our route lay ten miles across the Island a very tolerable road, & through several very pretty Plantations. It being Crop time a general cheerfulness seems to prevail in both whites and blacks – the very animals look fatter & happier. – The situations of the Sugar Works, & often of the dwelling Houses on the Plantations are extremely pretty. The Negro Huts placed frequently on the declivity of a hill, & always interspersed with fruit trees & little patches of vegetables, form the most picturesque objects, indeed, nothing can be more inviting than the Scenery of Clumps & Groves of Palms, Coconut, Plantains, Oranges, Limes, Sour Grapes (the favorite fruit of the Negroes), even the Manchineel Tree, which though poisonous is extremely beautiful & bears fruit which pleases by its fragrance ...[103]

Lady Nugent offers a comparably picturesque panorama of Jamaica as seen from the "indescribably lovely" Clifton estate in the foothills of the Blue Mountains:

> Imagine an immense amphitheatre of mountains, irregular in their shape and various in their verdure; some steep and rugged, others sloping gently, and presenting the thickest foliage, and the most varied tints of green, interspersed with the gardens of little settlements, some of which are tottering on the very brinks of precipices, others just peep out from the midst of cocoa-nut trees and bamboos, the latter looking really like large plumes of great feathers. The buildings are like little Chinese pavilions, and have a most picturesque effect ... The plain, from the Liguanea mountains, covered with sugar estates, *penns*, negro settlements, &c. and then the city of Kingston, the town of Port Royal, all so mixed with trees of different sorts, and all so new to an European eye, that it seemed like a Paradise; and Clifton, where I stood, the centre of the blissful garden.[104]

Nugent's reliance upon paradise discourse here – e.g. "blissful garden" – accords with Liston's picturesque language, as well as other propagandistic accounts of the British West Indies. Similarly, from the vantage point of William Dunbar's lofty plantation in Antigua, the Eleanora, Janet Schaw insists: "it is almost impossible to conceive so much beauty and riches under the eye in one moment."[105] In fact, so mind-bogglingly beautiful is the scenery spread before her that Schaw prefers not to offer any particular details, "till I recover my senses sufficiently to do it cooly: for at present, the beauty, the Novelty, the ten thousand charms that this Scene presents to me, confuse my ideas."[106] And later she goes on to describe the more mountainous parts of St. Kitts as a place "where every thing most beautiful in nature is mixed in delightful confusion."[107]

It seems apropos that Liston brought with her to Antigua a carriage to facilitate her tour of the island since the perspective that she offers of plantation life is so very safely removed from the abject realities of slave labor. That is, while Nugent clearly was familiar with the dreadful business of harvest time – circumstances that inform her claim, "I would not have a sugar estate for the world!"[108] – it is impossible to say whether Liston was equally aware of these horrors; like Fanny Barlow, the female protagonist in Edward Kimber's transatlantic novel, *The History of the Life and Adventures of Mr. Anderson* (1754), she might have been kept a stranger to the discipline of the plantation system, or purposely sheltered from such harsh realities by a doting mother. At least, in the aforementioned passages Liston chooses *not* to recognize the distresses of slavery, but instead prefers to situate the "Negro-Houses" in a picturesque scene of tropical splendor.

However, despite this cultural insensitivity, it may be worth noting that her attention in these passages is drawn not solely to those valuable non-native citrus fruits that figure in many early modern European idealizations of the Caribbean, including Richard Ligon's *True and Exact History of the Island of Barbadoes* (1657) and Daniel Defoe's *Robinson Crusoe* (1719), but, rather, to two indigenous American plant species – namely, the sea grape (*Coccoloba uvifera*) and the manchineel tree (*Hippomane mancinella*). The gnarled sour grape, or sea grape, has since become an important element of Afro-Caribbean identity vis-à-vis St. Lucian poet, Derek Walcott's 1976 collection, *Sea Grapes*, which addresses questions of hybrid identity and diaspora, among other subjects. And so, in hindsight, it may come as a surprise to see Liston – who seems otherwise blind to the horrors of plantation life – take this important historical symbol of hybridized Afro-Caribbean culture into account.[109] But even more intriguing is the attention she gives to the manchineel tree, which is supposed to be pleasant in appearance and fragrance, but highly poisonous. This fact is supported by Griffith Hughes, who observes in his *Natural History of Barbados* (1750), that the "Juice of this Tree is confessedly poisonous," and may cause an "Eruption of painful corrosive Blisters" if it comes into contact with one's skin. Aside from citing one "instance of its Malignancy" in which a planter was poisoned by "a certain Slave," Hughes notes, that, "if some of this crude milky Juice falls upon even a Horse, the Hair from the Part affected, soon falls off, and the Skin rises up in Blisters, which will require a long time to heal."[110]

Unlike Hughes, Liston notes the toxicity of this tree, but only in passing. What she seems most preoccupied with remembering is the tree's aesthetically pleasing appearance and sweet fragrance. This emphasis that she places upon the manchineel's ornamental value suggests, I would argue, important ways for us to think about Liston's diary (and other examples of British empire writing too).[111] Concealed beneath the rosy veneer of her picturesque descriptions is a highly toxic reality, including perhaps the "ancient war between obsession and responsibility" that Walcott refers to in his poem, "Sea Grapes."[112] And yet, unlike pieces of propaganda that were carefully composed to solicit British investment in the sugar trade, this travel journal was never intended for publication, but instead, like her other travel diaries, as North suggests, it was meant to serve as merely an aide-memoire.[113] Her focus on the picturesque arrangement of things, thus, appears to be mainly an unselfconscious side effect of her privileged upbringing on Antigua – *not* a rhetorical maneuver, per se. That is, she truly does regard the Caribbean as a gardener's paradise.

Furthermore, as noted earlier, Liston's preoccupation with the manchineel tree may be of particular significance, since, I argue, its appearance in the diary offers us a way to think about the nature of empire writing, including her own West Indian travel diary. Much as the manchineel's ornamental value tends to outweigh its toxicity, Liston's diary paints a romantic picture of the West Indies. And it is this image – the Caribbean as gardener's "paradise" – that persistently obscures the poisonous realities of chattel slavery and the plantation economy upon which the British Empire was built.

Would it not be useful for us to consider Liston's diary or, more importantly, A. C. Carmichael's proto-ethnographic account of West Indian 'domestic manners' as having an ornamental value that conceals the very toxicity of the plantation culture she claims to represent faithfully? Or, rather, in as much as we might define an American garden, or wilderness, as one carefully designed to obscure the work of the gardener – as carefully constructed to give the false appearance of something occurring naturally – perhaps it would be helpful for us to consider this art of deception as very much in keeping with the duties of the planter's (or, in Liston's case, the diplomat's) wife. Liston appears not to have any knowledge of the horrors of slavery. In her eyes, Antigua remains a picturesque compilation of quaint dwellings and kitchen gardens, and the West Indies as a whole represents a gardener's paradise. And yet, the evidence offered by Lady Nugent and Mary Prince (and Sansay too) suggests otherwise – i.e. that Creole women were not only thoroughly familiar with the brutal regimen of the plantation economy, but active participants, either as instigators or (as both *The History of Mary Prince* and Sansay's *Secret History* highlights) as *victims* of extreme violence.

While it's possible that Carmichael may be exaggerating the dutiful wife's role in superintending livestock, poultry, etc. – a scenario which resonates with the labor of women and children at home and in other extractive zones, including the slag heaps of the silver mining industry of Potosí, Bolivia[114] – one's job (as a planter's wife) was clearly to engage in a variety of activities carefully designed to promote or advance the plantation economy. Whether through the establishment of important transatlantic trade networks in marriage or by representing oneself as a spectacle of wealth and prosperity – that is, as a conspicuous consumer of transoceanic merchandise (e.g. the "rich embroideries, painted silks, flowered Muslins, with all the

Manufactures of the Indies" that Schaw mentions in her journal), and thereby invested with the same ornamental value as a picturesque provision ground – Creole women helped to disguise, if not justify the horrors upon which the plantation economy depended. Schaw's appalling racism, for example, manifests in her efforts to naturalize the corporeal punishment of slaves: "as to the brutes it inflicts no wound on their mind, whose Natures seem made to bear it, and whose sufferings are not attended with shame or pain beyond the present moment."[115]

The former contribution – the wife who presents herself as an embodiment of surplus wealth and prosperity through her conspicuous consumption of material goods, including Madras handkerchiefs – certainly informs Sansay's depiction of Creole women in her novel, and the grossly extravagant social events where these women were paraded about as objects of desire. Of course, this explains why Schaw may claim, that, "London itself cannot boast of more elegant shops than you meet with at St John's, particularly Mrs. Tudhope, a Scotch Lady ... at whose shop I saw as neat done up things as ever I met with in my life."[116] However, while certain mistresses might be inclined, as Mary Prince observes, to use their own "hard heavy fist[s]"[117] as disciplinary tools, the real secret history that Sansay's novel obliges us to consider is how women, including planter's wives, are routinely victimized within an economy designed to satisfy the interests of wealthy, powerful men.

Consider that, at the very outset of her autobiography, Mary Prince observes how her kind-hearted mistress, Mrs. Betsey Williams, lived in fear of her husband, "the master of a vessel which traded to several places in America and the West Indies":

> My master ... was a very harsh, selfish man; and we always dreaded his return from sea. His wife [Mrs. Williams] was herself much afraid of him; and, during his stay at home, seldom dared to shew her usual kindness to the slaves. He often left her, in the most distressed circumstances, to reside in other female society, at some place in the West Indies of which I have forgot the name. My poor mistress bore his ill-treatment with great patience, and all her slaves loved and pitied her.[118]

That the dreaded return of Prince's master effects an alteration in Mrs. Williams's usual kindness towards her slaves, I think, offers some insight into the cyclical nature of such violence / domestic abuse. Bearing in mind Olaudah Equiano's assessment of the slave trade's tendency to "debauch men's minds, and harden them to every feeling of humanity"[119] – and especially his claim, that, "it is the fatality of this mistaken avarice [the transatlantic slave trade], that it corrupts the milk of human kindness, and turns it into gall"[120] – I think it useful for us to regard the kindhearted Mrs. Williams and the savage Mrs. I---- as both deprived of their virtue by an economic system that prioritizes not merely profit, but also, first and foremost (as Sansay's novel suggests), the satisfaction of particular masculine interests / desires. It's useful to note, too, that the scenario depicted by Prince here (an account of domestic abuse) directly parallels the relationship (or secret horror) that unfolds at the center of Sansay's novel – that is, between Clara and her abusive plantation owner-husband, St. Louis.

Secret Her-stories

Secret History; or the Horrors of St. Domingo, in a Series of Letters, written by a Lady at Cape Francois. To Colonel Burr, the late Vice-President of the United States, Principally During the Command of General Rochambeau (Philadelphia, 1808) is an epistolary novel, featuring thirty-two letters composed by two sisters, Mary and Clara. Mary is responsible for the vast majority of these epistles, which focus primarily upon her sister's "precipitate" marriage to a debauched French officer named St. Louis. Exceedingly jealous of the special attention that Clara receives from competing French officers, including General Rochambeau, St. Louis appears in Mary's letters to be an overbearing sort of husband, and Clara's marriage to him an unhappy, if not utterly stifling sort of relationship. And so, arguably, the most significant of these thirty-two letters are the few composed by Clara, detailing the awful, Female Gothic nature of her marriage, as well as her eventual escape to Cuba. Although there is a general lack of information available about Leonora Sansay's life, she is supposed to have been raised in Philadelphia, where she evidently met Aaron Burr (possibly at the Sign of the Half Moon, the inn that was run by her late father, William Hassell), though the nature of their relationship remains debatable. Whether she figured as Burr's "sometimes mistress, confidante, and, perhaps, a political operative as well," Michael J. Drexler describes Sansay as "a public woman, a coquette ... capricious, witty, and inconstant in her attachments."[121] And, most importantly, it may have been at Burr's suggestion that Leonora traveled to Haiti in the company of her husband, Louis Sansay, precisely as General Leclerc was preparing to invade Le Cap in a last ditch effort by Napoleon to reassert French / white control over the island. As Burnham observes: "Leonora married Louis Sansay, a French planter who had sold his Saint Dominguan plantation to the revolutionary black leader Toussaint Louverture before fleeing to New York in an effort to 'escape the retribution meted out against the former slave holders of the revolted French colony.'" "By 1802," she continues, "some degree of order seemed to have been restored to Saint Domingue and numerous French planters and their families," including Louis Sansay and his wife, Leonora, "returned to the island hoping to recover their lost estates and income."[122] Accordingly, the novel is widely regarded as a fictionalized account of the actual letters that Sansay wrote to Burr from Saint Domingue.

And yet, strangely, for a Gothic novel that is supposed to be about the horrors of the Haitian Revolution, Sansay's narrator only sporadically provides us with glimpses of this political conflict's unfolding in the background. Her attention far more often focuses upon the various, and extraordinarily lavish social events to which she and Clara have been invited, including the following account of a ball hosted by the admiral aboard ship:

> Boats, covered with carpets, conveyed the company from the shore to the vessel, which was anchored about half a mile from the land, and on entering the ball room a fairy palace presented itself to the view ... Innumerable lusters of chrystal and wreaths of natural flowers ornamented the ceiling; and rose and orange trees, in full blossom, ranged round the room, filled the air with fragrance. The seats were elevated, and separated from the part appropriated to dancing, by a light balustrade. A gallery for the musicians was placed round the main-mast, and the whole presented to the eye an elegant saloon, raised by magic in a wilderness of sweets. (74)

This is just one, very striking example of the sorts of ecstasies / social events detailed in Mary's narration – providing, as it were, very little sense or notion of the revolution raging in the background.

However, it is not until very late in the novel (and from Clara herself) that the reader discovers what they may have suspected all along – namely, that Clara is a victim of domestic abuse: "Often returning at a late hour from the gaming table, he has treated me with the most brutal violence – this you never knew; nor many things which passed in the loneliness of my chamber, where, wholly in his power, I could only oppose to his brutality my tears and my sighs" (137). Such a revelation invites us to draw parallels between two oppressive institutions: marriage and the sugar plantation.

And it is no coincidence that Clara's flight path away from her abusive husband leads to El Cobre, Cuba – "the site for a large slave revolt at the state-run copper mines" (n.139). However, that Sansay pays only slight, peripheral attention to the uprising slave population in Haiti (and elsewhere) raises several important questions.

First, over the course of the eighteenth century, Saint Domingue would become the "most profitable of all of Europe's colonies," nearly matching all of the British West Indies in sugar production, and responsible for some 60 percent of all coffee consumed by Europeans.[123] It was a "prodigy of wealth,"[124] notes Cheney, a most valuable asset to the French Empire, the loss of which prompted Napoleon to recalibrate France's interest in the Americas. And so, given the widespread, socio-economic and political significance of the Haitian Revolution, especially as it relates to the so-called manifest destiny of the United States, why doesn't Sansay devote more attention to the actual slave uprisings? Why does this important historical unfolding serve merely as a backdrop to the amorous intrigues of the French and Creole men and women? And, second, how might the contrasting attention that she gives to the lives of such men and especially women impact our understanding of the sugar trade and its relationship to the growth of world capitalism? Gender clearly takes precedence here. And, accordingly, as I see it, Sansay's novel links the global spread of capitalism (vis-à-vis sugar) *not* to avarice, but, rather, sexual appetite (and a peculiarly masculine, and misogynistic notion of sexual appetite at that). In doing so, her novel helps explain why there are more people (and especially women) enslaved today than at the height of the transatlantic slave trade in the eighteenth century. (The Global Slavery Index estimates that there were 40.3 million people in "modern slavery" in 2016, 71 percent of which were women.)[125]

Sweetness-Sugar-Sexuality

My argument builds upon the fact that Sansay repeatedly confuses women and plants and animals, and that she relies upon the discourse of sugar (sweetness) to convey the sexual appeal of women. Siân Silyn Roberts similarly points out, that in Sansay's St. Domingue "there is no sharp division between culture and nature that allows the individual to convert raw, passive nature into personal property."[126] Roberts alerts us to the possibility of the novel's posing a serious challenge to Locke's social contract theory, the validity of which rests upon the sovereignty of the autonomous individual. He compellingly argues, that, "the novel helps expose the severe limitations of Enlightenment theories of the autonomous individual and contractual relations as a means of organizing life in a circum-Atlantic world where people and things circulate a vast, politically volatile geography."[127] Roberts builds a strong case for reading the novel as such, and I completely agree that the novel lends itself to the conceptualization of a new "mobile form of humanity defined less by nation, origin, or the household to which they belong and more by the cultural information to which they [Mary and Clara] are granted access."[128] However, Sansay's confusion of nature and culture does more than challenge basic social contract theory, I argue; it raises a number of provocative questions about the very *nature* of capitalism.

Sweetness is a term that Sansay marshals throughout to convey the attractive qualities of particular men and women, whether it's the "sweetness" expressed by Madame LeClerc's face (64), General Rochambeau's "sweet mouth" (72) (ironically, as Burnham observes, Rochambeau was "known equally for his excessive acts of violence against blacks and for his excessive indulgence in opulent luxury and sexual conquest"),[129] and/or the sweet modulations of General Boyer's voice: "his form and face are models of masculine perfection; his eyes sparkle with enthusiasm, and his voice is modulated by a sweetness of expression which cannot be heard without emotion" (67). Or, consider the sweetness that renders the Creole women the "most irresistible creatures that the imagination can conceive" (71). Mary characterizes the Creole women as follows:

> The Creole ladies have an air of voluptuous languor which renders them extremely *interesting*. Their eyes, their teeth, and their hair are remarkably beautiful, and they have acquired from the habit of commanding their slaves, an air of dignity which adds to their charms. Almost too indolent to pronounce their words they speak with a drawling accent that is very agreeable: but since they have been roused by the pressure of misfortune many of them have displayed talents and found resources in the energy of their own minds which it would have been supposed impossible for them to possess.
>
> They have naturally a taste for music, dance with a lightness, a grace, an elegance peculiar to themselves, and those who, having been educated in France, *unite the French vivacity to the Creole sweetness*, are the most irresistible creatures that the imagination can conceive. In the ordinary intercourse of life they are delightful ... (Italics mine, 70–1)

Certain scholars are apt to read the Creole women that appear in the novel as Gothic monsters of sorts. Abby L. Goode, for example, in her intriguing, eco-Gothic treatment of the theme of fertility in the novel aligns the Creoles with the horrors of hybridity and interconnectedness – an "interconnectedness that assumes the blurriness of racial and species distinctions."[130] This is an interesting notion, to be sure (and I applaud Goode's efforts to situate the novel in an ecological context). However, Goode's reading, I think, tends to confuse cultural and racial hybridity, and, more importantly, her argument neglects to account for the pains taken by the narrator, Mary, to distinguish between Creole and mulatto women. Indeed, as Melissa Adams-Campbell observes: "Mary reveals a wealth of contemporary assumptions about the differences between two classes of women in revolutionary-era Saint-Domingue: mixed race mulatto women and their rivals, white Creole women born in the Caribbean."[131] The above passage, for example, highlights the cultural (*not* the racial) hybridity of Creole women educated in France, and, more to the point, Mary employs the discourse of sugar to convey what is so very appealing (*not* horrifying) about such women. In this latter respect, there may be a useful connection between Mary's account of the sexual appeal of Creole women and Henrietta Liston's aforementioned assessment of the West Indies' vegetal marvels: "to an ardent lover of Plants, the West Indies is a Paradise – what in a Hot House in England may be a beautiful shrub is here a Superb flowering Tree."[132] Mary's evaluation of Caribbean-born European women's attractiveness has virtually the same implications as Liston's summary view of the St. Vincent Botanical Garden.

Moreover, that she also uses the term "interesting" to convey the Creole woman's appeal – a term that in the eighteenth century had economic value – reinforces this connection to the sugar plantation factory. In his *Treatise of Human Nature*, for instance, Hume uses the expression "interested affection" interchangeably with the terms avarice and/or greed, and the term "interest" crops up repeatedly in the final few pages of Equiano's autobiography. Notably, this occurs when Equiano details (in no uncertain terms) the economic advantages of abolition:

> It is trading upon safe grounds. A commercial intercourse with Africa opens an inexhaustible source of wealth to the manufacturing *interests* of Great Britain ... The manufacturing *interest* and the general *interests* are synonymous. The abolition of slavery would be in reality an universal good.[133] (Italics mine.)

But perhaps the most striking example of Sansay's marshaling of the discourse of sugar occurs in Mary's account of Clara's attendance at a ball hosted by General Rochambeau:

> Dressed in a robe ornamented with wreaths of flowers, she joined the sweetness of Flora [Roman goddess of flowers] to the lightness of the youngest graces. (98)

In this same scene (and roughly the same breath), Mary describes the hairdressing of another attendee of the ball, Madame V----, the only other "new face worth looking at," as prepared "*a la Ninon de l'Enclos*" (99), an allusion to Anne Louise Germaine de Stael. Sansay's evident familiarity with Germaine de Stael's *Influence of the Passions* (1796) highlights her considerable familiarity with contemporary literature. And Michael J. Drexler notes too, that, "Madame de Stael may have offered more than intellectual inspiration to Sansay. She was the model of the highly educated, witty, world-savvy, influential, and independent woman one can imagine Sansay aspiring to become."[134] However, Mary's reference to Flora here suggests that Sansay's search for models of female agency extended beyond the Enlightenment to the Classical period, including Ovid's *Fasti*, Book V. Indeed, a quick survey of the Roman mythology surrounding Flora, the goddess of flowers (Figure 3.1), yields some interesting connections to not only Sansay's gender politics, but also the ecology of Empire.

According to Ovid, Juno was angry that Jupiter had produced Minerva from his own head, and, in response, Flora offered to help her become pregnant with Mars through the touch of a magical flower – a flower capable of transforming a barren heifer into a mother. This is interesting for two reasons. First, the story of Flora is about collaboration: one woman helping another woman rebel against patriarchy, anticipating, as it were, Clara's flight to Cuba. Relevant to this particular reading would be Flora's status as a rape victim – something that Ovid carefully highlights in the preamble to the story of Juno's revenge. The punctuation of Sansay's novel with similar anecdotes of sexual violence towards women lends Mary's fleeting (and seemingly innocuous) allusion to Flora particular political significance.

Second, the story of Flora has *Frankenstein*-like qualities because it is a story about a man's usurpation of a woman's reproductive agency / rights. Is that not precisely what angers Juno? As Ovid explains: "Holy Juno grieved that Jupiter had not needed her services

Figure 3.1 Giovanni Tiepolo, "The Triumph of Flora" (c. 1743). Available in the public domain via Wikimedia Commons.

when Minerva was born without a mother," and "she went to complain of her husband's doings to Ocean."[135] To couch this scenario in Darwinian terms of evolutionary biology, perhaps it would be helpful to read Jupiter's unnatural actions as a form of *artificial* selection, if not bioengineering. Indeed, the Minerva that Jupiter has produced independently of Juno, and (for that matter) the Mars that Flora helps Juno produce independently of Jupiter, resonates with humankind's Frankenstein-like manipulations of agricultural produce and livestock – i.e. profit-driven efforts very much in keeping with the wholesale (and devastating) ecological transformation of the Caribbean into an alluring sea of cane fields, as well as the bioengineering of seeds that Shiva links to the mechanization of female bodies.[136] Consider, again, Liston's assessment: "the West Indies is a 'Paradise.'" The key thing to note here is the geographical engineering of the Caribbean; Barbados, Jamaica, Antigua, etc. at this juncture are quite literally human-engineered / built environments. That is, there is an important, implicit connection between the ornamentation of Clara's figure and Liston's so-called paradise: both are carefully constructed (and, as noted in Chapters 1 and 2, *co-produced* by manifold species, a combination of human and extra-human natures) to satisfy the interests / desires of "capitalist slaveholders" (i.e. European men). In short, Sansay's allusion to the Roman mythology of Flora reinforces my overarching interpretation of the novel as one that treats artificial selection as a form of domestic abuse.

Flora's solution, however, represents no less a magical manipulation of biology, and, in this regard, I think it important that Ovid carefully defines Flora as not merely the "queen only of dainty garlands," but agriculture. Ovid notes that her "divinity has to do with the tilled fields":

> If the crops have blossomed well, the threshing-floor will be piled high; if the vines have blossomed well, there will be wine; if the olive-trees have blossomed well, most buxom will be the year; and the fruitage will be according to the time of blossoming. If once the blossom is nipped, the vetches and beans wither, and thy lentils, O Nile that comest from afar, do likewise wither ... Honey is my gift. 'Tis I who call the winged creatures, which yield honey, to the violet and the clover, and the grey thyme. 'Tis I, too, who discharge the same function when in youthful years spirits run riot and bodies are robust.[137]

In as much as the survival (and prosperity) of the Roman Empire rests upon Flora's agricultural agency, so too does France's imperial power depend upon Caribbean sugar and coffee. Notably too, this passage neatly confuses plant fertility and pollination with human sexuality, a youthful amorousness. And, accordingly, Sansay adorns Clara's body with vegetal abundance, thereby confusing sexual and economic desire. This scene accords with Burnham's overarching point about how in the novel women's bodies figure as revelations of this confused circuitry of individual desire and capitalist drive. Adorned with flora, she is a female embodiment of the paradise discourse that was marshaled to advance European interests in the Caribbean.

This muddling of sexual and economic desire crops up repeatedly in the novel, notably when Mary recounts two Creole women's efforts to escape the Haitian Revolution. Consider, for example, Letter XXV, which details the story of Coralie. The significance of this distressing and romantic subplot lies, I argue, in an American merchant's concealment of the two women – Coralie and her sister – "in his store, among sacks of coffee and boxes of sugar" (130):

> Her mother and herself [Coralie] had been persuaded to remain at the Cape, after the evacuation, by a brother on whom they entirely depended, and who, seduced by the hope of making a fortune, staid and shared the melancholy fate of the white inhabitants of the place. Coralie and her sister were concealed by an American merchant in his store, among sacks of coffee and boxes of sugar. Their mother had been led, with the rest of the women, to the field of slaughter. (129–30)

The situation of these two women among sacks of coffee and boxes of sugar raises an important question: is the widespread commodification / exploitation of women's bodies no less central to the growth of capitalism than the cultivation of cash crops: coffee, tobacco, and (most importantly) sugar? Were Frenchmen motivated by avarice to transform Haiti into a sugar cane monoculture? Or was the appeal of the plantation economy that it afforded Frenchmen an opportunity to gratify, with a most a disturbing ferociousness, their sexual appetites? This latter question corresponds with Deckard's claim about how the lucrative sugar industry effected a transformation in paradise discourse, in which (again) "the pursuit of mystical bliss was replaced by the craving for physical pleasures."[138]

This – not a Garden of Eden – is precisely the sort of thing that Sansay has in mind when she writes, "St. Domingo was formerly a garden":

> Every inhabitant lived on his estate like a Sovereign ruling his slaves with despotic sway, enjoying all that luxury could invent, or fortune procure.
> The pleasures of the table were carried to the last degree of refinement. Gaming knew no bounds, and libertinism, called love, was without restraint. The Creole is generous, hospitable, magnificent, but vain, inconstant, and incapable of serious application; and in this abode of pleasure and luxurious ease vices have reigned at which humanity must shudder. (70)

Sansay's description of pre-revolutionary St. Domingo recalls Lady Nugent's account of the disgusting excess that characterizes the pleasures of the table at Bushy Park plantation in Jamaica. And Paul Cheney gives the example of one Jean-Baptiste Corbier, a student of the law and the upwardly mobile son of an Anjou innkeeper, who arrived in Saint Domingue in 1774 to manage Étienne-Louis's plantations on the Cul de Sac,[139] and would eventually grow disgusted with the debauchery of the island's planter elites. "He had come to the colony to strike it rich in the plantation economy," explains Cheney, but deplored all the cultural effects so easily traced to its existence: a feverish, casino-like atmosphere that perverted business ethics; wasteful displays of wealth, and above all, the promiscuous confusion of classes and races that seemed to constantly undermine decent order ... Corbier feared that his son would become one of the island's licentious tyrants, habituated from an early age to easy profits, the love of domination, and sexually available women of color.[140]

Janet Schaw's sense of this licentiousness comes across in her overtly racist assessment of the crowds of "Mullatoes, which you meet in the streets" of St. John's:

> Alas! my friend, tho' children of the Sun, they are mortals, and as such must have their share of failings, the most conspicuous of which is, the indulgence they give themselves in their licentious and even unnatural amours, which appears too plainly from the crouds of Mullatoes, which you meet in the streets, houses, and indeed every where; a crime that seems to have gained sanction from custom, tho' attended with the greatest inconveniences not only to Individuals, but to the publick in general ... and as even a mulattoe child interrupts their pleasures and is troublesome, they have certain herbs and medicines, that free them from such incumbrance, but which seldom fails to cut short their own lives, as well as that of their offspring. By this many of them perish every year.[141]

Aside from laying bare Schaw's appalling racism, this passage not only showcases the routine victimization of black women in a plantation economy designed to satisfy the interests of powerful white men, but also highlights greed's failure to counteract lust. And that she elects not to draw a veil over this most disturbing component part of the planter elite's character suggests too, that, despite her obvious racism, Schaw may have felt some measure of sympathy for the plight of these women.

In any case, Mary's assessment of pre-revolutionary Saint Domingue – "the most profitable plantation colony in the New World"[142] – clearly contradicts the trending Enlightenment revaluation of greed as a potential countervailing passion. The commerce in sugar and coffee has obviously not "remove[d] all relish for pleasure and expence," as Hume supposes, in "Of Interest"; the love of gain has not prevailed over the love of pleasure.[143] To the contrary, the colony (this so-called former garden) that Mary describes as one in which vice reigns with luxurious ease raises the question (again) of motivation: were Europeans attracted to this colonial enterprise merely in pursuit of wealth? Or was it the very immorality of the plantation economy that appealed to them – the license that a colony like Haiti afforded European men to gratify their most base appetites, including (as the novel highlights) their appetite for sexual violence against women? Consider, again, Mary's observation:

> The French appear to understand less than any other people the delights arising from an union of hearts. They seek only the gratification of their sensual appetites. They gather the flowers, but taste not the fruits of love. They call women the "*beau sexe*," and know them only under the enchanting form of ministers of pleasure. (96)

Again, that the institution of slavery has not collapsed – but, rather, according to the Global Slavery Index, has gained strength since the height of the transatlantic slave trade – that it has grown in conjunction with the spread of global capitalism, and now preys mainly upon women – I think, supports the latter view.[144]

Needless to say, the irony of the Haitian Revolution – an irony that was likely not lost on Sansay because of her connection to Aaron Burr (and, notably, the Burr conspiracy) – lies in that while important abolitionists viewed the revolution as a major blow to the institution of slavery (in his Lecture on Haiti, for example, Frederick Douglass claims to owe his freedom to the Haitian Revolution), the resulting sale of Louisiana to the United States had the opposite effect. Dubois and Garrigus observe, for example, that, "the revolutionary transformation in the French Caribbean during these years had a profound impact in the Atlantic world":

> It led directly to a major reconfiguration of imperial power in the Americas, since it was Napoleon Bonaparte's defeat in Haiti that caused him to sell France's territory of Louisiana to the United States. Ironically, therefore, Haiti's freedom led to the expansion and solidification of slavery in the United States.[145]

Dubois and Garrigus note too, that, "the emergence of a neighboring black republic and the arrival of thousands of French colonial refugees strengthened the already existing racial ideology in the United States."[146]

Together these three things – the Haitian Revolution, Louisiana Purchase, and severing of U.S.-Haitian trade relations via Senator George Logan's 1806 embargo – would have a profound impact upon slavery in the United States. That is, not only did the Louisiana Purchase expand the U.S. slave economy to newly acquired western territories, a circumstance that would, according to Elizabeth Dillon and Michael Drexler, alter the very "geographical imaginary" of the United States. According to Dillon and Drexler, as the U.S. shifted its attention to areas west of the Mississippi (or simply turned its back upon an Atlantic economy, the center of which was the Caribbean), "the geography of the United States assumed a westward face, and it was this westward face that would, in turn, cement itself in the mythology of the American frontier and the doctrine of manifest destiny central to the history of the nineteenth-century United States."[147] The advent and implementation of new technologies in the cotton industry would also intensify what was already a brutal slave regime in the southern states, supported by pro-slavery advocates who adopted a far more aggressive, less apologetic defense of that economy. (In effect, primarily racist rather than economic justifications for the enslavement of African Americans took root as a backlash to the liberal progress taking place in Haiti and elsewhere, including Britain, the Parliament of which voted to approve William Wilberforce's Act for the Abolition of the Slave Trade in 1807. Furthermore, it would catapult both the U.S. cotton industry and Cuban sugar into the limelight of global commerce. Indeed, the ironic ending of Sansay's novel – that Clara manages to escape her abusive husband by ascending the mountain just beyond El Cobre, Cuba (143) parallels the irony of the Haitian Revolution because Cuba would soon succeed Haiti as the primary supplier of sugar to European markets in the nineteenth century. In other words, the irony lies in that the site of Clara's newfound freedom is soon to become the center of a booming sugar trade built upon the backs of slaves.

The Land Crab Migration

Finally, perhaps the most intriguing human-non-human connection that figures in the novel is the one that Sansay uses to frame the entire narrative. The novel opens with a descriptive account of Creole women fleeing into the mountains above Cape François / Cap-Français to escape the devastation of the revolution:

> The ladies, bearing their children in their arms, or supporting the trembling steps of their aged mothers, ascended in crowds the mountain which rises behind the town. Climbing over rocks covered with brambles, where no path had been ever beat, their feet were torn to pieces and their steps marked with blood. Here they suffered all the

> pains of hunger and thirst; the most terrible apprehensions for their fathers, husbands, brothers and sons; to which was added the sight of the town in flames: and even these horrors were increased by the explosion of the powder magazine. (62)

The scenario described here is precisely what took place in the wake of General Victor-Emmanuel Leclerc's arrival in Le Cap (Cape François) harbor with five thousand French troops. Leclerc had been sent to Saint Domingue by his brother-in-law, Napoleon Bonaparte, with the primary objective of reasserting French control of the island; indeed, as Dillon and Drexler observe, Haiti was a central piece in Napoleon's grand American plan: in keeping with the Old Regime's mercantilist policies, "Napoleon envisioned a closed French circuit of production and profit," in which Louisiana would feed the colonies that, in turn, would produce sugar and coffee for sale in Europe, thereby enriching the metropole.[148] This explains his massive military investment in the region, "sending forty thousand troops to St. Domingue in 1801."[149] However, according to Carolyn Fick:

> When Leclerc did land, Le Cap was little more than a pile of ashes. The city had been evacuated, all of the main government buildings burned-out, and the gunpowder factory blown up. It was not a spontaneous riot, but a strategically organized act of military resistance, and the most devastating war in the entire history of Saint Domingue had now begun.[150]

The significance of Leclerc's arrival (and subsequent failure to fulfill Bonaparte's wishes) raises a similar question for Sansay's readers: if this was the launch of what historians regard as the most devastating part of the Haitian Revolution, and basically the chronological springboard to Sansay's narrative – again, as the novel opens, readers are presented with an image of women and children fleeing into the mountains above a devastated Le Cap anticipating LeClerc's landing – then why doesn't it play a more significant role in the novel?

In keeping with her Gothic fiction forebears, including Ann Radcliffe and Charlotte Smith, Sansay prioritizes the politics of gender (the 'Female Gothic,' as it were) throughout the novel, and, accordingly, this opening scene makes the most sense when read in juxtaposition to a scene that unfolds much later on. That is, towards the end of the novel, and in one of the few illuminating letters that Clara composes to Mary (the letter that not only reveals Clara's *secret history* as the helpless victim of St. Louis's most brutal

Capitalism and Domestic Violence in Secret History 199

violence, but also provides an account of her taking refuge in the mountains beyond El Cobre in eastern Cuba), Sansay treats us to a most spectacular biological phenomenon – namely, the female land crab's annual migration to the sea to lay her eggs:

> my slumbers were interrupted by a most unaccountable noise, which seemed to issue from all parts of the room, not unlike the clashing of swords; and, as I listened to discover what it was, a shriek from Madame V---- increased my terror. In sounds scarcely articulate, she said a large cold animal had crept into her bosom, and in getting it out, it had seized her hand.
>
> Frightened to death I opened the door and called the guide ... When I asked for a light to search for what had disturbed us, he said it was nothing but land crabs, which, at this season, descend in countless multitudes from the mountain, in order to lay their eggs on the sea shore.
>
> The ground was covered with them, and paths were worn by them down the sides of the mountain. They strike their claws together as they move with a strange noise, and no obstacle turns them from their course. (145)

This passage neatly summarizes one of the greatest, most spectacular mass migrations on earth – the annual march of a peculiarly *unruly nature*, the female red crabs (*Gecarcinus ruricola*), to the Caribbean Sea. The event occurs each year in Cuba during the rainy season because this particular species of crab, like its prehistoric seafaring ancestor (*Gecarcoidea*), still uses gills to breathe, and it can last for several weeks depending on how far the crabs must travel to reach the coastline (sometimes as far as six miles). It is a dangerous journey, to be sure – as the crabs must avoid lengthy exposure to sunshine or risk dehydration and death, but, of course, it is absolutely necessary, as the propagation of the species depends upon their reaching the sea, whereupon each crab will plunge into the water just long enough to cast away its pouch of fertilized eggs into the sea. The hatchlings will remain in the water for about a month, before crawling back to shore to restart the cycle over again.[151] Furthermore, it is (as I've already suggested) a most spectacular, potentially sublime event because the march typically numbers in the millions, so that one can certainly understand why Sansay (via Clara) insists: "no obstacle turns them from their course" (145). Indeed, that Sansay includes the land crab migration in her Gothic novel about domestic violence, and, more importantly, that she frames this biological phenomenon within the aesthetics of the sublime certainly merits extra critical attention.

This scene merits consideration as Sansay's Caribbean version of the ghostly, peculiarly Old World hauntings – the low hollow sounds inspiring "deadly ideas" – that punctuate Ann Radcliffe's quintessential Gothic novels, including *A Sicilian Romance*.

The linkage between these two scenes (the women fleeing uphill and the female crabs descending the mountain to the sea) is most striking. But what's the point? The point may be to inspire women to rise up in "countless multitudes" against structures of oppression: marriage, the plantation, Catholic church, etc.. And, notably, that she compares the "strange noise" of the crab's crustaceous locomotion to the "clashing of swords" (145) connects nicely to the novel's ostensible topic: revolutionary warfare. As noted earlier, this scenario depicted in the novel invites readers to rebuild connections – to restore the very cycles of regeneration disrupted by man's efforts to engineer the world[152] – as well as to view things through an anarcho-feminist lens, or perspective that "moves beyond the cycloptic colonial view, envisioning ... solidarities that ... extractive capitalist economies cannot fully capture."[153] That Gómez-Barris refers to such decolonial perspectives as "submerged" neatly resonates with Sansay's invocation of the female land crab's regenerative, annual return to the sea.[154]

Of course, Sansay would not be the first novelist to advocate for such a gender-based cultural revolution. Bluestocking author, Sarah Scott's 1762 novel, *Millenium Hall*, for example, not only treats the establishment of a separatist feminist utopia, but also raises important questions about the influx of dirty money from Britain's sugar plantations in Jamaica. Scott's novel celebrates the local economy above and beyond a global economy (transoceanic system of exchange) tainted by its association with the institution of slavery. And, of course, Mary Wollstonecraft's unfinished, and posthumously published Gothic novel, *The Wrongs of Woman*, insistently rails against the institutionalized oppression of women. Wollstonecraft anticipates the MeToo Movement in her novel that aims to unite women from various social classes on the basis of their shared experiences of rape, sexual assault, and domestic violence. Indeed, the very name of the novel's main character, Maria, invites speculation about Sansay's familiarity with Wollstonecraft's work. And, in *The Story of Henrietta*, which was originally published as the second volume in the five-volume series *The Letters of a Solitary Wanderer* (1800), Charlotte Smith not only invites her readers to think about the politics of horror in a contemporaneous colonial setting (that is, without the veil of historical distance that conveniently obscures the late eighteenth-century Gothic novel's radical, if not risqué political views).[155] She also very affectively translates a number of common Gothic tropes and devices into this new Caribbean context. For example, Radcliffe's familiar banditti of Renaissance Sicily, Italy, and France become Smith's Maroons of Jamaica – that is, the insurgent, runaway slaves occupying the woods and ravines in the Blue Mountains (if not the Cockpit mountains around Trelawny Town in western Jamaica, which was the site of the 1795–6 Maroon War).[156] The uncanny (a recurring Gothic device) factors into Henrietta Maynard's surprising discovery of her mulatto half siblings – a troubling moment in the narrative, to be sure, which calls into consciousness Henrietta's latent racism, or as George Boulukos refers to it, the "horror of hybridity."[157] Like the house of Mazzini (or castle) which lies in ruins at the outset of Radcliffe's *A Sicilian Romance*, Henrietta's family home, the Maynard plantation, is laid to waste by a troop of runaway slaves – a plot point that both precipitates the main characters' retreat to England, and conveniently foreshadows (if not calls for) the end of Great Britain's participation in the slave system (i.e. the Slave Trade Act of 1807 and the Slavery Abolition Act of 1833). And, finally, drawing upon the work of Ann Radcliffe, Regina Maria Roche, Eliza Parsons, et al., Smith's novel partakes of a Female Gothic tradition that, as Anna Shajirat suggests, pushed the discussion of Gothic ruins beyond "moldering castles and crumbling historical monuments" to consider the psychological decay of women coping under patriarchal structures of oppression – i.e. another sort of ruin: "the physical and mental decay the Gothic heroine undergoes on the path from childhood innocence to adult experience."[158] Given the attention that Smith gives to Henrietta's "calamitous condition,"[159] one cannot help but read the novel as at least partially, if not predominantly Female Gothic – bearing in mind, of course, that Smith folds into this Gothic standard a series of linked concerns about the horrors of slavery and contagion of racism spreading throughout the Atlantic world at this historic juncture (i.e. on the eve of Haitian independence). In other words, Smith's clever transposition of the Female Gothic to the British West Indies may well have provided Sansay with the inspiration for *Secret History* – that is, to reimagine her personal experiences in Saint Domingue in the form of a Female Gothic narrative / novel. For, as Burnham explains, "*Secret History* is generally recognized as a fictionalized transformation of Sansay's actual letters to [Aaron] Burr, written while she was trapped in the small portion of the city of Le Cap . . . that remained in French control before it finally fell to the black army."[160] Given the novel's obvious links to this Female Gothic tradition, it's easy to see why one might be encouraged to read this land crab migration scene as the inspiration for women to rise up in "countless multitudes" against patriarchal structures of oppression.

However, that Clara's route through Cuba leads to El Cobre, the historical site of an important slave revolt, simultaneously reinforces *and* complicates this reading. On the one hand, there is an unmistakable resonance between Clara's escape from an abusive relationship and the rebellious, runaway slaves who established themselves in the mountains beyond the copper mines of El Cobre. To be sure, Sansay's decision to situate the conclusion of Clara's narrative in and around El Cobre in eastern Cuba does not seem at all coincidental, as the slaves of El Cobre were particularly determined to obtain their freedom through various different avenues, including legal petition, revolt, and marronage. For starters, in 1670, as a result of the original copper mining company's bankruptcy, the slaves (and any other physical property associated with the mine) reverted to the monarchy of Castile. "The slaves of El Cobre became royal slaves with significant traditional privileges," which, as Franklin W. Knight notes, they evidently understood "better than the officials at the royal court." For much of the eighteenth century, "the slaves exploited Spanish laws and customs to establish a viable self-governing community" (something like a pueblo), "in which their town council supervised free people."[161] Indeed, as María Díaz observes, "the *royal slaves* of El Cobre were able to capitalize on what they deemed to be their special status and relation to the king, linking it, with some success, to a number of prerogatives, including the option to live as a *pueblo*."[162] Although they were required by the Crown to not only participate in the *mita* – that is, supply temporary workers to build fortifications – but also "form a defense militia in service of the king," Aline Helg points out that otherwise, "in daily life, [the slaves] had near-total autonomy: men largely concentrated on farming and women on copper mining."[163] Populations increased steadily, and, according to Helg, "between 1700 and 1769, 167 slaves (predominantly men) were able to purchase their freedom through coartación ... In the 1770s, El Cobre numbered nearly 900 'slaves' without masters and 450 *libres de color*."[164] However, through a series of circumstances, the mines were eventually reprivatized by the end of the century, and a new category of cheap labor was invented – the wage slave – as Knight explains: "Africans who had purchased their freedom were indeed free," while "those still determined to be enslaved had to be paid a wage by the new operators."[165]

Sansay's choice of locations in eastern Cuba does not seem at all coincidental. She cleverly invites us to compare Clara's escape from her awful marriage to St. Louis to the slaves of El Cobre, and their carefully determined efforts to live autonomously – an historical unfolding which Knight calls a "most anomalous situation in the American slave system: enslaved people with more extensive privileges than freeholders."[166] Of course, it may be worth noting too that, after the Spanish abandoned the mine, a British gentleman reopened it in the early 1830s as El Compañía Consolidada de Minas del Cobre (Cobre Mining Co.)[167] – but, again, the important thing here is the considerable critical resonance between Clara's and the royal slaves' efforts to live autonomously.

On the other hand, the narrative's relocation in Cuba recalls the irony of the Haitian Revolution. While (as noted earlier) Haiti's independence inadvertently "led to the expansion and solidification of slavery in the United States as new slave states were created in the territory of the Louisiana Purchase,"[168] a second, similarly significant side effect was the expansion of sugar production elsewhere in the Atlantic world. The Spanish and Portuguese, for example, were quick to grasp the economic significance of the revolution in terms of its disruption to the global sugar trade, seizing the opportunity to step up production in Cuba and Brazil. Antonio Benítez-Rojo refers to this phase in Cuban history as the Creole (or plantation) machine. Highlighting the environmental consequences of such a dramatic increase in Cuba's sugar production, he writes:

> It is possible to observe in short order the demolishing stride of the sugar mill through the length and breadth of the island . . . Spreading along the roads that led out of Havana, the sugar plantations extended toward the west, the south, and the east of the city. With my imagination . . . I'll take the southern road toward the valley of Güines: in 1780, I see the chimneys of only two sugar mills; by 1792, there are nine of them; by 1804, twenty-six; in 1827, I count forty-seven; in 1846, seventy-six; in 1859, the entire region is smoking with the fire of eighty-nine chimneys . . .[169]

Because Europeans' demand for sugar did not suddenly drop off in the wake of the Haitian Revolution, but, rather, has increased steadily through to the present day, France's bust in the Caribbean would mean Spain's boom. "The development of sugar in Cuba in the nineteenth century was spectacular," continues Benítez-Rojo: "there were periods in which the annual increase in sugar production was 25 percent."[170]

Again, the Haitian Revolution not only catapulted the U.S. into a starring role in the global economy, as Dillon and Drexler explain: "the value of cotton shot up just after the Haitian Revolution and was fundamental to the growth of the U.S. economy,"[171] but Cuba also would become the shining star of nineteenth-century sugar production.

And so, is it not ironic that Clara finds freedom on an island that is not safely removed from, but all the more thoroughly entrenched in a plantation economy that was not only "inescapably transoceanic and tragically destructive," as Burnham suggests,[172] but also deliberately designed to satisfy the interests / desires of capitalist slaveholders / powerful European men? If not to inspire women to rise up in multitudes against structures of oppression, then, perhaps Sansay intended the women's flight / land crab migration scene to situate cycles of capitalist exploitation (boom and bust) in the web of life (birth and death). Perhaps the point is to elicit a comparison between the familiar boom and bust cycles of resource extraction and the routine exploitation of women. The close connections between the labor of childbirth and death for women in the eighteenth and nineteenth centuries would reinforce this boom and bust / birth and death reading. And, for example, Cheney notes that, "in a process analogous to the islands of the Caribbean, intensive [agricultural] development [in Haiti] occurred sequentially from plain to plain."[173] As the soil of one plain became depleted through intensive sugar cultivation, plantations would rapidly fill other as yet unused areas of the island, thereby inaugurating a new boom period there. This "familiar cycle of declining soil fertility in established plains and the migration to new ones" also helps to explain why, in the wake of the Haitian Revolution, Cuba – "with its great expanses of comparatively virgin soil," would become the "new Eldorado of the Caribbean littoral in the early nineteenth century."[174] The question that Sansay's novel raises, then, is whether women are not fated to endure a similarly troubling boom and bust phase as their beauty blossoms and then fades in the eyes of such privileged men as Clara's husband, Louis, or General Rochambeau.

The secret history that lies at the center of Sansay's novel is not merely one woman's – i.e. Clara's – limited experience of domestic violence, but a much more general history of violence that applies to both human and extra-human natures, including (most importantly) the brutality to which *all* women are subjected in a plantation economy designed to satisfy the interests of powerful men. And in this respect, I argue, Sansay's *Secret History* invites us to grapple with the misogyny that continues to inform global capitalism in the twenty-first century.

Notes

1. Henrietta Marchant Liston, Caribbean Travel Diary (1801), Unpublished. Special Collections, National Library of Scotland, p. 39.
2. John Smith, *A Description of New England* (1616), *Captain John Smith: Writings, With Other Narratives of Roanoke, Jamestown, and the First English Settlement of America* (New York: The Library of America, 2007), 143.
3. This gesture resonates with Barbara Fuchs's notion of colonial quotation. See Fuchs, "Conquering Islands: Contextualizing *The Tempest*," *Shakespeare Quarterly* 48, no. 1 (Spring 1997), 45–62.
4. See Woodes Rogers, *A Cruising Voyage Round the World: First to the South-Seas, thence to the East-Indies, and homewards by the Cape of Good Hope* . . . (1712) (Amsterdam: N. Israel, 1969).
5. Richard Ligon, *A True and Exact History of the Island of Barbados* (1657) (Indianapolis: Hackett Publishing, 2011).
6. A. C. Carmichael, *Domestic Manners and Social Condition of the White, Coloured, and Negro Population of the West Indies*, Two Volumes (London: Whittaker, Treacher, and Co., 1833).
7. Beth Fowkes Tobin, *Colonizing Nature: The Tropics in British Arts and Letters, 1760–1820* (Philadelphia: University of Pennsylvania Press, 2005), 74–5.
8. Janet Schaw, *Journal of a Lady of Quality; Being a Narrative of a Journey from Scotland to the West Indies, North Carolina, and Portugal, in the years 1774 to 1776*, edited by Evangeline Walker Andrews, in collaboration with Charles McLean Andrews (New Haven: Yale University Press, 1923), 91.
9. *Lady Nugent's Journal of her residence in Jamaica from 1801–1805*, edited by Philip Wright (Kingston, Jamaica: Institute of Jamaica, 1966), 25.
10. Leonora Sansay, *Secret History; or, The Horrors of St. Domingo* (1808), edited by Michael J. Drexler (Peterborough, ON: Broadview Press, 2008), 70. Further citations will be parenthetical.
11. Michael Pollan, *The Botany of Desire: A Plant's-Eye View of the World* (New York: Random House, 2001), xxii.
12. Pollan, *Botany of Desire*, 30.
13. Charles Darwin, *On The Origin of Species by Means of Natural Selection or the Preservation of Favoured Races in the Struggle for Life* (1859) (Oxford: Oxford University Press, 2008), 34.
14. Pollan, *Botany of Desire*, xvii.

15. Darwin, *Origin of Species*, 27.
16. Jason Moore, *Capitalism in the Web of Life: Ecology and the Accumulation of Capital* (London: Verso, 2015), 36.
17. Paul Cheney, *Cul de Sac: Patrimony, Capitalism, and Slavery in French Saint-Domingue* (Chicago: University of Chicago Press, 2017).
18. Quoted in Cheney, *Cul de Sac*, 53.
19. Moore, *Capitalism*, 17.
20. Michelle Burnham, *Transoceanic America: Risk, Writing, and Revolution in the Global Pacific* (Oxford: Oxford University Press, 2019), 19.
21. Burnham, *Transoceanic*, 179.
22. Sharae Deckard, "Early Modern Paradise and the Age of Imperialism," in *Paradise Discourse, Imperialism, and Globalization: Exploiting Eden* (New York and London: Routledge, 2010), 12.
23. Moore, *Capitalism*, 14.
24. Sidney W. Mintz, *Sweetness and Power: The Place of Sugar in Modern History* (New York: Penguin, 1986), xviii. Laurent Dubois and John D. Garrigus note too, that, in the eighteenth century, Saint Domingue was "the most profitable plantation colony in the New World," responsible for the production of "40 percent of Europe's sugar and 60 percent of its coffee." See Dubois and Garrigus, *Slave Revolution in the Caribbean, 1789 – 1804: A Brief History with Documents* (New York: Bedford/St. Martin's Press, 2006), 8.
25. Helen Hunt, "'Fascinate, Intoxicate, Transport': Uncovering Women's Erotic Dominance in Leonora Sansay's *Secret History*," *Legacy: A Journal of American Women Writers* 33, no. 1 (2016), 31–54.
26. Burnham, *Transoceanic*, 19.
27. Burnham, *Transoceanic*, 180.
28. See Albert O. Hirschman, *The Passions and the Interests: Political Arguments for Capitalism before Its Triumph*, Twentieth Anniversary Edition (Princeton: Princeton University Press, 1997).
29. Mintz, *Sweetness and Power*, xxvii.
30. Vandana Shiva, *Biopiracy: The Plunder of Nature and Knowledge* (Boston: South End Press, 1997), 63.
31. Macarena Gómez-Barris, *The Extractive Zone: Social Ecologies and Decolonial Perspectives* (Durham, NC: Duke University Press, 2017), 124.
32. Hirschman, *Passions*.
33. David Hume, *Essays Moral, Political, and Literary*, Vol. 1, edited by T. H. Green and T. H. Grose (London: Longmans, 1898), 176. Quoted in Hirschman, *Passions*, 54.
34. Hirschman, *Passions*, 41.
35. David Hume, *A Treatise of Human Nature* (1739–40) (Oxford: Clarendon Press, 1978), 492.

36. Anthony Benezet, *Some Historical Account of Guinea, Its Situation, Produce and the general Disposition of its Inhabitants. With An inquiry into the Rise and Progress of the Slave-Trade, its Nature and Lamentable Effects* (Philadelphia: Joseph Crukshank, 1771), 143–4.
37. Olaudah Equiano, *The Interesting Narrative and Other Writings*, edited by Vincent Carretta (New York: Penguin, 1995), 233–4.
38. David Hume, "Of Interest," *Essays Moral, Political, and Literary*, edited by Eugene F. Miller (Indianapolis: Liberty Fund, 1994), 301.
39. Richard Steele, *The Spectator*, no. 11 (13 March 1711), *The Commerce of Everyday Life: Selections from* The Tatler *and* The Spectator, edited by Erin Mackie (New York: Bedford/St. Martin's, 1998), 194.
40. Steele, *Spectator*, no. 11, 194.
41. Steele, Spectator, no. 11, 195.
42. Sudan, *The Alchemy of Empire: Abject Materials and the Technologies of Colonialism* (New York: Fordham University Press, 2016), 5.
43. Carloyn Fick, *The Making of Haiti: The Saint Domingue Revolution from Below* (Knoxville: University of Tennessee Press, 1990), 16.
44. Deckard, *Paradise Discourse*, 12.
45. Cheney, *Cul de Sac*, 150.
46. Cheney, *Cul de Sac*, 150.
47. Mintz, *Sweetness and Power*, 46–7.
48. Cheney, *Cul de Sac*, 6.
49. Mintz, *Sweetness and Power*, xxvii.
50. Tobin, *Colonizing Nature*, 74–5.
51. Christopher S. Campbell, "Poaceae," *Encyclopedia Britannica* (7 October 2016), available at <https://britannica.com/plan/poaceae>. Accessed 14 November 2020.
52. Mintz, *Sweetness and Power*, 19.
53. See Fick, *Making of Haiti*, and also Cheney, *Cul de* Sac, 6, 49–50.
54. Cheney, *Cul de Sac*, 49.
55. Rev. James Ramsay, *An Essay on the Treatment and Conversion of African Slaves in the British Sugar Colonies* (1784), quoted in John Gilmore, *The Poetics of Empire: A Study of James Grainger's* The Sugar-Cane (London: Athlone Press, 2000), 210.
56. *Lady Nugent's Journal*, 62.
57. *Lady Nugent's Journal*, 62–3.
58. Cheney, *Cul de Sac*, 63.
59. Cheney, *Cul de Sac*, 60.
60. Quoted in Mintz, *Sweetness and Power*, 47–8.
61. Laurent Dubois and John D. Garrigus, *Slave Revolution*, 10–11.
62. Paul Virilio, *Speed and Politics*, translated by Mark Polizzotti (Cambridge, MA: MIT Press, 2006).
63. Mintz, *Sweetness and Power*, 114.
64. Burnham, *Transoceanic*, 184.

65. Schaw, *Journal*, 115.
66. Schaw, *Journal*, 130.
67. Schaw, *Journal*, 135.
68. Schaw, *Journal*, 137.
69. Burnham, "Female Bodies," 184.
70. Gómez-Barris, *Extractive Zone*, 114.
71. Moore, *Capitalism*, 29.
72. *Lady Nugent's Journal*, 68.
73. *Lady Nugent's Journal*, 69.
74. *Lady Nugent's Journal*, 68.
75. *Lady Nugent's Journal*, 68.
76. *Lady Nugent's Journal*, 69.
77. *Lady Nugent's Journal*, 69.
78. Shiva, *Biopiracy*, 5.
79. T. M. Devine, *Scotland's Empire: The Origins of the Global Diaspora* (London: Penguin, 2003), 240.
80. Devine, *Scotland's Empire*, 240.
81. Evangeline Walker Andrews, "Introduction," *Journal of A Lady of Quality* (New Haven: Yale University Press, 1923), 7.
82. Schaw, *Journal*, 104.
83. Schaw, *Journal*, 104.
84. Quoted in Dubois and Garrigus, *Slave Revolution*, 168.
85. Quoted in Dubois and Garrigus, *Slave Revolution*, 168.
86. Quoted in Dubois and Garrigus, *Slave Revolution*, 169.
87. Cheney, *Cul de Sac*, 130.
88. Schaw, *Journal*, 113.
89. *Lady Nugent's Journal*, 58.
90. Carmichael, *Domestic Manners*, 20.
91. Carmichael, *Domestic Manners*, 18.
92. Cheney, *Cul de Sac*, 133.
93. *Lady Nugent's Journal*, 41.
94. *Lady Nugent's Journal*, 57.
95. Deckard, *Paradise Discourse*, 12.
96. Schaw, *Journal*, 95.
97. Schaw, *Journal*, 95.
98. Tobin, *Colonizing Nature*, 73.
99. Mary Prince, *The History of Mary Prince, a West Indian Slave. Related by Herself.* (London: F. Westley and A. H. Davis, 1831), 6.
100. Carmichael, *Domestic Manners*, 21.
101. Louise V. North, "Introduction," *The Travel Diaries of Henrietta Marchant Liston: North America and Lower Canada, 1796–1800* (Lanham, MD: Lexington Books, 2014), xiii–xvii.
102. See North, "Introduction," *Travel*, i–xvii.
103. See the 1801 Caribbean travel diary of Henrietta Marchant Liston, 13–14.

104. *Lady Nugent's Journal*, 25.
105. Schaw, *Journal*, 90.
106. Schaw, *Journal*, 91.
107. Schaw, *Journal*, 126.
108. *Lady Nugent's Journal*, 63.
109. See Derek Walcott, *Sea Grapes* (New York: Farrar, Strauss, and Giroux, 1976).
110. Griffith Hughes, *The Natural History of Barbados* (London: Printed for the Author, 1750), 123–4.
111. Again, I use the term *empire writing* to describe texts that not only reflect the global expansion and consolidation of the British Empire, but also to those that make this historical-ecological transformation possible.
112. Walcott, *Sea Grapes*, 3.
113. North, "Introduction," xi.
114. Gómez-Barris, *Extractive Zone*, 114.
115. Schaw, *Journal*, 127.
116. Schaw, *Journal*, 115.
117. Prince, *History*, 6.
118. Prince, *History*, 1.
119. Equiano, *Interesting Narrative*, 111.
120. Equiano, *Interesting Narrative*, 111.
121. Michael J. Drexler, "Introduction," *Secret History* (Peterborough, ON: Broadview Press, 2008), 27.
122. Burnham, *Transoceanic*, 181.
123. Cheney, *Cul de Sac*, 1.
124. Cheney, *Cul de Sac*, 1.
125. See the Global Slavery Index. Available at <https://www.globalslaveryindex.org/2018/findings/highlights>. Accessed 14 August 2020.
126. Siân Silyn Roberts, *Gothic Subjects: The Transformation of Individualism in American Fiction, 1790–1861* (Philadelphia: University of Pennsylvania Press, 2014), 253.
127. Roberts, *Gothic Subjects*, 252.
128. Roberts, *Gothic Subjects*, 251.
129. Burnham, "Female Bodies," 180.
130. Abby L. Goode, "Gothic Fertility in Leonora Sansay's 'Secret History,'" *Early American Literature* 50, no. 2 (2015), 451.
131. Melissa Adams-Campbell, "Romantic Revolutions: Love and Violence in Leonora Sansay's *Secret History, or The Horrors of St. Domingo*," *Studies in American Fiction* 39, no.2 (2012), 125.
132. Liston, Caribbean travel diary, 39.
133. Equiano, *Interesting Narrative*, 234.
134. Michael J. Drexler, "Appendix B: Literary Selections," *Secret History* (Peterborough, ON: Broadview Press, 2008), 262.
135. *Ovid's Fasti*, translated by Sir James George Frazer (London: William Heinnemann, 1931), 277.

136. Shiva, *Biopiracy*, 57.
137. *Ovid's Fasti*, 279–81.
138. Deckard, *Paradise Discourse*, 12.
139. Cheney, *Cul de Sac*, 34–5.
140. Cheney, *Cul de Sac*, 150.
141. Schaw, *Journal*, 112–13.
142. Dubois and Garrigus, *Slave Revolution*, 10.
143. Hume, "Of Interest," 301.
144. See the Global Slavery Index. Available at <https://www.globalslaveryindex.org/2018/findings/highlights> Accessed 14 August 2020.
145. Dubois and Garrigus, *Slave Revolution*, 8.
146. Dubois and Garrigus, *Slave Revolution*, 39.
147. Elizabeth Maddox Dillon and Michael Drexler, eds. *The Haitian Revolution and the Early United States: Histories, Textualities, Geographies* (Philadelphia: University of Pennsylvania Press, 2016), 10.
148. Dillon and Drexler, *Haitian Revolution*, 7.
149. Dillon and Drexler, *Haitian Revolution*, 7.
150. Fick, *Making of Haiti*, 211.
151. For a spectacular summary of the red land crab's migration in Cuba, see the PBS's *Nature* series episode devoted to "Cuba: Wild Island of the Caribbean," available at <https://pbs.org/wnet/nature/cuba-wild-island-of-the-caribbean-cuban-crab-invasion/1247/>. Accessed 1 June 2023.
152. Shiva, *Biopiracy*, 63.
153. Gómez-Barris, *Extractive Zone*, 124.
154. Gómez-Barris, *Extractive Zone*, 124.
155. Examples include *A Sicilian Romance* (1790), in which Ann Radcliffe's proto-feminist Gothic heroine, Julia, boldly challenges patriarchal structures of oppression, including the institution of marriage and the Catholic Church. Julia's most outspoken feminist statement occurs near the novel's end when she says to her a mother, who for many years has been incarcerated in the southern fabric of Castle Mazzini: "Oh! Let me lead you to light and life ... Surely heaven can bless me with no greater good than by making me the deliverer of my mother." Ann Radcliffe, *A Sicilian Romance* (1790) (Oxford: Oxford University Press, 1998), 182. Or consider Victoria's violent contravention of traditional notions of femininity in Charlotte Dacre's *Zofloya, or the Moor* (1806).
156. Smith's male protagonist, Denbigh, mentions the Blue Mountains in Letter III, but as Janina Nordius points out, it's more than likely that Smith confused the geography of Jamaica here, since it was the Cockpit mountains around Trelawny Town in western Jamaica, not the Blue Mountains to the northeast of Kingston, that figure in the 1795–6 Maroon War. Noted in the Valancourt edition of Charlotte

Smith's *The Story of Henrietta*, edited by Janina Nordius (Kansas City, MO: Valancourt Books, 2012), n.105.
157. George Boulukos, "The Horror of Hybridity: Enlightenment, Anti-Slavery and Racial Disgust in Charlotte Smith's *The Story of Henrietta* (1800)," *Slavery and The Cultures of Abolition: Essays Marking the Bicentennial of the British Abolition Act of 1807*, edited by Brycchan Carey and Peter J. Kitson (Cambridge: D. S. Brewer, 2007), 87–109.
158. Anna Shajirat, "'Bending her gentle head to swift decay': Horror, Loss, and Fantasy in the Female Gothic of Ann Radcliffe and Regina Maria Roche," *Studies in Romanticism* 58, no. 3 (Fall 2019), 383.
159. Charlotte Smith, *The Story of Henrietta* (1800), edited by Janina Nordius (Kansas City, MO: Valancourt Books, 2012), 49. Further citations will be parenthetical.
160. Burnham, *Transoceanic*, 181.
161. Franklin W. Knight, "Slavery," *Encyclopedia of African-American Culture and History*, Volume 5, Second Edition (Gale: 2006), 2061.
162. María Elena Díaz, "To Live as a *Pueblo*: A Contentious Endeavor; El Cobre, Cuba, 1670s–1790s," *Afro-Latino Voices: Narratives from the Early Modern Ibero-Atlantic World, 1550–1812*, edited by Kathryn Joy McKnight and Leo J. Garofalo (Indianapolis: Hackett Publishing Co., 2009), 127.
163. Aline Helg, *Slaves No More: Self-Liberation before Abolitionism in the Americas*, translated by Lara Vergnaud (Chapel Hill: University of North Carolina Press, 2019), 69.
164. Helg, *Slaves No More*, 69.
165. Franklin W. Knight, "Review," *Slaves No More: Self-Liberation before Abolitionism in the Americas* by Aline Helg, *The Americas* 77, no. 1 (January 2020), 153.
166. Knight, "Slavery," 2061.
167. See the Cornish in Latin America. Available at <https://projects.exeter.ac.uk/cornishlatin/cobre.html>. Accessed 14 August 2020.
168. Dubois and Garrigus, *Slave Revolution*, 8.
169. Antonio Benítez-Rojo, "Sugar and the Environment in Cuba," translated by James Maraniss, *Caribbean Literature and the Environment: Between Nature and Culture*, edited by Elizabeth DeLoughrey, Renée K. Gosson, and George B. Handley (Charlottesville: University of Virginia Press, 2005), 40.
170. Benítez-Rojo, "Sugar," 41.
171. Dillon and Drexler, *Haitian Revolution*, 12.
172. Burnham, *Transoceanic*, 19.
173. Cheney, *Cul de Sac*, 4.
174. Cheney, *Cul de Sac*, 5–6.

Chapter 4

Robert Louis Stevenson and the "Horror of Creeping Things"

In his essay, "Isla Incognita" (1973), Saint Lucian poet, Derek Walcott draws our attention to the significance of noise as language, while simultaneously stressing the important, yet often unacknowledged role that both metaphor (figurative language) and walking play in human apprehension of the natural world:

> It has taken me over thirty years, and my race hundreds, to feel the fibers spread from the splayed toes and grip this earth, the arms knot into boles and put out leaves. When that begins, this is the beginning of seasons, cycle time. The noise my leaves make is my language. In it is tunneled the roar of seas of a lost ocean. It is a fresh sound. Let me not be ashamed to write like this, because it supports this thesis, that our only true apprehensions are through metaphor, that the old botanical names, the old processes cannot work for us. Let's walk.[1]

As I argue in this chapter, the work of Robert Louis Stevenson (no stranger to the eco-poetics of walking) similarly foregrounds the power of metaphor (and simile) to root humanity in nature. And, notably, in a letter that keenly draws upon one of his numerous walking excursions in Samoa, he aptly draws our attention to the ecological significance of the tropical bush as soundscape: "there, where I was, I just put down the sound to the mystery of the bush; where no sound now surprises – and any sound alarms."[2]

"Waves of Translation"

The village of Braemar lies in the shadows of *Am Monadh Ruadh* (the Russet-colored Mountains, or Cairngorms), just south of the confluence of the rivers Dee and Clunie in the eastern Highlands of Scotland (Aberdeenshire). Comprised of solidly built stone cottages and stalkers' lodges, the village is supposed to be one of the coldest places in Scotland. And it was here, residing amidst this impressive haven for wildlife in one of these sturdy retreats that Stevenson composed the bulk of one of his most cherished works, *Treasure Island*, an adventure tale about greed that evidently sprung from his cartographic imagination between the months of August and September 1881 (the narrative is famously supposed to have been built around a map sketched by Stevenson). Although the motivation for this undertaking was primarily parental in scope – presumably it was to produce a yarn sufficiently action-packed to entertain his stepson, Lloyd – this place (the Cairngorms) seems an odd place to launch into a seafaring adventure. There is no shortage of fresh water in and around Braemar, to be sure, but the Cairngorms feel just about as far removed from the sea as you can possibly get in Scotland. Red squirrels may still be seen leaping from branch to branch like "tufted acrobats" in among the pine trees that straddle the village. And, aside from the surrounding mountains and ancient Caledonian and Birkwood forests, perhaps the most striking feature of this particular region is the chorus of birdsong that fills the crisp air – a feature that would not have been lost on Stevenson, who, according to his cousin and biographer, Graham Balfour, was "very sensitive" to the songs of birds.[3] Red grouse, for example, perched on lichen-covered rocks sing a melancholy song – a sort of existential measure of staccato to offset the steady roll of the burn – that tends to make the lonely walker feel even more so, though by no means adversely. When startled the grouse dart from the moorland heather in a frenzy of flapping wings.[4]

I cite the composition of *Treasure Island* in Braemar in part because I think it curious that Stevenson's island literature begins *not* in Wick, nor the Outer Hebrides, not on the isle of Mull, nor Orkney and Shetland, which he had visited in the company of his lighthouse engineering father aboard the yacht, Pharos (14–29 June 1869). Instead, *Treasure Island* was born in the comparatively landlocked Cairngorm mountains, and I am encouraged to read this imaginative coincidence of land and sea as symptomatic of the fact that the sea, however far removed it may seem, is always "around us," a fact that is perhaps all the more obvious today owing to climate change. As marine biologist Rachel Carson explains in her influential book, *The Sea Around Us*, "in its broader meaning, that other concept of the ancients remains" – namely, that "outside, bathing the periphery of the land world, was Oceanus":[5]

> For the sea lies all about us. The commerce of all lands must cross it. The very winds that move over the lands have been cradled on its broad expanse and seek ever to return to it. The continents themselves dissolve and pass into the sea, in grain after grain of eroded land. So the rains that rose from it return again in rivers. In its mysterious past it encompasses all the dim origins of life and receives in the end ... the dead husks of that same life. For all at last return to the sea – to Oceanus, the ocean river, like the ever-flowing stream of time, the beginning and the end.[6]

Carson provides here a remarkably poetic account of the ocean's central role in the cycle of life on earth. Her description of the slow dissolution of the continents into the sea – "in grain after grain of eroded land" – speaks to the inevitable, ongoing communication between land and sea, a circumstance that figures in Elizabeth DeLoughrey's debunking of the myth of isolated island space: *Routes and Roots*. DeLoughrey relies on a similarly dynamic, or dialectical model of geography – one that takes into account the cyclical rhythms of the ocean – to "position island cultures in the world historical process."[7] Notably, Carson's highlighting the incredible distance traveled by a single wave suggests that there is no island on earth truly isolated. The sea is not a barrier between land masses, but a sort of medium that enables information (physical, biological, etc.) to be carried across great distances from one place to another. Indeed, one of the examples that Carson offers in her detailing of the life histories of waves are those which pass over a hydrodynamic recorder lying at the bottom of the sea at Land's End. "Most of the waves that roll over the recorder," explains Carson, "are born in the stormy North Atlantic eastward of Newfoundland and the south of Greenland":

> Some can be traced to tropical storms on the opposite side of the Atlantic, moving through the West Indies and along the coast of Florida. A few have rolled up from the southernmost part of the world, taking a great-circle course all the way from Cape Horn to Land's End, a journey of 6000 miles.[8]

So sublime are the forces of wind and water that it boggles the mind (and not merely from a meteorological standpoint) to think of the "messages" that these waves carry from such "far-off places." Darwin records an interesting example in *The Voyage of the Beagle* of his having caught a considerable number of beetles floating in the ocean some seventeen miles off the shores of Argentina. His explanation speaks to the ocean's role as message carrier:

At first I thought that these insects had been blown from the shore, but upon reflecting that out of the eight species four were aquatic, and two others partly so in their habits, it appears to me more probable that they were floated into the sea by a small stream which drains a lake near Cape Corrientes.[9]

I think Stevenson profoundly understood Carson's point about the encircling sea, so much so that even in Braemar he felt its presence. This may be owing to the education he received from his father, Thomas, a lighthouse engineer who dedicated himself to the study of waves. Indeed, one of Thomas Stevenson's great claims to fame is that of being the first man to ever measure the force of an ocean wave, something which he accomplished through his use of a dynamometer, a tool that he invented to gauge the force of waves pummeling the coasts of Scotland, waves such as those which tore away the breakwater (an 800-ton block of concrete) at Wick in December 1872. Of course, the sea is a most *unruly nature*, and with this mechanism Stevenson's father determined that "in winter gales the force of a wave might be as great as 6000 pounds to the square foot."[10] R. L. Stevenson, too, was similarly fascinated with the force of such waves, as is evident in a letter he wrote from Wick to his mother in September 1868, while he was preparing to become a lighthouse engineer (a pursuit that he would obviously abandon to focus on writing):

> I stood a long while at the cape watching the sea below me; I hear its dull, monotonous roar this moment below the shrieking of the wind; and there came ever recurring to my mind the verse I am so fond of: –
> "But yet the Lord that is on high
>   Is more of might by far
> Than noise of many waters is
>   Or great sea-billows are."
> The thunder at the wall when it first struck – the rush along ever growing higher – the great jet of snow-white spray some forty feet above you – and the "noise of many waters," the roar, the hiss, the "shrieking" . . . as it fell head over heels at your feet.[11]

As the citation of Psalm 93: 4 here suggests, Stevenson was clearly inspired by the poetry of the sea around him. Similarly, a survey of Thomas Stevenson's papers reveals someone concerned not solely with documenting the sublime force of sea waves with his dynamometer, though he was, indeed, thoroughly preoccupied with such careful measurements (his diaries are filled with these details). He also occasionally displays an aesthetic appreciation for the nature of wave motion. Consider, for example, the following passage from Thomas Stevenson's Skerryvore Diary (1843) – "Nothing can be more beautiful than to see the harmonious intersections of these waves" (23 Sunday).[12] He goes on to explain that, "all sea waves are to a greater and less extent waves of translation."

The sort of careful observation required to draw such a conclusion recalls R. L. Stevenson's descriptions of waves in his story, "The Merry Men." The title of this story refers to a cluster of waves that batter the southwest end of Aros, a fictional islet based on the actual tidal islet of Erraid, which lies off the southwestern edge of the Isle of Mull near the village of Fionnphort:

> At the seaward end there comes the strongest bubble; and it's here that these big breakers dance together – the dance of death, it may be called – that have got the name, in these parts, of the Merry Men. I have heard it said that they run fifty feet high; but that must be the green water only, for the spray runs twice as high as that. Whether they got the name from their movements, which are swift and antic, or from the shouting they make about the turn of the tide, so that all Aros shaked with it, is more than I can tell.[13]

Erraid, as I explain later, plays a significant role in Stevenson's writing. This passage, in particular, though, reveals the considerable influence of his father's scientific study of the force of waves. Indeed, *The Merry Men* is not merely a story about family, greed, and murder – the sinfulness of Gordon Darnaway's plundering of local shipwrecks. As the title implies, it is a story first and foremost about the sea that encircles the Isle of Mull (and islet of Erraid), and how that sea implicates an otherwise isolated family / region / culture in the sin of the world (i.e. global capitalism) at large. As Gordon Darnaway explains to his nephew, Charlie (the story's protagonist): "There's a sair sprang o' the auld sin o' the world in yon sea."[14] This is an important point, one that clearly invites us to reflect upon what Michelle Burnham describes as a "network of connections" that manifest between otherwise disparate / distant geographies when one reads literature in a "maritime global context."[15] In *The Merry Men*, Stevenson invites his readers to do precisely that – specifically, to think about maritime connections between the islet of Erraid, Spain, Africa, and the Caribbean. Or, rather, the implication here is that no island – not even a desert place like Aros / Erraid – merits consideration as truly isolated (or safely removed) from the sins of the world. Perhaps this explains Darnaway's prior exclamation, "O, sirs ... the horror – the horror o' the sea!"[16] But without offering any other particulars to define the horror in question, except that Darnaway's overpowering greed appears to stem from his communion with the Merry Men, I think we can safely assume that it is a horror inspired by the awful greed that precipitates Europeans' construction of a global economy – a world that, as Burnham observes (and, no doubt, Stevenson fully understood) was built upon not merely transatlantic, but also a variety of global transoceanic connections, thereby taking into account the boundless nature of oceanic water itself. And I say this, in part, because the racist discourse that punctuates Charlie's narrative after a black castaway turns up in Sandag Bay on Aros invites us to link that greed to the sinfulness of the transatlantic slave trade, which, of course, played an integral role in the sugar revolution and corresponding exponential growth of Britain's transoceanic maritime empire. Let us not forget, for example, the Spanish efforts to settle the Juan Fernández archipelago in the Pacific (Chapter 1), including the introduction of goats, turnips, etc. without which Selkirk might never have lived to provide Defoe with a model for Robinson Crusoe. And, as noted, in Chapters 2 and 3, the British East India Company's monopoly of tea growing in India played a crucial role in sugar's rising economic and cultural significance.[17]

Indeed, in as much as Olaudah Equiano, in his *Interesting Narrative*, relies upon a metaphor of contagion in his insistence that the institution of slavery "taints what it touches!" – so too does Darnaway appear to be infected by the greed that travels on the ocean. This is another good example of the double-internality that informs Jason Moore's critical analysis of capitalism in the web of life – i.e. the nature-in-capitalism / capitalism-in-nature. *The Merry Men* (and Darnford's madness) reveals to us the sheer impossibility of even the most seemingly isolated community living outside the boundaries of capitalist development. Charlie's recognition – "They seemed, indeed, to be part of the world's evil and the tragic side of life"[18] – reinforces these connections. In short, the sea always seems to figure into Stevenson's literary imagination. And is this not the basis of Stevenson's potential sympathetic identification with Darnaway, who is infected with "a constant haunting thought of the sea"?[19]

Furthermore, it is not solely the awesome power of Nature that intrigues Stevenson, but also the subtle, insinuation of nature into one's life. Consider, for example, his insightful analysis of the human significance of roads. In a quaint little essay aptly titled, "Roads," Stevenson celebrates the "quieter kinds of English landscape." He observes how footpaths and roadways alert us (as *trespassers*) to things we might take for granted otherwise: namely, the "subdued note[s]" of the landscape. He writes:

> From its subtle windings and changes of level there arises a keen and continuous interest that keeps the attention ever alert and cheerful. Every sensitive adjustment to the contour of the ground, every little dip and swerve, seems instinct with life and an exquisite sense of balance and beauty. The road rolls upon the easy slopes of the country, like a long ship in the hollows of the sea.[20]

Although the key phrase here – "instinct with life" – recalls Henry David Thoreau's insistence, "life consists with wildness,"[21] perhaps the most important element of this passage lies in the *translation* of landscape into seascape. Stevenson's language here functions like a "wave of translation."[22] Surprisingly, in the midst of an otherwise earthly essay – a piece in which we find Stevenson musing upon "homely and placid agricultural districts" and upon the benefits of tracing the contours of a country road – a maritime simile appears out of nowhere, comparing the road to a "long ship in the hollows of the sea."[23] This is no insignificant gesture, but a good example of the unruly intervention of the ocean in Stevenson's writing (his work seems always to be saturated with saltwater) and a reminder to the reader seeking to further understand his ecological imagination, that, again, as Carson suggests, the "sea lies all about us" regardless of our proximity to the coast. Not all Scottish authors share Stevenson's peculiarly tidal dialectical imagination; not all seem to appreciate (as thoroughly as Stevenson) Carson's important point.

However, I invoke "Roads" here not only to emphasize Stevenson's profound appreciation of the sea's omnipresence, but for the valuable advice that this essay offers to those who travel by foot, and, most importantly, for the clues that it provides concerning his emerging ecological consciousness. Notably, Stevenson prioritizes a thorough and systematic study of nature that unfolds over time, through close attention to the "constant recurrence of similar combinations of colour and outline":

> This is the true pleasure of your "rural voluptuary," – not to remain awestricken before a Mount Chimborazo ... but day by day to teach himself some new beauty – to experience some new vague and tranquil sensation that has before evaded him ... A man must have thought much over scenery before he begins to fully enjoy it ... most people's heads are growing bare before they can see all in a landscape that they have the capability of seeing ... .[24]

At the heart of Stevenson's celebration of the "rural voluptuary" is an implicit dismissal of the aesthetics of the Sublime, the art of which focuses upon overwhelming demonstrations of Nature's majesty and (most importantly) power, the elemental forces that figure in nineteenth-century landscape paintings, such as Thomas Moran's *The Wilds of Lake Superior* (1864) (Figure 4.1) or *Moonlit Shipwreck at Sea* (1901), or the lore surrounding the ocean's mind-boggling destruction of the concrete breakwater at Wick in 1872 and, five years later, the "new pier, weighing about 2600 tons."[25] Instead, Stevenson frequently prioritizes "small sequestered loveliness" – the sort of beauty that reveals itself through repeated close inspection. It's the "subdued note of the landscape" that he refers to first and foremost, implying that, to develop "minute knowledge" of any particular ecosystem, one must look and listen. Perhaps this close attention to environmental particularities (to the quieter aspects of one's surroundings) also explains Stevenson's persistent fascination with so-called desert places. For, in one sense, what is a desert but a historically underappreciated ecosystem, and, as such, one that requires us to pay careful attention to discover its not-so-obvious value?

Employed by Stevenson, the term "desert" has special anthropomorphic value, since it does not indicate any essential characteristic

Figure 4.1 Thomas Moran, "The Wilds of Lake Superior" (1864). Available in the public domain via Wikimedia Commons.

of a desert proper (arid and lacking in fresh water), but reflects some degree of human intervention. It is a term that not only reflects the value we humans confer upon the land, but one that also registers, to use Michael Niblett's key term, considerable ecological force – a "pivot in humanity's capacity to rework life, land, and the body."[26] Accordingly, Stevenson's frequent usage of the term to describe not deserted islands per se, but specific tracts of land in the Highlands of Scotland has additional significance.

Consider, for example, Stevenson's description of Rannoch Moor, as it appears in his novel, *Kidnapped*:

> The mist rose and died away, and showed us that country lying as waste as the sea; only the moorfowl and the peewees crying upon it, and far over to the east, a herd of deer, moving like dots. Much of it was red with heather; much of the rest broken up with bogs and hags and peaty pools; some had been burnt black in a heath fire; and in another place there was quite a forest of dead firs, standing like skeletons. A wearier looking desert man never saw . . .[27]

Obviously, there is no lack of fresh water or vegetation here, but an abundance of both. So, Balfour refers to Rannoch as a desert precisely because it is not only uninhabited by humans, but also requires (as I shall discuss later) David and Alan Breck to "play at being hares" to cross it safely.[28]

Evidently, such desert places in Scotland held the greatest sway over Stevenson's imagination. And, in his *Records of a Family of Engineers*, Stevenson confesses as much when he offers the following account of his grandfather's efforts to find a suitable location for the Cape Wrath lighthouse:

> About noon they reached the Kyle of Durness and passed the ferry. By half-past there they were at Cape Wrath . . . and beheld upon all sides of them unfrequented shores, an expanse of desert moor, and the high-piled Western Ocean . . . Perhaps it is by inheritance of blood, but I know few things more inspiring than this location of a lighthouse in a designated space of heather and air, through which the sea-birds are still flying.[29]

This claim, that there are "few things more inspiring" than the location of a lighthouse, reinforces my point about Stevenson's great fondness for such desert places. And, here again, the term desert figures in Stevenson's account of a place vacated by any human inhabitants, and therefore deemed (by capitalism's standards) largely value-less – except in so far as it now serves as a firing range for the

British Navy. Consider too the *Crusoe*-esque remoteness of which he highlights in the following passage (also from *Records*):

> To go round the lights, even today, is to visit past centuries . . . They are farther from London than St. Petersburgh, and except for the towers, sounding and shining all night with fog-bells and the radiance of the light-room, glittering by day with the trivial brightness of white paint, these island and moor-land stations seem inaccessible to the civilization of to-day, and even to the end of my grandfather's career the island was far greater.[30]

Indeed, that Cape Wrath (a desert of sorts) has been converted into a British Navy firing range serves as a testament to the devaluation of such desert places. It takes a poet, perhaps, not unlike Stevenson to recognize the value of life that exists here, from bog cotton (or cotton-grass) and heath-spotted orchids to cuckoos and dragonflies. The entrance to the range warns trespassers to steer clear and not to touch anything that looks like military debris because it may explode and kill you. Such warnings are inclined to make the wary walker feel as though they're walking through a minefield. And yet, even this road that winds for roughly eleven miles through a vast, seemingly empty stretch of peaty moorland is instinct with life, as Stevenson suggests in "Roads." Its gentle undulations make room for close inspection and quiet rumination – the sort that Thoreau equates with camels or perhaps even that which Stevenson equates with beachcombing in the South Pacific . . . the vegetating, for example, that characterizes Robert Herrick's state in the opening few chapters of "The Ebb-Tide." Similar to desert, a term which Stevenson loads with special significance, the word "vegetating" smartly draws to our attention the humanity-in-nature / nature-in-humanity, and it is precisely this sort of sympathetic union that, I argue, lies at the heart of Stevenson's ecological consciousness.

Sympathy is a key term for the Scottish Enlightenment philosopher, David Hume, who, in his *Treatise of Human Nature*, treats this faculty of mind as integral to the communication of emotion between humans and, however remarkably, as Tobias Menely astutely points out, across species. Hume insists, for example, that,

> no quality of human nature is more remarkable, both in itself and in its consequences, than that propensity we have to sympathize with others, and to receive by communication their inclinations and sentiments, however different from, or even contrary to our own . . . A good-natur'd man finds himself *in an instant* of the same humour

with his company ... Hatred, resentment, esteem, love, courage, mirth and melancholy; all these passions I feel more from communication than from my own natural temper and disposition. (Italics mine.)[31]

The element of speed here is crucial, as there is no time for critical or analytical reflection in this instantaneous communication of emotion – a circumstance that gets thoroughly explored by the early American author, Charles Brockden Brown, in his Gothic novel, *Edgar Huntly; Or, Memoirs of a Sleepwalker* (1799). Indeed, the sheer fluidity of such emotional exchanges may call into question the very integrity of the individual self. That is, does this confusion of emotion that Hume describes not make it practically impossible to determine the origins of one's emotions? Human neurology reinforces this confusion.[32] And in this particular regard, I think, sympathy offers a useful way for us to think about the co-dependency / interrelationship of organisms within any given ecosystem, an idea that evidently corresponds with Hume's ideas about cross species communication.

Menely points out, for example, that, "animals serve, for Hume, not to instigate skepticism – to measure the limits of human knowing and the unavailability of other minds – but rather as an antidote to skepticism."[33] That is, the key thing here is how Hume's ideas about the communication of emotion, challenge individual identity – the so-called discreet and stable self that he describes elsewhere in his *Treatise* as a necessary fiction constructed to mask the fact that one is constantly changing:

> I may venture to affirm of the rest of mankind, that they are nothing but a bundle or collection of different perceptions, which succeed each other with an inconceivable rapidity, and are in a perpetual flux and movement ... Thus we feign the continu'd existence of the perceptions of our senses to remove the interruption; and run into the notion of a *soul*, and *self*, and *substance*, to disguise the variation.[34]

Again, for Hume the very notion of a stable, discreet, and independent self is a necessary fiction constructed to mitigate (or cope with) the otherwise overwhelming perceptual flux and fluidity that defines every single moment of one's life. Furthermore, as Menely puts it,

> for Hume, sympathy is intrinsically remarkable as the enigmatic communicative channel that enables the "contagious" quality of passions, their propensity to pass from one self to another such that

the affective immediacy that would seem to guarantee individual identity, a given person's uniquely felt finitude, may always already derive from another.[35]

The metaphor of contagion often crops up in discussions of the mechanics of sympathy, but perhaps it would be helpful to think in terms of oceanic water here too, bearing in mind, of course, that Hume (not unlike Stevenson) was born in Edinburgh, Scotland, in close proximity to the North Sea. Much as "oceanic water only merges, melds, and mixes with more water – with bays, inlets, with rivers, gulfs, and seas, but also with other oceans," as Burnham observes – it is the oceanic, water-like fluidity of emotions that, for Hume, calls into question the notion of human individuality. No island is entirely isolated from the rest of the world, and "no man," to quote John Donne, "is an island entire of itself."

But what is perhaps the most remarkable aspect of Hume's treatment of sympathy is his embracing the possibility of affective communication across species. As Menely observes, "Hume sees us as most resolutely human, in our capacity to convey passions and join interests, where we are most akin to our fellow creatures, for "*sympathy*, or the communication of passions, takes place among animals, no less than men."[36] This is most intriguing, as Menely suggests, because symbolic communication frequently figures in discussions of what makes humans unique. And yet, Hume appears to be very forward thinking here, in so far as he regards the communication of emotion as something we share with other animals, if not the very thing that binds human-extra-human natures together in one coherent biotic community. At least, this is how I plan to use the term sympathy here – as a convenient expression for the intimacy that humans enjoy with other species. However, unlike Menely, who is first and foremost concerned with creaturely voices, and/or that which Hume characterizes as a "fundamental 'correspondence of *passions* in men and animals,'"[37] this chapter takes into account the intimacy humans enjoy with plants and, most especially, with Stevenson's uncanny relationship to a particular species / *unruly nature* – namely, *Mimosa pudica*, or the sensitive plant.

Of course, it is important too that Hume suggests sympathy is felt in proportion to resemblance and contiguity – that is, one is more apt to feel stronger sympathy for someone they resemble or someone with whom one is familiar or closely linked (geographically, and so on):

> where, beside the general resemblance of our natures, there is any peculiar similarity in our manners, or character, or country, or language, it facilitates the sympathy. The stronger the relation is betwixt ourselves and any object, the more easily does the imagination make the transition ... Nor is resemblance the only relation, which has this effect ... The sentiments of others have little influence, when far remov'd from us, and require the relation of contiguity, to make them communicate themselves entirely.[38]

However, while this stress that Hume puts on resemblance and contiguity seems fairly straightforward at first glance, offering a convenient explanation for racism, nationalism, gender biases, etc., the fact that he sees a "correspondence of *passions* in men and animals" invites us to see ourselves as all the more intimately connected to (alike, resembling, and contiguous with) those organisms with whom we share space, whether animal or plant.

Accordingly, this chapter explores how walking and weeding, in particular, helped Stevenson to develop an appreciation for the uncanny resemblance of animals and plants, but also to vegetate, or sympathetically identify with those plant species with whom he was most closely connected. So thoroughly preoccupied does Stevenson become with clearing ground at Vailima (his Pacific island home in Samoa) that these so-called creeping things – i.e. those peculiarly *unruly natures* that form the jungle underbrush, including the sensitive plant – begin to invade his sleep, thereby cementing his sympathetic identification with them:

> And in my dreams I shall be hauling on recalcitrants, and suffering stings from nettles, stabs from citron thorns, fiery bites from ants, sickening resistances of mud and slime, evasions of slimy roots, dead weight of heat, sudden puffs of air, sudden starts from birdcalls in the contiguous forest – some mimicking my name, some laughter, some the signal of a whistle; and living over again at large the business of my day.[39]

*****

A considerable amount of recent critical attention has been paid to Robert Louis Stevenson's colonial imagination.[40] Of these studies, Ann C. Colley's book, *Robert Louis Stevenson and the Colonial Imagination* (2004), stands out for situating Stevenson's writing in the context of missionary work in the South Pacific, as well as for drawing our attention to the complicated nature of his relationship to British imperialism. Colley correctly encourages readers of Stevenson's South Seas tales to pay close attention to the particulars and relativities that may undermine the imperial framing of his work.[41] And she does a fine job (along with Jenni Calder) of linking Scotland and Samoa, with her suggestion that Scotland's past provided Stevenson with access to the South Seas, but also placed him in an ambiguous position as someone who felt at once like an "intrusive colonial" and, as a Scot, a "victim of English cultural imperialism."[42]

This latter sentiment is especially manifest in a speech Stevenson delivered to a gathering of Samoan chiefs in celebration of the construction of an "important piece of road approaching his house." Quoted in his stepson, Lloyd Osbourne's *A Letter to Mr. Stevenson's Friends*, a compilation of remembrances published for private circulation in the wake of Stevenson's death in 1894, Stevenson's speech takes an example from Scotland's past – specifically, the Highland Clearances – as a case study of what *not* to do when one's land is under threat of colonial occupation. Stevenson implores that, "if you do not occupy and use your country, others will . . . You and your children will . . . be cast out into outer darkness where shall be weeping and gnashing of teeth."[43]

Clearly the powerful sympathy that Stevenson felt for his Samoan neighbors was fueled by his affection for the Scottish Highlands and islands. The characteristic tension between unity and fragmentation that (according to Susan Manning) informs Scottish literature and culture can also be seen in his wavering appreciation of such infrastructural developments in Samoa.[44] For, although in this particular speech Stevenson frankly celebrates road construction as one way to defend Samoa against European interests, elsewhere he uses terms like "ruinous" to describe the encroachments of Western civilization. Moreover, Stevenson, I think, well understood that, as is suggested in *The Travels of Hildebrand Bowman*, a 1778 novel based on James Cook's explorations in the Pacific Ocean, navigable roads "very much approximate places to one another."[45]

However, while scholars like Colley have provided us with useful ways to think about the cultural interactions that took place between Europeans and South Pacific islanders, there remains a relative shortage of scholarship on Stevenson's intriguing environmental imagination and, in particular, on his sympathetic relationship to the non-human building blocks of empire. This is surprising not only because of the abundance of current research on biological invasion in the South Pacific, but also because Stevenson's letters describing his daily activities on Samoa are punctuated with numerous passages that testify to the author's preoccupation with exploring his physical surroundings on horseback and on foot. The dual natural-historical process that Stevenson refers to as "sheep feeding" in the aforementioned speech recalls both Jason Moore's treatment of capitalism as "co-produced by manifold species," a notion that has considerable world-ecological implications,[46] as well as Rebecca Woods's study of the transportation of British breeds across the globe. Woods observes, for example, that, so-called "improved" types of native British breeds of sheep and cattle were enlisted as

> hoof-soldiers in the great agropastoral expansion of the British Empire from the mid nineteenth-century to its close, contributing to both the rationale and the material presence necessary for the expansion of British interests, capital, and settlers into previously un- or otherwise-occupied territories, all in the service of feeding the great maw that was industrial London.[47]

Accordingly, this chapter partially aims to fill this knowledge gap through careful consideration of the environmental orientation of Stevenson's South Pacific writings. I was initially drawn to the topic by a curious coincidence – namely, that, in 1893, the year that Stevenson published *Island Nights' Entertainments*, the Hawaii-based naturalist Robert Cyril Lawton Perkins would discover a bird pox on the island of Oahu, an avian disease spread by mosquitoes that were accidentally introduced to the island "when the crew of a Central American ship emptied their casks of stagnant water, and the larvae living in it, into a stream on Maui."[48] A few years later, Perkins would also draw attention to the threat posed to the island's bird population by another non-native species – namely, cats – such as the cat scarcely visible in the photo that Stevenson's cousin, Sir Graham Balfour, took of Hawaiians peeling taro (see Figure 4.2). Perkins writes:

> The four first birds of Oahu (got 40 years ago) are now utterly extinct & between the mongoose (which swarms there), cats and mynah birds, not to mention the wholesale clearing, which is taking place for coffee planting, those on Hawaii must follow before many years.[49]

In as much as we may be surprised to discover a cat in Balfour's photo, Perkins's fieldwork alarms not because of his tracing Oahu's environmental degradation – in this case, species extinction – to the coffee industry (the wholesale clearing of forests to make room for coffee plantations). It is a conspiracy of natures, or the combined

Stevenson and the "Horror of Creeping Things" 227

Figure 4.2 "Hawaiians peeling Taro," from the photo albums of Sir Graham Balfour. Courtesy of the Special Collections, National Library of Scotland, Edinburgh.

forces of several non-indigenous species – human *and* animal *and* plant – that leads to this most startling reduction in the island's biodiversity.

While I have no reason to believe Stevenson ever met the barefooted naturalist, the timing of Perkins's fieldwork in Hawaii corresponds with the insightful attention that Stevenson pays to the biological conditions of capitalism upon Samoa, culminating in what he terms, "cocoanut alley," a series of eerily silent, large-scale German coconut plantations. A close reading of Stevenson's writings in Samoa suggests that he understood the ecosystems of Hawaii and Samoa to be especially fragile and vulnerable to biological invaders, such as the cats that appear in Balfour's photos, including Figure 4.2, in which a white cat sits between a group of pigs and Hawaiians peeling taro. (Of course, one can't help but think of the cats that figure in the story of Alexander Selkirk here too.) But to what extent did he link the encroachment of European commercial interests (a historical process facilitated by innovations in navigation and transportation) to environmental degradation – specifically, to the diminution of biological diversity? More importantly, to what extent does Stevenson acknowledge his own presence (and labor) upon the island as symptomatic of a transoceanic, global ecology of commerce and empire that works not merely upon an otherwise externalized Nature, but, as Moore suggests, *through* nature?

To answer these questions, this chapter explores how both walking and weeding contributed to Stevenson's writing (especially his South Pacific poetry and prose) and to his increasing awareness of what contemporary economists and ecologists regularly call our shrinking world. Like Colley, I am concerned with particulars here, but instead of the particularities of cultural exchange, I focus upon Stevenson's inter-subjective relationship to non-human, or environmental particularities, especially as they relate to larger transoceanic, or global questions and concerns about biological invasion.

In his endeavor to situate capitalism in the *web of life*, Moore insists that, "capitalism is a co-produced history of human-initiated projects and processes bundled with (and within) specific natures."[50] Moore's work challenges us to view capitalism as both project and *process*,[51] and this, I argue, is the provocative realization that dawned upon Stevenson during the final years of his life in Samoa. Ultimately this chapter seeks to highlight the various ways in which Stevenson anticipates Moore's treatment of capitalism as world-ecology. Focusing in particular upon Stevenson's poem, "The Woodman," the conception of which occurred while he was clearing ground outside his home, Vailima, on the Pacific island of Samoa, I argue that Stevenson's interactions with a particular invasive plant species – namely, tuitui (otherwise known as *Mimosa pudica* or "giant sensitive" or simply the "sensitive plant," a native of South and Central America) – would lead him to sympathetically adopt a plant's-eye view of transoceanic commerce, as well as to acknowledge the co-productive role that "extra-human natures"[52] play in the accumulation of capital. Like the "submerged perspectives" that figure in Macarena Gómez-Barris's study of social ecologies in *The Extractive Zone*, the sympathy that forms between Stevenson and the "sensitive plant" offers the possibility of "renewed perception," as it were, a reclamation, and revalorization of the "hidden worlds that form the nexus of human and nonhuman multiplicity."[53] Not only does Stevenson's psycho-geographic conflation of Scotland and Samoa reflect the shrinking biodiversity of his world, as a consequence of global commerce. He also implicitly establishes a troubling parallel between capitalism's acceleration of turnover time and this particular invasive plant species' takeover of the Samoan rainforest, a natural-historical unfolding that he aptly refers to in his letters as the "horror of creeping things."[54] Furthermore, the sympathy that forms between Stevenson and the invasive sensitive plant – a correspondence that triggers his recognition of the co-productive role the he plays in the "whole silent battle, murder, and slow death of the contending forest"[55] – effectively replaces what Lucinda Cole describes, in her treatment of Bruno Latour's theory of *actants*, as the fundamental question of Western philosophy – who am I? – with another, much more provocative, however unsettling a question: "'what is my place in the system?'"[56] And, for Stevenson, herein again lies the "horror of creeping things."

Walking with Stevenson

In his essay on Henry David Thoreau, a loosely drawn outline of the American author's character and opinion, Stevenson claims that Thoreau "composed seemingly while he walked, or at least exercise and composition were with him intimately connected."[57] Rightly so, Stevenson encourages us to regard Thoreau as among the peripatetic authors, who, like William Wordsworth, composed lines of verse and prose afoot, *deliberately* moving through a landscape. So closely linked were these two activities in Thoreau's imagination that it may be possible to gather an understanding of the contours of the earth upon which he walked simply by paying close formal attention to his rather poetic prose. The aphorisms that punctuate his masterpiece, *Walden*, for example – lines such as "Olympus is but the outside of the earth every where"[58] – announce themselves like fallen limbs or rocky outcroppings in that they oblige readers to pause deliberately and scramble for meaning.

Coincidentally, the British poet and novelist, Sydney Royse Lysaght observed a similar connection between Stevenson's walking and writing. Or, at least, he employs similar terms to describe Stevenson's distinctive bearing:

> he was barefooted and walked with a long and curiously marked step, light but almost metrical, in accord, it seemed, with some movement of his mind. It was his constant habit to pace to and fro as he conversed and his step and speech seemed in harmony.[59]

Lysaght landed in Samoa on Easter Sunday in 1894, and, after observing Stevenson *deliberately* pace to and fro on his verandah at Vailima, he rightly suggests that this sort of locomotion played an integral role in his writing. We know too from Lysaght's recollection that the two authors discussed rhythm in poetry, "especially as to a tendency towards subtler and less regular rhythmical effects."[60] Stevenson's apparent aspiration to develop "more complex harmonies" in his late verse neatly coincides with his arrival on the island, and therefore suggests an interesting connection to his walking through the "tangled forests"[61] of Mt. Vaea – the roughly 1500 ft. mountain overshadowing Samoa's capital, Apia, and lying just east of Stevenson's home (see Figure 4.3).

Providing ample opportunities for wandering afoot, Vaea evidently fed Stevenson's environmental imagination, including his fascination with birdsong. However, as James H. Mulligan recollects, despite the ecological peculiarities of the tropical rainforest, "these mountains [on Samoa] spoke to him of Scotland; these dashing streams sang to him the same wild songs brawled into the ears of boyhood, in the Highlands."[62] This may seem odd (or even ironic) because if one walks through Scotland today – or, for that matter, in Stevenson's day too – one is constantly reminded of the historic division of the landscape into enclosures for livestock. Whatever comparative freedom Thoreau enjoyed on the outskirts of Lancaster, Massachusetts, walkers in Scotland from at least the eighteenth century onward have had to straddle fences, and pass through gates

Figure 4.3 Vailima (Stevenson's home in Samoa), with Mt. Vaea in the background. Courtesy of the Special Collections, National Library of Scotland, Edinburgh.

everywhere because even in the most so-called *desert* of places – a term that Stevenson uses repeatedly in his writing – one encounters soft evidence of grazing cattle or sheep, barbed wire, stone walls, or the occasional telltale sign of an industry, an ongoing collaboration of mammals that has transformed ecosystems throughout the world.[63]

Of course, there are still some places in Scotland that may make one *feel* utterly removed from the village, as Thoreau puts it.[64] And this may be especially true if one heeds Stevenson's advice in "Roads," and thus measures the wildness of such places by *listening* to the water, wind, birds, and insects or, rather, by listening to the general absence of human-generated noises. The bubble of water, perpetual birdsong, faint buzz of a bumblebee, and, of course, the constant whistling of heather and grass in the wind – these are the sounds that may accompany the walker plodding through, say, Rannoch Moor, one of Stevenson's so-called deserts – a stark open space in an otherwise compartmentalized, subdivided landscape of agribusiness.

That Stevenson understood the value of these escapes is apparent in his novels and short stories, many of which contain passages that keenly take into account the *quieter* aspects of the landscape. It might even be more appropriate to call these "soundscapes," given his preoccupation with how each environment sounds. Take, for example, the following passage from his unfinished novel, *Weir of Hermiston* (1896):

> The road to Hermiston runs for a great part of the way up the valley of a stream ... full of falls and pools, and shaded by willows and natural woods of birch ... The manse close by ... finds harbourage in a grove of rowans, and is all the year round in a great silence broken only by the drone of the bees, the tinkle of the burn, and the bell on Sundays ... All beyond and about is the great field, of the hills; the plover, the curlew, and the lark cry there; the wind blows as it blows in a ship's rigging, hard and cold and pure; and the hill-tops huddle one behind another like a herd of cattle into the sunset.[65]

This is a remarkably accurate account of the sounds that punctuate such landscapes. It is also curious that the landscape via metaphor (and simile) becomes at once a seascape: "the wind blows as it blows in a ship's rigging." In this way, Stevenson cleverly draws to our attention the significance of the encircling sea. In the midst of an otherwise earthly passage, a maritime metaphor appears out of nowhere, comparing the manse to a ship in harbor. This is no insignificant gesture, but one that recalls Derek Walcott's important point – "that our only true apprehensions are through metaphor"[66] – and, as I suggested earlier, it is a convenient reminder to the reader seeking to further understand Stevenson's environmental imagination that, as Carson suggests, the "sea lies all about us"[67] – that is, regardless of our proximity to the coast.

But perhaps the most famous example of Stevenson's landscape or, rather, soundscape painting occurs in *Kidnapped* vis-à-vis David Balfour's Robinson Crusoe-esque struggle with shipwreck and desertion on the islet of Erraid:

> With my stepping ashore I began the most unhappy part of my adventures. It was half-past twelve in the morning, and though the wind was broken by the land, it was a cold night. I dared not sit down (for I thought I should have frozen), but took off my shoes and walked to and fro upon the sand, barefoot, and beating my breast, with infinite weariness. There was no sound of man or cattle; not a cock crew, though it was about the hour of their first waking; only the surf broke outside in the distance, which put me in mind of my perils and those of my friend. To walk by the sea at that hour of the morning, and in a place so desert-like and lonesome, struck me with a kind of fear.[68]

In this passage that corresponds to one of the author's own formative walking experiences in Scotland (see *Memoirs of an Islet*),[69] Stevenson pays close attention to what can be heard from Balfour's situation, and, notably, he uses the absence of particular familiar sounds – "there was no sound of man or cattle; not a cock crew" – to emphasize the desert-like status of Erraid.

****

The term "desert" presumably worked like a charm upon Stevenson's imagination, as it repeatedly appears throughout his work. For example, in *Kidnapped*, an emphatically peripatetic novel, he uses it to describe the islands and highlands through which Balfour and Alan Breck walk. Consider, again, the following description of Rannoch Moor, a 50-square mile expanse of blanket bogs, gentle streams, and brilliant moss-covered rocky outcroppings:

> The mist rose and died way, and showed us that country lying as waste as the sea; only the moorfowl and the peewees crying upon it, and far over to the east, a herd of deer, moving like dots. Much of

it was red with heather; much of the rest broken up with bogs and hags and peaty pools; some had been burnt black in a heath fire; and in another place there was quite a forest of dead firs, standing like skeletons. A wearier looking desert man never saw . . .[70]

Note here, again, how the unruly sea manages to intervene in Stevenson's treatment of moorland – "that country lying as waste as the sea." Though clearly Stevenson intended the vast and foreboding appearance of Rannoch to harmonize neatly with Balfour's dire straits, he must also have been mysteriously attracted to these so-called weary looking deserts, as he claims in his account of exploring the Hawaiian island of Molokai via horseback, that "there is a poetry in empty lands."

Indeed, the term "desert" not only appears over again in "Memoirs of an Islet," *Kidnapped*, and virtually every other Scottish novel, but it also crops up repeatedly in his South Seas letters and fiction. It appears, for example, in *The Beach of Falesá* to describe the island's supposedly haunted high bush – that side of the island without any human settlements. And it also appears in his posthumously published cultural study of Pacific islanders, *In the South Seas* (1896), to describe an empty beach on the Pacific atoll of Fakarava:

> I lay down to sleep, and woke again with an unblunted sense of my surroundings. I was never weary of calling up the image of that narrow causeway, on which I had my dwelling, lying coiled like a serpent, tail to mouth, in the outrageous ocean, and I was never weary of passing . . . from the shady, habitable shores of the lagoon to the blinding desert and uproarious breakers of the opposite beach. The sense of insecurity in such a thread of residence is more than fanciful.[71]

Although the term obviously signifies a precarious sort of desolation, it also connotes something positively exhilarating. Stevenson seems to rely on this particular key word to convey the restless excitement that he experienced in such places, denoted here by his pacing to and fro between the sheltered lagoon and the exposed beach where the sea regularly "burst[s] upon the island like a flood."[72] In Molokai he gives this exhilaration yet another term – "poetry" – implying the Thoreau- or even Walcott-like inspiration that Stevenson evidently derived from these desert places:

> A sense of survival attended me upon my ride, and the nervous laughter of Apaka sounded in my ears not quite unpleasantly. The place of the dead is clean; there is a poetry in empty lands.

> A greener track received us; smooth, shoreside grass was shaded with groves and islets of acacias; the hills behind, from the red colour of the soil and the singularity of the formation, had the air of a bare Scottish moorland in the bleak end of autumn; and the resemblance set a higher value on the warmth of the sun and the brightness of the sea.[73]

The invocation of Scotland here suggests the psycho-geographic value of the term "desert." Aside from simply denoting the absence of humans, it offers an imaginative through line (the basis of a sympathetic identification) connecting Scotland and Hawaii (Scots and Hawaiians) past and present. The desert, in this sense, becomes ocean-like, in that, as Margaret Cohen suggests, oceans link both geographical spaces and timelines.[74] And here, again, Stevenson's work invites us to reflect upon a "network of connections" that manifest between otherwise disparate / distant geographies, as it were, in keeping with Burnham's efforts to read American literature in a "maritime global context."[75]

****

Stevenson's account of Fakarava also marks an important shift in his perception of the Pacific islands' so-called remoteness, as he further explains that, "insect life is sometimes dense ... and even in Fakarava the mosquitoes were a pest. The land crab may be seen scuttling to his hole, and at night the rats besiege the houses and the artificial gardens."[76] This passage contains a familiar cast of *unruly natures* – namely, mosquitoes, land crabs, and rats (creatures featured in Selkirk's Juan Fernandez, Grainger's St. Kitts, and Sansay's Haiti). Stevenson's turning of his attention, however briefly, to the atoll's unruly / pesky mosquitoes, land crabs, and rats (those imperfect creatures that figure in Lucinda Cole's reading of *Robinson Crusoe* (see Chapter 1))[77] serves to remind us that no island – much less a tidal islet such as Erraid – is truly desert, or ever really entirely cut off from the rest of the world. It is an important gesture, one that anticipates Elizabeth DeLoughrey's use of Kamau Brathwaite's key term, "tidalectic," to describe the ongoing communication of land and sea, as well as Greg Dening's point, that "every living thing on an island has been a traveler. Every species of tree, plant, and animal on an island has crossed the beach."[78] And yet, this is not the first time that Stevenson would challenge this sort of *Robinson Crusoe*-esque mythology of island desertion. In *Kidnapped,* David Balfour's first impression of Erraid turns out to be completely mistaken – a "pitiful illusion," or panicky misapprehension of the islet's removal from the mainland. Balfour eventually discovers that, as a tidal islet, Erraid "can be entered and left twice in every twenty-four hours, either dry-shod, or at the most by wading."[79] While the naive fantasy of desertion may have been too powerful for Balfour to accurately perceive his surroundings, the main thing that Stevenson teaches us with this episode from *Kidnapped* is that such feelings of desertion are merely illusory. There is no escape from civilization or, specifically, the increasingly wide net of capitalist development, which, to this day, remains almost entirely contingent upon maritime transport. Indeed, as Cohen points out, "ships continue to convey over ninety percent of the world's freight."[80]

This idea – that there is no escaping the global economy – recalls Darnaway's point, in *The Merry Men*, that, "there's a sair sprang o' the auld sin o' the world in yon sea."[81] Michelle Burnham similarly invites us to "reimagine global relations in more oceanic terms."[82] And, in doing so, she makes a point of citing Epeli Hau'ofa's observation, that, "Pacific island peoples have long engaged in a kind of 'world enlargement' that makes 'nonsense of all national and economic boundaries, borders that have been defined only recently, crisscrossing an ocean that had been boundless for ages before Captain Cook's apotheosis.'"[83] But does transoceanic travel in Stevenson's mind merit consideration as a similar sort of world enlargement? Or does the endless criss-crossing of the Atlantic and Pacific oceans – that which remains an integral feature of the twenty-first-century's global supply chain – not result in the approximation of one place to another, a confusion of ecologies harkening back to what Schiebinger and Swan describe in terms of the colonial botanist's efforts to reconfigure and redistribute the earth's flora?[84] And would world shrinkage not more accurately describe what Stevenson presciently considers as the environmental fallout of such a transoceanic, global economy?

Stevenson, who occasionally fantasized about becoming a trader, clearly seems to have understood the significance of transoceanic travel in terms of time-space convergence. In many respects, Stevenson anticipates Cohen's vital point about how oceans "knot together" geographical spaces and timelines,[85] in part because he views Samoa's future in light of Scottish history. In his aptly titled, *A Footnote to History: Eighty Years of Trouble in Samoa*, for example, he claims that, "Apia, the *port and mart*, is the seat of the political sickness in Samoa."[86] Although he formerly claims the "whole extent of the South Seas" to be "desert of ships," living near the capital of Samoa enabled Stevenson to properly gauge the extent of European commerce (and influence).[87] That he uses a metaphor of contagion to describe the Samoans' subjugation to German, British, and U.S. interests, makes it patently clear that he views these historical developments – the influx of stores, offices, and barracks – mainly in a negative light. For Stevenson, the trouble in Samoa is practically identical to the Highland clearances in Scotland.

Yet perhaps the most interesting feature of this work remains Stevenson's preoccupation with walking:

> At the foot of a peaked, woody mountain, the coast makes a deep indent, roughly semicircular. In front the barrier reef is broken by the fresh water of the streams ... and along the fringeing coral which follows the configuration of the beach, the surf breaks with a continuous uproar ... The western horn is Mulinuu, the eastern, Matautu; and from one to the other of these extremes, I ask the reader to walk. He will find more of the history of Samoa spread before his eyes in that excursion, than has yet been collected in the blue-books or the white-books of the world.[88]

This passage may explain why Stevenson titled the book, *A Footnote*. It was not simply to convey his understanding of Europeans' marginalization of Samoan history. The title does more than imply that this is the sort of material that biased Eurocentric empire writers typically relegate to footnotes. Rather, the passage makes it clear that he regarded walking – one's becoming acquainted with the lay of the land – as an integral component of historical work. Stevenson takes his readers on an imaginative walk through Apia because he wishes them to plainly see how roads that wind through a landscape function as technologies of power. The son of a Scottish engineer would no doubt have been familiar with the role that road construction played in neutralizing radical elements in the Highlands of Scotland, especially the roads built by General George Wade (1673–1748) in the aftermath of the 1745 Jacobite rebellion.[89] Thus, Stevenson claims, that real Samoa begins at the "boundary of the *Eleele Sa*" (neutral territory), or, basically, where the roads either cease or are rendered "impassable by native pig-fences," where bridges are "quite unknown," and the "houses of the whites ... become at once a rare exception."[90] In other words, the indigenous, or local wisdom gleaned from walking *on* (and not merely reading about) Samoa has evidently taught Stevenson to see roads in a new light. Roads, in this instance, are not necessarily "instinct with life" – a point that he makes in his early essay titled "Roads" – but, rather, seen as symbols of encroaching capitalist development and harbingers of environmental change.

A "Desert of Food"

Nowhere is this idea – that roadways are not necessarily "instinct with life," but may prefigure disastrous natural-historical changes, such as creating a more hospitable (i.e. disturbed) habitat for invasive plant species (see Chapter 1) – more evident than in the chapter titled, "Sorrows of Laupepa," wherein Stevenson takes his readers on a tour of a German plantation:

> You ride in a German plantation and see no bush, no soul stirring; only acres of empty sward, miles of cocoanut alley: a *desert of food*. In the eyes of the Samoan the place has the attraction of a park for the holiday schoolboy, of a granary for mice. We must add the yet more lively allurement of a haunted house, for over these empty and silent miles there broods the fear of the negrito cannibal. For the Samoan besides, there is something barbaric, unhandsome, and absurd in the idea of thus growing food only to send it from the land and sell it. A man at home who should turn all Yorkshire into one wheat field, and annually burn his harvest on the altar of Mumbo-Jumbo, might impress ourselves not much otherwise.[91] (Italics mine.)

This is a wonderfully intriguing passage, in part because the term "desert" crops up again, but without the same allure as it formerly had for Stevenson. A "desert of food": the term no longer signifies escape from civilization. Instead, Stevenson uses it to convey all the "barbaric, unhandsome, and absurd" consequences of European agribusiness – specifically, the crop monoculture of "cocoanut alley." However, it is not merely the crop monoculture that strikes the Samoan as both barbaric and absurd here, according to Stevenson, so much as the idea of growing crops for sale in a global marketplace, as it were, to be shipped overseas. Such absurdity speaks to the so-called economic efficiency of our present-day global supply chain, as, for example, *Wall Street Journal* columnist Christopher Mims points out, that cod fish caught in Scotland are typically frozen and "sent to China and Southeast Asia to be filleted, and then shipped back to Scotland to be sold": "it's a journey of many thousands of miles, because transporting that cod [aboard gigantic container ships roughly the same size as the Empire State Building in New York

City] is so much cheaper than paying domestic workers to prepare that cod."[92] For Stevenson this Samoan "desert of food" is an effect of global capitalism, in keeping with precedent imperialist agricultural practices in the Caribbean (the sugar revolution). Or consider the enormous cornfields that started to appear in the Midwestern United States beginning in the 1860s, as innovations in agricultural technology transformed the region into a massive, monocultural cash crop region.[93] Moreover, Stevenson's application of the term stems from the fact that silence predominates here.

Indeed, Stevenson appears to be utilizing the eeriness of this particular silence to stress how European agribusiness disrupts the delicate balance of nature in Samoa. The haunted house allusion reinforces this purpose, and in this way Stevenson provocatively transforms what for so many prior generations of empire writers appeared as a picturesque symbol of imperial expansion – the orderly plantation – into a Gothic ruin of imperial-agricultural excess (or transoceanic, global capitalism). Indeed, if we measure wildness in terms of sound, then there are few places in the world that afford us an opportunity to feel as though we have left civilization behind. Gordon Hempton claims, in *One Square Inch of Silence*, that, even in the expansive U.S. wilderness areas and national parks, the "average daytime noise-free interval . . . has shrunk to less than five minutes."[94] Of course, this partly explains Thoreau's preoccupation with the Fitchburg railroad. For the scream of the train's whistle makes it practically impossible for him to forget the village.

And yet, even the most so-called remote wildernesses are rarely ever truly silent. Hempton explains:

> When you're in a place of natural silence, you're not alone, and you can feel it. Whether it's birdcalls from miles away or the proximity of a giant tree whose warm tones you can *feel*, there's a presence. It's a quieting experience.[95]

Accordingly, in the passage from *Kidnapped* I cited earlier, Stevenson makes a point of drawing our attention to other sounds that invariably break the silence: "All is silent, *except* for the sound of the waves crashing upon the islet" (italics mine). Similarly, in *Weir of Hermiston*, "the manse close by . . . is all the year round in a great silence broken only by the drone of the bees, the tinkle of the burn . . ."[96] The silence that figures in these passages corresponds with Hempton's notion of natural silence. These are not examples of absolute silence, but (in Hempton's terms) *quieting scenarios*.

Such qualifications, however, do not figure in Stevenson's recollection of the eerie silence that predominates in Upolu's cocoanut alley. Remarkably, this place does not resound with tree frogs or the "shrill cries" of birds that figure in Stevenson's other descriptions of the island, especially those detailing the tropical bush.[97] And so, one may be encouraged to regard this particular passage as disconcerting because true silence in nature usually betokens some sort of environmental catastrophe. In *Roughing It*, Mark Twain employs the phrase – "Sabbath stillness" – to account for the ecological after-effects (degradation) of California's gold rush.[98] Or, consider, for example, the silence that now prevails in the forests on the Pacific island of Guam. Anyone (such as Stevenson) who has walked through a tropical rainforest will remember (perhaps above all else) the singing of birds; for instance, the bell minor's distinctive sonar-like ping echoes in the rainforest of the Blue Mountains in New South Wales, Australia, as does the sulfur-crested cockatoo's alarming squawk. On Fakarava Stevenson tells us – "Crickets sang; some shrill thing whistled in a tuft of weeds; and the mosquito hummed and stung."[99] In fact, as noted earlier, Graham Balfour insists, that, "to the song of birds" Stevenson was "very sensitive," which, judging from his *Letters*, certainly appears to be the case. In a letter to Edward L. Burlingame, for example (7 October 1890, Vailima, Apia – Samoa), Stevenson notes:

> there is an endless voice of birds; I have never lived in such a heaven ... how the birds and the frogs are rattling and piping, and hailing from the woods! Here and there a throaty chuckle; here and there, cries like those of jolly children who have lost their way.[100]

Sympathetic human-animal comparisons / resemblances abound in Stevenson's imagination. In a letter to Lloyd Osbourne dated 29 September 1890, he similarly notes:

> a bird that fills Vaea Mountain every evening with cries, like those of schoolboys hailing each other, is now near done; the tree frogs are in full cry; later, in the dead of night, a singular bird begins, I whistled its call to a native (our friend Faalelei of Tanugamanono) and he said it was called the *maoma'o* (catch not very strong).[101]

He remarks upon the humanness of their calls: "Vaea mountain about sundown sometimes rings with shrill cries, like the hails of merry, scattered children."[102] And, perhaps most importantly, in "Forest Notes: Idle Hours" (1876), he had already proved to be an especially keen observer of forest ecosystems. Here he offers the following insightful account of the forest at Fontainbleau, France:

> The forest – a strange thing for an Englishman – is very destitute of birds. This is no country where every patch of wood among the meadows gives up an incense of song ... And this rarity of birds is not to be regretted on its own account only. For the insects prosper in their absence, and become as one of the plagues of Egypt. Ants swarm in the hot sand; mosquitoes drone their nasal drone; wherever the sun finds a hole in the roof of the forest you see a myriad of transparent creatures coming and going in the shaft of light ...[103]

This is an interesting passage because it not only reveals Stevenson's sensitivity to birdsong – that which suggests, according to John Veitch, that he had the ear of a "true poet."[104] His remarks upon the proliferation of the "transparent creatures" (insects) in the absence of birds suggest that he understood the forest as a delicately balanced interconnected community of organisms (i.e. an ecosystem). Stevenson's reliance upon these sorts of sympathetic human-animal resemblances offers a convenient way for us to think about the nature of ecosystems.

Weeding with Stevenson

Someone as keenly sensitive to the nature of forests and birdsong as Stevenson would no doubt find the current status of the tropical rainforests on Guam to be utterly disorientating. Indeed, as Claire Martin observes, "visitors to Guam's forests find them quiet – eerily so," because "no chirping of birds can be heard overhead."[105] The unnerving avian silence on Guam serves as a visceral indicator of the island's "invasional meltdown" due to the U.S. military's accidental introduction of the brown tree snake (*Boiga irregularis*) sometime between the years 1945 and 1950.[106] Transportation of the brown tree snake to an unsuspecting (and delicately balanced) island ecosystem has effectively converted this formerly innocuous arboreal creature (a native of Australia and Indonesia) into a raging menace on Guam – one that has practically obliterated the island's bird population; at least ten of the island's twelve native species, including the lovely Mariana fruit dove, the Guam Flycatcher, Rufous Fantail, and Cardinal Honeyeater have been rendered extinct. Prior to the brown tree snake's arrival, explains Alan Burdick, "the only snake on Guam was the hapless Braminy." Today, however, "Guam hosts more brown tree snakes – more snakes of any kind, for that matter – per square mile than anywhere else in the world," notes Burdick, and "this distinction has come largely at the expense of Guam's native bird population, which the snake's boundless appetite has almost entirely eliminated."[107] Moreover, that scientists now believe they can link the absence of seed dispersing birds to the gradual thinning of the island's forests suggests the power of such bio invasions – in this case, a synergistic interaction of two non-native species (snakes and geckos) – to have a cross-kingdom impact. Indeed, if the tones of trees can be felt, as Hempton suggests, then an even more eerie silence lies in Guam's not-too-distant future.

A similar silence, I would argue, figures in Stevenson's poem, "The Woodman," which was inspired by his laboring to clear a patch of ground behind his house on Samoa. The poem begins as follows:

> In all the grove, nor stream nor bird
> Nor aught beside my blows was heard,
> And the woods wore their noonday dress –
> The glory of their silentness.
> From the island summit to the seas,
> Trees mounted, and trees drooped, and trees
> Groped upward in the gaps. The green
> Inarboured talus and ravine
> By fathoms. By the multitude
> The rugged columns of the wood
> And bunches of the branches stood;
> Thick as a mob, deep as a sea,
> And silent as eternity.[108]

The speaker envisions a garden in the clearing he has created with his axe; however, these plans are delayed indefinitely once he discovers a "foe more resolute to live, / the toothed and killing sensitive" – namely, the tropical forest undergrowth of vines and so-called weeds, including *Mimosa pudica* (the sensitive plant). The poet, thus, proceeds to elucidate the awful competition for sunlight that takes place between these plants:

> Thick round me in the teeming mud
> Brier and fern strove to the blood:
> The hooked liana in his gin
> Noosed his reluctant neighbours in:
> There the green murderer throve and spread,
> Upon his smothering victims fed,
> And wantoned on his climbing coil.

> Contending roots fought for the soil
> Like frightened demons: with despair
> Competing branches pushed for air.
> Green conquerors from overhead
> Bestrode the bodies of their dead:[109]

And he continues:

> So hushed the woodland warfare goes
> Unceasing; and the silent foes
> Grapple and smother, strain and clasp
> Without a cry, without a gasp.[110]

In an essay on Stevenson's poetry, Penny Fielding provides an insightful and compelling interpretation of this poem as one that not only resonates with Andrew Marvell's seventeenth-century wrangling with the relationship between art and nature, but also stands apart from contemporary works, such as Richard Le Galliene's "Tree Worship," vis-à-vis its refusal to offer any meaningful popular-historical framework through which to grasp an otherwise incommensurable and alienating nature. Stevenson's woods "remain 'unmeaning,'" suggests Fielding: "the [forest] gods of the poem are 'disinvested' . . . suggesting not only have they lost their formal investiture as gods, but also that no one is investing any faith in them anymore."[111] Fielding, furthermore, reads the poem as concerned with questions of geographical dislocation, not unlike other poems in the posthumously published collection, *Songs of Travel and Other Verses* (1896), poems such as "The Tropics Vanish." The silence, according to Fielding, paints a scene that "cannot be easily measured" – as unfathomable as the deep sea. The "uniform green" that appears in the poem obscures geographical distinctions, and, accordingly, the poem "grows almost as out of control as the undergrowth, although he remains in command of his careful metre."[112]

Fielding's point about disinvestment in the forest gods is an excellent one because it speaks to the poem's resonance with the colonial history of Samoa, and, in particular, with the clearing of forests to make room for German plantations, such as the "cocoanut alley" described in Stevenson's *Footnote*. However, I would argue that it is *not* Nature that remains incommensurable here, but the anthropocentric clearing of forests and corresponding death of particular natures. That the forest is "silent as eternity" reinforces this idea, as death is frequently couched in such terms, and this eternal silence lends the poem a sort of mixed eco-Gothic-apocalyptic quality. Or, rather, as I see it, the silence that figures in Stevenson's poem uncannily anticipates the silence that prevails now in Guam's forests because, as the speaker clearly observes in the very first stanza – "In all the grove, nor stream, *nor bird* / Nor aught beside my blows was heard" (italics mine). Indeed, the stark absence of birdsong immediately alerts readers to the fact that something is truly wrong with this particular forest. It also enables us to read this eternal silence in terms of species extinction – the offshoot of some precedent environmental catastrophe. For a forest without birds is not a healthy forest.

Furthermore, if we take a moment to remember the context in which the poem was conceived (namely, Stevenson's clearing ground) it will become apparent that it is not solely the woodman's work – his "killing," or murderous rampage against trees – but a combination of forces, the co-production of both plant and human, that disrupts the delicate balance of this particular tropical island ecosystem. In his *Letters*, Stevenson explains that he was clearing a patch of ground on Samoa at the time that he composed the poem. And, most importantly, Stevenson not only identifies the particular plant that he was wrangling with at this point in time – namely, tuitui, or *Mimosa pudica* (commonly referred to as sensitive plant, shame plant, or sleeping grass in English or as la'au fefe in American Samoa).[113] (See Figure 4.4.)[114] But he also cleverly acknowledges the plant as *not* indigenous to the island:

> Right in the wild lime hedge which cuts athwart of us just homeward of the garden, I found a great bed of kuikui [sic] – sensitive plant – our deadliest enemy. A fool brought it to this island in a pot, and used to lecture and sentimentalize over the tender thing. The tender thing has now taken charge of this island, and men fight it, with torn hands, for bread and life. A singular, insidious thing, shrinking and biting like a weasel; clutching by its roots as a limpet clutches to a rock. As I fought him, I bettered some verse in my poem, *The Woodman*, the only thought I gave to letters. Though the kuikui [sic] was thick, there was but a small patch of it, and when I was done I attacked the wild lime, and had a hand-to-hand skirmish with its spines and elastic suckers.[115]

This is the first paragraph of several pages in which Stevenson carefully outlines his epic struggle to contain the invasive tuitui. A second passage speaks to the strange effect that weeding has had on his imagination:

Figure 4.4 *Mimosa pudica*, from Henry Charles Andrews, *The Botanist's Repository* (1807–8). Courtesy of the Beinecke Rare Book and Manuscript Library, Yale University.

> My long, silent contests in the forest have had a strange effect on me. The unconcealed vitality of these vegetables, their exuberant number and strength, the attempts – I can use no other word – of lianas to enwrap and capture the intruder, the <u>awful silence</u>, the knowledge that all my efforts are only like the performance of an actor, the thing of a moment, and the wood will silently and swiftly heal them up with fresh effervescence; the cunning sense of the *tuitui*, suffering itself to be touched with the wind-swayed grasses and not minding – but let the grass be moved by a man, and it shuts up; the whole <u>silent battle, murder, and slow death of the contending forest</u>; weigh upon the imagination.[116] (Underscoring mine.)

That he describes this plant's insidious takeover as a "silent battle, murder, and slow death of the contending forest" directly mirrors the "hushed" and "unceasing" "woodland warfare" – or "killing" – that we encounter in "The Woodman." Indeed, the "toothed and killing sensitive" in the poem is without doubt the "sensitive plant" that he struggled unsuccessfully to weed out of his own property, and that he regards as engaged in a violent competition for sunlight with other species of plants. In this respect, the plant's strange effect consists of alerting Stevenson to a particular biological truth – namely, that "all species 'build' environments – they are 'ecosystem engineers,'" but, as Moore points out, "some engineers are more powerful than others."[117] Moore has humans in mind here – in particular, distinctive extroversions that favor hominoid evolution: "a smaller digestive system and use of fire as an external stomach," etc.[118] But for Stevenson it is the sensitive plant's peculiar, or uncanny human-like defense mechanism – its "cunning" ability to discern the touch of man and "shut up" – that provides it with a potential biological advantage over other plants. Although scientists do not know for certain why the sensitive plant changes its leaf orientation when stimulated (a trait known as *seismonastic* movement), some interpret the plant's touch-me-not approach as a useful defense against animal and insect herbivores.[119]

The eco-poetic brilliance of this poem lies in Stevenson's anticipation of journalist and environmental activist, Michael Pollan's work in *The Botany of Desire*.[120] Indeed, what horrifies the woodman most is perhaps not simply the uncontrollable undergrowth, but the extent to which he now sees himself as either complicit or (worse) a pawn in the plant's "silent assault." In other words, what the woodman does here is begin to see things from a "plant's eye view," and, I argue, this sort of interspecies (human-plant) sympathetic identification is precisely the strange effect – an emergent alternative to the extractive view (Gómez-Barris)[121] – that Stevenson claims weeding had on his imagination. For, in as much as the sensitive plant and lianas compete with trees for valuable sunlight, the woodman's work makes it possible for such plants to not merely survive, but also thrive. In creating open space for a garden, he has also inadvertently created opportunities for these so-called lowly weeds to climb up the ladder of power in the biotic community. How apropos is it that the woodman refers to himself as a "beast"? Cattle – one of humankind's favorite creatures of empire[122] – similarly facilitate the growth of various grasses by keeping trees in check. Cattle ranches are responsible for "chewing up" forests throughout the world,[123] and the presence of cattle on the German plantations near Apia suggests the likelihood of Stevenson's familiarity with the environmental impact of their grazing.[124] And so, I argue, Stevenson's woodman comes to see himself as a co-conspirator in the sensitive plant's rise to power, in part due to his *beastly* removal of those trees that are responsible for keeping this undergrowth in check.

Such a reading corresponds with Stevenson's reflections upon weeding in his *Letters*. It all begins in a letter to his mother describing his new life in Samoa as "wonderful strife," and the following confession: "I love weeding even, but clearing bush is heaven."[125] This theme continues in a letter to R. D. Blackmore (October 1890), wherein he claims to prefer weeding over against his passion for writing –

> I find myself a landholder and a farmer, with paths to hew in tropical bush, weeds to deracinate, weeders and diggers to supervise. You at least will sympathize when I tell you how this work seizes and enthralls me; I would rather do a good hour's work weeding <u>sensitive</u> – our deadliest enemy – than write two pages of my best: conscience embraces that work, congratulates the worker; I come back from an hour or two of vegetable trucidation, and conscience smiles on me like a full moon; my blood runs sweet: ah, we must still be killing somewhat! But the fight is fair; I do but defend <u>allies</u>. (Underscoring mine.)[126]

And not long afterwards, in a letter to Sydney Colvin dated 2 November 1890, Stevenson insists that there is nothing so interesting as weeding:

> This is a hard and interesting and beautiful life that we lead now: our place is in a deep cleft of Vaea Mountain, some six hundred feet above the sea, embowered in forest, which is our strangling enemy, and which we combat with axes and dollars. I went crazy over outdoor work ... *Nothing* is so interesting as weeding, clearing and path-making ... it is quite an effort not to drop into the farmer; and it does make you feel so well. To come down covered with mud and drenched with sweat and rain after some hours in the bush, change, rub down, and take a chair in the verandah, is to taste a quiet conscience.[127]

And, then, approximately four and a half months later, in a letter dated 19 March 1891, Stevenson confesses to Colvin how thoroughly intertwined his life has become with the life of plants, so much so that his unconscious mind appears to be sympathetically brimming with the bush. "It was 9.5 this morning," writes Stevenson,

> when I set off to the streamside to my weeding; where I toiled, manuring the ground with the best enricher, human sweat, till the conch shell was blown from our verandah at 10.30. At eleven we dine; about half-past twelve I tried (by exception) to work again, could make nothing on't, and by one was on my way to the weeding, where I wrought till three ... .[128]

Notably, in the next passage Stevenson appears not to be able to think (or, rather, dream) about anything but weeding, thereby giving new meaning to the term "vegetating" – a term that, I argue, encourages us to see resemblances between animals / humans and plants:

> when I shut my eyes to sleep, I know I shall see before them ... endless vivid deeps of grass and weed, each plant particular and distinct, so that I shall lie inert in body and transact for hours the mental part of my day business, choosing the noxious from the useful. And in my dreams I shall be hauling on recalcitrants, and suffering stings from nettles, stabs from citron thorns, fiery bites from ants, sickening resistances of mud and slime, evasions of slimy roots, dead weight of heat, sudden puffs of air, sudden starts from birdcalls in the contiguous forest – some mimicking my name, some laughter, some the signal of a whistle; and living over again at large the business of my day.[129]

And, finally, he begins to grapple with the significance of his newfound passion in more philosophical terms linking it to writing:

Figure 4.5 Clearing ground (wrestling with vegetable life) at Vailima (Stevenson's home in Samoa). Courtesy of the National Library of Scotland, Edinburgh.

> Though I write so little, I pass all my hours of fieldwork in continual converse and imaginary correspondence. I scarce pull up a weed, but I invent a sentence on the matter to yourself . . . methought you asked me – frankly, was I happy. Happy (said I), I was only happy once . . . But I know pleasure still; pleasure with a thousand faces, and none perfect . . . High among these I place this delight of weeding out here alone by the garrulous water, under the silence of the high wood, broken by incongruous sounds of birds . . .
>
> So far and much further, the conversation went, while I groped in slime and viscous roots, nursing and sparing little spears of grass, and retreating (even with outcry) from the prod of the wild lime. I wonder if anyone had ever the same attitude to nature as I hold, and have held for so long? This business fascinates me like a tune or a passion; yet all the while I thrill with a strong distaste. The horror of the thing, objective and subjective, is always present to my mind; <u>the horror of creeping things</u>, a superstitious horror of the void and the powers about me, the horror of my own devastation and continual murders. <u>The life of plants comes through my fingertips</u>, their struggles go to my heart like supplications. I feel myself blood-boltered; then I look back on my cleared grass, and count myself an <u>ally</u> in a fair quarrel, and make stout my heart.[130] (Underscoring mine.)

Despite the obvious pleasure that Stevenson derives from weeding alone by the garrulous water, the language that he employs here (and also in one of the previous citations too) – "ally" – reflects both the discourse of sympathy and the language of co-production. Again, I am reminded of Menely's point, that "Hume sees us as most resolutely human, in our capacity to convey passions and join interests, where we are most akin to our fellow creatures."[131] However, it is not merely that seeing things from the sensitive plant's perspective alerts Stevenson to his own humanity. Rather, it provides him with a clear idea of the critical, co-productive role he has played in the "slow death of the contending forest." And, by extension, it offers an ominous foreshadowing of the potentially catastrophic environmental consequences of transoceanic commerce and empire, particularly since (as Stevenson tells us) it was a naive European who introduced the "toothed and killing sensitive" to the island's delicately balanced ecosystem. This co-production, I argue, partly explains the sublime "horror of creeping things." I say "sublime" to emphasize the delightful terror that accompanies Stevenson's realization of how closely connected his life is with plant life – i.e. his recognition of the humanity-in-nature and nature-in-humanity. Or, again, this passage gives new meaning to the term "vegetating."

The equation that Stevenson establishes between the woodman's labor and the sensitive plant's "silent battle" also ties in very nicely with Moore's treatment of capitalism as "co-produced by manifold species."[132] We may be encouraged to read the woodman's labor as not merely an embodiment of European commercial interests, but a particular expression of capitalism's socio-spatial relations. And, since this clearing of ground to create space for a plantation has the unintended consequence of providing the sunlight necessary to fuel the invasive sensitive plant's silent takeover of the forest, the poem, thus, resonates neatly with the idea that capitalism works for nature, in as much as nature works for capitalism. Both the woodman and the invasive weed are united in their silent battle against the forest, and in this particular respect the poem invites us to reflect upon the co-productive role that extra-human natures play in the accumulation capital.

Finally, that the sensitive plant is an invasive species speaks to the shrinking of Stevenson's world – the very navigability of those deep and seemingly unfathomable seas, and the resulting approximation of places to one another. Stevenson's registration of this shrinkage recalls Woodes Rogers's (and others') early promotion of "Trade to the *South-Sea*,"[133] and how, as Schiebinger and Swan note, "European colonial expansion touched off an unprecedented widespread movement of flora globally that . . . deeply restructured the world agricultural map."[134] The following lines from the poem, in particular, account for this shrinking of the world, and the corresponding threat that invasive species pose to biodiversity:

> Here too thy banners move abroad:
> Forest and city, sea and shore,
> And the whole earth, thy threshing-floor![135]

These few lines provide some idea of the obscuring of geographical distinctions that Fielding discusses – specifically, the merging of land and sea. But one may also be reminded of the cyclical rhythms of the ocean here, or, rather, the "dynamic model of geography" that DeLoughrey employs to "position island cultures in the world historical process."[136] The presence of this species in Samoa, which Stevenson says was brought to the island by a "fool" who "used to lecture and sentimentalise over the tender thing," and its having taken "charge of this island" serves to not only complicate the popular mythology of Pacific island isolation (see also my Introduction and Chapter 1), but also to stress the delicate balance and vulnerability of island ecosystems throughout the world. "The Woodman" is not merely a poem about the relationship between art and nature – i.e. human efforts to contain an otherwise uncontainable Nature. It is a poem about the unruly nature of biological invasions. Walking may have made Stevenson aware of the "subdued note" of the landscape ("Roads") both in Scotland and Samoa, but weeding has taught him to sympathetically identify with plants – i.e. to see things from a plant's-eye view. Perhaps this is why Stevenson insists that, "*Nothing* is so interesting as weeding,"[137] for at one point in his meditations upon weeding, he notes, "*Tuitui* is a truly strange beast, and gives food for thought."[138] In this respect, I argue that weeding (and *Mimosa pudica*, in particular) has triggered a seismic, ecological shift in Stevenson's thinking. This alternative view calls into focus the otherwise "hidden worlds that form the nexus of human and nonhuman multiplicity."[139] Or, as noted earlier, the sympathy that forms between Stevenson and the sensitive plant – a correspondence that triggers his recognition of the co-productive role the he plays in the "whole silent battle, murder, and slow death of the contending forest"[140] – prompts a shift in attention away from questions of identity or humanity – i.e., who am I? – in favor of consideration of one's place in relationship to other organisms in the ecosystem.[141] For Stevenson, I argue, the horror of creeping things lies in this recognition of their agency, as it were, a recognition of the unruliness of particular natures and their capacity to not only upset anthropocentric notions of who we are, but also (drawing once more on Cole's treatment of Latour's theory of actants) to destabilize the very "idea of system itself."[142]

Thus, I argue, the weeding of *Mimosa pudica* also explains why Stevenson was inspired to compose his most famous South Seas tale, *The Beach of Falesá*, for the violent antagonism that develops between the two British traders in this story, Wiltshire and Case, is comparable to the competition for sunlight that typifies the tropical rainforest ecosystem and which he carefully describes in "The Woodman." Stevenson's South Pacific writings may afford us an opportunity to not only think through crises relating to biological invasion and crop monoculture – that is, providing we remain attentive to environmental particularities, to the "subdued note of the landscape," as well as to the types of animals and plants that appear over again. "The Woodman," in particular, also provides a horrifying glimpse of environmental degradation linked to transoceanic commerce and trade. In this poem Stevenson provides a most insightful and unforgiving catastrophic vision of capitalism as world-ecology.

Plant Action and Stevenson's Tragic Jungle

It was during Stevenson's epic struggle to contain the invasive *Mimosa pudica* that, in addition to composing "The Woodman," he conceived of what he would later describe as his "first realistic South Sea story"[143] – namely, *The Beach of Falesá*. In a letter to Sydney Colvin that he wrote on 7 November 1890, Stevenson details his inspiration for the narrative:

> My poem "The Woodman" stands; but I have taken refuge in a new story, which just shot through me like a bullet in one of my moments of awe, alone in that <u>tragic jungle</u>. *The High Woods of Ulufanua* ... It is very strange, very extravagant, I daresay; but it's varied, and picturesque, and has a pretty love affair, and ends well. *Ulufanua* is a lovely Samoan word, *ulu* = grove, *fanua* = land, grove land – "the tops of the high trees."[144] (Underscoring mine.)

Lending credence to Stephen Gwynn's early assessment of the fiction that Stevenson produced in Samoa, this letter alerts us to the degree to which the story was inspired by his "material environment."[145] Distinguished for its realism, or, say, Stevenson's devotion to "plain physical sensations plainly and expressly rendered,"[146] *The Beach of Falesá* turns upon not merely the personal, but also, as Roslyn Jolly carefully notes, the global. "The stories ... are the product of Stevenson's exposure to both the indigenous and imperialist cultures of the Pacific," writes Jolly, in her "Introduction," to *South Sea Tales*, "and, they demonstrate the inseparability of these two elements in the cultural constitution of the region."[147] This is an astute observation, to be sure. And I completely agree with Jolly's overarching assessment that "these works offer valuable insights into the transformation of nineteenth-century imperial culture into twentieth-century global culture."[148] They do this, to be sure. But, to paraphrase Michel Serres, let us not forget the world of things, as the point of this chapter continues to be that of remembering *not* merely the cultural, but also the natural-historical implications of this transformation. As the above letter encourages us to consider the *tragic jungle*'s role in Stevenson's creative process, in what follows I offer a more thorough exploration of the ecological implications of this inseparability of not merely indigenous and imperialist cultures, but also humans, animals, plants, and minerals.

In the same long letter I cited above (7 November 1890), for example, Stevenson continues to dwell upon *Mimosa pudica*, highlighting for Colvin the considerable sway it held over his imagination:

> The guid wife had bread to bake . . . O! But between whiles she was down with me weeding sensitive in the paddock. The men have but new passed over it; I was round in that very place to see the weeding was done thoroughly, and already the reptile springs behind our heels. <u>Tuitui is truly a strange beast, and gives food for thought.</u> I am nearly sure – I cannot yet be quite, I mean to experiment, when I am less on the hot chase of the beast – that, even at the instant it shrivels up his leaves, he strikes his prickles downward so as to catch the uprooting finger: instinctive, say the gabies; but so is man's impulse to strike out. One thing that takes and holds me is to see the strange variation in the propagation of alarm among these rooted beasts; at times it spreads to a radius (I speak by the guess of the eye) of five or six inches; at times only one individual plant appears frightened at a time. We tried how long it took one to recover; 'tis a sanguine creature; it is all abroad again before (I guess again) two minutes. It is odd how difficult in this world it is to be armed. The double armour of this plant betrays it . . . a touch on the leaves, and its fine sense and retractile action betrays its identity at once. Yet it has one gift incomparable. Rome had virtue and knowledge: Rome perished. The sensitive plant has indigestible seeds – so they say – and it will flourish forever. I give my advice thus to a young plant: have a strong root, a weak stem, and an indigestible seed: so you will outlast the eternal city, and your progeny will clothe mountains, and the irascible planter will blaspheme in vain. The weak point of *tuitui* is that its stem is strong.[149] (Underscoring mine.)

The focused attention that Stevenson gives to the plant (e.g. that he offers measurements, and he intends to conduct further experiments) clearly reveals someone peculiarly obsessed with its uncanny animal-like qualities, denoted here too by terms like "reptile" and "beast." His fascination appears to be so overwhelming that one cannot help but wonder about the plant's influence upon *The Beach of Falesá* itself, a connection reinforced by the masculine gender that Stevenson gives to it. Is, for example, the plant's volatility (and supposed hostility) not comparable to either Wiltshire or Case's volatility in *Falesá*?

Of course, Stevenson was not the first major British author to have discovered food for thought in plant sensitivity. Evidently fueled by the eighteenth-century's cult of sensibility – "the cultural movement devoted to tear-demanding exhibitions of pathos and unqualified virtue"[150] – the imaginations of Romantic-era writers

Percy Shelley and Sydney Owenson were similarly nourished by *Mimosa pudica*, and its appearance in greenhouses throughout Britain, a phenomenon that merits closer inspection to distinguish Stevenson's peculiar – i.e. sympathetic – fascination with the plant.

Furthermore, as the original title and characters' names imply, the narrative is rooted in the tropical rainforest surrounding his home on Samoa. As such, we are encouraged to take a closer look at this so-called "tragic jungle"[151] that figures in the story, though perhaps not merely for its role in shrouding in mystery the strange power that the story's antagonist, a crooked English trader named Case, wields over the island's indigenous population. What is the motivation for Stevenson's characterization of Samoa's tropical rainforest as tragic? And what makes the high bush of Falesá a similarly "tragic jungle"? Is it merely because of the human tragedy that unfolds in the darkness of the forest? Or does he intend for us to view Falesá's jungle itself as the victim of European agribusiness / global capitalism, not unlike Samoa's cocoanut alley? Or, rather, exactly what sort of "food for thought" did the invasive sensitive plant provide Stevenson (as compared with literary predecessors: Erasmus Darwin, Percy Shelley, and Sydney Owenson)? How might the plant's biology – and, by extension, forest ecology – have informed Stevenson's composition of *The Beach of Falesá*?

****

At the outset of the story, Stevenson couches the protagonist, Mr. Wiltshire's arrival on the island in notably similar terms to those that he previously used to describe the curative properties of mountain air. Wiltshire observes: "Here was a fresh experience: even the tongue would be quite strange to me; and the look of these woods and mountains, and the rare smell of them, renewed my blood."[152] The sentiment clearly echoes Stevenson's suggestion in *Forest Notes* that, "it is not so much for its beauty that the forest makes a claim on men's hearts, as for that subtle something, that quality of the air, that emanation from the old trees, that so wonderfully changes and renews a weary spirit."[153] Wiltshire views the change of scenery as positively transforming. However, his expectations for a fresh start are complicated, in as much as Case contrives to marry him to an "out-islander" against whom there is a standing taboo. As a result, Wiltshire finds himself tabooed by proxy to his wife, Uma, shortly after his arrival, thereby enabling Case to maintain his monopoly of the copra trade. (Copra is the dried kernel of the coconut, from which valuable oil is extracted.)[154] The ensuing plot revolves around Wiltshire's efforts to remove the taboo. And this leads to his exploration of the island's high bush, which he believes holds the secret to Case's mysterious power over the islanders. Of course, it turns out that the high bush is not haunted by the devil, Tiapolo, as the islanders suspect, but that Case has merely rigged up the trees with Aeolian harps ("a candle-box" with "banjo strings stretched so as to sound when the wind blew" (53)), as well as crafted wooden figures ("bogies") decorated with luminous paint to frighten trespassers, conceal the storage of trade goods, and, in effect, reinforce his authority. It is no fresh experience that Wiltshire enjoys upon the island, but something old, or *uncanny* that haunts his marriage to Uma.

Stevenson's choice of the Aeolian harp as the device used to frighten those who venture into this uncultivated section of the island invites us to situate Case's treachery in a particular historical period – namely, the Romantic era during which this musical instrument became a relatively common household item in Britain. The appearance of the harp in several important Romantic-era poems, including, of course, Coleridge's "The Eolian Harp," serves as a testament to its popularity in the British imagination at this juncture – a period that (not surprisingly) follows in the wake of considerable Pacific exploration, including, most famously, the three expeditions led by Captain James Cook in 1768–71, 1772–5, and 1776–9. In fact, from the 1760s onward, a number of "ambitious voyages of discovery" were sponsored by both England and France, including those led by Bougainville, Byron, Wallis, Carteret, Cook, La Pérouse, and Vancouver.[155] And, of course, numerous commercial voyages followed shortly thereafter. "By the late 1780s and throughout several subsequent decades," notes Burnham,

> the Pacific was also traversed by numerous British, American, French, and Russian commercial voyages seeking profits from the lucrative China trade as well as from sealing and whaling. During the late eighteenth century, then, a multinational array of goods and bodies moved with some regularity around the Pacific Ocean, its American and Asian coastlines, and Polynesia.[156]

Burnham notes too, that, "this international explosion in Pacific travel was accompanied by an equally international print explosion in Pacific travel writing."[157] That is, while publications by Dampier and Rogers (see Chapter 1) clearly whetted early eighteenth-century British readers' appetites for global maritime travel literature – hence, the popularity of Daniel Defoe's adventure capitalism in novels like *The Life and Strange Surprizing Adventures of Robinson Crusoe* (1719), *The Farther Adventures of Robinson Crusoe* (1719), and *The Life, Adventure, and Pyracies of the Famous Captain Singleton* (1720) – this international print explosion that Burnham describes, including John Hawkesworth's 1773 collection of the English voyages of Byron, Wallis, Carteret, and Cook, rendered the idea of transoceanic travel a key component of the British cultural / national / imperial imagination, clearly anticipating the Empire's exponential growth in the nineteenth century. And so, given this coincidence of the Aeolian harp's popularity with, say, Cook's efforts (vis-à-vis Hawkesworth) to enfold Pacific islands into British consciousness, it does not seem at all strange for Case to have such a device at his disposal. What is rather more curious is the similar Romantic-era fascination with *Mimosa pudica*, the presence of which Stevenson treats as a distinguishing feature of the cultivated Western section of the island.

****

In *The Action Plant* (1992), an important study of movement and nervous behavior in plants, Paul Simons writes:

> There are living beings in your garden that are not animals, yet they move. They have no proper muscles, yet the contents of their cells churn around using muscle proteins. They have no nerves, yet they have nerve-like electrical signals. They have no brains, but they have senses of taste, vision, touch, gravity, temperature, humidity, pressure, electricity and sometimes magnetism. Some of them even catch and eat meat by their own movements. These organisms are called plants.[158]

Simons's study of plant action not only challenges us to acknowledge the artificiality of the long-established boundaries biologists have set up to distinguish between living organisms, and especially animals and plants, but also offers us an important glimpse into the operations of *Mimosa pudica* (or sensitive plant), that so-called freak of nature that lies at the heart, I argue, of Stevenson's prescient grasp of animal-plant sympathies.

For starters, Simons points out, that, while the Venus flytrap's carnivorous behavior might seem really strange, the fact remains that "an enormous variety of plants have special movements for a variety of survival strategies."[159] *Mimosa pudica*'s sensitivity – its ability to feel the touch of a potentially life-threatening herbivore, and, through "rapid water release from specialized cells located at the bases of leaflets and leaf stalks,"[160] defend itself accordingly – has particular animal-like qualities. Plant action as such not only calls to mind Lucinda Cole's point (vis-à-vis Bruno Latour) about how so-called imperfect creatures are, "like humans, *actants* in the world ... [they] 'modify other actors'; they are not subjects, but 'interveners.'"[161] The automatic nature of the plant's reaction to given stimuli also resonates, however uncannily, with Hume's treatment of the mechanics of sympathy, as (again), "a good-natur'd man finds himself in an instant of the same humour with his company."[162] The mechanical, involuntary, or, rather, instinctive nature of this sympathetic bonding is key.

Moreover, Simons's metaphor to explain how plant mobility (as such) works – a battlefield – resonates neatly with Stevenson's own metaphorical depictions of the tropical underbrush. He explains: "think of it as a battlefield. The soldiers at the battlefront see that they are under attack (perception), and so they radio to the rear for help (signaling the excitation) and fresh guns are delivered (executing the action)."[163] This battlefield metaphor is useful because it recalls precisely the type of language that Stevenson relies upon to describe the competition for sunlight that takes place in the tropical underbrush: "So hushed the woodland warfare goes / Unceasing; and the silent foes / Grapple and smother, strain and clasp / Without a cry, without a gasp."[164]

Of course, it may be worth noting too that the early American botanist, William Bartram, was quite keen to explore similarities between plants and animals. In the "Introduction" to his *Travels through North and South Carolina, Georgia, and East and West Florida, the Cherokee Country, The Extensive Territories of the Muscogulges, or Creek Confederacy, and the Country of the Chactaws* (Philadelphia, 1791), for example, Bartram reflects upon the familiarity between animals and plants, a train of thought that he aptly launches with a characteristically poetic account of "the extraordinary Dionea muscipula!," or Venus flytrap, which happens to be native to the subtropical wetlands in the southeastern United States (North and South Carolina) through which he traveled:

> Astonishing production! see the incarnate lobes expanding, how gay and sportive they appear! Ready on the spring to intrap incautious deluded insects! what artifice! there behold one of the leaves just closed upon a struggling fly; another has gotten a worm; its hold is sure, its prey can never escape – carnivorous vegetable! Can we after

viewing this object, hesitate a moment to confess, that vegetable beings are endued with some sensible faculties or attributes, familiar to those that dignify animal nature; they are organical, living and self-moving bodies, for we see here, in this plant, motion and volition.[165]

Bartram offers a further example of climbing plants:

> What power or faculty is it, that directs the cirri of the Cucurbita, Momordica, Vitis, and other climbers, towards the twigs of shrubs, trees, and other friendly support? we see them invariably leaning, extending, and like the finger of the human hand, reaching to catch hold of what is nearest, just as if they had eyes to see with . . . is it sense or instinct that influences their actions?[166]

And, finally, drawing upon these (and other) careful observations of plant action, Bartram offers the following prescient assertion of a connection between animals and plants:

> The vital principle or efficient cause of motion and action, in the animal and vegetable system, perhaps may be more familiar than we generally apprehend.[167]

Given what we now know about plant cells and electricity, such claims may not seem so surprising. But, considering the historical period into which Bartram was born, the Enlightenment – a period that also gave birth to the Linnaean system of classification, as it were, geared towards a hierarchical separation of organisms into distinct groups (domains, phyla, classes, orders, families, genera, species, etc.) – it is amazing to find a botanist so very quick to establish common ground across plant and animal kingdoms. Bartram's poetical highlighting of an *uncanny* resemblance (if not sympathy) that exists between animals and plants sets him apart from his scientific peers, but perhaps also endears him to the Romantic poets, who were similarly attracted to the phenomenon of plant sensitivity.

Indeed, the very curiosity of plant mobility no doubt contributed to *Mimosa pudica*'s popularity in Britain and elsewhere. That is, the defense mechanism designed to guard against herbivores basically ensured that it would be cultivated by humans as a curiosity in greenhouses throughout the world. And Stevenson clearly understood this, having noted (again) that it was first introduced to Samoa by a fool who used to "sentimentalise over the tender thing." As Henry Charles Andrews explains, in *The Botanist's Repository* (1807–8), *Mimosa pudica* was "neither new nor rare" at this time, though "nevertheless very interesting" because it had "not hitherto made its appearance in any modern publication; nor is there any colored figure of it extant. Our representation of it, therefore, is in part a novelty however old and familiar the plant itself may be":

> According to the observations of Linnaeus, it opens or expands its foliage at three in the morning, and closes it about six in the evening. Its singular quality of shrinking from the touch is supposed to be owing to its being strongly saturated with oxygen gas, which it disengages upon the slightest provocation, and its place for a short time is supplied by the atmospheric air . . .[168]

Reinforcing Andrews's assessment of cultivators' familiarity with this so-called bashful Mimosa, Thomas Green, in *The Universal Herbal, or, Botanical, Medical, and Agricultural Dictionary, Containing an Account of All the known Plants in the World* (1824), insists that "it is the most common of any species in the islands of the West Indies, and in the English gardens. The seeds are sold in the seed shops by the name of Humble Plant."[169] Indeed, while the plant first appears in Carl Linnaeus's 1753 *Species Plantarum*, it is its presence in Romantic poetry that indicates the degree to which this indigenous American plant species (a native of South and Central America) had become, by the early nineteenth century, effectively incorporated into British consciousness, as it were, "commonly grown as a curiosity in greenhouses."[170]

Aside from basic human curiosity, another reason for the plant's popularity lies in the linkage between plant action – *Mimosa pudica*'s "unusually quick response to touch" – and the cult of sensibility. In Sydney Owenson's poetic fragment, "The Sensitive Plant," for example, leaf movement serves as a convenient metaphor through which to explore human emotional sensitivity – the sensibility that, as Janet Todd explains, "jangled the nerves of Europe." "Little used before the mid-eighteenth century," explains Todd, sensibility "came to denote the faculty of feeling, the capacity for extremely refined emotion and a quickness to display compassion for suffering."[171] The first stanza of Owenson's poem reads as follows:

> Sweet timid trembling thing,* no more
> Shalt thou beneath each rude breath sink;
> Thy vestal attribute is o'er,
> E'en from the softest sigh to shrink.**[172]

Owenson draws upon plant action here to establish a contrast between feminine sensibility – that power of feeling that distinguishes a truly elevated human soul – and the unfeeling harshness, or "rude breath" of Enlightened (i.e. scientific, rational, and patriarchal) British society. The annotations reinforce this, as she clearly privileges "SENTIMENT" over Science:

> *This little impromptu arose from observing a sprig of the Sensitive Plant dead on a very *feeling* and *affectionate* bosom.
> ** "Every vegetable as well as the Sensitive Plant shrinks when wounded," says the Naturalist. But SENTIMENT, unwilling to relinquish the delicate attribute of its own sweet shrub, replies to Science, "It is true; but in other plants, even when wounded, the motion is too slow to be perceptible; while the vibration of the Sensitive Plant, even to the faintest touch, is as quick as it is *visible*."[173]

Erasmus Darwin, in *The Botanic Garden*, similarly draws upon plant action to convey an ideology of sensibility:

> Weak with nice sense, the chaste Mimosa stands,
> From each rude touch withdraws her timid hands;
> Oft as light clouds o'er-pass the Summer-glade,
> Alarm'd she trembles at the moving shade;
> And feels, alive through all her tender form;
> Shuts her sweet eye-lids to approaching night,
> And hails with freshen'd charms the rising light.[174]

Although the following line – "So sinks or rises with the changeful hour / The liquid silver in its glass tower" – neatly corresponds with the science behind *Mimosa pudica*'s movement (its reliance upon "rapid water release from specialized cells located at the bases of leaflets and leaf stalks")[175] – Darwin anthropomorphically equates plant sensitivity with feminine innocence and sensibility, whereas Shelley's poem, *The Sensitive Plant*, a "mysterious song of beauty and death,"[176] neatly invites us to consider the plant's mobility as a bridge between two worlds – animal and plant:

> But none ever trembled and panted with bliss
> In the garden, the field, and the wilderness,
> Like a doe in the noontide with love's sweet want,
> As the companionless Sensitive Plant.[177]

For Owenson and other Romantic-era authors / poets, *Mimosa pudica* figures as a convenient device through which to explore how human sensibility, though idealized, becomes a liability or source of unhappiness in an unfeeling world – not a flaw exactly, but a character trait that, as in Susanna Rowson's remarkably popular *Charlotte Temple* (London, 1791 / Philadelphia, 1794), frequently figures in the female protagonist's tragic – i.e. tear-jerking – demise. Or, consider P. W. Latham's *The Floral Festival*, a didactic series appearing in the American periodical, *The Family Circle*. Volume XIV, Number IV–VII features "The Sensitive Plant" (1856), a cautionary tale about overindulgence in sentimentality. Accompanied by the following curious engraving, Latham maps the tragic downfall of a young woman, whose "extreme sensibility" and "mimosa-like susceptibility" are ultimately responsible for her having to "sigh out her existence in loneliness and poverty" – a "warning to all, that in abusing God's gifts we must become miserable."[178]

However, it is important to point out here that such representations of *Mimosa pudica* in Romantic and Victorian literature and culture typically do not correspond with the actual biology of plant action. *Mimosa pudica*'s sensitivity likely serves as a defense against herbivores. Simons explains, that, "an enormous variety of plants

Figure 4.6 "The Sensitive Plant," from P. W. Latham's "The Floral Festival" in *The Family Circle* periodical (New York, 1856). Courtesy of the American Antiquarian Society, Worcester, MA.

have special movements for a variety of reasons," including: "catching animals for food, defending themselves from animals, enhancing their prospects for cross-pollination, scattering fruits or spores to new homes, keeping their photosynthesis mechanism well supplied with sunlight, water, and air," etc.[179] Plant sensitivity is, therefore, no liability – but, rather, a considerable strength. Or, to couch this in Darwinian evolutionary terms, sensitivity generally contributes to a plant's survival in an otherwise hostile environment. In his book-length study of plants that rely on sensitivity to catch insects, *Insectivorous Plants*, for example, Darwin invokes the evolutionary concept of a struggle for survival – "the battle for life" – as he carefully details the animal-like advantages of plant action as such.[180] Notably, Darwin claims that his interest in this topic began in the summer of 1860, when he was "surprised by finding how large a number of insects were caught by the leaves of the common sun-dew (*Drosera rotundifolia*) on a heath in Sussex":

> I gathered by chance a dozen plants, bearing fifty-six fully expanded leaves, and on thirty-one of these dead insects or remnants of them adhered; and, no doubt, many more would have been caught afterwards by these same leaves, and still more by those as yet not expanded ... On one large leaf I found the remains of thirteen distinct insects. Flies (Diptera) are captured much oftener than other insects. The largest kind which I have seen caught was a small butterfly (Cænonympha pamphilus) but the Rev. H. M. Wilkinson informs me that he found a large living dragon-fly with its body firmly held by two leaves. As this plant is extremely common in some districts, the number of insects thus annually slaughtered must be prodigious.[181]

Notably too, Darwin occasionally compares plant and animal sensitivity. He insists, for example, that the human tongue is not nearly as sensitive as the tentacles of the sun-dew:

> extremely minute particles of glass, cinders, hair, thread, precipitated chalk, &c., when placed on the glands of the outer tentacles, caused them to bend ... Larger particles than those ... cause no sensation when placed on the tongue, one of the most sensitive parts of the human body.[182]

However, as the title of his study suggests, Darwin's primary concern is with plant action that figures not as a reactive form of defense, but as a proactive, offensive mechanism designed to satisfy the plant's hunger for life. And, of course, let us not forget, that, *Dionea muscipula,* or the Venus flytrap's carnivorous behavior depends upon a similar sort of sensitivity as that which figures in *Mimosa pudica*'s seismonastic movement. Would Shelley have likely romanticized the sensitivity of *Mimosa pudica* had he understood its close relationship to the Venus flytrap's bloodthirstiness?

To Stevenson's great credit, he (unlike his Romantic- and Victorian-era predecessors) appears to have understood plant sensitivity as precisely a defensive / offensive mechanism, providing *Mimosa pudica* with an undeniable advantage – "its cunning sense"[183] – over other plants in Samoa's tropical rainforest. The ideas (and dreams) that spring from Stevenson's close encounters with the plants and animals in the tropical underbrush – i.e. the food that *Mimosa pudica* provides for thought – evokes Bruno Latour's heterarchical theory of actants, in which humans, animals, and plants all act upon one another in "dynamic and interlocking systems."[184] And, notably, Stevenson's revaluation of the plant corresponds with Case's improvisation with the Aeolian harp to defend against trespassers in the jungle that he has staked out to serve as his secret storehouse. The comparison between *Mimosa pudica* seems pretty obvious when we consider the mechanics of the Aeolian harp – i.e. that it generates music by virtue of the sensitivity of its strings to the wind. And it seems apt too for the Romantics to have latched onto both figures as convenient symbols for the sensibility – the "capacity for extremely refined emotion and a quickness to display compassion for suffering"– they imagined serving as the basis for a sort of spiritual transcendence and sociopolitical revolution.[185]

However, that a symbol of Romantic sensibility (the Aeolian harp) gets strategically reappropriated to serve the interests of such a ruthless trader, lacking in any sort of moral or ethical compass, as Case, who is engaged in the big, transoceanic business of copra / coconut oil, suggests the failure of Romanticism to stem the tide of laissez-faire capitalism. Indeed, the insightfulness of *The Beach of Falesá* lies partly in this critical reappraisal of Romanticism. But is the Aeolian harp's uncanny appearance in the narrative supposed to establish a neat equation between the Romantic poet's overvaluation of sensibility and the islanders' superstitious naivety? Or is it Coleridge, and his poem, "The Eolian Harp," that Stevenson questions, in particular? Is Coleridge too preoccupied with human genius and emotion (too anthropocentric)? Are his views of Nature in the poem not mistaken?

The latter would tie in nicely with the aforementioned Romantic and Victorian authors' failure to appreciate the real, scientific significance of plant sensitivity. And, of course, the violent economy of particular natures that Stevenson explores in "The Woodman" differs from the overwhelmingly beautiful sort of Nature (upper-case N) that Coleridge celebrates in "The Eolian Harp":

> And what if all of animated nature
> Be but organic Harps diversely fram'd,
> That tremble into thought, as o'er them sweeps
> Plastic and vast, one intellectual breeze,
> At once the Soul of each, and God of all? (l. 44–8)[186]

Indeed, the unity between man and Nature that figures in Coleridge's "Eolian Harp" has little to do with the cross-species (human-extra-human) collaboration that unfolds in "The Woodman." The former has particular transcendental value, whereas the latter is firmly rooted in the physical-material world – a non-transcendental, animal-plant-human sympathy geared towards basic survival. The former relationship, in so far as it has special transcendental or religious significance, remains (at heart) an anthropocentric enterprise – i.e. "one intellectual breeze" – whereas the latter, I argue, acknowledges the non-Cartesian human place *in* nature / nature *in* humanity. The latter is a leveling gesture, prioritizing neither plant nor animal species. And this is where the uncanny plays a role in Stevenson's narrative.

In his remarkably influential essay, "The Uncanny," Freud defines the uncanny (*unheimlich*) not as something that frightens because it is unfamiliar, but rather something so very deeply familiar (long forgotten or thoroughly repressed) that when it does manifest it appears strange. "The uncanny," explains Freud, "proceeds from something familiar that has been repressed."[187] Although one might be inclined to attribute the uncanny feelings aroused by plant action to some measure of anthropomorphism, such as the projection that clearly factors into Shelley's poem, "The Sensitive Plant," such a view does not account for Stevenson's experience in Samoa – i.e. the intimate knowledge that he acquires through his futile efforts to eradicate *Mimosa pudica*. The uncanny that Stevenson experiences as he becomes more thoroughly acquainted with the plant's behavior has, I argue, primarily to do with the revelation of a thoroughly repressed – i.e. long forgotten (at least in the Western tradition) ecological truth – namely, the deep familiarity and ties (sympathetic and otherwise) that exist between animals and plants. *Mimosa pudica* has an uncanny effect upon Stevenson because its motion and volition remind him of the interrelationship of all things. It is not a matter of projection, but *reflection*. Stevenson recognizes aspects of his own self and, broadly speaking, the human experience reflected in the plant's "strange variation," "double armor," and its "cunning sense."

What's more, in *The Beach of Falesá,* Stevenson obliges us to consider this uncanny, ecological interrelationship not merely through the sensitive plant's appearance in the narrative – a cameo that occurs when describing the one half of the island settled by humans (both Indigenous and European) – but also through his usage of such key terms as "vegetating." This occurs during one of the confrontations between the two traders, in which Case confesses that he hasn't any desire to kill Wiltshire, so long as he continues to "vegetate":

> I give you my word I don't want to shoot you. Why should I? You don't hinder me any. You haven't got one pound of copra but what you made with your own hands, like a negro slave. You're vegetating – that's what I call it – and I don't care where you vegetate, nor yet how long. Give me your word you don't mean to shoot me, and I'll give you a lead and walk away. (56)

Case's use of the word here to emphasize Wiltshire's idleness corresponds with the typical usage of the intransitive verb, vegetate: "to lead a passive existence without exertion of body or mind" (*Webster's Dictionary*). In her critical introduction to the tale, Roslyn Jolly claims, that, "Wiltshire's emotional attachment to Uma [unusual for Stevenson's mostly homosocial work] outweighs his desire for profit."[188] Perhaps that is what vegetating means here – an unruly nature, or unwillingness to contribute to the advancement of what appears in the Samoan's eyes as a barbaric and absurd global economy.[189] At the very outset of his novella, *The Ebb-Tide,* for example, the term clearly seems to be associated with one's failure to prosper in the Pacific:

> Throughout the island world of the Pacific, scattered men of many European races and from almost every grade of society carry activity and disseminate disease. Some prosper, some vegetate. Some have mounted the steps of thrones and owned islands and navies. Others again must marry for a livelihood; a strapping, merry, chocolate-coloured dame supports them in sheer idleness ... they sprawl in palm-leaf verandahs and entertain an island audience with memoirs of the music-hall.[190]

However, that the term quite literally means to "grow in the manner of a plant" (*Webster's Dictionary*), and, further, that it derives from the Latin, *vegetātus,* to invigorate – alerts us to the possibility of its having uncanny, ecological significance too. By which I mean, is Stevenson's use of the term here not somehow relevant to his own weeding? Invigorating work, to be sure, weeding (as I have argued) enables Stevenson to sympathetically adopt a plant's-eye view of things. Is Wiltshire's vegetating supposed to reflect his occupation of a similar vantage point or are we meant to interpret this as more symptomatic of his alienation from the global capitalist economy (a side effect of that taboo against Uma)? Is it a matter of his timing – his living outside capitalism's accelerated turnover time, as appears to be the case for the vegetating Europeans in *The Ebb-Tide*? Is it even possible to live outside such a transoceanic, global economy?

That Wiltshire ultimately defeats Case, thereby securing his monopoly of the island's copra trade begs a similarly important question: is plant growth – or, specifically, the spread of such a cunning invasive species as *Mimosa pudica* – not comparable to the development of global capitalism? Perhaps the answer depends on the vegetable. Stevenson's correspondence implies that this particular species offered itself as a peculiar sort of model of the inveterate capitalist's relentless pursuit of profit. Perhaps Stevenson used *Mimosa pudica*'s cunning invasion of Samoa as a model not merely for Case's "readiness and invention," of which, as the missionary Tarleton observes, "there is no end" (42). Perhaps the sensitive plant's volatility and motion informed Stevenson's depiction of Wiltshire's triumph too. His name, Wiltshire – i.e. WILT SURE – supports this connection, as it mirrors the plant's seismonastic movement: the sudden and apparent wilting of its leaves. Furthermore, while the undoubted sympathy and love that Wiltshire experiences for Uma perhaps corresponds with the plant's role in the Romantic-era cult of sensibility, we must also consider the role that sensibility plays in Wiltshire's cunning. Is sensibility not part and parcel of the cunning that enables Wiltshire to triumph over Case in the end, much as the plant's sensitivity led it to become a favorite curiosity in British greenhouses throughout the world? (We mustn't forget the so-called sentimental fool who, according to Stevenson, was responsible for the plant's introduction to Samoa.)[191] After all, it is precisely that sympathy, for example, that Wiltshire extends to Uma that implicates her in his efforts to outsmart Case, and that sympathy too which obscures his true motives. (Here, again, I think it worth drawing a parallel between the automatic nature of plant sensitivity and Hume's treatment of the mechanics of sympathy – i.e. the idea that "a good-natur'd man finds himself in an instant of the same humour with his company.")[192] Perhaps Wiltshire is / was content to live happily (and properly) married to Uma, as it were, neglecting to actively participate in the island's transoceanic copra trade. But, after he succeeds in removing his competition (Case), are his true motives not revealed to us when we discover his lingering resentment for having to trade fairly with the island inhabitants? Bearing in mind Stevenson's "advice to a young plant" – namely, "have a strong root, a weak stem, and an indigestible seed: so you will outlast the eternal city, and your progeny will clothe mountains, and the irascible planter will blaspheme in vain"[193] – the comparison seems apt because Wiltshire outlives Case to monopolize the island's trade:

> So there was I, left alone in my glory at Falesá; and when the schooner came round I filled her up, and gave her a deck-cargo half as high as the house. I must say Mr. Tarleton did the right thing by us; but he took a meanish kind of revenge.
> "Now, Mr Wiltshire," said he, "I've put you all square with everybody here. It wasn't difficult to do, Case being gone; but I have done it, and given my pledge besides that you will deal fairly with the natives. I must ask you to keep my word." (70)

That Case confesses he was bothered by this obligation to have to trade fairly with "the natives," and how (despite his success on Falesá) he was "half glad when the firm moved me on to another station, where I was under no kind of pledge and could look my balances in the face" (70) suggests that he had never lost sight of his true motive – profit / the accumulation of capital – throughout.

In short, Stevenson's work, as well as his letters detailing his peculiar fascination with *Mimosa pudica*, encourage us to remember that animals and plant "are," as Latour suggests, "like humans, *actants* in the world . . . [they] 'modify other actors'; they are not subjects, but 'interveners.'"[194] That Wiltshire owes his triumph over Case to his "cunning sense" represents precisely this particular invasive species, the sensitive plant's intervention in Stevenson's writing, and thereby invites us to redefine the key term, "vegetating." Perhaps vegetating implies not merely to live like a plant, but also to acquire a plant's-eye view of both the tropical rainforest and the world / global economy. Perhaps the term serves as some measure of Wiltshire's ecological consciousness – that is, very much in keeping with Stevenson's own keen sense of the uncanny similarities and cooperation between animals and plants. Analogies, including similes, often figure in Stevenson's work as reminders of this interrelationship between animals and plants, whether it's the mosquitoes that hum like bees (8), the comparison of Case to a parasite, crawling and feeding upon old Captain Randall "like the flies" (9), Uma "crying and sobbing to herself with no more noise than an insect" (68), or the butterflies that flop up and down "like dead leaves" (51). And, in *Kidnapped* too, the survival of David Balfour and Alan Breck rests precisely upon their sympathetic identification with various animals. A good example of this would be when Alan explains to David that, in order to cross Rannoch Moor safely, "we'll have to play at being hares."[195] The success of this gesture – a strategy that builds on the same idea as Stevenson's own sympathetic identification with *Mimosa pudica* – I think rests entirely on what Menely describes (via Hume) as a "fundamental 'correspondence of *passions* in men and animals.'"[196] The scenario unfolds as follows:

> With that he began to run forward on his hands and knees with an incredible quickness, as though it were his natural way of going. All the time, too, he kept winding in and out in the lower parts of the moorland where we were the best concealed. Some of these had been burned or at least scathed with fire; and there rose in our faces (which were close to the ground) a blinding, choking dust as fine as smoke. The water was long out; and this posture of running on the hands and knees brings an overmastering weakness and weariness, so that the joints ache and the wrists faint under your weight.[197]

The experience of crossing Rannoch hare-like utterly transforms Alan, if not simply David's perception of him, as he explains: "his breath cried and whistled as it came; and his voice, when he whispered his observations in my ear during our halts, *sounded like nothing human*" (italics mine).[198] Of course, the transformation that unfolds here is no supernatural metamorphosis; it is, rather, that Alan's play at being a hare illustrates to David a profound ecological truth – that humanity and nature are not divided, but united. Alan's play raises David's ecological consciousness; it results in his profound recognition of the humanity-in-nature / nature-in-humanity.

Perhaps the same is true of Wiltshire's living like a plant. Stevenson reinforces the metaphorical linkage between Wiltshire's and the sensitive plant's struggle for survival with his careful division of the island into two parts conveniently separated by a "long mound of stones." Pacific Islanders and European traders inhabit the western section of the island, whereas the eastern section consists primarily of high bush or jungle, and, thus, appears to be yet another one of Stevenson's desert places for lack of human intervention. At least, this is the term that the narrator, Wiltshire, employs throughout to describe this area:

> The beginning of the *desert* was marked off by a wall, to call it so, for it was more a long mound of stones ... Up to the west side of the wall, the ground has been cleared, and there are cocoa-palms and mummy-apples and guavas, and lots of sensitive. Just across, the bush begins outright: high bush at that, trees going up like the masts of ships, and ropes of liana hanging down like a ship's rigging, and nasty orchids growing in the forks like funguses ... I saw many green pigeons ... A number of butterflies flopped up and down along the ground like dead leaves; sometimes I would hear a bird calling, sometimes the wind overhead, and always the sea along the coast. (51)

This is an intriguing passage, though not simply because Stevenson displays his particular cartographic imagination in detailing the island's geographical features. Indeed, we do get a clear sense of the division of the island into civilized and deserted, cultivated and wild parts. That the "sensitive" appears to grow only upon the cleared ground, along with cocoa-palms, mummy-apples, and guavas, links the presence of this plant species to human intervention in the island's natural history. Indeed, as Daniel Simberloff explains, "disturbed habitats are particularly susceptible to [biological] invasion."[199] The sensitive plant is implicitly earmarked as an invasive species here, and, as such, raises several important questions. Is Stevenson not comparing the insidiousness of the plant to European influence? Perhaps this interpretation alone sufficiently accounts for the sensitive plant's active role in the story's conception – i.e. this particular *unruly nature*'s intervention in Stevenson's writing. But, more importantly, what are we to make of Wiltshire's similes here? Is his comparison of the island's tall trees to "the masts of ships" merely an example of imperialist sublimation (or what Sudan calls, the "alchemy of empire,")[200] comparable, as it were, to Captain James Cook's careful survey of Pacific islands? Or is the simile employed here a recognition of the co-productive role played by trees in Great Britain's commercial expansion overseas? Is the point not to emphasize how the British Empire's growth resembles (and is contingent upon) the growth of trees in the tropical rainforest as such? Or, rather, do the maritime similes employed by Stevenson here (the "trees going up like the masts of ships," and the "ropes of liana hanging down like a ship's rigging") not link deforestation to the transoceanic expansion of the British Empire and, by extension, global capitalism?

That Stevenson's conception of *Falesá* coincides with his weeding of *Mimosa pudica* invites a comparison between Case and Wiltshire's hostility / violent antagonism towards one another and the competition for sunlight that unfolds in the tropical underbrush of "The Woodman." And, more importantly, this link between the two invites further speculation about the ecology of global capitalism, not to mention empire writing. That is, if Stevenson was inspired by his weeding and clearing of ground in Samoa (the first impulse of an archetypal British colonist not unlike Robinson Crusoe) to compose this story, then I think it's fair to say that the story anticipates Moore's point about capitalism working through nature. *Falesá* is, on one level (and as Stevenson explains in his letter to Colvin) a picturesque love story that ends well. However, the bulk of the narrative begs to be read otherwise: as an allegorical treatment of one of the foundational principles of any capitalist economy – namely, competition. This may be the strange extravagance that Stevenson refers to here: "It is very strange, very extravagant, I daresay; but it's varied, and picturesque, and has a pretty love affair, and ends well."[201]

The story ends well for Wiltshire, to be sure – but let us not forget the *tragic* jungle. Let us learn from Stevenson's writing to remember the fundamental, or uncanny correspondences between animals and plants, and try as best we can to sympathetically recognize the "cunning sense"[202] of all plants, including *Mimosa pudica*. Let us remember to vegetate.

Notes

1. Derek Walcott, "Isla Incognita" (1973), *Caribbean Literature and the Environment*, edited by Elizabeth Deloughrey, Renée K. Gosson, and George B. Handley (Charlottesville: University of Virginia Press, 2005), 57.
2. Robert Louis Stevenson to Sydney Colvin, Vailima, Samoa, 15 December 1891, *The Letters of Robert Louis Stevenson*, Vol. 7 (New Haven: Yale University Press, 1995), 213.
3. Sir Graham Balfour, "Notes and Papers," Manuscript Archives and Special Collections, National Library of Scotland, Edinburgh, p. 123.
4. For more on the red grouse, see the Royal Society for the Protection of Birds. Available at <https://www.rspb.org.uk/birds-and-wildlife/bird-and-wildlife-guides/bird-a-z/r/redgrouse/>. Accessed 27 February 2023.
5. Rachel Carson, *The Sea Around Us* (1950) (Oxford: Oxford University Press, 1989), 199.
6. Carson, *Sea Around Us*, 212.
7. Elizabeth M. DeLoughrey, *Routes and Roots: Navigating Caribbean and Pacific Island Literatures* (Honolulu: University of Hawaii Press, 2007), 3.

8. Carson, *Sea Around Us*, 112.
9. Charles Darwin, *Journal of Researches into the Geology and Natural History of Various Countries Visited by the H.M.S. Beagle, 1832–1836* (1839) (New York: Modern Library, 2001), 142.
10. Quoted in Carson, *Sea Around Us*, 121.
11. Robert Louis Stevenson to Mrs. Thomas Stevenson, September 1868, *The Letters of Robert Louis Stevenson*, edited by Sydney Colvin (New York: Charles Scribner's Sons, 1923), 26.
12. Thomas Stevenson, "Skerryvore Diary," Manuscript Archives and Special Collections, National Library of Scotland, Edinburgh, p. 14.
13. Robert Louis Stevenson, *The Merry Men and Other Tales and Fables* (1887) (London: Chatto & Windus, 1905), 5.
14. Stevenson, "Merry Men," 48.
15. Michelle Burnham, *Transoceanic America: Risk, Writing, and Revolution in the Global Pacific* (Oxford: Oxford University Press, 2019), 4.
16. Stevenson, "Merry Men," 16.
17. Sidney W. Mintz, *Sweetness and Power: The Place of Sugar in Modern History* (New York: Penguin, 1986), 14.
18. Stevenson, "Merry Men," 58.
19. Stevenson, "Merry Men," 40.
20. Robert Louis Stevenson, "Roads," *Essays of Travel and in the Art of Writing* (New York: Charles Scribner's Sons, 1923), 101.
21. Henry David Thoreau, "Walking," *Nature Walking* (Boston: Beacon Press, 1991), 97.
22. Thomas Stevenson, "Skerryvore Diary," 14.
23. Stevenson, "Roads," 101.
24. Stevenson, "Roads," 99.
25. Carson, *Sea Around Us*, 121.
26. Michael Niblett, *World Literature and Ecology: The Aesthetics of Commodity Frontiers, 1890 – 1950* (Cham: Palgrave Macmillan, 2020), 3.
27. Robert Louis Stevenson, *Kidnapped* (1886) (New York: Penguin Books, 1994), 153.
28. Stevenson, *Kidnapped*, 154.
29. Robert Louis Stevenson, *Records of a Family of Engineers* (London: Chatto & Windus, 1912), 59.
30. Stevenson, *Records*, 60.
31. David Hume, *A Treatise of Human Nature* (1739–40) (Oxford: Clarendon Press, 1978), 316–17.
32. See Jonathan Turner, *On the Origins of Human Emotions: A Sociological Inquiry into the Evolution of Human Affect* (Palo Alto, CA: Stanford University Press, 2000).
33. Tobias Menely, *The Animal Claim: Sensibility and the Creaturely Voice* (Chicago: University of Chicago Press, 2015), 58.

34. Hume, *Treatise*, 252–4.
35. Menely, *Animal Claim*, 58–9.
36. Menely, *Animal Claim*, 3.
37. Menely, *Animal Claim*, 61.
38. Hume, *Treatise*, 318.
39. Stevenson, *Letters*, Vol. 7, 92–3.
40. See, for example, Ann C. Colley, *Robert Louis Stevenson and the Colonial Imagination* (Aldershot: Ashgate, 2004); Roslyn Jolly, *Robert Louis Stevenson in the Pacific: Travel, Empire, and the Author's Profession* (Farnham: Ashgate, 2009); Timothy S. Hayes, "Colonialism in R. L. Stevenson's South Seas Fiction: 'Child's Play in the Pacific,'" *English Literature in Transition, 1880–1920* 52, no. 2 (2009), 160–81; Linda Dryden, "Literary Affinities and the Postcolonial in Robert Louis Stevenson and Joseph Conrad," *Scottish Literature and Postcolonial Literature: Comparative Texts and Critical Perspectives*, edited by Michael Gardiner, Graeme MacDonald, and Neall O'Gallagher (Edinburgh: Edinburgh University Press, 2011); and Lawrence Phillips, *The South Pacific Narratives of Robert Louis Stevenson and Jack London: Race, Class, Imperialism* (London: Continuum, 2012).
41. Wary of generalizations, Colley regards her work as very much in sympathy with a group of scholars, including Jonathan Lamb, Vanessa Smith, and Nicholas Thomas, "who have become increasingly attendant to the particular rather than the universal aspects of colonial encounter." Colley, *Colonial*, 7.
42. Colley, *Colonial*, 5. See also Jenni Calder, *Robert Louis Stevenson: A Life Study*. New York: Oxford University Press, 1980.
43. Lloyd Osbourne, *A Letter to Mr. Stevenson's Friends*. (1894) Published "for private circulation." Manuscript Archives and Special Collections, National Library of Scotland, Edinburgh, pp. 10–11.
44. See Susan Manning, *Fragments of Union: Making Connections in Scottish and American Writing* (Houndmills, Palgrave, 2002).
45. Anonymous, *The Travels of Hildebrand Bowman* (1778), edited by Lance Bertelsen (Peterborough, ON: Broadview Press, 2016), 161.
46. Jason Moore, *Capitalism in the Web of Life: Ecology and the Accumulation of Capital* (London: Verso, 2015), 4
47. Rebecca J. H. Woods, *The Herds Shot Round the World: Native Breeds and the British Empire, 1800–1900* (Chapel Hill: University of North Carolina Press, 2017), 3.
48. Alan Burdick, *Out of Eden: An Odyssey of Ecological Invasion* (New York: Farrar, Strauss, and Giroux, 2005), 87.
49. Robert Cyril Lawton Perkins, *Barefoot on Lava: The Journals and Correspondence of Naturalist R. C. L. Perkins in Hawai'i, 1892–1901*, edited by Neal L. Evenhuis (Honolulu: Bishop Museum Press, 2007), 306.
50. Moore, *Capitalism*, 18.

51. Moore, *Capitalism*, 36.
52. Moore, *Capitalism*, 17.
53. Macarena Gómez-Barris, *The Extractive Zone: Social Ecologies and Decolonial Perspectives* (Durham, NC: Duke University Press, 2017), 1, 5.
54. Stevenson, *Letters*, Vol. 7, 93.
55. Stevenson, *Letters*, Vol. 7, 27.
56. Lucinda Cole, *Imperfect Creatures: Vermin, Literature, and the Sciences of Life, 1600–1740* (Ann Arbor: University of Michigan Press, 2016), 9.
57. Robert Louis Stevenson, "Henry David Thoreau: His Character and Opinions" (1880), *Familiar Studies of Men and Books* (London: Chatto and Windus, 1917), 148.
58. Henry David Thoreau, *Walden; or, Life in the Woods* (1854) (New York: Penguin, 1983), 129.
59. Sydney Royse Lysaght, "Easter 1894," from the Notes and Notebooks of Sir Graham Balfour, Manuscript Archives and Special Collections, National Library of Scotland, Edinburgh, p. 189–90.
60. Lysaght, "Easter 1894," 194.
61. Osbourne, *Letter*, 188.
62. Osbourne, *Letter*, 16.
63. Goats, sheep, and cattle have been known to cause considerable environmental havoc. See, for example, Alexander Beatson, *Papers Relating to the Devastation Committed by Goats on the Island of St. Helena . . .* (St. Helena: J. Coupland, 1810); and Richard Grove, *Green Imperialism: Colonial Expansion, Tropical Island Edens, and the Origins of Environmentalism, 1600–1860* (Cambridge: Cambridge University Press, 1995).
64. Thoreau writes: "In my afternoon walk, I would fain forget about all my morning occupations and my obligations to society. But it sometimes happens that I cannot easily shake off the village." Thoreau, "Walking," 78.
65. Robert Louis Stevenson, *Weir of Hermiston* (1896) (New York: Bamboo Books, 2015), 45.
66. Walcott, "Isla Incognita," 57.
67. Carson, *Sea Around Us*, 212.
68. Stevenson, *Kidnapped*, 91.
69. See Robert Louis Stevenson, "Memoirs of an Islet," *Memories and Portraits* (1887) (New York: Charles Scribner's Sons, 1923).
70. Stevenson, *Kidnapped*, 153.
71. Robert Louis Stevenson, *In the South Seas* (1896) (New York: Penguin, 1998), 116.
72. Stevenson, *South Seas*, 116.
73. Robert Louis Stevenson, *Travels in Hawaii*, edited by A. Grove Day (Honolulu: University of Hawaii Press, 1973), 75–6.

74. See Margaret Cohen, "Literary Studies on the Terraqueous Globe," *PMLA* 125, no.3 (2010), 657–62.
75. Burnham, *Transoceanic*, 4.
76. Stevenson, *South Seas*, 117.
77. See Cole, *Imperfect Creatures*.
78. Greg Dening, *Islands and Beaches. Discourse on a Silent Land: Marquesas, 1774–1880* (Carlton: Melbourne University Press, 1980), 31.
79. Stevenson, *Kidnapped*, 98.
80. Cohen, "Literary Studies," 658.
81. Stevenson, "Merry Men," 48.
82. Burnham, *Transoceanic*, 9.
83. Quoted in Burnham, *Transoceanic*, 9.
84. Londa Schiebinger and Claudia Swan, *Colonial Botany: Science, Commerce, and Politics in the Early Modern World* (Philadelphia: University of Pennsylvania Press, 2005), 8–10. See also Marie-Noëlle Bourguet, "Measurable Difference: Botany, Climate, and the Gardener's Thermometer in Eighteenth-Century France," *Colonial Botany: Science, Commerce, and Politics in the Early Modern World* (Philadelphia: University of Pennsylvania Press), 270–86.
85. Cohen, "Literary Studies," 659.
86. Robert Louis Stevenson, *A Footnote to History: Eighty Years of Trouble in Samoa* (London: Cassell & Company, Limited, 1892), 20.
87. Stevenson, *South Seas*, 117.
88. Stevenson, *Footnote*, 20–1.
89. See Louis Kirk McAuley, *Print Technology in Scotland and America, 1740–1800* (Lewisburg: Bucknell University Press, 2013), 12–14.
90. Stevenson, *Footnote*, 25.
91. Stevenson, *Footnote*, 40.
92. Quoted in Dave Davies' interview with Christopher Mims, "The global supply chain is amazingly efficient. So why did it break down?," *Fresh Air*, National Public Radio, 5 January 2022. Available at <https://www.npr.org/2022/01/05/1070514847/the-global-supply-chain-arriving-today-christopher-mims>. Accessed 15 January 2022. See also Christopher Mims, *Arriving Today: From Factory to Front Door – Why Everything Has Changed About How and What We Buy* (New York: Harper Collins, 2021).
93. John Fraser Hart, "Change in the Corn Belt," *Geographical Review* 76, no. 1 (January 1986), 51–72.
94. Gordon Hempton and John Grossman, *One Square Inch of Silence: One Man's Quest to Preserve Quiet* (New York: Free Press, 2009), 13.
95. Gordon Hempton, "Quiet Please: Gordon Hempton On The Search For Silence In A Noisy World." Interview with Leslee Goodman. *The Sun*, Issue 417 (September 2010). Available at <https://www.thesunmagazine.org/issues/417/quiet-please>. Accessed 4 June 2023.

96. Stevenson, *Weir of Hermiston*, 45.
97. See, for example, Stevenson, *Letters*, Vol. 7, pp. 8, 25.
98. Mark Twain, *Roughing It* (1872) (New York: Penguin Books, 1985), 413.
99. Stevenson, *South Seas*, 115.
100. Stevenson, *Letters*, Vol. 7, 12.
101. Stevenson, *Letters*, Vol. 7, 8.
102. Stevenson, *Letters*, Vol. 7, 25.
103. Robert Louis Stevenson, "Forest Notes: Idle Hours" (1876), *An Apology for Idlers*. (New York: Penguin Books, 2009), 110–11.
104. See John Veitch, *The Feeling for Nature in Scottish Poetry* (Edinburgh: William Blackwood and Sons, 1887). For a valuable discussion of Veitch, see Louisa Gairn, *Ecology and Modern Scottish Literature* (Edinburgh: Edinburgh University Press, 2008.)
105. Claire Martin, "Where Have the Trees of Guam Gone? Scientists are investigating whether the obliteration of the island's bird species is thinning the tree canopy and could alter the forests' structure," *Smithsonian Magazine*, 11 April 2013. Available at <https://www.smithsonianmag.com/science-nature/where-have-the-trees-of-guam-gone-19756341/>. Accessed 4 June 2023.
106. Daniel Simberloff and Betsy Von Holle define invasional meltdown as an ecological invasion in which two or more species cooperate (symbiotically) to establish themselves. In the case of Guam, the brown tree's invasion was aided by the introduction of non-native skinks and geckos, which currently occupy the place of the extinguished bird population in the island's food chain. Daniel Simberloff and Betsy Von Holle, "Positive interactions of nonindigenous species: invasional meltdown?" *Biological Invasions*, no. 1 (1999), 21–32. See also Burdick, *Out of Eden*, 89–92.
107. Burdick, *Out of Eden*, 4.
108. Robert Louis Stevenson, "The Woodman," *Songs of Travel and Other Verses* (London: Chatto & Windus, 1896), 69.
109. Stevenson, "Woodman," 72–3.
110. Stevenson, "Woodman," 73.
111. Penny Fielding, "Stevenson's Poetry," *The Edinburgh Companion to Robert Louis Stevenson*, edited by Penny Fielding (Edinburgh: Edinburgh University Press, 2010), 116.
112. Fielding, "Stevenson's Poetry," 116.
113. For further details pertaining to tuitui (or *Mimosa pudica*), see the Global Invasive Species Database. Available at <http://www.iucngisd.org/gisd/speciesname/Mimosa+pudica>. Accessed 27 February 2023. It's worth noting that the Cook Islands Biodiversity database lists *Mimosa invisa*, a variety of giant sensitive weed as "the worst agricultural weed on the island [Aitutaki]." See Cook Islands Biodiversity and Natural Heritage. Available at <http://cookislands.

bishopmuseum.org/species.asp?id=6399>. Accessed 27 February 2023.
114. See also *Poetic Botany: Art and Science of the Eighteenth-Century Vegetable World*, a digital exhibition curated by Ryan Feigenbaum, New York Botanical Garden. Available at <https://www.nybg.org/poetic-botany/#start>. Accessed 5 November 2020.
115. Stevenson, *Letters*, Vol. 7, 26.
116. Stevenson, *Letters*, Vol. 7, 27.
117. Moore, *Capitalism*, 11.
118. Moore, *Capitalism*, 11.
119. For a discussion of plant defenses, including leaf movement, see P. D. Coley and J. A. Barone, "Herbivory and Plant Defenses in Tropical Forests," *Annual Review of Ecology and Systematics*, no. 27 (1996), 305–35.
120. See Michael Pollan, *The Botany of Desire: A Plant's-Eye View of the World* (New York: Random House, 2001).
121. Gómez-Barris, *Extractive Zone*, 4–5.
122. This phrase derives from Virginia DeJohn Anderson, *Creatures of Empire: How Domestic Animals Transformed Early America* (Oxford: Oxford University Press, 2006).
123. The following 2009 Greenpeace blog post claims that "cattle ranching is now the biggest cause of deforestation in the Amazon." Available at <http://www.greenpeace.org.uk/blog/forests/how-cattle-ranching-chewing-amazon-rainforest-20090129>. Accessed 20 May 2016.
124. See C. A. Berendsen, "WESTERN SAMOA," *Journal of the Royal Society of Arts* 85, no. 4383 (1936), 29–48. Available at <www.jstor.org/stable/41360872>. Accessed 5 November 2020. See also Tony Brunt. *"To Walk Under Palm Trees": The Germans in Samoa: Snapshots from Albums – Part One*. Auckland, New Zealand, March 2016. Available at <https://archive.org/details/towalkunderpalmtrees>. Accessed 4 June 2023.
125. Stevenson, *Letters*, Vol. 7, 14.
126. Stevenson, *Letters*, Vol. 7, 18.
127. Stevenson, *Letters*, Vol. 7, 19–20.
128. Stevenson, *Letters*, Vol. 7, 92.
129. Stevenson, *Letters*, Vol. 7, 92–3.
130. Stevenson, *Letters*, Vol. 7, 93–4.
131. Menely, *Animal Claim*, 3.
132. Moore, *Capitalism*, 4.
133. Woodes Rogers, *A Cruising Voyage Round the World: First to the South-Seas, thence to the East-Indies, and homewards by the Cape of Good Hope . . .* (1712) (Amsterdam: N. Israel, 1969), 137.
134. Schiebinger and Swan, *Colonial Botany*, 9.
135. Stevenson, "Woodman," 73.
136. DeLoughrey, *Routes and Roots*, 3.

137. Stevenson, *Letters*, Vol. 7, 20.
138. Stevenson, *Letters*, Vol. 7, 28.
139. Gómez-Barris, *Extractive Zone*, 5.
140. Stevenson, *Letters*, Vol. 7, 27.
141. Cole, *Imperfect Creatures*, 9.
142. Cole, *Imperfect Creatures*, 9.
143. Stevenson, *Letters*, Vol. 7, 161.
144. Stevenson, *Letters*, Vol. 7, 27–8.
145. Roslyn Jolly, "Introduction," Robert Louis Stevenson's *South Sea Tales* (Oxford: Oxford University Press, 2008), xxxii.
146. Jolly, "Introduction," xxxii.
147. Jolly, "Introduction," xxxiii.
148. Jolly, "Introduction," xxxiii.
149. Stevenson, *Letters*, Vol. 7, 28.
150. Janet Todd, *Sensibility: An Introduction* (1986), quoted in Susanna Rowson, *Charlotte Temple* (New York: W. W. Norton, 2011), 284.
151. Stevenson, *Letters*, Vol. 7, 27.
152. Robert Louis Stevenson, *The Beach of Falesá* (1893), collected in *South Sea Tales*, edited by Roslyn Jolly (Oxford: Oxford University Press, 2008), 3. Further citations will be parenthetical.
153. Gairn, *Ecology*, 36.
154. Mary Newman and Constance L. Kirker observe, that, "beginning in the mid-nineteenth century, the major European colonial powers began coconut cultivation in their various spheres of influence, from India to Sri Lanka, Africa, the East Indies and the Pacific region," and that "large-scale planting of coconuts for commercial export of oil and dried copra began in South Pacific regions." They also point out that, "in 1887 F. W. Loder invented a process for refining coconut oil that would make it more palatable and, therefore, a suitable substitute for oleo oil and margarine." Indeed, the coconut boom that occurred between the 1890s and 1920s was largely motivated by growing demand for edible oils and oils for soap-making in the United States and Europe, though copra was also used to create industrial oil. See Constance L. Kirker and Mary Newman, *Coconut: A Global History* (London: Reaktion Books, 2022).
155. Burnham, *Transoceanic*, 28.
156. Burnham, *Transoceanic*, 28.
157. Burnham, *Transoceanic*, 28.
158. Paul Simons, *The Action Plant: Movement and nervous behavior in plants* (Oxford: Blackwell, 1992), 1.
159. Simons, *Action Plant*, 2.
160. "Sensitive Plant," *Encyclopedia Britannica*. Available at <https://www.britannica.com/plant/sensitive-plant>. Accessed 26 September 2020.

161. Cole, *Imperfect Creatures*, 9. See also Bruno Latour, *Politics of Nature: How to Bring the Sciences into Democracy*, translated by Catherine Porter (Cambridge, MA: Harvard University Press, 2004), 75.
162. Hume, *Treatise*, 316–17.
163. Simons, *Action Plant*, 11.
164. Stevenson, "Woodman," 73.
165. William Bartram, *Travels through North and South Carolina, Georgia, and East and West Florida, the Cherokee Country, The Extensive Territories of the Muscogulges, or Creek Confederacy, and the Country of the Chactaws. Containing An Account of the Soil and Natural Productions of Those Regions; Together with Observations on the Manners of the Indians*, Second Edition (London: J. Johnson, 1794), xiii.
166. Bartram, *Travels*, xiv.
167. Bartram, *Travels*, xiv.
168. Henry Charles Andrews, *The Botanist's Repository, Comprising Colour'd New and Rare Plants Only, with Botanical Descriptions in Latin and English, after the Linnaean System*, Volume 8 (London: The Author, 1807–8), 543.
169. Thomas Green, *The Universal Herbal; or, Botanical, Medical, and Agricultural Dictionary; containing An Account of All the known plants in the World, Arranged According to the Linnean System* . . . (London: Caxton Press, 1824), 129.
170. "Sensitive Plant," *Encyclopedia Britannica*. Available at <https://www.britannica.com/plant/sensitive-plant>. Accessed 26 September 2020.
171. Todd, *Sensibility*, 283.
172. Sydney Owenson, "The Sensitive Plant," *The Lay of an Irish Harp; or, Metrical Fragments* (London: Robert Phillips, 1807), 87.
173. Owenson, "Sensitive Plant," 87.
174. Erasmus Darwin, *The Botanic Garden; A Poem, In Two Parts* (London: J. Johnson, 1791), 31–3.
175. "Sensitive Plant," *Encyclopedia Britannica*. Available at <https://www.britannica.com/plant/sensitive-plant>. Accessed 26 September 2020.
176. Laurence Housman, "Introduction" to Percy Bysshe Shelley's *The Sensitive Plant* (New York: Haskell House, 1972), 7.
177. Percy Bysshe Shelley, *The Sensitive Plant*, edited by Laurence Housman (New York: Haskell House,1972), 20.
178. P. W. Latham, "The Sensitive Plant," from *The Floral Festival*, which appeared in *The Family Circle* XIV, nos. IV–VII (1856), 122.
179. Simons, *Action Plant*, 2.
180. Charles Darwin, *Insectivorous Plants* (New York: Appleton and Company, 1896), 357.

181. Darwin, *Insectivorous Plants*, 3–4.
182. Darwin, *Insectivorous Plants*, 263.
183. Stevenson, *Letters*, Vol. 7, 27.
184. Cole, *Imperfect Creatures*, 9.
185. Todd, *Sensibility*, 283.
186. Samuel Taylor Coleridge, "The Eolian Harp," *Selected Poetry*, edited by Richard Holmes (Penguin: London, 1996).
187. Sigmund Freud, "The Uncanny," first published in *Imago*, translated by Alix Strachey (1919), 16.
188. Jolly, "Introduction," xv.
189. Stevenson, *Footnote*, 40.
190. Robert Louis Stevenson and Lloyd Osbourne, "The Ebb-Tide: A Trio and Quartette" (1894), collected in *South Sea Tales*, edited by Roslyn Jolly (Oxford: Oxford University Press, 2008), 123.
191. Stevenson, *Letters*, Vol. 7, 26.
192. Hume, *Treatise*, 316–17.
193. Stevenson, *Letters*, Vol. 7, 28.
194. Cole, *Imperfect Creatures*, 9. See also Latour, *Politics of Nature*, 75.
195. Stevenson, *Kidnapped*, 154.
196. Menely, *Animal Claim*, 61.
197. Stevenson, *Kidnapped*, 154.
198. Stevenson, *Kidnapped*, 155.
199. Daniel Simberloff, *Invasive Species: What Everyone Needs to Know* (Oxford: Oxford University Press), 48–9.
200. Rajani Sudan, *The Alchemy of Empire: Abject Materials and the Technologies of Colonialism* (New York: Fordham University Press, 2016), 5.
201. Stevenson, *Letters*, Vol. 7, 27.
202. Stevenson, *Letters*, Vol. 7, 27.

Afterword

Unruly / Uncanny Natures in Kingston, Jamaica (2013)

In June 2013, I traveled to Kingston, Jamaica, accompanied by a colleague and friend from the School of Economic Sciences at Washington State University in Pullman. Kingston is supposed to offer a glimpse of real Jamaica – Jamaica unfiltered through the posh splendor of an enclosed (à la *Robinson Crusoe*) resort, catering to the indulgent, materialist demands of mostly white, comparatively well-to-do tourists. The decadence of such Caribbean resorts would appear to be inherited from the colonial period in which, as Paul Cheney suggests, planter elites felt it was necessary to conspicuously consume all sorts of material goods in order to set themselves apart from an otherwise confusing mixture of social classes and races.[1] Indeed, the all-inclusive resort catering to the pleasure-seeking tourist calls to mind those disgustingly "profuse" meals that figure in Lady Nugent's account of the Bushy Park estate, not to mention the grossly overindulgent banquets and balls that inform Leonora Sansay's Female-Imperial Gothic novel about the Haitian Revolution, *Secret History* (see Chapter 3). Lady Nugent writes:

> I don't wonder now at the fever the people suffer from here – such eating and drinking I never saw! Such loads of all sorts of high, rich, and seasoned things, and really gallons of wine and mixed liquors as they drink . . . – in short, it was all as astonishing as it was disgusting.[2]

One cannot help but wonder at the resonance between what Lady Nugent describes here at the Bushy Park estate in the early nineteenth century and the sorts of indulgences that tourists enjoy inside posh resorts throughout the Caribbean today. Of course, in stark contrast to these rich meals that are featured in both Nugent's journal and the present-day Caribbean tourist industry, there is awful poverty widespread throughout Kingston, especially in and around the infamous housing projects, or, as Bob Marley put it, concrete jungles of Trench Town (legendary birthplace of reggae music), Jones Town, and Tivoli Gardens. And, of course, the razor wire and security guards employed across the city are not reassuring signs, but constant reminders of the precariousness of life (and Black lives especially) caught up in an unrelenting legacy of Empire – namely, the bust phase of a commodity frontier worn down, if not *ruined* (to use a key Gothic term) by the capitalist appropriation of so-called 'cheap natures.' Indeed, as I write this Afterword I am reminded of the fact that just several weeks ago protests erupted on 22 March 2022 outside the British High Commission in Kingston in anticipation of a visit from the British Royals – namely, Prince William and Kate. Carrying signs with phrases like "Seh Yuh Sorry!" and "Apologize Now!," the protestors gathered in the wake of a "publicized letter," penned by prominent public figures and leaders in Jamaica, demanding an apology and slavery reparations from Britain. According to NPR's reportage of the event, "the group protesting the royal visit noted in its letter that the British raped and killed thousands of slaves as it sought an apology for sixty reasons, including 'for refusing to acknowledge the historic trade in Africans as a crime against humanity,' and for 'pretending that the British led the abolition movement, when our ancestors worked, prayed and fought hard for this.'"[3]

However, the primary objective of my trip to Jamaica was not to explore present-day socio-economic conditions in Kingston, but rather to investigate (from an ecocritical standpoint) the print culture of colonial Jamaica at the National Library, a very modest sort of greyish building in downtown Kingston, which is supposed to house the most comprehensive collection of Jamaican newspapers dating back to 1718. Sadly, though, as I dug into my research at the library, carefully reading through such intriguing materials as the *Jamaica Magazine* (1812–13), a local, gentlemanly periodical comprised of original work (essays, poetry, etc.), "together with interesting sketches, biographical and political, from the latest European publications,"[4] I gradually became aware of the damage sustained by the National Library during the landfall of Hurricane Sandy on 24 October 2012. Archival materials were sorely damaged by the storm, to such an extent that the card catalog of materials no longer accurately reflected the library's holdings. Each time I put in a request to view certain materials it was a bit like taking a shot in the dark, as there was no guarantee the item I requested was not lost or damaged beyond use. This was both frustrating and sad, to be sure – to think about the erasure of historical documents, the rendering of valuable print culture from colonial Jamaica inaccessible to future generations of scholars, et al. And yet, as I pause to reflect upon this experience now (nearly ten years later), it seems oddly fitting for my research to have been interrupted by particular natures in this way – a violent storm, not unlike the awful thunderstorm which forces Roland, the missionary in Cynric Williams's novel, *Hamel*, to see his own history as shared with the Obeah man's,[5] and also the mold and mildew that is apt to live off water-damaged organic printed materials like newspapers and books. Is Hurricane Sandy not comparable to the storm that obliges the British missionary to not only confront that other body – the Obeah man – buried deep within his unconscious mind, but also to acknowledge their shared histories? In other words, it occurs to me to remember the havoc Hurricane Sandy wrought upon Jamaica in 2012 as an *unruly nature* – a critical, oceanic / meteorological intervention, and one that should make us all pause to think not only about the sea around us, as Rachel Carson put it,[6] but also climate change *and* of the countless ways in which we are inextricably united with the rest of nature in the web of life.

Of course, the aftermath of Hurricane Sandy was not the only reminder I received of these crucial facts of life in our global economy. In the evenings my colleague and I were apt to sit outside, encircled by tropical flora and fauna, marveling at the thumping music from the street parties in Kingston below, music that somehow managed to drift up to us in the foothills of the Blue Mountains. That is, our bed and breakfast was supposed to be quietly situated on the outskirts of Kingston (by no means an enclosed resort, but a privileged remove from the urban center nonetheless), yet somehow the air was always filled with the pulsating music of the city. However, most importantly, these were not the only sounds / the only music to catch my ear while we were sitting outside. Another, more startling sound was a peculiar rustling that emanated from the verdant intricacy of the forest canopy at the edges of the yard. When I asked the caretaker, Billy, what was the cause of this noise, he explained to me that rats were eating mangoes in the trees. This struck me as somewhat horrifying – that is, to think that the rustling was a sign of rats feeding upon mangoes ripening in the trees. Or, rather, to my mind, this was a stark, horrifying, and uncanny reminder of James

Grainger's suggestion, in *The Sugar Cane*, that, "there is a species of East-Indian animal, called a Mungoes [i.e. mongoose], which bears a natural antipathy to rats": "Its introduction into the Sugar-Islands would, probably, effectuate the extirpation of this destructive vermin."[7] To be sure, tree-climbing rats like those in the forest canopy surrounding us at the time, are apt reminders that the Javan mongoose was introduced to Jamaica in 1872, which (as I note in Chapter 2) biologists regard as one of the greatest environmental disasters of its kind. Not only did this introduction of the mongoose not solve the rat problem in Jamaica (the rats were merely driven up into the forest canopy, as evidenced by those I listened to rustling about in the mango trees in 2013), but, as Stuart McCook explains, the mongoose increased in population "until they spread over the whole island and became a greater pest than the rats on account of their wholesale destruction of poultry, game, ground-nesting birds of various kinds, reptiles, and even fruits ... the decrease in birds was followed by a marked increase in certain insect pests," especially ticks.[8] So, here again I find myself uncannily reminded by an inglorious sort of furry nature – i.e., invasive rats, the very so-called "imperfect creatures"[9] that are supposed to have disturbed the sleep of castaway Alexander Selkirk by gnawing upon his feet – of our shared histories, and how humans and extra-human natures are knit together "within a gravitational field of endless accumulation."[10] And, as I argue throughout this book, such interventions by unruly animals, plants, and minerals play a key role in determining / registering the ecology of British and American empire writing.

Notes

1. See Paul Cheney, *Cul de Sac: Patrimony, Capitalism, and Slavery in French Saint-Domingue* (Chicago: University of Chicago Press, 2017), 150.
2. *Lady Nugent's Journal of her residence in Jamaica from 1801–1805*, edited by Philip Wright (Kingston, Jamaica: Institute of Jamaica, 1966), 57.
3. From the Associated Press via National Public Radio, "As British royals visit Jamaica, protestors demand slavery reparations." Available at <https://www.npr.org/2022/03/23/1088167278/protesters-in-jamaica-spurn-british-royals-ahead-of-official-visit>. Accessed 28 April 2022.
4. See *The Jamaica Magazine; Containing Original Essays, Moral Philosophical, and Literary: Together with Interesting Sketches, Biographical and Political, From the Latest European Publications* ...;

And on Subjects of Generality, Comprehending Selections from Recent Tracts; The Latest Discoveries and Inventions, in Science and Fine Arts; Various Gleanings and Remarks, Collected by a Gentleman of General and Extensive Readings . . . (Kingston: Jamaica, 1812–1813).
5. See Cynric Williams, *Hamel, the Obeah Man* (1827) (Peterborough, ON: Broadview Editions, 2010).
6. As marine biologist Rachel Carson explains in her influential book, *The Sea Around Us*, "in its broader meaning, that other concept of the ancients remains" – namely, that "outside, bathing the periphery of the land world, was Oceanus." Rachel Carson, *The Sea Around Us* (1950) (Oxford: Oxford University Press, 1989), 199.
6. Carson, *Sea Around Us*, 212.
7. James Grainger, *The Sugar-Cane: A Poem in Four Books. With Notes* (1764), *Caribbeana: An Anthology of English Literature of the West Indies, 1657–1777*, edited by Thomas W. Krise (Chicago and London: University of Chicago Press, 1999), 201.
8. Although the mongoose's introduction initially did have some impact upon the rats, McCook explains that, "over the longer term, the rat population adapted to the mongoose by shifting their habitat up into trees, where the mongooses did not climb." See Stuart McCook, "The Neo-Columbian Exchange: The Second Conquest of the Greater Caribbean, 1720–1930," *Latin American Research Review* 46, Special Issue (2011), 26–7.
9. See Lucinda Cole, *Imperfect Creatures: Vermin, Literature, and the Sciences of Life, 1600–1740* (Ann Arbor: University of Michigan Press, 2016).
10. Quoted in Michael Niblett, *World Literature and Ecology: The Aesthetics of Commodity Frontiers, 1890–1950* (Cham: Palgrave Macmillan, 2020), 7.

Bibliography

Adams-Campbell, Melissa. "Romantic Revolutions: Love and Violence in Leonora Sansay's *Secret History, or The Horrors of St. Domingo.*" *Studies in American Fiction* 39, no. 2 (2012), 125–46.

Ahuja, Neel. *Bioinsecurities: Disease Interventions, Empire, and the Government of Species*. Durham, NC and London: Duke University Press, 2016.

Anderson, Virginia DeJohn. *Creatures of Empire: How Domestic Animals Transformed Early America*. Oxford: Oxford University Press, 2006.

Andrews, Evangeline Walker. "Introduction." *Journal of A Lady of Quality*. New Haven: Yale University Press, 1923, 7.

Andrews, Henry Charles. *The Botanist's Repository, Comprising Colour'd New and Rare Plants Only, with Botanical Descriptions in Latin and English, after the Linnaean System*. Vol. 8. London: The Author, 1807–8.

Anonymous. *The Travels of Hildebrand Bowman* (1778). Edited by Lance Bertelsen. Peterborough, ON: Broadview Press, 2016.

Balfour, Sir Graham. "Notes and Papers." Manuscript Archives and Special Collections, National Library of Scotland, Edinburgh.

Bartram, William. *Travels through North and South Carolina, Georgia, and East and West Florida, the Cherokee Country, The Extensive Territories of the Muscogulges, or Creek Confederacy, and the Country of the Chactaws. Containing An Account of the Soil and Natural Productions of Those Regions; Together with Observations on the Manners of the Indians*. Second Edition. London: J. Johnson, 1794.

Baugh, Edward. "Literary Theory and the Caribbean: Theory, Belief, and Desire, or Designing Theory." *Journal of West Indian Literature* 15, no. 1/2 (November 2006), 3–14.

Beard, J. S. *The Natural Vegetation of the Windward and Leeward Islands*. Oxford: Clarendon Press, 1949.

Beatson, Alexander. *Papers Relating to the Devastation Committed by Goats on the Island of St. Helena, From the period of their Introduction to the Present Time; Comprising Experiments, Observations & Hints, Connected with Agricultural Improvement And Planting, &c. &c. &c.* St. Helena: J. Coupland, 1810.

—. *Tracts relative to the island of St Helena, Written during a residence of five years*. London: W. Bulmer & Co., 1816, lxiii.
—. *Flora Sta. Helenica*. St. Helena: Printed by J. Boyd, 1825.
Beckert, Sven. *Empire of Cotton: A Global History*. New York: Knopf, 2015.
Bender, John. *Ends of Enlightenment*. Palo Alto, CA: Stanford University Press, 2012.
Benezet, Anthony. *Some Historical Account of Guinea, Its Situation, Produce and the general Disposition of its Inhabitants. With An inquiry into the Rise and Progress of the Slave-Trade, its Nature and Lamentable Effects*. Philadelphia: Joseph Crukshank, 1771.
Benítez-Rojo, Antonio. "Sugar and the Environment in Cuba." Translated by James Maraniss. *Caribbean Literature and the Environment: Between Nature and Culture*. Edited by Elizabeth DeLoughrey, Renée K. Gosson, and George B. Handley. Charlottesville: University of Virginia Press, 2005.
Berendsen, C. A. "WESTERN SAMOA." *Journal of the Royal Society of Arts* 85, no. 4383 (1936), 29–48.
Biermann, Frank, et al. "Down to Earth: Contextualizing the Anthropocene." *Global Environmental Change*, no. 39 (2016), 341–50.
Blom, Philip. *To Have and to Hold: An Intimate History of Collectors and Collecting*. Woodstock: The Overlook Press, 2003.
Boisseron, Bénédict. *Afro-Dog: Blackness and the Animal Question*. New York: Columbia University Press, 2018.
Boulukos, George. "The Horror of Hybridity: Enlightenment, Anti-Slavery and Racial Disgust in Charlotte Smith's *The Story of Henrietta* (1800)." *Slavery and The Cultures of Abolition: Essays Marking the Bicentennial of the British Abolition Act of 1807*. Edited by Brycchan Carey and Peter J. Kitson. Cambridge: D. S. Brewer, 2007, 87–109.
Bourguet, Marie-Noëlle. "Measurable Difference: Botany, Climate, and the Gardener's Thermometer in Eighteenth-Century France." *Colonial Botany: Science, Commerce, and Politics in the Early Modern World*. Edited by Londa Schiebinger and Claudia Swan. Philadelphia: University of Pennsylvania Press, 2005.
Branch, Michael P., and Scott Slovic. "Surveying the Emergence of Ecocriticism." *The ISLE Reader: Ecocriticism 1993–2003*. Edited by Branch and Slovic. Athens: University of Georgia Press, 2003, xiv–xv.
Brathwaite, Kamau. *Barabajan Poems, 1492–1992*. Kingston, Jamaica and New York: Savacou North, 1994.
Brunt, Tony. *"To Walk Under Palm Trees": The Germans in Samoa: Snapshots from Albums – Part One*. Auckland, New Zealand: March 2016, http://germansinsamoa.net/wp-content/uploads/2013/09/Palm_Trees_Ebook.pdf. Accessed 1 June 2016.
Buell, Lawrence. *The Environmental Imagination: Thoreau, Nature Writing, and the Formation of American Culture*. Cambridge, MA: Belknap Press, 1996.

Burdick, Alan. *Out of Eden: An Odyssey of Ecological Invasion*. New York: Farrar, Straus, and Giraux, 2005.
Burnham, Michelle. "Female Bodies and Capitalist Drive: Leonora Sansay's *Secret History* in Transoceanic Context." *Legacy* 28, no. 2 (2011), 177–204.
—. *Transoceanic America: Risk, Writing, and Revolution in the Global Pacific*. Oxford: Oxford University Press, 2019.
Calder, Jenni. *Robert Louis Stevenson: A Life Study*. New York: Oxford University Press, 1980.
Carmichael, A. C. *Domestic Manners and Social Condition of the White, Coloured, and Negro Population of the West Indies*. 2 volumes. London: Whittaker, Treacher, and Co., 1833.
Carney, Judith. "Out of Africa: Colonial Rice History in the Black Atlantic." *Colonial Botany: Science, Commerce, and Politics in the Early Modern World*. Edited by Londa Schiebinger and Claudia Swan. Philadelphia: University of Pennsylvania Press, 2005.
Carson, Rachel. *The Sea Around Us* (1951). Special Edition. Oxford: Oxford University Press, 1991.
—. *Silent Spring* (1962), 50th Anniversary Edition. Boston: Mariner Books, 2002.
Casid, Jill. *Sowing Empire: Landscape and Colonization*. Minneapolis: University of Minnesota Press, 2005.
Cheney, Paul. *Cul de Sac: Patrimony, Capitalism, and Slavery in French Saint-Domingue*. Chicago: University of Chicago Press, 2017.
Chynoweth, March, Christopher Lepczyk, and Creighton M. Litton, "Feral Goats in the Hawaiian Islands: Understanding the Behavioral Ecology of Nonnative Ungulates with GPS and Remote Sensing Technology." *Proceedings 24th Vertebrate Pest Conference*. Edited by R. M. Timm and K. A. Fagerstone. Davis: University of California, Davis, 2010.
Cody, Lisa Forman. *Birthing the Nation: Sex, Science, and the Conception of Eighteenth-Century Britons*. Oxford: Oxford University Press, 2005.
Cohen, Margaret. "Literary Studies on the Terraqueous Globe." *PMLA* 125, no. 3 (2010), 657–62.
—. *The Novel and the Sea*. Princeton: Princeton University Press, 2010.
Cole, Lucinda. *Imperfect Creatures: Vermin, Literature, and the Sciences of Life, 1600–1740*. Ann Arbor: University of Michigan Press, 2016.
Coleridge, Samuel Taylor. "The Eolian Harp." *Selected Poetry*. Edited by Richard Holmes. Penguin: London, 1996.
Coley, P. D., and J. A. Barone. "Herbivory and Plant Defenses in Tropical Forests." *Annual Review of Ecology and Systematics*, no. 27 (1996), 305–35.
Colley, Ann C. *Robert Louis Stevenson and the Colonial Imagination*. Aldershot: Ashgate, 2004.
Coverley, Merlin. *Psychogeography*. Harpenden: Pocket Essentials, 2010.

Cronon, William. "The Trouble with Wilderness; or, Getting Back to the Wrong Nature." *Uncommon Ground: Rethinking the Human Place in Nature*. Edited by William Cronon. New York: W. W. Norton, 1995, 69–90.

Crosby, Alfred W. *Ecological Imperialism: The Biological Expansion of Europe, 900–1900*. Cambridge: Cambridge University Press, 2004.

Dampier, William. *A New Voyage Round the World, Describing particularly the Isthmus of America, several Coasts and Islands in the West Indies, the isles of Cape Verde, the Passage by Terra del Fuego, the South-Sea Coasts of Chili, Peru, and Mexico* ... (1697). New York: Dover, 1968.

Darwin, Charles. *Journal of Researches into the Geology and Natural History of Various Countries Visited by the H.M.S. Beagle, 1832–1836* (1839). New York: Modern Library, 2001.

—. *On The Origin of Species by Means of Natural Selection or the Preservation of Favoured Races in the Struggle for Life* (1859). Oxford: Oxford University Press, 2008.

—. *Insectivorous Plants*. New York: Appleton and Company, 1896.

Darwin, Erasmus. *The Botanic Garden; A Poem, In Two Parts*. London: J. Johnson, 1791.

De Certeau, Michel. *The Practice of Everyday Life*. Berkeley: University of California Press, 1988.

Deckard, Sharae. *Paradise Discourse, Imperialism, and Globalization: Exploiting Eden*. New York and London: Routledge, 2010.

Defoe, Daniel. *The Storm: Or, A Collection of the Most Remarkable Casualties and Disasters Which happen'd in the Late Dreadful Tempest Both By Sea and Land*. London: G. Sawbridge, 1704.

—. *The Farther Adventures of Robinson Crusoe; Being the Second and Last Part of his Life, and the Strange Surprizing Accounts of his Travels Round Three Parts of the Globe*. London: W. Taylor, 1719.

—. *The Life and Strange Surprizing Adventures of Robinson Crusoe of York, Mariner: Who lived Eight and Twenty Years, all alone in an uninhabited Island on the Coast of America, near the Mouth of the Great River of Oroonoque; Having been cast on Shore by Shipwreck, where in all the Men perished but himself* ... (London: W. Taylor, 1719). Edited by John Richetti. New York: Penguin Books, 2001.

—. *A Journal of the Plague Year* (1722). Oxford: Oxford World's Classics, 1990.

—. *A New Voyage Round the World. The Works of Daniel Defoe* (1724). *The Works of Daniel Defoe*. Vol. 7. Philadelphia: John D. Morris & Company, 1903.

—. *A Plan of the English Commerce. Being a Compleat Prospect of The Trade of this Nation, as well the Home Trade as the Foreign*. London: Charles Rivington, 1728.

DeLoughrey, Elizabeth M. *Routes and Roots: Navigating Caribbean and Pacific Island Literatures*. Honolulu: University of Hawaii Press, 2007.

DeLoughrey, Elizabeth, Renée K. Gosson, and George B. Handley. "Introduction." *Caribbean Literature and the Environment: Between Nature and Culture*. Charlottesville: University of Virginia Press, 2005.

Dening, Greg. *Islands and Beaches. Discourse on a Silent Land: Marquesas, 1774–1880*. Carlton: Melbourne University Press, 1980.

Devine, T. M. *Scotland's Empire: The Origins of the Global Diaspora*. London: Penguin, 2003.

Díaz, María Elena. "To Live as a *Pueblo*: A Contentious Endeavor; El Cobre, Cuba, 1670s–1790s." *Afro-Latino Voices: Narratives from the Early Modern Ibero-Atlantic World, 1550–1812*. Edited by Kathryn Joy McKnight and Leo J. Garofalo. Indianapolis: Hackett Publishing Co., 2009.

Dillon, Elizabeth Maddox, and Michael Drexler, eds. *The Haitian Revolution and the Early United States: Histories, Textualities, Geographies*. Philadelphia: University of Pennsylvania Press, 2016.

Djikic, Maja, Keith Oatley, and Mihnea C. Moldoveanu. "Reading other minds: Effects of literature on empathy." *Scientific Study of Literature* 3, no. 1 (2013), 28–47.

Drexler, Michael J. "Introduction." *Secret History*. Peterborough, ON: Broadview Press, 2008.

Dryden, Linda. "Literary Affinities and the Postcolonial in Robert Louis Stevenson and Joseph Conrad." *Scottish Literature and Postcolonial Literature: Comparative Texts and Critical Perspectives*. Edited by Michael Gardiner, Graeme MacDonald, and Neall O'Gallagher. Edinburgh: Edinburgh University Press, 2011.

Dubois, Laurent, and John D. Garrigus. *Slave Revolution in the Caribbean, 1789–1804: A Brief History with Documents*. New York: Bedford/St. Martin's Press, 2006.

Dugatkin, Lee Alan. *Mr. Jefferson and the Giant Moose: Natural History in Early America*. Chicago: University of Chicago Press, 2009.

Elton, Charles S. *The Ecology of Invasions by Animals and Plants* (1958). With a new Foreword by Daniel Simberloff. Chicago: University of Chicago Press, 2000.

Environment and Empire. The Oxford History of the British Empire Companion Series. Edited by William Beinart and Lotte Hughes. Oxford: Oxford University Press, 2009.

Equiano, Olaudah. *The Interesting Narrative and Other Writings*. Edited by Vincent Carretta. New York: Penguin, 1995.

Fick, Carolyn. *The Making of Haiti: The Saint Domingue Revolution from Below*. Knoxville: University of Tennessee Press, 1990.

Fielding, Penny. "Stevenson's Poetry." *The Edinburgh Companion to Robert Louis Stevenson*. Edited by Penny Fielding. Edinburgh: Edinburgh University Press, 2010.

Freud, Sigmund. "The Uncanny." *Imago*. Translated by Alix Strachey (1919).
Frost, Amy. "Big Spenders: The Beckford's and Slavery." 30 October 2014. Available at <http://www.bbc.co.uk/wiltshire/content/articles/2007/03/06/abolition_fonthill_abbey_feature.shtml>. Accessed 4 June 2023.
Fuchs, Barbara. "Conquering Islands: Contextualizing *The Tempest*." *Shakespeare Quarterly* 48, no. 1 (Spring 1997), 45–62.
Gairn, Louisa. *Ecology and Modern Scottish Literature*. Edinburgh: Edinburgh University Press, 2008.
Gerbi, Antonello. *Nature in the New World: From Christopher Columbus to Gonzalo Fernández de Oviedo*. Pittsburgh: University of Pittsburgh Press, 1985.
Gilmore, John. *The Poetics of Empire: A Study of James Grainger's* The Sugar-Cane. London: Athlone Press, 2000.
Gómez-Barris, Macarena. *The Extractive Zone: Social Ecologies and Decolonial Perspectives*. Durham, NC: Duke University Press, 2017.
Goode, Abby L. "Gothic Fertility in Leonora Sansay's 'Secret History.'" *Early American Literature* 50, no. 2 (2015), 449–73.
Gottlieb, Evan. *Feeling British: Sympathy and National Identity in Scottish and English Writing, 1707–1832*. Lewisburg, PA: Bucknell University Press, 2007.
Grainger, James. *The Sugar-Cane: A Poem in Four Books. With Notes* (1764). *Caribbeana: An Anthology of English Literature of the West Indies, 1657–1777*. Edited by Thomas W. Krise. Chicago and London: University of Chicago Press, 1999.
Green, Thomas. *The Universal Herbal; or, Botanical, Medical, and Agricultural Dictionary; containing An Account of All the known plants in the World, Arranged According to the Linnean System . . .* London: Caxton Press, 1824.
Greimler, Josef, Patricio Lopez S., Tod F. Stuessy, and Thomas Dirnböck, "The Vegetation of Robinson Crusoe Island (Isla Masatierra) Juan Fernández Archipelago, Chile." *Pacific Science* 56, no. 3 (2002), 263–84.
Grivetti, Louis E., and Howard-Yana Shapiro. *Chocolate: History, Culture, and Heritage*. Hoboken: Wiley, 2009.
Grove, Richard. *Green Imperialism: Colonial Expansion, Tropical Island Edens, and the Origins of Environmentalism, 1600–1860*. Cambridge: Cambridge University Press, 1995.
—. "The Island and History of Environmentalism." *Nature and Society in Historical Context*. Edited by Mikaláš Teich, Roy Porter, and Bo Gustaffson. Cambridge: Cambridge University Press, 1997.
Guilding, Rev. Lansdown. *An Account of the Botanic Gardens in the Island of St. Vincent, From Its Establishment to the Present Time*. Glasgow: Richard Griffin & Company, 1825.
Handler, Jerome S. "Diseases and Medical Disabilities of Enslaved Barbadians From the Seventeenth Century to around 1838." *The Journal of Caribbean History* 40, no. 1 (2006), 1–38.

Hart, John Fraser. "Change in the Corn Belt." *Geographical Review* 76, no. 1 (January 1986), 51–72.
Hayes, Timothy S. "Colonialism in R. L. Stevenson's South Seas Fiction: 'Child's Play in the Pacific.'" *English Literature in Transition, 1880–1920* 52, no. 2 (2009), 160–81.
Helg, Aline. *Slaves No More: Self-Liberation before Abolitionism in the Americas*. Translated by Lara Vergnaud. Chapel Hill: University of North Carolina Press, 2019.
Hempton, Gordon, and John Grossman. *One Square Inch of Silence: One Man's Quest to Preserve Quiet*. New York: Free Press, 2009.
Heng, Geraldine. "Reinventing Race, Colonization, and Globalisms across Deep Time: Lessons for the Longer *Durée*." *PMLA* 130 no. 2 (March 2015), 358–66.
Hirschman, Albert O. *The Passions and the Interests: Political Arguments for Capitalism before Its Triumph*. Twentieth Anniversary Edition. Princeton: Princeton University Press, 1997.
Houston, Alexander, and Company's Foreign Letter Book No E, Commencing at Glasgow the 4th March 1776 and Ending the 24 April 1778, Special Collections, *National Library of Scotland*, Edinburgh.
Howard, R. A., and E. S. Howard. *Alexander Anderson's The St Vincent botanic garden*. Cambridge, MA: Harvard University Press, 1983.
Huggan, Graham and Helen Tiffin. *Postcolonial Ecocriticism: Literature, Animals, Environment*. Abingdon: Routledge, 2010.
Hughes, Griffith. *The Natural History of Barbados*. London: Printed for the Author, 1750.
Hume, David. *A Treatise of Human Nature* (1739–40). Oxford: Clarendon Press, 1978.
—. *Essays Moral, Political, and Literary*. Vol. 1. Edited by T. H. Green and T. H. Grose. London: Longmans, 1898.
—. "Of Interest." *Essays Moral, Political, and Literary*. Edited by Eugene F. Miller. Indianapolis: Liberty Fund, 1994.
Hunt, Helen. "'Fascinate, Intoxicate, Transport': Uncovering Women's Erotic Dominance in Leonora Sansay's *Secret History*." *Legacy: A Journal of American Women Writers* 33, no. 1 (2016), 31–54.
Hunt, John Dixon, and Peter Willis, eds. *The Genius of Place: The English Landscape Garden, 1620–1820*. Cambridge, MA: MIT Press, 1988.
The Jamaica Magazine; Containing Original Essays, Moral, Philosophical, and Literary: Together with Interesting Sketches, Biographical and Political, From the Latest European Publications . . .; And on Subjects of Generality, Comprehending Selections from Recent Tracts; The Latest Discoveries and Inventions, in Science and Fine Arts; Various Gleanings and Remarks, Collected by a Gentleman of General and Extensive Readings. Kingston, Jamaica, 1812–13.
Jolly, Roslyn. "Introduction." Robert Louis Stevenson's *South Sea Tales*. Oxford: Oxford University Press, 2008.

—. *Robert Louis Stevenson in the Pacific: Travel, Empire, and the Author's Profession*. Farnham: Ashgate, 2009.
Ker, John. *The Journal of John Ker, Surgeon's Mate in the Royal Navy – a manuscript account describing his service in the West Indies, 1778–1782*. Special Collections, National Library of Scotland, Edinburgh.
The Kingston *Daily Advertiser*, printed by Strupar, Bennett, & Doddington, in Harbour-street, Kingston, Jamaica.
Kirker, Constance L., and Mary Newman, *Coconut: A Global History*. London: Reaktion Books, 2022.
Knight, Franklin W. "Slavery." *Encyclopedia of African-American Culture and History*, Vol. 5, Second Edition. Farmington Hills, MI: Gale, 2006.
—. "Review." *Slaves No More: Self-Liberation before Abolitionism in the Americas* by Aline Helg. *The Americas* 77, no. 1 (January 2020), 153.
Knox, Robert. *An Historical Relation of the Island of Ceylon in the East-Indies: Together with an Account of the Detaining in Captivity the Author and divers other* Englishmen *now Living there, and of the Author's Miraculous ESCAPE*. London: Printed by Richard Chiswell, 1681.
Kosek, Jake. *Understories: The Political Life of Forests in Northern New Mexico*. Durham, NC: Duke University Press, 2006.
Krise, Thomas W., ed. *Caribbeana: An Anthology of English Literature of the West Indies, 1657–1777*. Chicago: University of Chicago Press, 1999.
Lamb, Jonathan. "'The Rime of the Ancient Mariner,' A Ballad of Scurvy." *Pathologies of Travel*. Edited by Richard Wrigley and George Revill. Amsterdam: Editions Rodolpi B.V., 2000.
—. *Preserving The Self in the South Seas, 1680–1840*. Chicago: University of Chicago Press, 2001.
—. *Scurvy: The Disease of Discovery*. Princeton: Princeton University Press, 2016.
Lambert, Andrew. *Crusoe's Island: A Rich and Curious History of Pirates, Castaways and Madness*. London: Faber & Faber, 2016.
Latham, P. W. "The Sensitive Plant." From *The Floral Festival*. *The Family Circle* XIV, nos. IV–VII (1856).
Latour, Bruno. *We Have Never Been Modern* (1991). Translated by Catherine Porter. Cambridge, MA: Harvard University Press, 1993.
—. *Politics of Nature: How to Bring the Sciences into Democracy*. Translated by Catherine Porter. Cambridge, MA: Harvard University Press, 2004.
Lefebvre, Henri. *The Production of Space*. Translated by Donald Nicholson-Smith. Malden, MA: Wiley-Blackwell, 1992.
Lever, Christopher. *Naturalized Animals: The Ecology of Successfully Introduced Species*. London: T. & A. D. Poyser, 1994.
Ligon, Richard. *A True and Exact History of the Island of Barbados* (1657). Indianapolis: Hackett Publishing, 2011.
Lingis, Alphonso. *Dangerous Emotions*. Berkeley: University of California Press, 2000.

Liston, Henrietta Marchant. 1801 Caribbean Travel Diary. Unpublished. Special Collections, National Library of Scotland, Edinburgh.

Lobis, Seth. *The Virtue of Sympathy: Magic, Philosophy and Literature in Seventeenth-Century England*. New Haven: Yale University Press, 2015.

Locke, John. *Two Treatises of Government*, ed. Mark Goldie. London: Everyman, 1993, 2000.

Loss, Scott R., Tom Will, and Peter P. Marra. "The impact of free-ranging domestic cats on wildlife in the United States." *Nature Communications* 4, no. 1396 (29 January 2013).

Lugo, Ariel E., Ralph Schmidt, and Sandra Brown. "Tropical Forests in the Caribbean." *Ambio* 10, no. 6, (1981), 318–24.

Lysaght, Sydney Royse. "Easter 1894." From the Notes and Notebooks of Sir Graham Balfour, Manuscript Archives and Special Collections, National Library of Scotland, Edinburgh.

Mabberley, D. J. "Anderson, Alexander (1748?–1811)." *Oxford Dictionary of National Biography*. Oxford University Press, 2004. Available at <http://www.oxforddnb.com/view/article/465>. Accessed 24 November 2015.

McAuley, Louis Kirk. *Print Technology in Scotland and America, 1740–1800*. Lewisburg, PA: Bucknell University Press, 2013.

McCook, Stuart. "The Neo-Columbian Exchange: The Second Conquest of the Greater Caribbean, 1720–1930." *Latin American Research Review* 46, Special Issue (2011), 11–31.

McKibben, Bill. *The End of Nature* (1989), Reissue. New York: Random House Trade Paperback, 2006.

McLeod, Bruce. *The Geography of Empire in English Literature, 1580–1745*. New York: Cambridge University Press, 1992.

McNeil, J. R. *Mosquito Empires: Ecology and War in the Greater Caribbean, 1620–1914*. Cambridge: Cambridge University Press, 2010.

Maddox Dillon, Elizabeth and Michael Drexler, eds. *The Haitian Revolution and the Early United States: Histories, Textualities, Geographies*. Philadelphia: University of Pennsylvania Press, 2016.

Manning, Susan. *Fragments of Union: Making Connections in Scottish and American Writing*. Houndmills and New York: Palgrave, 2002.

Marshall, P. J. "Introduction." *The Oxford History of the British Empire, Volume II, The Eighteenth Century*. Oxford: Oxford University Press, 1998.

Marzec, Robert P. "Enclosures, Colonization, and the *Robinson Crusoe* Syndrome: A Genealogy of Land in a Global Context." *Boundary 2* (Summer 2002), 129–56.

Menely, Tobias. *The Animal Claim: Sensibility and the Creaturely Voice*. Chicago: University of Chicago Press, 2015.

—. *Climate and the Making of Worlds: Toward a Geohistorical Poetics*. Chicago: University of Chicago Press, 2021.

Miller, John. *Empire and the Animal Body: Violence, Identity, and Ecology in Victorian Adventure Fiction*. London: Anthem Press, 2012.

Mills, Beth. "'The Bad Old Days Look Better': Enlightened Colonial Land Management Practices and Land Reform in the British Windward Islands." *Environmental Planning in the Caribbean*, Edited by Jonathan Pugh and Janet Henshall Momsen. Aldershot: Ashgate, 2006.

Mimosa pudica. Sensitive Plant. Cook Islands Biodiversity and Natural Heritage database. Available at <http://cookislands.bishopmuseum.org/species.asp?id=6399>. Accessed 27 February 2023.

—. Sensitive plant. Global Invasive Species Database. Available at <http://www.iucngisd.org/gisd/speciesname/Mimosa+pudica>. Accessed 27 February 2023.

Mims, Christopher. *Arriving Today: From Factory to Front Door – Why Everything Has Changed About How and What We Buy*. New York: Harper Collins, 2021.

Mintz, Sidney W. *Sweetness and Power: The Place of Sugar in Modern History*. New York: Penguin, 1986.

Momsen, Janet Henshall, and Pamela Richardson, "Caribbean Cocoa: Planting and Production." *Chocolate: History, Culture, and Heritage*. Edited by Louis E. Grivetti and Howard-Yana Shapiro. Hoboken, NJ: Wiley, 2009.

Moore, Jason W. *Capitalism in the Web of Life: Ecology and the Accumulation of Capital*. London: Verso, 2015.

Niblett, Michael. *World Literature and Ecology: The Aesthetics of Commodity Frontiers, 1890–1950*. Cham: Palgrave Macmillan, 2020.

North, Louise V. "Introduction." *The Travel Diaries of Henrietta Marchant Liston: North America and Lower Canada, 1796–1800*. Lanham, MD: Lexington Books, 2014.

Nugent, Mary. *Lady Nugent's Journal of her residence in Jamaica from 1801–1805*. Edited by Philip Wright. Kingston, Jamaica: Institute of Jamaica, 1966.

Nussbaum, Martha, and Alison LaCroix, eds. *Subversion and Sympathy: Gender, Law, and the British Novel*. Oxford: Oxford University Press, 2013.

Osbourne, Lloyd. *A Letter to Mr. Stevenson's Friends* (1894). Published "for private circulation." Manuscript Archives and Special Collections, National Library of Scotland, Edinburgh.

Ovid. *Fasti*. Translated by Sir James George Frazer. London: William Heinnemann, 1931.

Owenson, Sydney. "The Sensitive Plant." *The Lay of an Irish Harp; or, Metrical Fragments*. London: Robert Phillips, 1807.

The Oxford History of the British Empire, Volumes I–V. Wm. Roger Louis, Editor-in-Chief. Oxford: Oxford University Press, 1998.

The Oxford History of the British Empire Companion Series, including *Environment and Empire*. Edited by William Beinart and Lotte Hughes. Oxford: Oxford University Press, 2009.

Paravisini-Gerbert, Lizabeth. "Deforestation and the Yearning for Lost Landscapes in Caribbean Literatures." *Postcolonial Ecologies: Literatures of the Environment*. Edited by Elizabeth DeLoughrey and George B. Handley. Oxford: Oxford University Press, 2011.

Parker, Matthew. *The Sugar Barons: Family, Corruption, Empire, and War in the West Indies*. New York: Walker & Company, 2011.

Parrish, Susan Scott. *American Curiosity: Cultures of Natural History in the Colonial British Atlantic World*. Chapel Hill: University of North Carolina Press, 2006.

Pauley, Benjamin. "On Teaching Another Defoe." *Digital Defoe: Studies in Defoe and His Contemporaries*, no. 1 (Spring 2009), p. 115, n.4, <http://english.illinoisstate.edu/digitaldefoe/archive/spring09/teaching/pauleynotes.shtml>. Accessed 29 May 2023.

Pearl, Jason H. "Desert Islands and Urban Solitudes in the *Crusoe* Trilogy." *Studies in the Novel* 44, no. 2 (Summer 2012).

Perkins, Robert Cyril Lawton. *Barefoot on Lava: The Journals and Correspondence of Naturalist R. C. L. Perkins in Hawai'i, 1892–1901*. Edited by Neal L. Evenhuis. Honolulu: Bishop Museum Press, 2007.

Phillips, Lawrence. *The South Pacific Narratives of Robert Louis Stevenson and Jack London: Race, Class, Imperialism*. London: Continuum, 2012.

Pollan, Michael. *The Botany of Desire: A Plant's-Eye View of the World*. New York: Random House, 2001.

Portuondo, María M. *Secret Science: Spanish Cosmography and the New World*. Chicago: University of Chicago Press, 2009.

Poyntz, John. *The Present Prospect of the Famous and Fertile Island of Tobago: With a Description of the Situation, Growth, Fertility, and Manufacture of the said Island*. London: George Larkin, 1683.

Prince, Mary. *The History of Mary Prince, a West Indian Slave. Related by Herself*. London: F. Westley and A. H. Davis, 1831.

Raffaele, Herbert A. and James W. Wiley, *Wildlife of the Caribbean*. Princeton: Princeton University Press, 2014.

Ramachandran, Ayesha. *The Worldmakers: Global Imagining in Early Modern Europe*. Chicago: University of Chicago Press, 2015.

Ramsay, Rev. James. *An Essay on the Treatment and Conversion of African Slaves in the British Sugar Colonies*. London: James Phillips, 1784.

Richardson, Bonham C. *Caribbean Migrants: Environment and Human Survival on St. Kitts and Nevis*. Knoxville: University of Tennessee Press, 1983.

Richetti, John, ed. "Introduction." *Robinson Crusoe*. London: Penguin Books, 2001.

—. *The Life of Daniel Defoe*. Malden, MA: Blackwell Publishing, 2005.

Roberts, Siân Silyn. *Gothic Subjects: The Transformation of Individualism in American Fiction, 1790–1861*. Philadelphia: University of Pennsylvania Press, 2014.

Rogers, Woodes. *A Cruising Voyage Round the World: First to the South-Seas, thence to the East-Indies, and homewards by the Cape of Good Hope . . .* (1712). Amsterdam: N. Israel (1969).
Roxburgh, Dr. W. "Directions for taking care of growing Plants at Sea." *The Annual Register, or A View of the History, Politics, and Literature for the Year 1810*. Second Edition. London: Baldwin, Cradock, and Joy, 1825.
Sansay, Leonora. *Secret History; or, The Horrors of St. Domingo* (1808). Edited by Michael J. Drexler. Peterborough, ON: Broadview Press, 2008.
Schaw, Janet. *Journal of a Lady of Quality; Being a Narrative of a Journey from Scotland to the West Indies, North Carolina, and Portugal, in the years 1774 to 1776*. Edited by Evangeline Walker Andrews, in collaboration with Charles McLean Andrews. New Haven: Yale University Press, 1923.
Schiebinger, Londa and Claudia Swan, eds. "Introduction." *Colonial Botany: Science, Commerce, and Politics in the Early Modern World*. Philadelphia: University of Pennsylvania Press, 2005.
Seed, Patricia. *Ceremonies of Possession in Europe's Conquest of the New World, 1492–1640*. Cambridge: Cambridge University Press, 1995.
Serres, Michel. *The Natural Contract*. Translated by Elizabeth MacArthur and William Paulson. Ann Arbor: University of Michigan Press, 1995.
—. *The Parasite*. Minneapolis: University of Minnesota Press, 2007.
Shajirat, Anna. "'Bending her gentle head to swift decay': Horror, Loss, and Fantasy in the Female Gothic of Ann Radcliffe and Regina Maria Roche." *Studies in Romanticism* 58, no. 3 (Fall 2019), 383–412.
Shelley, Percy Bysshe. *The Sensitive Plant*. Edited by Laurence Housman. New York: Haskell House, 1972.
Shiva, Vandana. *Monocultures of the Mind: Perspectives on Biodiversity and Biotechnology*. London: Zed Books, 1993.
—. *Biopiracy: The Plunder of Nature and Knowledge*. Boston: South End Press, 1997.
Simard, Suzanne. *Finding the Mother Tree: Discovering the Wisdom of the Forest*. New York: Knopf, 2021.
Simberloff, Daniel. *Invasive Species: What Everyone Needs to Know*. Oxford: Oxford University Press, 2013.
Simons, Paul. *The Action Plant: Movement and nervous behavior in plants*. Oxford and Cambridge, MA: Blackwell, 1992.
Singleton, John. *A General Description of the West-Indian Islands, As far as relates to the British, Dutch, and Danish Governments, from Barbados to Saint Croix* (1767). *Caribbeana: An Anthology of English Literature of the West Indies, 1657–1777*. Edited by Thomas W. Krise. Chicago: University of Chicago Press, 1999.
Skottsberg, Carl, ed. *The Natural history of Juan Fernández and Easter Island*. Uppsala: Almqvist & Wiksells Boktryckeri, 1920.

Sloane, Hans. *A Voyage to the Islands of Madera, Barbados, Nieves, S. Christophers and Jamaica, with the Natural history of the Trees, Four-footed Beasts, Fishes, Birds, Insects, Reptiles, etc. of the Last of those Islands.* London: Printed by B. M. for the Author, 1707.

Smith, Charlotte. *The Story of Henrietta* (1800). Edited by Janina Nordius. Kansas City, MO: Valancourt Books, 2012.

Smith, Edward. *The Life of Sir Joseph Banks.* Cambridge: Cambridge University Press, 2011.

Smith, John. *A Description of New England* (1616). *Captain John Smith: Writings, With Other Narratives of Roanoke, Jamestown, and the First English Settlement of America.* New York: The Library of America, 2007.

Smithson, Robert. "Entropy Made Visible" (1973). *Robert Smithson: The Collected Writings.* Edited by Jack Flam. Berkeley: University of California Press, 1996.

Souhami, Diana. *Selkirk's Island: The true and strange adventures of the real Robinson Crusoe* (New York: Harcourt, 2001).

Speck, W. A. *The Butcher: The Duke of Cumberland and the Suppression of the '45.* Caernarfon Gwynedd, Cymru: Welsh Academic Press, 1995.

Steele, Richard. *The Spectator*, no. 11 (13 March 1711). *The Commerce of Everyday Life: Selections from* The Tatler *and* The Spectator. Edited by Erin Mackie. New York: Bedford/St. Martin's, 1998.

Stevenson, Robert Louis. "Forest Notes: Idle Hours" (1876). *An Apology for Idlers.* New York: Penguin Books, 2009.

—. "Henry David Thoreau: His Character and Opinions" (1880). *Familiar Studies of Men and Books.* London: Chatto & Windus, 1917.

—. *Kidnapped* (1886). New York: Penguin Books, 1994.

—. "Memoirs of an Islet," *Memories and Portraits* (1887). New York: Charles Scribner's Sons, 1923.

—. *The Merry Men and Other Tales and Fables* (1887). London: Chatto & Windus, 1905.

—. *A Footnote to History: Eighty Years of Trouble in Samoa.* London: Cassell & Company, Limited, 1892.

—. "The Beach of Falesá." (1893). *South Sea Tales.* Edited by Roslyn Jolly. Oxford: Oxford University Press, 2008.

—. "The Ebb-Tide: A Trio and Quartette" (1894). *South Sea Tales.* Edited by Roslyn Jolly. Oxford: Oxford University Press, 2008.

—. *In the South Seas* (1896). New York: Penguin, 1998.

—. *Songs of Travel and Other Verses.* London: Chatto & Windus, 1896.

—. *Weir of Hermiston* (1896). New York: Bamboo Books, 2015.

—. *Records of a Family of Engineers.* London: Chatto & Windus, 1912.

—. *The Letters of Robert Louis Stevenson.* Edited by Sydney Colvin. New York: Charles Scribner's Sons, 1923.

—. "Roads." *Essays of Travel and in the Art of Writing.* New York: Charles Scribner's Sons, 1923.

—. *Travels in Hawaii*. Edited by A. Grove Day. Honolulu: University of Hawaii Press, 1973.

—. *The Letters of Robert Louis Stevenson*. Vol. 7. New Haven: Yale University Press, 1995.

Stevenson, Thomas. "Skerryvore Diary" (1843). Manuscript Archives and Special Collections, National Library of Scotland, Edinburgh.

Sudan, Rajani. *The Alchemy of Empire: Abject Materials and the Technologies of Colonialism*. New York: Fordham University Press, 2016.

Taylor, Alan. *American Colonies: The Settling of North America*. New York: Viking Penguin, 2001.

Thoreau, Henry David. *Walden; or, Life in the Woods* (1854). New York: Penguin, 1983.

—. "Walking." *Nature Walking*. Boston: Beacon Press, 1991.

Todd, Janet. *Sensibility: An Introduction*. London: Methuen, 1986. Quoted in *Charlotte Temple* by Susanna Rowson (and edited by Marion L. Rust). New York: W. W. Norton, 2011.

Tobin, Beth Fowkes. *Colonizing Nature: The Tropics in British Arts and Letters, 1760–1820*. Philadelphia: University of Pennsylvania Press, 2005.

Turner, Jonathan. *On the Origins of Human Emotions: A Sociological Inquiry into the Evolution of Human Affect*. Palo Alto, CA: Stanford University Press, 2000.

Twain, Mark. *Roughing It* (1872). New York: Penguin Books, 1985.

Veitch, John. *The Feeling for Nature in Scottish Poetry*. Edinburgh: William Blackwood and Sons, 1887.

Virilio, Paul. *Speed and Politics* (1977). Translated by Mark Polizzotti. Cambridge, MA: MIT Press, 2006.

Walcott, Derek. "Isla Incognita" (1973). *Caribbean Literature and the Environment*. Edited by Elizabeth Deloughrey, Renée K. Gosson, and George B. Handley. Charlottesville: University of Virginia Press, 2005.

—. *Sea Grapes*. New York: Farrar, Strauss, and Giroux, 1976.

Webber, Herbert John. "History and Development of the Citrus Industry." *The Citrus Industry*. Edited by Walter Reuther, Herbert John Webber, and Leon Dexter Batchelor, Revised Edition. Berkeley: University of California Press, 1967.

Werlhof, Claudia Von. "Women and Nature in Capitalism." *Women: The Last Colony*. Edited by Maria Mies. London: Zed Books, 1989.

Williams, Cynric. *Hamel, the Obeah Man* (1827). Peterborough, ON: Broadview Editions, 2010.

Williams, Michael. *Deforesting the Earth: From Prehistory to Global Crisis*. Chicago: University of Chicago Press, 2003.

Wohlleben, Peter. *The Hidden Life of Trees: What They Feel, How They Communicate – Discoveries from a Secret World*. Vancouver, BC: Greystone Books, 2016.

Woods, Rebecca J. H. *The Herds Shot Round the World: Native Breeds and the British Empire, 1800–1900.* Chapel Hill: University of North Carolina Press, 2017.

Wratt, G. S., and H. C. Smith, *Plant Breeding in New Zealand.* Wellington: Butterworths, 1983.

Wright, Laura. *"Wilderness into Civilized Shapes": Reading the Postcolonial Environment.* Athens: University of Georgia Press, 2010.

Yaeger, Patricia. "Editor's Column: Sea Trash, Dark Pools, and The Tragedy of the Commons." *Publications of the Modern Language Association (PMLA)* 125, no. 3 (2010), 523–42.

Zahedieh, Nuala. "Economy." *The British Atlantic World, 1500–1800.* Edited by David Armitage and Michael J. Braddick. Houndmills: Palgrave Macmillan, 2002.

Index

Note: page numbers in *italic* refer to figures.

abolitionism, 165–6, 179, 190, 197
actants, theory of, 6, 10, 73, 229, 256, 262
Adams-Campbell, Melissa, 190
Aeolian harps, 254, 255, 262
agribusiness, 43, 48, 115–16, 160, 164, 231, 237–8; *see also* sugar industry
Ahuja, Neel, 38, 45
Alexander Houston & Co., 111
Anderson, Alexander, 132–4
Anderson, Virginia, 112
Andrews, Henry Charles, 244, 257–8
animal species
    animal sensitivity, 261
    birds, 35–6, 69–70, 126, 140–1, 213, 239–40
    brown tree snakes, 35–6, 240–1
    Burmese pythons, 36
    camels, 89, 146
    cats, 3, 7, 33–4, 67–71, 69, 140, 226, 227, 227
    cattle, 226, 245
    deer, 70, 91
    dogs, 116, 140, 141
    as food, 139, 141–3
    goats, 2, 11, 13, 33, 37, 64–6, 67, 69, 70, 83, 85–6, 90–1, 92–3, 127–8, 129–30
    hogs, 128–9
    land crabs, 11, 164, 199–200, 201–2, 204, 234
    mongooses, 34, 44, 70, 140–1, 281–2
    monkeys, 137–9
    rabbits, 92
    rats, 2, 3–4, 5, 7, 27–8, 33, 67–8, 69–71, 78, 116, 138, 139–40, 141, 142–3, 234, 281–2
    seals, 66–7
    Selkirk and, 73

sheep, 226
tree frogs, 239
Anthropocene, 23–4
Antigua, 110–11
anthropocentrism, 129
anthropomorphism, 27–8, 138
avarice, 14, 48, 165–8, 186, 190; *see also* greed

Bacon, Francis, 161
Baldwin, Robert, 113
Balfour, Graham, 213, 239
    cats/Hawaiian photo albums, 34, 35, 67, 226, 227, 227
barley, 1, 3–4, 6–7, 15–16, 28, 75–6, 91
Bartram, William, 19, 256–7
Bates, Jonathan, 115
Baugh, Edward, 28
Beach of Falesá, The (Stevenson), 36, 233, 250, 251–4, 262, 264, 265–8
Beatson, Alexander, 116, 126–32, 133
    and deforestation, 129–30
    and environmentalism, 126–7
    and goats, 129–30
    green imperialism, 143
Beckford, William, 110
Benezet, Anthony, 165–6
Benítez-Rojo, Antonio, 13, 27, 124, 203
bio-invasion, 75, 113, 99
biopiracy, 9, 29, 47–8, 175
bioregionalism, 115
birds, 69–70
    Guam, 36, 239, 240
    Stevenson, 239–40
black-animal subtext, 28, 82, 84
Blackmore, R. D.: letter to, 246
Bligh, William, 132
Boisseron, Bénédict, 27–8, 82, 84

Botanic Garden, The (Darwin), 259
botanical gardens, 134
Botanist's Repository, The (Andrews), 244, 257–8
botany, 1–2, 235; *see also* plant species
Boulukos, George, 201
Bourguet, Marie-Noëlle, 13, 39, 120, 131
Boyle, Robert, 3
Brathwaite, Kamau, 27, 234
breadfruit, 39, 132
British East India Company, 112, 116, 172, 217
Brown, Charles Brockden, 41–2, 222
Brown, Sandra, 147–8
brown tree snakes, 35–6, 240–1
Buffon, Comte de (Georges-Louis Leclerc), 133
Bull of Donation (papal bull, 1493), 9
Burdick, Alan, 31, 95, 240–1
Burlingame, Edward L.: letters to, 239
Burmese pythons, 36
Burnham, Michelle, 13, 14, 27, 32, 38, 40–2, 63–4
   domestic violence, 163
   on exploitation of women, 43
   on global capitalism, 172, 217
   on global economy, 111, 162
   global relations in oceanic terms, 235
   on movement of water, 96–7
   on Pacific travel writing, 254–5
   on Sansay, 30–1, 162, 163, 187, 201, 204
   on seas/oceans, 223
   on Stevenson, 216
   on violence, 43–4
Burr, Aaron, 186, 187, 196, 201

cabbage trees, 64, 65–6
cacao, 79, 81, 90, 121, 182, 242, 268
Cairngorms, 212–13
camels, 89, 146
cannibalism, 83, 87
capitalism, 175–6, 265
   global capitalism, 111, 161–2, 265
   Moore on, 21, 22–3, 71, 95, 129, 161, 173, 217, 226, 228
   as world-ecology, 22–3, 228, 250
capitalism-in-nature/nature-in-capitalism, 78, 79, 217
Capitalocene, 23, 24
Caribbeanness, 27, 28
Carmichael, A. C., 159, 177–9, 180, 184
Carney, Judith, 10–11, 61

Carson, Rachel, 9, 39–40, 78
   on seas/oceans, 213–14, 218, 232
Casid, Jill, 2, 76–7
Catalogue of Plants in His Majesty's Garden on the Island of St. Vincent (Anderson), 133
cats, 3, 7, 33–4, 67–71, 69, 140, 226, 227, 227
cattle, 226, 245
cereals, 6, 93, 169
   barley, 1, 3–4, 6–7, 15–16, 28, 75–6, 91
   rice, 3, 6, 10–11, 61
Charlotte Temple (Rowson), 259–60
Cheney, Paul, 161, 169, 171, 177, 188, 194–5, 204, 279
Chew, Kristina, 135
chocolate, 81, 112
citrus fruit, 79–81, 82, 87, 88, 89, 90, 121
climate change, 44, 54n94, 125, 170
coconut palms, 93–4, 122–3
Cody, Lisa Forman, 30
coffee, 34, 112, 193–4, 226
Cohen, Margaret, 40, 71, 118, 234, 235, 236
Cole, Lucinda, 2, 3, 4, 5, 7, 10, 46, 73, 78, 93, 139
   on cats, 68
   identity, 11
   on rats, 67, 68, 78
   theory of actants, 10, 73, 229, 256
Coleridge, Samuel Taylor, 262–3
Colley, Ann C., 224–5
Columbian Exchange, 1
Columbus, Christopher, 1, 74, 81, 121
Columbus charter, 9
Colvin, Sidney: letters to, 246, 251–2
Constitution of the French Colony of Saint-Domingue (L'Ouverture), 176
copper mining, Cuba, 188, 202–3
Corbier, Jean-Baptiste, 194–5
copra, 253–4
cotton, 197, 204
Council of the Indies, Spain, 4–5
Creole women, 160, 177, 189–90
   characterization of, 189
   and escape from Haitian Revolution, 193–4, 197–8
   Liston, 117, 131–2, 133–4, 158, 179, 180–1, 182–4, 190, 192–3
   and violence, 43, 184, 185
Crevecoeur, J. Hector St. John de, 160
Cronon, William, 22, 78, 133
Crosby, Alfred W., 1

Cruising Voyage round the World, A (Rogers), 26, 60, 61, 91, 158
Cuba, 199
   mining industry, 202–3
   sugar industry, 13, 203–4

Daily Advertiser, Kingston, 111, 116, 141
Dampier, William, 61, 62, 64–5
Darwin, Charles, 160, 214–15, 261
   Insectivorous Plants (Darwin), 261
   Natural History of Various Countries Visited by the H.M.S. Beagle, 31–2
   The Voyage of the Beagle (Darwin), 214–15
Darwin, Erasmus, 259
DDT (dichloro-diphenyl-tricholoro-ethane), 8–9
de Stael, Anne Louise Germaine, 191
Deckard, Sharae, 36, 38, 71, 87–8, 123, 125, 126, 146
   myth of paradise, 124, 130, 147, 194
   on paradise as consumer Eden, 125, 162
deer, 70, 91
Defoe, Daniel, 1–10, 15–16, 83
   and Dampier's travel journal, 62
   and environmental issues, 96
   Journal of the Plague Year, 100
   Weekly Review of the Affairs of France, 76, 101
   see also *Farther Adventures of Robinson Crusoe, The* (Defoe); *Robinson Crusoe* (Defoe)
deforestation, 125–6, 145–8
   Beatson and, 129–30
   Caribbean, 111–12, 113–14, 129–30
   and climate change, 125
   Easter Island, 92
   goats and, 33, 127–8
DeLoughrey, Elizabeth, 26–7, 31, 40, 94, 113, 214, 234, 249
Dening, Greg, 93, 234
Descartes, René, 13
Description of New England, A (Smith), 134
Devine, T. M., 20, 110, 111, 175
Diario (Columbus), 74
Díaz, María, 202
Dillon, Elizabeth, 196–7, 198, 204
disasters, 143–9
dogs, 116, 140, 141
Domestic Manners and Social Conditions of the White, Coloured, and Negro Populations of the West Indies (Carmichael), 159, 177–8
domestic violence, 30, 163, 187
Donne, John, 223
Douglass, Frederick, 196
Drexler, Michael J., 186, 191, 196–7, 198, 204
Dubois, Laurent, 171–2, 196
Durante (physician-poet), 139, 141

Easter Island: deforestation, 92
'Ebb-Tide, The' (Herrick), 221
Ebb-Tide, The (Stevenson), 264, 265
echo-criticism, 117–18
ecosystems, 219, 250
   ecosystem engineering, 80, 86, 93, 124, 245
   island ecosystems, 5, 76, 80, 91, 240, 243
Edgar Huntly; Or, Memoirs of a Sleepwalker (Brown), 222
Elton, Charles S., 26, 70, 74–5, 90–2, 113
empire writing: definition of, 24
Enclosure Movement, 76
enclosures, 76–7, 82, 92–3
Englishman, The, 62, 91
entropicality (entropy, tropical), 112–13, 148
environmental issues, 96, 125–30
   conservation measures, 148–9
   deforestation, 33, 92, 111–12, 113–14, 125–6, 127–8, 129–30, 145–8
   environmental engineering, 12
   plantation economy and, 117
   soil erosion, 37, 38, 70, 91, 135, 145–6, 147–8, 149
'Eolian Harp, The' (Coleridge), 262–3
Equiano, Olaudah, 20, 166, 185–6, 190, 217
Erraid, 216, 232, 234–5
Essay on the Treatment and Conversion of African Slaves in the British Sugar Colonies, An (Ramsay), 170–1
Evelyn, John, 89
evolutionary biology, 160, 192, 261

Farther Adventures of Robinson Crusoe, The (Defoe), 6, 27, 61, 77, 86–7, 101, 169
Fasti (Ovid), 191–3
fences, 2, 76–7, 88
Fernández, Juan, 64–5
Fick, Carolyn, 168, 198

Fielding, Penny, 242
Flora Sta. Helenica (Beatson), 130–2, 133
Floral Festival, The (Latham), 260, *260*
Footnote to History: Eighty Years of Trouble in Samoa, A (Stevenson), 41, 235–7
Forest Notes (Stevenson), 239–40, 253
Freeman, Arthur, 120–1
Freud, Sigmund, 17, 263
Fuchs, Barbara, 113

gardens, 158–60, 164
Garrigus, John D., 171–2, 196
General Agreement on Tariffs and Trade (GATT) treaty (1947), 9
General Description of the West Indian Islands, A (Singleton), 36, 38, 114, 135
  unnatural disasters, 143–9
geographical agency, 134–49
Georgics (Virgil), 135
Gilmore, John, 142
global capitalism, 111, 161–2, 172–3, 217, 265
global economy, 2, 111, 115, 162, 172–3
goats, 1, 11, 13, 33, 37, 67, 69, 83, 85–6, 90–1, 92–3
  Beatson and, 129–30
  and deforestation, 127–8
  introduction to oceanic islands, 60–1
  Juan Fernández archipelago, 64–6
Gómez-Barris, Macarena, 15, 24, 29, 30, 87, 122, 164, 245
  on exploitation of women, 173
  extractive perspectives, 136
  submerged perspectives, 33, 200
Goode, Abby L., 190
Gothic genre, 116
  Female Gothic, 186, 198, 201–2
  uncanny, 201
  see also *Secret History; Or, the Horrors of St. Domingo* (Sansay); *Sicilian Romance, A* (Radcliffe); *Story of Henrietta, The* (Smith)
Gottlieb, Evan, 21
Grainger, James, 11, 12, 17, 27–8, 36, 44
  biopiracy, 47–8
  on his contribution to British poetry, 110
  see also *Sugar-Cane, The* (Grainger)
greed, 20, 21, 165–8, 173, 190, 195, 216–17; see also avarice
Green, Thomas, 258
green imperialism, 143

Green Thought, 14, 22
Greimler, Josef, 75
Grove, Richard, 88, 89, 96, 112, 114, 125, 132–3
  on Beatson's environmentalism, 126–7
  on botanical gardens, 134
  on forest conservation legislation, 148–9
  plant transfers, 131
  on soil-conservation measures, 148
Guam
  birds, 36, 239, 240
  snakes, 35–6, 240–1
Guibert, Hervé, 38, 147
Gwynn, Stephen, 251
gypsy moths, 8–10, 15, 34–5

Haiti, 31, 194, 204
Haitian Revolution (1791–1803), 13, 163, 196, 203–4
  constitution, 176–7, 179–80
  Creole women's escape from, 193–4, 197–8
  slave uprising, 188
Hakewill, James, 36–7, *37*
Handler, J. S., 117
Hau'ofa, Epeli, 32–3, 97, 235
hedonism, 195
Helg, Aline, 202
Hempton, Gordon, 238
Heng, Geraldine, 26, 31, 36
Herrick, Robert, 221
Hirschman, Albert O., 165, 168
Historical Relation of the Island of Ceylon, An (Knox), 74, 91
History of Mary Prince, A West Indian Slave, The (Prince), 179, 184
hogs, 128–9
Howard, R. A. and E. S., 133
Howell, John, *69*, 72
Huggan, Graham, 15, 16
Hughes, Griffith, 93–4, 122–6, 131, 134–5, 183
Hume, David, 17–18, 19, 20–1, 31, 190, 248
  on avarice, 165, 166
  love of pleasure, 195
  sympathy, 221–4, 256, 265
Hunt, Helen, 163
Hurricane Sandy, 280–1
Hutcheson, Francis, 20

In the South Seas (Stevenson), 233
Influence of the Passions (de Stael), 191

insect species, 214–15, 239, 240
  insect migration, 31–2
  mosquitoes, 146, 226, 234
  moths, 8–10, 15, 34–5
  spotted lanternflies, 99
  ticks, 140, 282
Insectivorous Plants (Darwin), 261
Interesting Narrative of the Life of Olaudah Equiano, or Gustavus Vassa, The African, The (Equiano), 20, 166, 217
International Union for Conservation of Nature (IUCN): Red List, 33
invasion biology, 6–7, 15, 45, 98, 99, 134, 137, 140
  disturbed habitats and, 66
  ecological health of ecosystems and, 74–5
  Elton on, 75, 113
  impact on forests, 241
  moths, 8–10, 15, 34–5
invertebrate species
  rosy wolf snails, 34
'Isla Incognita' (Walcott), 212
island ecosystems, 74, 97, 114, 116

Jamaica, 110–11, 112, 148, 174–5
Jamaica Magazine, The, 113–14, 118, 121–2
Jefferson, Thomas, 133
Johnson, Samuel, 116, 139
Jolly, Roslyn, 251, 264
Journal of a Lady of Quality; Being a Narrative of a Journey from Scotland to the West Indies, North Carolina and Portugal (Schaw), 42, 120–1, 159, 175–6
Journal of John Ker, Surgeon's Mate in the Royal Navy (Ker), 118–20, *119*, 122
Journal of the Plague Year (Defoe), 100
Juan Fernández archipelago, 1, 11, 25–6, 63, 64–7, 70
  animal species, 69
  discovery of Selkirk, 60–1
  fruit/vegetable production, 66
  significance of, 64–6

Ker, John, 118–20, *119*, 122
Kidnapped (Stevenson), 72–3, 220, 232–3, 234–5, 238, 267
King, Carole, 147
King's Hill Forest Act (1791), 125, 132–3, 170

Kingston, Jamaica, 279–80
Kirker, Constance L., 276n154
Knight, Franklin W., 202, 203
Knox, Robert, 74, 91
Kosek, Jake, 118
Kowaleski, Elizabeth, 109n146
Krise, Thomas, 143

Labat, Père, 139, 141
Lady Nugent's Journal, 174–5, 178, 181–2
Lamb, Jonathan, 158
Lambert, Andrew, 25, 26, 65–6, 81–2
land crabs, 11, 199–200, 201–2, 204, 234
lanternflies, 99
Latham, P. W., 260, *260*
Latour, Bruno, 3, 6, 10, 262
Le Galliene, Richard, 242
Leclerc, Georges-Louis, Comte de Buffon, 133
Leclerc, Victor-Emmanuel, 186–7, 198
Letter to Mr. Stevenson's Friends, A (Osbourne), 225
Letters (Stevenson), 239, 243, 246
Letters of a Solitary Wanderer, The (Smith), 37, 200
Life and Strange Surprizing Adventures of Robinson Crusoe, The (Defoe) see *Robinson Crusoe* (Defoe)
Ligon, Richard, 74, 82, 84–5, 125–6, 159, 183
  on citrus fruit, 87, 89
Linnaeus, Carl, 258
lionfish, 142
Liston, Henrietta Marchant, 117, 133–4, 158, 180–1, 190
  Caribbean paradise, 192–3
  travel journals, 131–2, 134, 179, 180–1, 182–4
literature as ecological force, 12
Locke, John, 65, 77, 106n91, 124
  labor theory of property, 76, 80
  social contract theory, 188–9
Loss, Scott R., 33
Louisiana Purchase, 196–7, 203
L'Ouverture, François Dominique Toussaint, 176–7, 179–80, 187
Lugo, Ariel E., 147–8
Lysaght, Sydney Royse, 229

Mabberley, D. J., 132
McCook, Stuart, 113, 140, 282
McKibben, Bill, 77
McNeil, J. R., 121, 124, 126, 145–6

manchineel trees, 134, 181, 183, 184
Manning, Susan, 17, 225
Marion Island, Southern Indian Ocean, 70
Marley, Bob, 280
Marra, Peter P., 33
marriage, 176–7
   planters' wives, role of, 179–80, 184–5
   in Sansay, 186
Martin, Claire, 240
Marvel, Andrew, 120, 242
Marzec, Robert, 76
Melville, Robert, 114, 125, 132
'Memoirs of an Islet' (Stevenson), 233
Menely, Tobias, 12, 18, 149, 221, 222–3, 248, 267
Merry Men, The (Stevenson), 216–17, 235
metaphors, 163–4, 212, 217, 231–2, 256
Millenium Hall (Scott), 200
Mills, Beth, 133
Mimosa pudica see sensitive plant (*Mimosa pudica*)
Mims, Christopher, 237
mining industry
   copper mining, Cuba, 188, 202–3
   silver mining, Bolivia, 29–30, 87, 173, 184
Mintz, Sidney W., 43, 112, 121, 164, 169–70, 172
misogyny, 204–5
   Sansay and, 31, 48, 49, 161–3
   and sexual appetite, 188
   sugar revolution and, 173
Momsen, Janet Henshall, 81
mongooses, 34, 44, 140–1, 281–2
monkeys, 137–9
monocultures, 115, 144, 148
   and soil erosion, 37, 38
   Stevenson, 237–40
   see also sugar cane
Moonlit Shipwreck at Sea (Moran), 219
Moore, Jason, 14, 44, 48, 63, 64, 93, 227, 245
   on capitalism, 21, 22–3, 71, 95, 129, 161, 173, 217, 226, 228
   on environmentalism, 129
   law of value, analysis of, 85
   myth of separation, 77
   rate of exploitation, 86
Moran, Thomas, 219, *219*
mosquitoes, 146, 226, 234
moths see gypsy moths
Mujeres Creando Communidad, 30
Mulligan, James H., 230

Napoleon Bonaparte, 186–7, 188, 196, 198
National Environmental and Planning Agency (NEPA), Jamaica, 142
National Oceanic and Atmospheric Administration, 142
Natural History of Barbados (Hughes), 93–4, 122–3, 125, 183
nature and society, 3, 6, 11–12
New England, 134
New Voyage Round the World, A (Dampier), 61
New Voyage Round the World, A (Defoe), 97
New Zealand
   bats, 33, 90–1
   red deer, 70, 73, 91
   soil erosion, 91
Newman, Maro, 276n154
Niblett, Michael, 2, 12–13, 14, 17, 42, 117, 220
North, Louise V., 180
Notes on the State of Virginia (Jefferson), 133
Novum Organum (Bacon), 161
Nugent, Lady Mary, 159, 171, 174–5, 180, 181–2, 194, 279
   and abolitionism, 179
   on women's agency, 177
numerical genres, 41–2

'Of Interest' (Hume), 166, 195
On The Origin of Species (Darwin), 160
Ormond; Or, the Secret Witness (Brown), 41–2
Osbourne, Lloyd, 225, 239
Ovid: Flora myth, 191–3
Oviedo y Valdéz, Gonzalo Fernández de, 81
Owenson, Sydney, 252–3, 258–9

Papers Relating to the Devastation Committed by Goats on the Island of St. Helena (Beatson), 116, 126–8
paradise
   as consumer Eden, 178
   myth of, 36, 130, 147, 194
Paradise (Guibert), 38, 147
Paredes, Julieta, 30
Parker, Matthew, 111
Pauley, Benjamin, 97
Pearl, Jason H., 76, 101

Perkins, Robert Cyril Lawton, 34, 140–1, 226–7
pest control, 139–41
Picturesque Tour of the Island of Jamaica, A (Hakewill), 36, 37
Plan of the English Commerce, A (Defoe), 82, 84
plant species
   barley, 1, 3–4, 6–7, 15–16, 28, 75–6, 91
   breadfruit, 39, 132
   cabbage trees, 64, 65–6
   cacao, 79, 81, 90, 121, 182, 242, 268
   cereals, 93, 169
   citrus fruit, 79–81, 82, 87, 88, 89, 90, 121
   coconut palms, 93–4, 122–3
   corn, 6
   manchineel trees, 134, 181, 183, 184
   plant action, 256–7, 260–2
   plant transfers, 131
   rice, 3, 6, 10–11, 61
   St. Helena, 133
   sea grapes, 181, 183
   sun-dew (*Drosera rotundifolia*), 261
   tea, 112, 172, 217
   Venus flytrap, 255, 256–7, 261–2
   yucca, 124
   see also sensitive plant (*Mimosa pudica*); sugar cane
plantation economy, 136, 161–2, 168–9
   and environmental degradation, 117
   and exploitation of women, 174–5, 184–5
   immorality of, 194–6
   landscape architecture, 120–1
Pollan, Michael, 160, 245
Portuondo, María M., 4–5, 24, 47, 62, 79
Poyntz, John, 88–9, 93
Present Prospect of the Famous and Fertile Island of Tobago, The (Poyntz), 88–9
Prince, Mary, 179, 185–6
private ownership, 76–7
property theory, 76, 80

rabbits, 92
Radcliffe, Ann, 162, 200, 201
Raffaele, Herbert A., 80, 94
Ramachandran, Ayesha, 6, 12, 17, 65, 120
Ramsay, James, 170–1, 172
rats, 2, 5, 27–8, 33, 67–8, 69–71, 116, 138, 139–40, 142–3, 234, 281–2
   consumption of, 141

   disappearance from island, 3–4, 7, 68, 78
Records of a Family of Engineers (Stevenson), 220–1
reforestation, 124, 128
religion: Defoe, 3–4, 15–16
reptile species
   brown tree snakes, 35–6
   Burmese pythons, 36
rice, 3, 6, 10–11, 61
Richardson, Bonham C., 112, 146
Richardson, Pamela, 81
Richetti, John, 78
'Roads' (Stevenson), 217–19, 221, 231, 236–7, 250
Roberts, Siân Silyn, 188–9
Robinson Crusoe (Defoe), 1–7, 21–2, 38, 45, 183
   as allegory, 96, 99
   barley, 1, 3–4, 6–7, 15–16, 75, 91
   black-animal subtext, 82, 84
   cacao, 79
   cereals, 93
   citrus fruit, 79–80, 82, 88
   Crusoe's deliverance, 73–9
   eastern side of island, 79–80
   fences, 88, 92–3
   footprint scene, 6, 28, 77–8, 94–5
   Friday, 7, 61, 82, 83, 85–6
   goats, 83, 85–6, 90–1, 92–3
   rats, 3–4, 5, 7, 68, 78
   setting, 1, 2–6
   sleep, 5
   sources, 25, 61, 62, 74, 88, 91
   Spanish wreck, 99–100
   and speed, 169
   tidal/oceanic consciousness, 98–101
Rogers, Pat, 76
Rogers, Woodes, 26, 60, 91, 158, 249
   on birds, 69
   on Selkirk, 60–2, 66–7, 71–3
   on South Sea trade, 62–3
Roman, Joe, 142
Roman mythology: Flora, 191–3, *192*
rosy wolf snails, 34
Roughing It (Twain), 239
Rowson, Susanna, 259–60
Roxburgh, W., 130
Royal Gazette (Jamaican newspaper), 139

St. Christopher (St. Kitts), 110–11, 112, 139, 148, 170–1
St. Eustatius, 42

St. Helena, 126–8, 130–1, 133, 143
St. Vincent Botanic Gardens, 39, 131, 132, 133–4, 190
Samoa, 148, 212, 225–8, 229–30, 235–9, 241–2, 246–8
  and Scotland, 41, 49, 225, 228, 230
  Vailima, 224, 228, 229, 230, 247
Sansay, Leonora, 13–14, 28, 38, 43, 48, 159
  Burnham on, 30–1, 162, 163, 187, 201, 204
  extra-human metaphors, 163–4
  marriage in, 186
  misogyny and, 31, 48, 49, 161–3
  sweetness/sugar/sexuality, 188–97
  see also *Secret History; Or, the Horrors of St. Domingo* (Sansay)
Schaw, Alexander, 175
Schaw, Janet, 42, 120–1, 159, 172–3, 182, 195
  attitude to planters' indulgence in luxuries, 178–9
  attitude to slavery/capitalism, 175–6
  on Creole women, 177
Schiebinger, Londa, 1, 131, 235, 249
Schmidt, Ralph, 147–8
scientific revolution, 44
Scott, Sarah, 200
sea grapes, 183
Sea Grapes (Walcott), 183
seals, 66–7
Second Treatise of Government (Locke), 77, 106n91, 134
Secret History; Or, the Horrors of St. Domingo (Sansay), 13–14, 28, 30–1, 38, 43, 48, 159, 160–5, 168, 173, 184, 185, 186–97
  land crabs, 199, 201–2, 204
  violence, 204–5
  women's escape from Haitian Revolution, 162, 176, 193–4, 197–8
Seed, Patricia, 76
Selkirk, Alexander, 1, 5, 11, 25, 66–8, 69, 70–3
  dancing with cats and goats, 68, 69, 70–1
  discovery/rescue of/story of, 60–3
  and goats, 71, 72
sensibility, 252–3, 258–9
sensitive plant (*Mimosa pudica*), 11, 41, 223, 224, 228, 241–2, 243–5, 244, 246, 249, 250, 251–3, 255–6, 257–60
  and capitalism, 265

and human sensibility, 258–60
mobility of, 257–9, 260
Stevenson, 262, 263–4, 265, 266, 267, 268–9
'Sensitive Plant, The' (Owenson), 258–9
Sensitive Plant, The (Shelley), 259, 263
separation myth, 77
Serious Reflections During the Life and Surprising Adventures of Robinson Crusoe (Defoe), 83
Serres, Michel, 116, 251
sexual violence, 30, 164, 191, 195–6
Shajirat, Anna, 201
sheep, 226
Shelley, Percy, 252–3, 259, 263
Shiva, Vandana, 9, 10, 29, 30, 64, 84, 136, 164
  on biopiracy, 175
  global economic system, 115
  instability of monocultures, 115
  mistreatment of women's labor, 87
Sicilian Romance, A (Radcliffe), 162, 200, 201
silver mining, Bolivia, 29–30, 87, 173, 184
Simberloff, Daniel, 6, 8, 33–5, 45, 54n94, 70, 74, 268
  on bio-invasion, 75, 99, 274n106
  on feral dogs, 116
  on rabbits, 92
similes, 218, 231, 266–7
Simons, Paul, 19, 255–6, 260–1
  battlefield metaphor, 256
Singleton, John, 36, 37, 38, 114
  on geographical agency, 143–9
  on unnatural disasters, 143–9
Skottsberg, Carl, 70
slavery/slave trade, 20, 37, 44, 82–3, 136
  abolition of, 165–6, 190
  modern slavery, 31, 188, 196, 197
  sugar-cane plantations, 112, 146
  US and, 196–7
sleep, 5, 224
Sloane, Hans, 82, 89–90
Smith, Adam, 110
Smith, Charlotte, 37, 200–1
Smith, John, 134, 158
Smithson, Robert, 112–13
snakes
  brown tree snakes, 35–6, 240–1
  Burmese pythons, 36
social contract theory, 188–9
society/nature binary, 77–8

Society of Arts, 131
soil erosion, 135, 147–8, 149
  deer and, 70
  goats and, 37
  monocultures and, 37, 38, 145–6
  New Zealand, 91
Some Historical Account of Guinea (Benezet), 165–6
Songs of Travel and Other Verses (Stevenson), 242
South Sea Tales (Stevenson), 251
Spain: Council of the Indies, 4–5
Species Plantarum (Linnaeus), 258
Speck, W. M., 138
Spectator, The: Inkle and Yarico story, 166–7
speed, 44, 169, 172, 222
spotted lanternflies, 99
Stael, Anne Louise Germaine de, 191
Steele, Richard, 61, 62, 67, 68, 91
Stevenson, Robert Louis, 32–3, 36, 41, 72–3, 216–21, 224–6, 234–46, 251–4, 262–9
  birds, 239–40
  desert of food, 237–40
  deserts, 230–4, 268
  Fakarava, 234, 239
  fascination with deserts, 219–21
  on Fontainbleau forest, 240
  A Footnote to History: Eighty Years of Trouble in Samoa, 41, 235–7
  Forest Notes, 239–40, 253
  In the South Seas, 233
  insects, 240
  on land crabs, 234
  metaphors, 231–2, 236
  on monocultures, 237–40
  mythology of island desertion, 234–5
  rats, 234
  roads, 236–7
  and sea/waves, 215
  and sensitive plant, 262, 263–4, 265, 266, 267, 268–9
  similes, 231, 266–7
  South Pacific writings, 226, 227
  speech to Samoan chiefs, 225
  sympathy, 228
  Thoreau essay, 229
  and tidal islet of Erraid, 216, 232
  Treasure Island, 213
  on transoceanic travel, 235–6
  vegetating, 32–3, 224, 247, 248, 264–5, 266
  walking, 212, 224, 229–32, 236, 250
  weeding, 224, 240–50, 265, 268–9
Stevenson, Thomas, 215–16
Story of Henrietta, The (Smith), 37, 200–1
Sudan, Rajani, 10, 38, 61, 116, 167–8
sugar cane, 1, 13, 31, 36, 37–8, 43, 44, 85, 87–8, 114–15, 121, 129–30
  cultivation of, 169–70
  and deforestation, 111–12
  sugar, production of, 170–2
  and sustainability, 124–5
Sugar-Cane, The (Grainger), 12, 36, 38–9, 44, 110–17, 148–9, 170
  and appropriation of cheap nature, 114–15
  as biopiracy, 47–8
  cats, 67
  geographical agency in, 135–43
  Preface, 110, 112, 113
sugar industry, 168–9
  in Antigua, 110–11
  in Cuba, 13, 203–4
  in Haiti, 31, 194, 204
  in Jamaica, 110–11, 112, 148, 174–5
  in St. Christopher (St. Kitts), 110–11, 112, 139, 148, 170–1
sugar plantations, 43, 112, 146–7, 159, 161, 168–9
sugar revolution, 112, 126, 172–3
sugar trade, 110–11
sun-dew (*Drosera rotundifolia*), 261
sustainability, 124–5
Sutherland, Thomas, 37
Swan, Claudia, 1, 131, 235, 249
sympathy, 17–21, 24, 31, 228
  human sympathy/empathy, 17–18
  Hume and, 221–4, 256, 265

Tailour, Dr., 136
Taylor, Alan, 116–17
tea, 112, 172, 217
Thoreau, Henry David, 218, 221, 229, 231, 238
ticks, 140, 282
tidalectic (tidal dialectic), 27, 234
Tiepolo, Giovanni, 192
Tiffin, Helen, 15, 16
Tobin, Beth Fowkes, 38, 159, 169, 179
Todd, Janet, 258
Travels of Hildebrand Bowman, The (anon.), 41, 225
Travels through North and South Carolina (Bartram), 19, 256–7

Treasure Island (Stevenson), 213
Treatise of Human Nature (Hume), 18, 165, 190, 221–4
tree frogs, 239
'Tree Worship' (Le Galliene), 242
Trouvelot, Etienne Leopold, 7–10, 14, 15, 17, 21
True and Exact History of the Island of Barbados, A (Ligon), 74, 125–6, 159, 183
Twain, Mark, 239
Tyron, Thomas, 171

uncanny, 17, 70–2, 201, 263–4
  ecological uncanny, 71–2
  Freud, 17, 263
'Uncanny, The' (Freud), 263
United States of America: manifest destiny, 70, 188, 197
Universal Herbal, or, Botanical, Medical, and Agricultural Dictionary, The (Green), 258

Vailima, Samoa, 224, 228, 229, 230, 247
value, law of, 85
vegetating, 32–3, 224, 247, 248, 264–5, 266
Veitch, John, 240
Venus flytrap, 255, 256–7, 261–2
violence, 43–4, 204–5
  domestic violence, 30, 163, 187
  sexual violence, 30, 164, 191, 195–6
  women and, 31, 184, 185–6
Virgil (Publius Vergilius Maro), 135
Virilio, Paul, 44, 172
Von Holle, Betsy, 274n106
Voyage of the Beagle, The (Darwin), 214–15
Voyage to the Islands of Madera, Barbados, Nieves, S. Christophers and Jamaica, A (Sloane), 82, 89

Walcott, Derek, 183, 212
Walden; or, Life in the Woods (Thoreau), 229
walking, 212, 224, 229–32, 236, 250
Watt, Ian, 2
Webber, Herbert John, 80, 81, 88
weeding, 224, 240–50, 265, 268–9
Weekly Jamaica Courrant, 113
Weekly Review of the Affairs of France (Defoe), 76, 101
Weir of Hermiston (Stevenson), 231, 238
West Africa, 83–4
  rice, 10–11, 61
wildernesses, 22, 133–4, 238
  biblical overtones, 77, 78, 134
  myth of, 28
Wilds of Lake Superior, The (Moran), 219, 219
Wiley, James W., 80, 94
Will (Moskito Indian), 61
Will, Tom, 33
Wollstonecraft, Mary, 200
women
  agency, 177
  anarcho-feminism, 29–30
  appropriation of work/energy, 86–7, 173–86
  childbearing, 30, 174–5
  domestic abuse, 176, 185, 186
  escape from Haitian Revolution, 162, 176, 193–4, 197–8
  exploitation of, 43, 161–2, 173, 174–5, 184–5
  and sexual violence, 30, 191, 195–6
  and violence, 31, 48, 184, 185–6
  see also Creole women
'Woodman, The' (Stevenson), 228, 241–3, 244–6, 249–50, 262–3, 268–9
Woods, Rebecca, 2, 226
worldmaking, 12
Wright, Laura, 17, 28
Wrongs of Woman, The (Wollstonecraft), 200

Yaeger, Patricia, 117
yuccas, 124

Zahedieh, Nuala, 110

EU representative:
Easy Access System Europe
Mustamäe tee 50, 10621 Tallinn, Estonia
Gpsr.requests@easproject.com

www.ingramcontent.com/pod-product-compliance
Lightning Source LLC
Chambersburg PA
CBHW050203240426
43671CB00013B/2231